IFIP Advances in Information and Communication Technology 320

IFIP – The International Federation for Information Processing

IFIP was founded in 1960 under the auspices of UNESCO, following the First World Computer Congress held in Paris the previous year. An umbrella organization for societies working in information processing, IFIP's aim is two-fold: to support information processing within its member countries and to encourage technology transfer to developing nations. As its mission statement clearly states,

IFIP's mission is to be the leading, truly international, apolitical organization which encourages and assists in the development, exploitation and application of information technology for the benefit of all people.

IFIP is a non-profitmaking organization, run almost solely by 2500 volunteers. It operates through a number of technical committees, which organize events and publications. IFIP's events range from an international congress to local seminars, but the most important are:

- The IFIP World Computer Congress, held every second year;
- Open conferences;
- Working conferences.

The flagship event is the IFIP World Computer Congress, at which both invited and contributed papers are presented. Contributed papers are rigorously refereed and the rejection rate is high.

As with the Congress, participation in the open conferences is open to all and papers may be invited or submitted. Again, submitted papers are stringently refereed.

The working conferences are structured differently. They are usually run by a working group and attendance is small and by invitation only. Their purpose is to create an atmosphere conducive to innovation and development. Refereeing is less rigorous and papers are subjected to extensive group discussion.

Publications arising from IFIP events vary. The papers presented at the IFIP World Computer Congress and at open conferences are published as conference proceedings, while the results of the working conferences are often published as collections of selected and edited papers.

Any national society whose primary activity is in information may apply to become a full member of IFIP, although full membership is restricted to one society per country. Full members are entitled to vote at the annual General Assembly, National societies preferring a less committed involvement may apply for associate or corresponding membership. Associate members enjoy the same benefits as full members, but without voting rights. Corresponding members are not represented in IFIP bodies. Affiliated membership is open to non-national societies, and individual and honorary membership schemes are also offered.

Michele Bezzi   Penny Duquenoy
Simone Fischer-Hübner   Marit Hansen
Ge Zhang (Eds.)

Privacy and Identity Management for Life

5th IFIP WG 9.2, 9.6/11.7, 11.4, 11.6/PrimeLife
International Summer School
Nice, France, September 7-11, 2009
Revised Selected Papers

 Springer

Volume Editors

Michele Bezzi
SAP Research Sophia-Antipolis, Security & Trust, SAP Labs France
805, Avenue du Docteur Maurice Donat, BP 1216, 06254 Mougins Cedex, France
E-mail: michele.bezzi@sap.com

Penny Duquenoy
Middlesex University, School of Computing Science
Bounds Green, London N11 2NQ, UK
E-mail: p.duquenoy@mdx.ac.uk

Simone Fischer-Hübner
Ge Zhang
Karlstad University, Department of Computer Science
Universitetsgatan 2, 651 88 Karlstad, Sweden
E-mail: {simone.fischer-huebner, ge.zhang}@kau.se

Marit Hansen
Independant Centre for Privacy Protection Schleswig-Holstein
Holstenstr. 98, 24103 Kiel, Germany
E-mail: uld6@datenschutzzentrum.de

CR Subject Classification (1998): C.2, K.6.5, D.4.6, E.3, H.4, J.1

ISSN   1868-4238
ISBN-10   3-642-42253-5 Springer Berlin Heidelberg New York
ISBN-13   978-3-642-42253-9 Springer Berlin Heidelberg New York

springer.com

© IFIP International Federation for Information Processing 2010

Softcover re-print of the Hardcover 1st edition 2010
Typesetting: Camera-ready by author, data conversion by Scientific Publishing Services, Chennai, India
Printed on acid-free paper   06/3180

Preface

New Internet developments pose greater and greater privacy dilemmas. In the Information Society, the need for individuals to protect their autonomy and retain control over their personal information is becoming more and more important. Today, information and communication technologies—and the people responsible for making decisions about them, designing, and implementing them—scarcely consider those requirements, thereby potentially putting individuals' privacy at risk. The increasingly collaborative character of the Internet enables anyone to compose services and contribute and distribute information. It may become hard for individuals to manage and control information that concerns them and particularly how to eliminate outdated or unwanted personal information, thus leaving personal histories exposed permanently. These activities raise substantial new challenges for personal privacy at the technical, social, ethical, regulatory, and legal levels: How can privacy in emerging Internet applications such as collaborative scenarios and virtual communities be protected? What frameworks and technical tools could be utilized to maintain life-long privacy?

During September 3–10, 2009, IFIP (International Federation for Information Processing) working groups 9.2 (Social Accountability), 9.6/11.7 (IT Misuse and the Law), 11.4 (Network Security) and 11.6 (Identity Management) held their 5th International Summer School in cooperation with the EU FP7 integrated project PrimeLife in Sophia Antipolis and Nice, France. The focus of the event was on privacy and identity management for emerging Internet applications throughout a person's lifetime.

The aim of the IFIP Summer Schools has been to encourage young academic and industry entrants to share their own ideas about privacy and identity management and to build up collegial relationships with others. As such, the Summer Schools have been introducing participants to the social implications of information technology through the process of informed discussion.

Following the holistic approach advocated by the involved IFIP working groups and by the PrimeLife project, a diverse group of participants ranging from young doctoral students to leading researchers in the field engaged in discussions, dialogues and debates in an informal and supportive setting. The interdisciplinary, and international, emphasis of the Summer School allowed for a broader understanding of the issues in the technical and social spheres.

All topical sessions started with introductory lectures by invited speakers in the mornings, followed by parallel workshops and seminars in the afternoons. The workshops consisted of short presentations based on the contributions submitted by participating PhD students, followed by active discussions.

Contributions combining technical, social, ethical or legal perspectives were solicited. Keynote speeches provided the focus for the theme of the Summer School—Lifelong Privacy, Privacy Aspects of Social Networks, Privacy of Data,

Transparency and Data subject Access, Privacy Principles for Identity Management, Economic Privacy Aspects, Identity and Legal, Technical and Economic
Aspects of a new regulatory Framework—and the contributions from participants enhanced the ideas generated by the keynote speeches. The Summer School
was a very successful event. More than 50 delegates from more than 15 countries
actively participated. We succeeded in initiating intensive discussions between
PhD students and established researchers from different disciplines.

These proceedings include both keynote papers and submitted papers accepted by the Program Committee, which were presented at the Summer School.
The review process consisted of two steps. In the first step, contributions for
presentation at the Summer School were selected based on reviews of submitted short papers by the Summer School Program Committee. The second step
took place after the Summer School, when the authors had an opportunity to
submit their final full papers addressing discussions at the Summer School. The
submissions were again reviewed, by three reviewers each, and those included in
these proceedings were carefully selected by the International Summer School
Program Committee and by additional reviewers according to common quality
criteria.

It is our pleasure to thank the members of the Program Committee, the
additional reviewers, the members of the Organizing Committee as well as all
the speakers. Without their work and dedication, this Summer School would not
have been possible. Last but not least, we owe special thanks to the PrimeLife
project, SAP, Microsoft Research, Eurecom, HumanIT at Karlstad University
as well as IFIP for their support.

March 2010   Michele Bezzi
                                                           Penny Duquenoy
                                                    Simone Fischer-Hübner
                                                             Marit Hansen

Organization

The PrimeLife/IFIP Summer School 2009 was organized by the EU FP7 Project PrimeLife and the IFIP Working Groups 9.2, 9.6/11.7, 11.4 and 11.6.

General Chair

Michele Bezzi   SAP Research, France

Program Committee Co-chairs

Penny Duquenoy	Middlesex University, UK, IFIP WG 9.2 Chair
Simone Fischer-Hübner	Karlstad University, Sweden, IFIP WG11.6 Vice Chair
Marit Hansen	Independent Centre for Privacy Protection Schleswig-Holstein, Kiel, Germany

Organizing Committee Chair

Jean-Christophe Pazzaglia   SAP Research, France

Program Committee

Jan Camenisch	IBM Research, Switzerland, IFIP WP 11.4 Chair
Mark Gasson	University of Reading, UK
Hans Hedbom	Karlstad University, Sweden
Tom Keenan	University of Calgary, Canada
Dogan Kesdogan	Siegen University, Germany
Kai Kimppa	University of Turku, Finland
Eleni Kosta	KU Leuven, Belgium
Ronald Leenes	Tilburg University, The Netherlands
Elisabeth de Leeuw	Ordina, The Netherlands, IFIP WG 11.6 Chair
Marc van Lieshout	Joint Research Centre, Spain
Javier Lopez	University of Malaga, Spain
Vaclav Matyas	Masaryk University, Brno, Czech Republic
Martin Meints	Independent Centre for Privacy Protection Schleswig-Holstein, Kiel, Germany
Jean-Christophe Pazzaglia	SAP Research, France
Uli Pinsdorf	Europäisches Microsoft Innovations Center GmbH/EMIC, Germany
Andreas Pfitzmann	TU Dresden, Germany

Charles Raab	University of Edinburgh, UK
Kai Rannenberg	Goethe University Frankfurt, Germany, IFIP TC11 Chair
Dieter Sommer	IBM Research, Switzerland
Sandra Steinbrecher	TU Dresden, Germany
Morton Swimmer	John Jay College of Criminal Justice, CUNY, USA
Jozef Vyskoc	VaF, Slovakia
Rigo Wenning	W3C, France
Diane Whitehouse	The Castlegate Consultancy, UK
Pierangela Samarati	Milan University, Italy
Gregory Neven	IBM Research Zurich, Switzerland

Additional Reviewers

Sebastian Clauß	TU Dresden, Germany
Benjamin Kellermann	TU Dresden, Germany
Katrin Borcea-Pfitzmann	TU Dresden, Germany

Table of Contents

Lifelong Privacy

Priavcy for Social Network Sites and Collabrative Systems

Privacy for eGovernment Applications

Privacy and Identity Management for eHealth and Ambient Assisted Living Applications

Anonymisation and Privacy-Enhancing Technologies

Identity Management and Multilateral Security

Usability, Awareness and Transparency Tools

Lifelong Privacy:
Privacy and Identity Management for Life

Andreas Pfitzmann and Katrin Borcea-Pfitzmann

Technische Universität Dresden, Faculty of Computer Science
D-01062 Dresden, Germany
{andreas.pfitzmann,katrin.borcea}@tu-dresden.de
http://dud.inf.tu-dresden.de

Abstract. The design of identity management preserving an individual's privacy must not stop at supporting the user in managing her/his present identities. Instead, since any kind of privacy intrusion may have implications on the individual's future life, it is necessary that we identify and understand the issues related to longterm aspects of privacy-enhancing identity management. Only that way, according solutions can be developed, which enable users to control the disclosure of their personal data throughout their whole lives, comprising past, present, and future.

This paper will give a general overview about concepts supporting privacy-enhancing identity management. Further, it introduces the reader to the problem field of privacy management by means of privacy-enhancing identity management during various stages of life as well as in various areas of life. Statements about required mechanisms will be given as well as directions regarding the three most important aspects to consider when managing one's identities: communication infrastructure as well as selection of communication partners and tools.

Keywords: Privacy, Identity Management, Lifelong Aspects, Stages of Life, Areas of Life.

1   Introduction

When starting to talk about lifelong privacy[1], first we have to state that we're talking about a timeframe of nearly 100 years. Inclusion of genetics and children inheriting DNA codes from their parents into the considerations may even extend this timeframe essentially. To give a point of reference, the military would be quite happy if they could keep their secrets for about 30 years. So, what the researchers in the field of lifelong privacy are talking about is an extremely long time span.

---

[1] "Privacy is the claim of individuals, groups, or institutions to determine for themselves when, how, and to what extent information about them is communicated to others." [Wes67]

M. Bezzi et al. (Eds.): Privacy and Identity, IFIP AICT 320, pp. 1–17, 2010.

During that timeframe, an individual's world changes a lot, i.e., information and communication technology develops (remember the changes in this area during the last 40 years, which were very impressive; an even more perceivable evolution is to be expected during the next decades), and each individual's appreciation of privacy will change several times in her or his life, too.

What is really hard and, to the authors opinion, not possible to achieve is to make data fade away. Each time a user is using the Internet, possibly, s/he creates lots of traces. What s/he cannot do is reliably cause data to be destroyed on other persons' or organizations' machines – be they smart phones, laptops, desktops, or servers. One particular copy of data can be deleted if the other person or organization cooperates. But nobody knows whether there are other copies somewhere on the Internet. The approach of this problem field is two-fold:

1. *Minimization of personal data* means giving *hiding priority over disclosing data* since "if data is given out, it is out". No-one can ever call it back. At this point, we have to admit that some applications would not work well with users not willing to share personal data. *Identity management* may prove to be the most important approach to cope with this dilemma. It provides a mindset, a means to support people in managing their personal data and in sharing data that they really want to share with those people they really want to share it with. Identity Management will be dealt with in the following section. That section will explain what identity as well as management of identities shall mean. Further, it will introduce means to make identity management privacy-enhancing.

2. *Long-term security* is the second means of enabling lifelong privacy. Thereby, information- theoretically secure cryptography should be used instead of comp-lexity-theoretically secure cryptography wherever possible. Information-theoretically secure cryptography, which is sometimes called unconditionally secure cryptography, provides secure crypto independent of the attacker's computing power and algorithmic knowledge, which may essentially develop further in, e.g., 50 years. Nevertheless, migration to platforms providing stronger security should be done when they become available.

A more detailed discussion about long-term security will not be given in this paper as it is explored to a large extent already (cf., e.g., [CGHN97]). In contrary to this, identity management with regard to long-term aspects can be considered as a rather new research area. Especially, preserving or – to soften that strong term a bit – managing privacy during such a very long period of time by means of identity management takes an interesting perspective on the topic. That is why the following sections will give a general overview on the concepts of *identity, identity management,* and how it can be used to support users in managing their privacy throughout their *whole lives* by considering different stages as well as different areas of their lives. We conclude this paper by summarizing those issues important to consider when managing one's lifelong privacy based on privacy-enhancing identity management.

2   Identities and Identity Management

When talking about the concepts of *identity* and *identity management*, the question "the identity of which data subject"[2] needs to be answered. Even if almost each person has in mind natural persons when referring to identities, this could also refer to the identity of legal persons or the identity of computers. The latter is true when a person (let's call him Bob) takes a computer (e.g., being a mobile phone) with him all the time. In this case, if Bob would allow others to have a location tracking service of his computer they could track where he moves. This little example very well shows the need for some identity management for computers acting in place of their owners as well.

The development of the entities being in the position to have identity characteristics during the next 50 years we assume as follows: while the number of natural persons will not change very much (at least in comparison to the other two kinds of entities) – it can be expected that the number of human beings will not exceed the limit of 10^{10} – the number of legal persons will essentially increase (about 10^{11}). The numbers of computers, however, will explode. We expect roughly 10^{14} computing devices in the year 2059.

2.1   Identity – What Is It?

Identity is a concept that is less clear than most people would expect. So, it is more than just talking about *names*, which are easy to remember for human beings. Identity is also more than *identifiers*, which usually are unique in a certain context. And, identity is even more than being a means for secure authentication. (If looking into the longer timeframe, i.e., a person's lifetime, identifiers and means of authentication experience much more change than names.) So, identity as we understand it is:

> *Identity* primarily is a set of attribute values related to one and the same data subject.

Some of the attribute values of an identity may change over time. But, if we add a timestamp to each attribute value for which that attribute value is valid[3], then attribute values never change. And, following this train of thoughts, we can further state:

> An *identity* as a set of attribute values valid at a particular time can stay the same or grow, but never shrink.

---

[2] By data subjects we refer to entities being able to interact via communication infrastructures with other entities, i.e., natural and legal persons as well devices used to represent them in interactions. Sometimes, even sets of persons are called data subjects.

[3] A *valid* attribute value means that it is used to represent its holder in a given setting.

This is true both for a global observer as well as for each party (or set of parties pooling their information) interacting with the entity represented by the identity. Therefore, if an attacker has no access to the change history of each particular attribute, the fact whether a particular subset of attribute values of an entity is an identity, which sufficiently identifies its holder within a set of data subjects, or not may change over time. If the attacker has access to the change history of each particular attribute, any subset of attribute values forming an identity, which sufficiently identifies its holder within a set of data subjects, will form such an identity from his perspective irrespective how attribute values change.

Any reasonable attacker will not just try to figure out attribute values per se, but the points in time (or even the timeframes) they are valid (in). This is because such change histories help a lot in linking data and, thus, in inferring further attribute values. Therefore, it may clarify one's mind to define each *attribute* in such a way that its value(s) cannot get invalid. So, instead of the attribute *location* of a particular individual person, take the set of attributes *location at time x*. Depending on the inferences one is interested in, refining that set as a list ordered concerning *location* or *time* may be helpful.

Partial Identities. Having in mind that identities usually grow over time and, thus, the probability of identification of the entity within the given subset of entities usually grows as well, a solution is needed to get a way out of that privacy-related dilemma. The idea is to subset the identity of an individual, the result of which should be a possibly very large set of so called *partial identities*. Thereby, each partial identity may have its own name, own identifier, and own means of authentication. In a certain sense, each partial identity might be seen as a full-fledged identity of someone or something.

The question that has to be answered now is how the attribute values have to be subset in order to establish reasonable partial identities. Obviously, if subsetting is done badly it won't help out of the privacy-related dilemma and it only makes the life of the related person more complicated. So, the right tools have to be used and subsetting of one's identity has to be done in the right way. Then this does not only help the person whose identity is under consideration, but also the people communicating with her or him since partial identities should consist of only those attribute values, which are really needed within that particular relationship or context.

Figure 1 shows a snapshot of a person's possible partial identities in different contexts. The dark-grey areas represent different partial identities of a person being parts of the full identity of that person represented by the light-grey area. While one may assume that this identity as well as its partial identities are related to activities of the individual in either the online world or the physical world, activities may also spread to the respective other world. The authors even assume that it is really hard to say if there will be any differentiation between those two "worlds" in the next 50 or 100 years. Ambient intelligence and ubiquitous/pervasive computing might make the boundaries blur or even disappear. This means that differentiating between identity-related data of the online and of the physical worlds might not make sense anymore. To conclude,

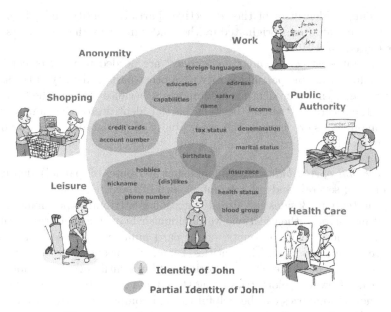

Fig. 1. Partial identities of an individual [HBPP05]

when looking into the future, subsetting the identity/ies is important whenever one strives for privacy.

Requirements for Using Partial Identities. Using partial identities requires a *basic understanding* by the data subject concerned. Of course, government and businesses have to understand it as well since managing one's (partial) identities makes sense only if the surrounding is willing to accept it.

Further, the authors assume that every person has at least one *personal computer* (or some device able to execute the according computations) administrating personal data and executing cryptographic protocols. Thereby, this personal computer is fully controlled by the user (otherwise there is no way to validate privacy properties).[4] The authors are fully aware of this today very daring assumption that all people have a computer being fully under their control. However, every time when people are talking about secure e-commerce they assume the same. So, since there are "major commercial forces" striving for that direction, it could be expected that the assumption the authors have made will become a more realistic one during the next 20 years.

By having a large set of (partial) identities, each of these (partial) identities needs its own means of authentication. Therefore, *digital pseudonyms* are needed to fulfill the requirement for secure authentication (otherwise there is no way to achieve accountability). With digital pseudonyms we refer to bit strings, which

---

[4] In contrast to the requirement indicated here, whenever somebody talks about digital rights management (DRM) then usually having the user fully in control is not what they have in mind.

represent unique identifiers of the respective (partial) identity and which are used to authenticate items originated by the holder in a way that recipients can check it (based on [PH09]).

Last but not least, *anonymous credentials*[5] are needed to transfer certified attribute values from one partial identity to another partial identity of the same identity. So, anonymous credentials are important because they are the basis for sharing authenticated attributes between partial identities of the same entity. Without anonymous credentials, the applicability of partial identities would be severely reduced.

Important Kinds of Attributes. When looking at attributes of (partial) identities, we can observe several kinds of attributes, each of them requiring a particular degree of protection. Besides the already mentioned attribute types name, identifier, and means of authentication, we distinguish biometrics, addresses (used for communication), bank accounts, credit card numbers etc. used for – to a large degree – uniquely identifying entities. Biometrics as one of these represents a well-known concept of the physical world used for identifying persons for hundreds of years. However, biometrics being stored and evaluated by computers is relatively new. Biometrics can be helpful to bind computing devices to a natural person. But, it can also by critical if it is used in contradiction to privacy attitudes of people. When considering long-time aspects, the authors expect a lot of change of identifiers, of means of authentication, in the field of biometrics, and also of addresses.

With respect to classification of identity-related attributes, there are different possibilities:

- One of the main distinctions that can be made with respect to attributes is if they are *authenticated* at all. If so, then there are two possibilities regarding who did authenticate the attribute: First option is that they are authenticated by the first party – the data subject. In this case, it would be a claim the data subject makes about her/himself and the claim would be as trustworthy as the data subject is trustworthy. The second option refers to authentication by a third party. The authors explicitly did not refer to a *trusted* third party. So, it should be quite natural to ask: The third party is trusted *by whom* and with respect *to what*?

---

[5] The concept of anonymous credentials has been introduced by David Chaum in [Cha85]. According to him, a credential provides evidence of a statement about a particular property (attribute) of a data subject. This evidence is provided by an entity, i.e., the credential issuer, about another entity, i.e., the data subject, adding authentication by the credential issuer. If that credential is transferable between different digital pseudonyms of one and the same holder and using it with these pseudonyms does not prove the sameness of their holder, then it is called an *anonymous credential*. Anonymous credentials can be brought in different representations and used towards different parties. If anonymous credentials are issued to several users, they provide a good level of privacy among those users sharing the same attribute in a certified way.

- Another approach of classification refers to *who knows* the attribute value, i.e., is the attribute value known only to the first party (the data subject) or also to second parties (the data subject's communication partner)?
- Attributes can be classified according to the *degree of changeability*. Could attributes values be changed easily or is this hard to do?
- *Variability* of attributes over time is also a possible classification whereby this could range from non-varying to fully varying. In this context: Can changes of attribute values be predicted?
- Attributes can be distinguished according to *who defines* the attribute values, i.e., are the attribute values given to the data subject by an external source or did the data subject her/himself choose the attribute values.[6]
- Another classification of attributes could be the actual *information* it contains. So, are we talking about *pure* attributes whereby the attribute values contain only information about themselves, or do the attribute values also contain significant side information?[7]
- Further, attributes can be classified according to the *relationships* the data subject is in. So, one could ask if an attribute value characterizes a single entity per se or an entity only in its relationship to other entities, e.g., entity A likes/loves/hates entity B.
- *Sensitivity* of attribute values in particular contexts can be seen as an additional means to classify attributes, though this might be a very subjective approach. However again, if considering long-term aspects, then attributes judged to be non-sensitive today, may become quite sensitive in future times (just think of a possible change of the social order).

From those approaches of classification, the question can be drawn regarding how much protection attributes or attribute values, respectively, need. Supposedly, some attribute values need much more privacy protection than others, e.g., those which

- are not easy to change,[8]
- do not vary over time or can be predicted,
- are given attribute values,
- might contain significant side information,[9] or
- are sensitive or might get sensitive, respectively, in at least one context.

These attribute values are part of the *core identity*. Of course, it would be nice to protect everything. But, to be realistic, this is almost not possible. So, whenever

---

[6] To give an example: if we refer to the attribute *color of hair* then its value can be a given (natural hair color) or a chosen (after chemical dyeing) attribute.

[7] Let's assume we use biometrics, i.e., an image of someone's face available in a high resolution. From this, some doctors possibly may conclude some diseases.

[8] To give an example for the necessity to protect those attributes, think of some biometrics gets to be known widely. Then, it might become necessary, but be very hard to change that biometrics (which could mean, e.g., handing out new fingerprints to everybody). In comparison to that, cryptographic keys can easily be revoked and new ones generated.

[9] Nobody knows which algorithms for analysis of side information will become available during the next years.

starting to manage identity attributes, one has to think what defines her or his core identity, i.e., what attributes really belong to that core identity and need, therefore, according protection. Advancements and use of technology may shift some attributes from core identity to non-core identity. E.g., the address of your house or flat is core, the current address of your laptop maybe not.

Biometrics – the extraordinary identity attribute. Biometrics has already been mentioned in this paper several times. But, since it is an eternal core-identity attribute, it represents the most important example for an attribute requiring outstanding protection. Pfitzmann discussed the issue "How to (not) use biometrics" in quite a detail in [Pfi08]. The main statements that have been made in that article relate to the following: Biometrics represents a really good concept if it is applied between a personal computing device of the person owning the biometric attribute value(s) and that person only. But it implies serious problems with regard to privacy if it is applied between, e.g., some kind of border control computer, which the person has no control over, and that person. The use of biometrics is, therefore, advised under the following conditions only:

- Biometrics is applied between a person and her/his devices only;
- Authentication is realized by possession and/or knowledge *and* biometrics;
- Classic forensic techniques are not to be devaluated (e.g., by foreign devices reading fingerprints, digital copies will make it into databases of foreign secret services and organized crime, enabling them to leave dedicated false fingerprints at the scenes of crime);
- Privacy problems by side information must be prevented when using biometrics (e.g., biometric-related measurements may also contain medical or psychological side information).

Since the safety problem remains unchanged by using biometrics between a person and her/his devices only, a possibility needs to be provided to switch off biometrics once and for all after successful biometric authentication.

2.2 Identity Management - How It Works

Identity management typically is not only between a person and its personal computer, which would imply some kind of authentication. But usually, identity management is applied within interactions between several persons and/or organizations.

Figure 2 demonstrates an example scenario where a person wants to do business with an organization. The typical data flow is as follows: The person uses a laptop. For authentication with her/his laptop, the person can use possession of the laptop, passwords, physical tokens, or biometrics. The laptop communicates to some infrastructure using addresses and encryption. This forwards the communication content to an end device within the organization.

However, such data flow is not what the person is really interested in. S/he wants to do a person-to-person communication by using names, icons, or pictures. Since interaction is mediated by a computer-based infrastructure,

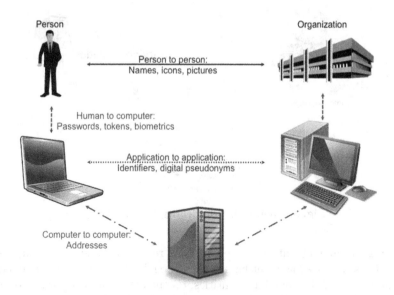

Fig. 2. Data Flows of Identity Management

application-to-application communication is required. At that level, cryptographic authentication is applied using identifiers, digital pseudonyms etc. So, whenever someone talks about digital pseudonyms, s/he is talking about computer-to-computer communication; it does not imply scenarios where human beings talk to each other addressing each other directly using digital pseudonyms.

An architecture of identity management looks like shown in Figure 3. Accordingly, a *user* communicates with a *service provider*. They use a *secure channel* for their communication. On each side, a component providing identity management (including authentication) functionalities is executed. For certain reasons, they may need services provided by so-called *Trusted Third Parties* (cf. our statements with respect to "trusted" third parties on page 6), e.g., identity brokers, PKI service, certification etc.

2.3   Presentation of Identities – Pseudonyms

Considering the use of partial identities in particular, one has to be aware that, first, partial identities have to be consciously created and established; and, second, the usage patterns of the partial identities[10] drive the kind of linkability of the attribute values and, thus, the conclusions that could be inferred. This means that users should do some partitioning of online activities according to contexts – so called context management [BDF+05].

---

[10] When referring to *usage patterns of partial identities*, we address different aspects, e.g., how frequently a partial identity is communicated; how fine-grained is the context defined in which the partial identity is used; what rules are applied when selecting a particular partial identity for an interaction.

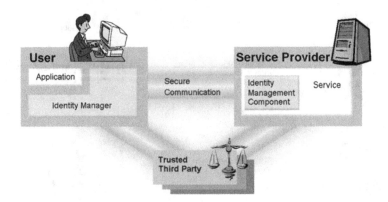

Fig. 3. Architecture of Identity Management

Identities or partial identities of an entity are represented using (digital) pseudonyms. Those are used as identifiers of the (partial) identities, on the one hand, and as addresses of the (partial) identities, on the other hand. In order to indicate holdership of a (partial) identity, an explicit link between the pseudonym and the holder of the attributes of that (partial) identity needs to be created. Thereby, different kinds of initial linking between a pseudonym and its holder can be distinguished:

- *Public pseudonym*: The linking between a pseudonym and its holder may be publicly known from the very beginning, e.g., the phone number with its holder listed in public directories.
- *Initially non-public pseudonym*: The linking between pseudonym and its holder may be known by certain parties (trustees for identity), but is not public at least initially, e.g., a bank account with the bank as trustee for identity.
- *Initially unlinked pseudonym*: The linking between pseudonym and its holder is – at least initially – not known to anybody (except the holder), e.g., biometric characteristics such as DNA (as long as not in some register).

As already mentioned, according to the usage patterns of using partial identities and, connected to them, their pseudonyms, various types of pseudonyms can be distinguished. That differentiation of pseudonyms is closely related to different levels of anonymity that are achievable by the usage patterns.

Figure 4 illustrates that interrelation. According to this, *person pseudonyms*, i.e., names or identifiers directly identifying a real person, imply the lowest degree of anonymity. Examples for such kinds of pseudonyms are numbers of identity cards or the well-known social security number, which are used with very diverse communication partners and in very manifold contexts. Further, they typically are associated with their holders over their whole lifetime. This means, each time a user communicates by indicating her/his person pseudonym, all of the person's activities could potentially be linked together. As a result, a quite detailed profile describing that person could be created.

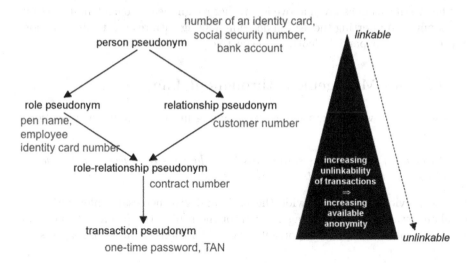

Fig. 4. Pseudonyms – Use in different contexts leading to partial order [PH09]

In comparison, *role pseudonyms* and *relationship pseudonyms* are pseudonyms used within particular contexts only. Thereby, a role pseudonym is used by its holder when acting in a certain role. An example for role pseudonyms are pen names. Similar to role pseudonyms are relationship pseudonyms. Those refer to entities within particular relationships, e.g., a pseudonym denoting someone in his or her relationship to a sports club. In this case, it does not matter if the person represents him- or herself as a trainer or as an athlete. So, the two pseudonym types are distinguished according to the following rules: Whenever a pseudonym specifies a person communicating *with* specified other entities, then we speak of a relationship pseudonym. Instead of this, if users specify *as what/whom* they communicate, then they are using role pseudonyms. Linkability is, therefore, restricted to the activities performed within the given relationship or when acting in a particular role and using the according pseudonym.

Even more privacy in terms of anonymity can be reached with help of role-relationship pseudonyms. The increase of conditions, i.e., used in a particular relationship while appearing in a special role, narrows the variety of a scenario where one and the same pseudonym is used essentially down. So, more role-relationships (and, connected with them, partial identities) have to be created for more specific contexts.

If the goal is to get utmost anonymity when communicating via a computer network, one should make use of transaction pseudonyms. So, individuals benefit from the one-time use of those transaction pseudonyms. Linkability of different actions of the pseudonym holder via the pseudonyms only is not possible any longer since the user would create a new pseudonym for each interaction that is visible outside the user's personal computer.

The classification as given above is a rather rough means to contribute to tool development supporting the user in decision making with respect to the selection of pseudonyms or partial identities, respectively.

3   Identity Management throughout Life

This section, we would like to start by summing up what the previous sections comprise:

> *An identity management system has to be the communicational gateway of its user to her/his outside world.*

So, the previous sections provide the basis and give necessary information to build on towards identity management throughout life. And passim, the authors already pointed to aspects important for considerations of long-time aspects.

3.1   Identity Management Spanning Areas of Life and Stages of Life

Identity management has to be supported by an identity management system, which needs hardware and software interfaces to, of course, legacy systems, but also to emerging systems. Thereby, the users need to be aware that their identity management systems as a hardware/software implementation will change throughout their lives several times. Further, people's attitudes regarding privacy will change, too, as all individuals run through various phases of life and are related to different areas of life.

Figure 5 is a try to depict disclosures of personal data during an individual's lifetime, which has been sketched in [CHP+09, HPS08]. Usually, even before a human being is born, a lot of personal data about the unborn child is gathered. Such gathering is continuing all the time during a human being's life. The data is stored with various data controllers involved. And, if this is being done well, thereby the data are partitioned into various partial identities: Each data controller should know only one partial identity of the human being. It would be even better if, even with respect to the same data controller, one has several distinct partial identities for distinct purposes.

Looking at a particular partial identity, there is a starting point where the partial identity is being established (in Figure 5, marked by "Establishment"). It evolves by either the person concerned adding data or by others appending data to that partial identity (in Figure 5, designated by "Evolvement"). And, finally it is terminated (in Figure 5, this is labeled by "Termination"). But, termination does not mean that the data disappears. In many cases the data will be stored further, e.g., in backups. So, data will stay for quite a long time. Assuming the person died in the moment where Figure 5 shows a coffin, still some data will be stored even after the funeral for quite a long time.

If looking at identity management today, usually it covers a short timeframe only. It takes some history of the past into account and, depending on the attitudes of the user and the possible settings of his or her identity management

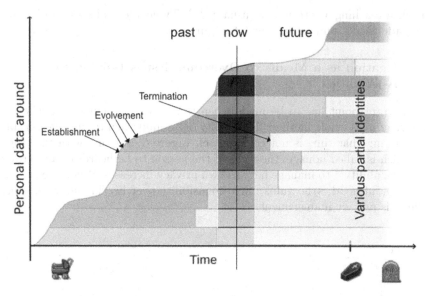

Fig. 5. Example of how partial identities develop throughout life and in various areas of life (based on [CHP⁺09])

system, it also looks a little bit into the future. What is actually required for comprehensively managing (partial) identities is a perspective taking into account the whole past and as much of the future as possible. Making a long story short, privacy throughout life means:

– covering the *full lifespan* by considering short-term as well as long-term effects;
– covering *all areas of life* by addressing context-specific as well as context-spanning aspects;
– covering *different stages of life* by respecting constant as well as changing abilities or behavior, respectively, of individuals.

When talking about *areas of life*, formal and informal areas are addressed. In formal areas, i.e., government, education, work, and health care, people have to participate whereas in informal areas, i.e., family, friends, shopping, and church, one may choose whether to participate or even others decide for the person, respectively.

A *stage of life* of an individual with respect to managing her/his privacy is a period of life in which his rights and abilities to do so remain between defined boundaries characterizing this stage of life. A concrete stage might be defined in different areas of life differently, e.g., in Christian churches, a young man becomes adult after his confirmation (typically at age between 12 or 14) whereas for the point of view of a national government, a young man becomes adult when reaching a certain age (usually 18). Typical formal stages of life are nonage, adulthood, and retirement (cf. Figure 6).

3.2   Delegation as a Means to Overcome Issues Related to (Dis-)Abilities

One important point has to be made when talking about managing one's privacy during one's whole lifetime: The ability of an individual to manage her/his privacy during that time is not constant, cf. Figure 6. Starting with the stage of life which is called nonage, the right of the person to be heard usually grows because the ability[11] to manage her/his own privacy increases. When the person arrives at adulthood, s/he gains full responsibility over her/his life and, thus, over her/his privacy management.

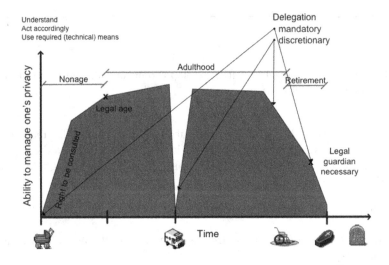

Fig. 6. Ability to manage one's private sphere during an individual's lifetime (based on [CHP+09])

The case of accidents, temporary hospitalizations etc. may severely reduce the capability of handling one's data and, related to this, the capability of managing one's privacy. If s/he does not pass away before, each human being will get old (stage of retirement), which again may start reducing her/his abilities including the ones to taking responsibility of her/his privacy. In an extreme case, a legal guardian is needed. So, when looking at the curve in Figure 6, some people will start experiencing a loss of ability with respect to managing their privacy. At the end of their lives, this may lead to an ability similar to the one of children or even of babies.

---

[11] The semantics of "ability" is: understanding a situation, to act accordingly, and to use the required (technical) means.

In result of the considerations regarding the different levels with respect to the ability to manage one's own privacy, a very important concept has to be taken into account: *delegation*. Rights of the child are delegated by law – usually to their parents. This is very similar to situations where people need legal guardians and their rights are delegated to their legal guardians, which, of course, has to include rights and duties concerning privacy. So, the parents should take care of the privacy of their kids as legal guardians have to do so.

Delegation may happen in a mandatory fashion imposed by law. And, it can be realized in a discretionary manner. To give an example for the latter: A person is waking up in a hospital after experiencing an accident and having to undergo an operation. That person may decide for her/himself that s/he will need another person (her/his surrogate) temporarily taking over authorities and duties of the patient. Also, in case of old age, it could be a good decision that the person concerned defines a surrogate who will take over responsibilities by the time when s/he is losing the according abilities.

3.3 Mechanisms

The prime technological concepts and mechanisms required to realize reasonable lifelong privacy based on identity management have been introduced in Section 2. The following list summarizes what concepts and mechanisms are already available:

- Much theoretical work exists describing how to *handle partial identities.*
- How to *minimize personal data* is also known in principle.
- *Enforceable rules for data processing* and how to handle them are known as well.
- Further, researchers elaborated and are still working on several kinds of *transparency functionality* including how to check and inspect computers.

Even though many of the indicated concepts are well-elaborated and studied in theory, it is still an open issue putting them into practice. In addition, there are open issues for research and discussion, which need development effort and/or adaptations:

- As many *areas of life as possible and sensible* have to be covered.
- The *variances of stages of life* have to be regarded.
- Elaborations have to address the *full lifespan* when developing support for the management of an individual's privacy.

4 Conclusion

The authors do not claim having provided *the* solution solving all the problems connected with lifelong privacy. Instead, the problem field has been framed and known solutions have been described.

However, this work has shown that managing one's lifelong privacy affects many aspects people are not yet aware of. So, one of the most important tasks of researchers, educators, government etc. is to tell people to be attentive to managing their identity implying the management of partial identities. Otherwise, others will manage them – in a way that might not foster their privacy.

While managing their privacy, people should find a compromise, which they consider being right, between their desire or need to interact and their privacy. For this, the following three issues have to be considered:

1. Finding a good compromise based on human (subjective) decision is and will be an issue as long as the according *tools* helping to achieve the required compromise are not available. Several project groups are currently working on such tools, e.g., PRIME[12] as well as its succeeding project PrimeLife[13].
2. Besides the mentioned tools, an according privacy-preserving *communication infrastructure* is needed. Such an infrastructure has to prevent attaching permanent identifiers to the communication partners (e.g., network addresses). I.e., if all communication activities of an individual use the same network address then the network address is a globally unique identifier allowing to link all these activities together and, thus, also to link all partial identities. That kind of communication infrastructure would make privacy-enhancing identity management at the application layer void.
3. Finally, the right *communication partners* have to be chosen, i.e., avoiding those which are unnecessarily privacy-invasive. Communication partners labeling themselves as trustworthy should cause quite some distrust with the privacy-aware individual.

Acknowledgments. We like to thank the attendees of the keynote talk related to this article for their very helpful comments. The research leading to these results has received funding from the European Community's Seventh Framework Programme (FP7/2007-2013) under grant agreement no. 216483.

References

[BDF+05] Borcea, K., Donker, H., Franz, E., Liesebach, K., Donker, H., Wahrig, H.: Intra-Application Partitioning of Personal Data. In: Proceeding of the Workshop on Privacy-Enhanced Personalization (PEP 2005), UC Irvine Institute for Software Research (ISR), July 2005, pp. 67–74 (2005)

[CGHN97] Canetti, R., Gennaro, R., Herzberg, A., Naor, D.: Proactive security: Long-term protection against break-ins. RSA Laboratories' CryptoBytes 3(1), 1–8 (1997)

[Cha85]   Chaum, D.: Security without Identification: Transaction Systems to Make Big Brother Obsolete. Communications of the ACM 28(10), 1030–1044 (1985)

[CHP+09] Clauß, S., Hansen, M., Pfitzmann, A., Raguse, M., Steinbrecher, S.: Tackling the challenge of lifelong privacy. In: eChallenges (October 2009)

---

[12] https://www.prime-project.eu/
[13] http://www.primelife.eu/

[HBPP05] Hansen, M., Borcea-Pfitzmann, K., Pfitzmann, A.: PRIME - Ein europäisches Projekt für nutzerbestimmtes Identitätsmanagement. It - Information Technology, Oldenbourg 6(47), 352–359 (2005)

[HPS08]   Hansen, M., Pfitzmann, A., Steinbrecher, S.: Identity management throughout one's whole life. Information Security Technical Report 13(2), 83–94 (2008)

[Pfi08]   Pfitzmann, A.: Biometrics – how to put to use and how not at all? In: Furnell, S.M., Katsikas, S.K., Lioy, A. (eds.) TrustBus 2008. LNCS, vol. 5185, pp. 1–7. Springer, Heidelberg (2008)

[PH09]   Pfitzmann, A., Hansen, M.: A terminology for talking about privacy by data minimization: Anonymity, Unlinkability, Undetectability, Unobservability, Pseudonymity, and Identity Management, December 2009, v0.32 (2009), https://dud.inf.tu-dresden.de/Anon_Terminology.shtml

[Wes67]   Westin, A.F.: Privacy and Freedom. New York Atheneum (1967)

Delegation for Privacy Management from Womb to Tomb – A European Perspective[*]

Marit Hansen[1], Maren Raguse[2], Katalin Storf[1], and Harald Zwingelberg[1]

[1] Unabhängiges Landeszentrum für Datenschutz Schleswig-Holstein,
Holstenstr. 98, 24103 Kiel, Germany
`{ULD6,ULD77,ULD65}@datenschutzzentrum.de`
[2] Ministerium für Arbeit, Soziales und Gesundheit Schleswig-Holstein,
Adolf-Westphal Str. 4, 24146 Kiel, Germany
`maren.raguse@sozmi.landsh.de`

Abstract. In our information society with processing of personal data in almost all areas of life, the legally granted right to privacy is quite hard to preserve. User-controlled identity management systems have been proposed as a means to manage one's own private sphere. Still there is no functioning concept how privacy protection can be effectively safeguarded over a long time period and how self-determination in the field of privacy can be maintained in all stages of life from the womb to the tomb. When user control and the capability to exercise rights can not yet or no longer be carried out by the data subject herself, the decisions concerning the processing of personal data may have to be delegated to a delegate. In this text, we elaborate on delegation of privacy-relevant actions under a lifelong perspective and point out possible legal, technological, and organizational measures to appropriately take up the arising challenges. For crucial gaps in current concepts we sketch solutions and explain implications on user-controlled identity management systems. Finally we give recommendations to stakeholders such as data controllers, application designers and policy makers.

Keywords: lifelong privacy, user-controlled identity management, delegation of privacy, incapability to exercise rights, privacy by delegate.

1 Introduction

Since the beginning of humankind, technological progress has led to a change of society. However, in a time of rapid development of technologies and applications it

---

[*] The research leading to these results has received funding from the European Community's Seventh Framework Programme (FP7/2007-2013) under grant agreement n° 216483. The information in this document is provided "as is", and no guarantee or warranty is given that the information is fit for any particular purpose. The above referenced consortium members shall have no liability for damages of any kind including without limitation direct, special, indirect, or consequential damages that may result from the use of these materials subject to any liability which is mandatory due to applicable law.

M. Bezzi et al. (Eds.): Privacy and Identity, IFIP AICT 320, pp. 18–33, 2010.

is hard for many people to keep pace with changing trends. Who could have predicted thirty years ago that personal computers, mobile phones, and navigation systems would become part of life of almost every individual in the industrialized world? And who has a clue what our information society will look like in another thirty years? Extrapolating from our quite young experience with information and communication technologies, we see a risk that certain traditional values and concepts – such as privacy protection – which have proven themselves good for a democratic society will be abandoned, probably more or less by accident. This calls for solutions how to maintain one's privacy throughout one's life as it is discussed in [1] and [2].

In this text we focus on privacy aspects of delegation as a means to support individuals in stages of life when they cannot act on their own – from prenatal stages over birth to death, and possibly even a bit beyond. Similarly individuals can be supported who are not willing to act on their own regarding some aspects of their privacy although they might be capable to do it. For a better understanding of the following sections, we give some definitions:

Stage of life: A **stage of life** of an individual with respect to managing her privacy is a period of life in which her ability to do so remains between defined boundaries characterizing this stage of life [1, 2]. Every individual during her lifetime passes through one or more stages during which she is incapable of managing her privacy on her own. Such an **incapability of managing one's privacy** means not having the ability to sufficiently understand the consequences of data processing relevant to one's private sphere or to (re)act upon them appropriately.

Delegation: Delegation is a process whereby a **delegate** (also called "proxy", "mandatory" or "agent") is authorized to act on behalf of a **person concerned** via a **mandate of authority** (or for short: mandate).

The mandate of authority usually defines in particular

(1) the **scope of authority** for the actions of a delegate on behalf of a person concerned and

(2) when and under which conditions the delegate gets the **power of authority** to act on behalf of the person concerned.

The delegate shall only act on behalf of the person concerned if the delegate has the actual power of authority and if his action lies within the scope of authority. The simple acting of the delegate with the existence of a mandate while not having the power of authority would not be sufficient. The difference between mandate and power of authority becomes clear in the following example: In working life the schedule of responsibilities may determine that person A should take over the work of colleague B if the latter is absent. The issuance of the mandate of authority to A is expressed by the schedule of responsibilities, but the A's actual power of authority only comes into existence if B is absent. Otherwise A must not act on behalf of B.

The mandate of authority is issued by the **delegator** (also called "mandator"). This may be the person concerned herself, but there are also cases where other entities explicitly decide on the delegation (e.g., in the case of incapacitation of a person the guardianship court rules on delegation) or where the delegation is foreseen in law (e.g., when parents are the default delegates of their young children). The mandate of authority is usually assigned for a specific period of time. Similar to the process of issuing a mandate, changing or revoking the mandate can be done by the delegator, i.e., by the person concerned herself or by other entities. The conditions and processes to issue, change, or revoke a mandate can be defined by the underlying contract or law.

Note that not always the delegate is aware of the mandate of authority or of the fact that he actually has the power of authority. So the delegator should implement an appropriate way of informing the delegate (and the person concerned if she is not the delegator herself) about the mandate and the power of authority.

For supervising purposes of the delegation and related actions by the parties involved, one or more impartial **delegation supervisors** may be appointed by one or more of the actors. In particular the person concerned may have the need to check whether the delegate really acts as agreed upon.

Delegation has been discussed by various authors, mainly aiming at technical solutions for specific scenarios. Putting the focus on privacy aspects and adding the legal perspective, we deviate slightly from the definitions used in [3] or [4].[1] In our setting, the person concerned is a natural person with some interest in her privacy; the other actors, in particular the delegate, may be natural persons, also caring for their individual privacy.

European data protection legislation: In this text we focus on the European view with respect to data protection and protection of one's private sphere: The baseline of this view is Art. 8 of the European Convention on Human Rights which provides a right to respect for one's "private and family life, his home and his correspondence". Several laws and by-laws substantiate privacy-relevant issues. For EC Member States, the European Data Protection Directive 95/46/EC and further directives in the areas of telecommunication or e-commerce harmonize data protection regulation. The European Data Protection Directive defines the following terms in its Art. 2:

"personal data' shall mean any information relating to an identified or identifiable natural person ('**data subject**'); an identifiable person is one who can be identified, directly or indirectly, in particular by reference to an identification number or to one or more factors specific to his physical, physiological, mental, economic, cultural or social identity";

"processing of personal data' ('**processing**') shall mean any operation or set of operations which is performed upon personal data, [...], such as collection, recording, organization, storage, adaptation or alteration, retrieval, consultation, use, disclosure by transmission, dissemination or otherwise making available, alignment or combination, blocking, erasure or destruction";

"[data] **controller**' shall mean the natural or legal person, [...] which alone or jointly with others determines the purposes and means of the processing of personal data; [...]";

"[data] **processor**' shall mean a natural or legal person, [...] which processes personal data on behalf of the controller".

Note that usually privacy management of individuals is intertwined with actions from other contexts of life (e.g., using a service or communicating with other persons) so that it is difficult to restrict delegation on privacy management only. On the other hand, delegation performed not specifically for the purpose of privacy management very often cannot be separated fully from privacy-relevant issues. For instance if a delegate is handling the financial affairs of a person concerned, this involves personal

---

[1] See also Section 5 on related work.

data of the person concerned, of all financial contacts, and finally of the delegate herself – and all these data can be relevant for managing the private sphere of the person concerned, and as we will see later, also of the delegate. In the following, we will speak about "delegation of privacy-relevant actions" which encompasses explicit privacy management activities such as the exercise of data subjects' rights as well as other issues which may be relevant to the privacy of the person concerned.

Delegation of privacy-relevant actions to third persons becomes a necessity within any stage of life where an individual is incapable to conduct them on her own, and specifically where she is incapable to care for her privacy needs on her own behalf [5]. After this introduction Section 2 analyzes privacy aspects of delegation. Relevant stages of life (determined, e.g., by childhood, temporary illness, or dementia) together with main legal regulations on delegation, corresponding challenges and possible solutions will be further discussed in Section 3. Section 4 elaborates on recommendations for implementing privacy-aware delegation. Related work is presented in Section 5. Finally, Section 6 concludes the text and gives an outlook.

2 Privacy-Relevant Challenges Concerning Delegation

Civil laws around the world provide sophisticated mechanisms on legal kinds of delegation such as representation and agency including a framework of rights for the time when the delegation ends. This might, depending on the legal system, include rules on liability or rules regarding minors' rights to nullify or resign from contracts concluded in their name by their parents. Also protective means against indebtedness of minors reaching maturity are regularly in place.[2] While debts can be legally nullified and contracts cancelled, a transmission of personal data including the resulting consequences once the information has been released may not be revoked as easily, if possible at all. Usually the actions of the delegate on behalf of the person concerned include disclosure of personal data of the person concerned and/or the delegate, so both may have to bear immediate or later consequences to their own privacy. In the following, several privacy-relevant challenges concerning delegation are pointed out.

2.1 Transparency of Privacy-Relevant Actions Performed by the Delegate

A precondition for managing a person's privacy is transparency on who processes one's personal data for which purpose and under which conditions. This also applies to past transactions or other disclosures of personal data. Getting this information should be easily possible for all individuals concerned, and of course also when involving a delegate. However, in the online world people scarcely know all aspects of data processing which may be relevant to their privacy, e.g., they are rarely aware of data trails like IP addresses or browser chatter in local or remote log files, they have no idea who can access their data on routers or servers, they do not know about profiling algorithms applied to their digital identities. Even in the offline world it is difficult to be sure who else gets access to personal data disclosed to one data controller

---

[2] For example, the German Civil Code (Bürgerliches Gesetzbuch – BGB) limits the liability of a young adult for debts assumed by the legal representatives to the person's assets when reaching majority age, § 1629a BGB.

because there may be further data processors involved, or the data may be transferred to other data controllers, or there may be a data breach giving access to unauthorized parties.

For online transactions, user-controlled identity management systems have been proposed [5, 6, 7] which – among others – can store privacy-relevant information on past transactions and provide the possibility to later find out about which data the user has disclosed to whom in a former transaction. In the PRIME/PrimeLife project this functionality is called "Data Track" [6]. The data track aims at providing a comprehensive overview of what personal data the user has released to whom, under which partial identity (in particular under which pseudonym), when, and under which conditions (including privacy policy statements such as the purpose, the retention time etc.) [7]. Transferring this concept to delegation entails that one can establish some kind of shared data track which enables the person concerned to know about privacy-relevant actions the delegate performed on her behalf and likewise gives input to the respective identity management systems of the person concerned and the delegate as far as their own partial identities are concerned.

Another solution is to get help from another party which can supervise the delegate's actions: The person concerned could appoint one or more impartial **delegation supervisors** which could see or check all other delegates' actions, but could not act otherwise. For transparency reasons, supervising actions of such a delegation supervisor in general have to be visible for all involved and supervised persons.

2.2 Making Actions from the Person Concerned and the Delegate Distinguishable

Many of today's services like web shops or online banking applications, or social networks are not designed to support delegates. In particular they don't enable them authentication [8] on their own and expressing the fact and extent of delegation. For services which use knowledge-based authentication mechanisms, e.g., account name combined with a password or PIN, a person concerned is frequently forced to reveal her identification credentials to the delegate who will then act under the name of the person concerned. In case the authentication is object-based and involves, e.g., a hardware token such as a chipcard, the person concerned would have to give this token to the delegate. Often the service's terms of use prohibit the transfer of authentication credentials. For the service it is not distinguishable whether actions are taken by the person concerned or the delegate or an identity thief. In [9] where a typology of various characteristics of "identity[3] change" among different actors is elaborated, "identity delegation" with consent of the "original identity bearer" is dissociated from "identity takeover" without the identity bearer's consent – but these two forms won't be distinguishable for the service when using the same credentials. At least in cases where the person concerned has never granted authority for the measures taken on her behalf and under her name, it becomes a problem if she cannot prove to the service that she didn't act on her own. Then she instead of the delegate would be held liable for the performed actions. This could be avoided when the underlying infrastructure would support that delegates act under their own partial identity, e.g., the person

---

[3] Note that [5] uses the term "identity" also for "partial identities".

concerned assigns certain rights to the delegate's account or issues specific credentials to the delegate also indicating the scope of the delegate's authority. The introduction of measures that enable delegates to act under their own name should be encouraged by all relevant stakeholders such as data protection commissions, administration, standardization bodies and the service providers themselves.

2.3 Guidelines for the Delegate

As people may feel very differently how it should be dealt with their personal data, a person concerned should be able to define preferences and guidelines or even set specific conditions for the use of her personal data. Lawmakers should provide general guidelines how delegates should – when other preferences are absent – treat personal information of an incapable person concerned. However, when a person concerned is able to stipulate certain preferences, she should be enabled to influence the treatment of her (partial) identities to a certain extent, e.g., extroverted persons may allow and encourage the use of their own photographs in social networks, while others may prefer to remain as anonymous as possible.

Applying data tracks raises further questions such as to which data track to write when a delegate exercises the rights of the person concerned under the delegate's name. In such cases both involved persons release personal data and thus could (or should) store this information for future reference. However, both the person concerned and the delegate process personal data about each other – it may even be discussed whether they may become data controllers in the sense of the European Data Protection Directive 95/46/EC themselves [10]. No matter whether it is a legally obliged data controller or another entity processing personal data, the processing entity bears some responsibility for the data which requires the provision of appropriate safeguards. Among others, a deletion period for the data could be indicated and enforced, or for enhancing trust, certain rights on the processing of each other's personal data could be stipulated.

2.4 Balancing the Interests of the Person Concerned and the Delegate

While a delegate should be bound to the general guidelines and expressed preferences, these requirements must not be overstrained. Otherwise possible delegates might refrain from volunteering due to fear of liability. Rather a fair balance must be struck with other duties conferred to the delegate, e.g., being an appointed custodian as well. Often delegates will not be professionals in data protection, but rather in a personal stress situation as a near relative or friend became unexpectedly incapable to act on her own behalf and privacy-related considerations are understandably only of minor significance compared to solving pressing problems such as getting a medical treatment or home care.

3 Delegation at Different Stages of Life

The challenges indicated in the previous section and possible solutions for a delegation of privacy-relevant actions may differ and require customization in accordance to the stage of life concerned. These stages and specific legal and factual characteristics are identified in the following.

The approach of user-controlled identity management [5, 7] as well as of exercising informational self-determination presupposes that the acting data subject sufficiently comprehends the effect of the data processing as a question and likewise can act accordingly. Every natural person during her lifetime passes through (a) stage(s) of life during which she does not have the ability to understand the consequences of data processing conducted by data controllers, or she is not capable to exercise her self-determination via the provided means, e.g., due to usability problems. During these phases a data subject needs to be represented by another person who exercises the right on behalf of her. This may start when a child is born, and it may continue in the case of adults that have temporary or permanent needs to get support, and it may finally end with the death of the data subject concerning her last will.

The current civil legal framework encompasses several instruments regulating legal representation or agency which have an effect also with regards to the exercise of fundamental rights: For minors the instrument of parental care is known in civil law. Most of the EC Member States also have legal regulations regarding the representation on children. The Article 29 Data Protection Working Party defined in its Opinion 2/2009 [11] principles regarding children's privacy which we generalize in the following to the relation of persons concerned and delegates regarding privacy-relevant actions:

- The delegate should act in the best interest of the person concerned. This may comprise protection and care which are necessary for the well-being of the person concerned.
- Guidelines for delegation should be defined beforehand.
- The person concerned and her delegates may have competing interests. If conflicts cannot be avoided, it should be clarified how to sort them out, possibly with the help of external parties. Note that a delegate does not necessarily stand in for all partial identities of the person concerned which may lead to additional conflicts of interest of parties involved.
- The degree of delegation should be geared to the capabilities of the person concerned regarding privacy and self-determination. This means that the degree of accountability of the person concerned has to be adapted over time, and regarding privacy-relevant decisions taken by the delegate, the person concerned has a right to be consulted.

It appears that the privacy protection rights of an individual are exercised by different people during the lifetime. This asks for a delegation system where it is clear for all parties involved who can perform which rights at which moment and in which context. The consequences of the delegate's actions may both influence the privacy of the person concerned and the delegate herself to a certain extent.

The following subsections explore various stages of life with respect to delegation.

3.1 Fruit of the Womb ("From womb …")

Privacy throughout life comprises a very early stage of life, the prenatal phase of an individual. Even in this stage of life there might be the need to protect personal data, e.g., considering the privacy implications of prenatal DNA tests. In many EC Member States there are discussions about the issue of genetic analysis and the threat a use of genetic data poses for individuals regarding their right to informational self-determination as well as potential discrimination. Regulations regarding requirements for genetic analysis and the use of genetic data could be a solution.

3.2 Children and Teenagers

Growing autonomy is an important issue in protection of children's rights, in any area of law. The complexity of situations involving minors is based on the fact that children, despite having full rights, need a representative to exercise these rights – including their privacy rights. Data protection for children starts within the first days after birth and the processing and storage of birth data or medicine data within the hospital. The protection of personal data of children resides more or less in the responsibility of parents or legal guardians. But when a child grows up, other responsible persons for data processing in different areas of life may become involved, such as teachers, doctors or supervisors [5].

The rights of the child and the exercise of those rights – including that of data protection – should be expressed in a way which recognizes as many as possible of the abovementioned aspects of the situation [11] as follows: until a certain age children have no way to monitor data processing, simply because they are too young to be involved in certain activities. If their parents decide, for example, to put the child's pictures on their profile in a social network, it is the parents who make the decision about the processing of their children's data and give the consent to do so on behalf of the child. Normally, putting pictures of another person in a social network profile requires consent of that person, the data subject. In the situation described here, the parents are entitled to express the consent in the name of the child. Such a situation may put the parents in the double role – of data controllers while publishing their child's personal information open on the web, and, at the same time, of consent issuers as the child's representatives. This double role may easily lead to conflicts. Parents must take great care not to cross the line of the child's best interest when processing the child's data.

It is necessary for the parents or other representatives to listen carefully to the interests of the child at least beginning from a certain age and consider those interests when making a privacy-relevant decision as that decision is binding for the child [11]. When the child reaches legal age and becomes an adult, it may want to change the recent decision of the parents. Therefore the child needs to know what decisions about processing of personal data were made by the representatives. Afterwards the child needs to give her explicit consent for the processing of personal data. This may be implemented in certain operations in a way that the operator is reminded that the person of legal age[4] and now the explicit consent is needed. This is relevant in many

---

[4] The definition of "legal age" of a person and the corresponding age in years differs within Europe. There are different categories of legal age, such as age of consent with respect to sexual activities, age of criminal responsibility, legal drinking age, marriage age, voting age or age of majority. The age of majority is in general the threshold of adulthood and defines the chronological moment when a minor ceases to legally be considered a child and assumes control over their personal actions and decisions. The age of majority means terminating the legal control and legal responsibility of the parents or other guardians. In the European Members States the age of majority is set to 18 years.

circumstances, e.g., medical matters, recreational activities of the child, school matters, or agreements made by the parents before the child's majority.

As children and teenagers are in the process of developing physically and mentally, the rights of the child and the exercise of those rights – including the rights of data protection – should be accomplished in a way which recognizes these aspects of the situation. Especially the adaptation of the degree of maturity of children and teenagers is a central aspect that has to be taken into account by their parents. Children gradually become capable of contributing to decisions made about them. It is natural that the level of comprehension is not the same in case of a 7-year-old child and a 15-year-old teenager.[5] This in particularity has to be recognized by the children's representatives. Therefore the children should be consulted more regularly about the exercise of their rights, including those relating to data protection.

The children's representatives should also think about a way to document privacy-relevant decisions so that when the children have become teenagers or young adults they can easily understand what personal data have been disclosed to whom and under which conditions. This would enable the grown-up children to actively approach certain data controllers to give or revoke consent concerning data processing or to request access, rectification or erasure of their personal data.

3.3 Adults Lacking Privacy Management Capabilities

For adults that may have temporary or permanent needs to get support or that others act on behalf concerning decisions on their private sphere, we distinguish between delegation for legally relevant actions and non-legally relevant actions. All legally relevant actions regarding processing of personal data are based on national legal regulations such as delegation or legal guardianship.

In case of non-legally relevant actions, such as help with a social network or the Internet in general the person concerned can freely decide what to do. The person concerned could choose a delegate to act in the name of the person on the basis of a contract to manage the private sphere. Then the person concerned should clearly define her expectations and needs regarding the representation and the power of disposal.

3.4 Deceased People ("… to tomb")

In situations where a person has died, the instrument of law of succession applies. The European Data Protection Directive 95/46/EC assigns the right of privacy and data protection to "natural persons" (Article 1). Deceased persons are no longer regarded as data subjects. Protection against an unregulated processing of data concerning deceased individuals in some European legal frameworks[6] is provided by means of a "post-mortal personality right". In some situations, the instrument offered by the law of succession might not be sufficient – further regulations are needed.

---

[5] The level of comprehension is defined in different ways. For instance the US-American Children's Online Privacy Protection Act (COPPA, Title XII – Children's online privacy protection, SEC. 1302) defines a child as an individual under the age of 13.

[6] Such as Germany: so-called "Mephisto decision" of the German Constitutional Court; BVerfGE 30, 173.

For instance, some users of social networks want their profile to exist even after death or at least would like to be informed how the provider handles the personal data and the profile after death. Here the action of providers of social networks is required to find mechanisms and concepts for handling of profiles after death of the user. Various mechanisms are thinkable, e.g., the user could determine how her profile should be handled after death within the registration process (deletion, blocking, delegate to contact, etc.). Therefore, SNS providers need to define clear measures and concepts to determine the handling of profiles after one's death. In some situations even the autonomous action of the SNS provider might be essential for the protection of users. For example if a SNS user dies and the press accesses the SNS site to copy pictures, contacts, etc. of the dead user, the provider has to balance the protection of the user's rights and her competence to, e.g., block the profile without the consent of the legal assignee (because this has to happen very quickly).

Meanwhile new services appear on the market which offer to send out secure messages to friends after the death of the user. Their goal is to give people a safe way to share account passwords, wills and other information. When users book the service against payment of a fee, they get options for when to send messages or to delete some messages permanently after their death. As already shown in Section 2.2, it is problematic if authentication credentials of the user have to be transferred to the service which opens the way to misuse because it is not distinguishable for others whether the user or the service acts.

4 Recommendations for Implementing Privacy-Aware Delegation

As in the networked world oblivion of negative facts is hindered or impossible and even neutral information may turn against the data subject years later, it had been our initial assumption that a need to provide for lifelong measures in respect of privacy rights exists [2, 5]. Measures must be taken urgently as also the current use and collection of data may have negative future implications on data subjects. This is not only necessary for persons who can handle their privacy interest on their own, but even more so for persons who are currently or permanently incapable to preserve their rights. In periods of incapability it becomes necessary that third persons act on behalf of the person concerned and that, if adequate, the person concerned may choose and instruct her delegates herself. Regarding privacy-aware delegation we derive a set of technical, legal, and societal recommendations and finally adapt our reflections on user-controlled identity management systems.

4.1 Recommendations for Data Controllers and Application Designers

Allowing delegation within the field of privacy requires that some preconditions are met from the involved technologies and underlying processes [5]. Implementing these is a task that is best addressed by data controllers and application designers as these stakeholders have control over the relevant technology and processes in their specific application setting. Data controllers, such as service providers, are responsible for the actual data processing and choose for that an implementation provided by an application designer. In the procurement process, data controllers should ask for the recommend functionality which should be provided by application designers. The implementation lies also within the well understood interest of these stakeholders, e.g., as the measures can increase security and especially accountability and legal enforceability of the data controller's transactions. The following measures should be implemented:

- **Technical representation of delegation:** Usually delegation is expressed by issuance of a "mandate certificate" to the delegate. Among the important procedures to be specified are: issuance of the mandate of authority to the delegate, activation of the actual power of authority, conducting actions under the name of the person concerned within the scope of the authority, verification of the authority, revocation of the authority from the delegate, and expression of acceptance of the mandate by the delegate [12]. For all these procedures it is important that they ensure the necessary level of security to prevent misuse.

- **The credentials of the person concerned must not be used by the delegate:** Delegation has to be enabled without transferring the original credentials (such as tokens or certificates) of the person concerned to prevent identity theft. Possible implementations include derived credentials for delegates or that the delegate uses own credentials to get access and then indicates that she acts in behalf of the person concerned.

- **Logging:** Actions taken by a delegate must be traceable by the person concerned or on her behalf.

- **Preferences and conditions:** Where possible, the person concerned should be enabled to define the scope of authority by declaring preferences and conditions, e.g., to partially or absolutely restrict certain disclosures, to stipulate preferences or by giving guidelines for data usage in form of preferences but allowing exceptions for transactions she is interested in regardless of the data required. The application should support both expressing these preferences and conditions and checking whether they have been adhered to.

- **Protection of the delegate's privacy:** The delegate's own desires for maintaining his privacy have to be considered in addition to the privacy requirements of the person concerned. Here **data minimizing** solutions, e.g., by anonymous authorizations, can help preserving the private spheres of both parties involved.

- **Supervision of the delegation:** As exercising privacy and other personal rights is a strictly individual decision, a person concerned should be enabled to choose one or more impartial delegation supervisors trusted by the person concerned to look after her interests. This is in particular necessary when a delegate was appointed by a third party (e.g., by a court).

- **Stipulations for post-mortal period:** Where applicable, as personal data will be processed and particularly distributed after a person's death such as in social networks, data controllers should clarify the use of such data in their privacy policies after the user's death. Users should be enabled to stipulate preferences for the post-mortal processing of their personal data.

4.2 Recommendations for Policy Makers

Several legal prerequisites are necessary to lay the foundation for effective and privacy-aware delegation. These requirements address policy makers such as parliaments for providing a solid legal foundation, but also standardization bodies and data protection authorities for ensuring practicability and consistent enforcement.

- **Delegation in privacy issues should be recognized by law** as far as legally possible, e.g., requiring actions in person only where private law acknowledges similar requirements (like the requirement that a will cannot be made by a delegate could correspond with a regulation that privacy rights for the post-mortal period require a specific written authorization). It must be compulsory for data controllers to accept declarations made by a delegate on behalf of a person concerned. Concerning the legally granted data protection rights of data subjects such as the "right of access", the "rights to rectify or to delete", and the "right to object", the "Joint Proposal for a Draft of International Standards on the Protection of Privacy with regard to the processing of Personal Data" [13] already states that data subjects should be able to exercise those rights "through a representative who shall satisfactorily establish his/her status to the responsible person". Thereby the proof of the identity of the person concerned and her consent as well as the mandate must not be too complicated or costly. Until a reliable eID infrastructure is available, policy makers should provide a respective means for offline use, e.g., with a harmonized form.

- **Delegate not acting under the (partial) identity of the person concerned:** Acting as a delegate should be done under the name of the delegate, under pseudonym, or anonymously while indicating the authorization of the person concerned to act on her behalf.

- **Supervision by the person concerned:** To enable the person concerned to supervise actions taken in her name, certain prerequisites must be met to enable a later revision of privacy-relevant actions in a manipulation-resistant log (e.g., in a shared data track). This supervision has to be transitive if the delegate herself has commissioned other delegates as her own stand-in. As a further consequence the person concerned should also be able to directly exercise her right of access with any data controller – without involving their regular delegate(s). Also minors should be enabled to get professional advice.

- **Specific legal regulations:** In accordance with the suggestions of the Article 29 Data Protection Working Party [11] we suggest that national legislation and interpretation of data protection law should consider minors and other persons incapable to exercise their privacy rights. Such a regulation should provide guidance and boundaries for delegates.

- **Protection of the delegate:** As persons that are (temporarily) incapable to act on their own with respect to privacy rights are dependant on delegates to act on their behalf, it is necessary that delegates are available. This requires that being a delegate does not comprise too many risks as otherwise only a few persons would volunteer for the task. Policy makers could contribute to this by limiting the liability of delegates. In addition, it would not be proportional to track each action of a delegate in detail as the delegate's privacy may be concerned, too. Here the interests of the person concerned and the delegate have to be balanced in a fair way.

- **Best practices for authorizations of delegates:** Data protection authorities or standardization bodies may provide for a set of predefined authorizations of delegates including definite descriptions of the respective scope of authority. This could possibly give start to research on a whole ontology of the types and causes for delegation and possible limitations of the scope of the authority necessary to comply with the cause's specific needs.

4.3 Societal Recommendations

Besides these legal and technical requirements for delegation it is necessary to raise awareness for privacy-related issues in the broad public beginning by including specific privacy-related topics in the curricula for school students. However, considering that parents act as delegates and that sports clubs and schools also publish information on minors, these groups bear high responsibility for data disclosures, underlining the need for specific awareness raising programs in these groups as well.

Teachers, doctors, trainers and other caretakers often take the position of factual delegates, temporarily representing the children's interests within a certain area of life. Here also self-determination and transparency are necessary as soon and as far as possible, requiring a communication with appointed or self chosen delegates of the person concerned. Such factual delegates should handle disclosure of personal data as restrictively as possible and acquire consent of the competent delegate. Especially these caretakers should work on empowering at least those who are only temporarily incapable of handling privacy-relevant actions instead of making themselves indispensible and provoking a lock-in effect.

4.4 Implementing Privacy-Aware Delegation in Identity Management Systems

For the implementation of user-controlled identity management systems the aspect of lifelong privacy also imposes specific requirements. As shown for the example of data tracks, which offer transparency for the person concerned, such technology imposes new challenges (see above Section 2.3).

- **Logging:** Actions taken by a delegate must be traceable for the person concerned (see Section 4.1) e.g., by writing into a data track accessible for both the person concerned and the delegate or by providing copies of the relevant entries. Also the data track of the delegate should indicate the fact of having acted as delegate and which data was released. However, in case of minors as persons concerned the logging requirements must not overstrain the capabilities of average parents.
- **Control over partial identities:** It must be possible for the person concerned to control which delegate can access and see specific partial identities.
- **Access to the data of the person concerned by the delegate:** Identity management systems should offer a possibility for persons concerned to grant access for data track entries and possibly additional data relevant for the situation to delegates. A delegate may need to base decisions on previously released data or to choose among partial identities of the person concerned in order to avoid linkability of such identities of the person concerned. This includes the possibility of access by delegation supervisors chosen by the person concerned. When allowing access to data tracks, it must be well considered whose track to use and which information should be visible as person concerned and delegate reveal personal data.
- **Support in supervising delegates:** Specific delegation supervisors should get access to all transactions performed by the delegates of the person concerned wishing for such an external supervision. For transparency reasons such accesses should

be logged and visible for the supervised persons. The delegation supervisors should not have the access rights to perform any actions except for controlling the delegates of the person concerned. Another controlling effect may be achieved if persons concerned choose multiple delegates which have to agree (or vote) on important decisions before taking action. Again, this would have to be reflected in the identity management systems.

- **Defined retention periods:** A predefined **deletion time for (partial respectively shared) data track entries** could be useful so that only those parts prevail that are necessary for further privacy management. In particular, data track entries which comprise privacy-relevant information for both the delegate and the person concerned may be cut apart, the person concerned may check the delegate's actions on the basis of the logged data, and then only the parts belonging to the person concerned may be kept.

- **Stipulations for post-mortal period:** Identity management systems should provide for a solution to store instructions in case the person concerned dies. This information must not be accessible by the delegates except for the case of explicit clearance by the person concerned or the death of the person concerned.

5   Related Work

As a matter of course, various topics in the privacy debate have delegation aspects, e.g., when discussing data protection issues in the health area (whether it be usable health cards, remote medical technologies, or ambient assisted living) or in labor relations (privacy rights of employees, stand-ins for absent colleagues, or representation of the organization as such). On the other hand, numerous publications [12, 14-17] deal with components of delegation from the technological perspective, elaborating specifics of access control, policy interpretation, or cryptographic certificates. In this section we limit our scope to those papers which contribute to implementing the vision of privacy-aware delegation.

Some delegation schemes were proposed explicitly for federated identity management systems, taking at least some privacy considerations of the user into account [14, 15]. In these papers, the delegate usually is not a natural person, but a provider or service component which acts on behalf of the user. A more generic and distinctly user-centric approach which considers also some legal demands (e.g., deals with the necessity of revocation) has been developed in [12]. The specific scenario of introducing a delegate as mediator between users and service providers which takes care of specific privacy issues of the persons concerned has been proposed in [16] and [17] – here the combination with anonymous credentials and an identity management system shows some similarities to the work on user-controlled identity management [5]. However, none of the approaches deals with persons concerned who are (temporarily) incapable to manage their private spheres and their need to be supported by delegates, and none considers potential desires or privacy rights of the delegate. And even papers that mention identity management do not present solutions how entries of logging components such as the different data tracks involved should be treated.

Further, specific research on aspects of lifelong privacy, arising problems, and possible solutions is ongoing research within the PrimeLife project resulting in a set of derived requirements for a lifelong privacy protection [2].

6   Conclusion and Outlook

We have shown that delegation is a necessary prerequisite for preserving lifelong privacy as in every individual's life there are stages of incapability to cover. However, at present many privacy-related technologies lack proper handling of delegation. Providing proper means to enable delegates requires not only further research and development in the field of information and communication technologies, but also a legal framework to establish the basis for handling privacy-aware delegation. As could be shown for delegation and the application of data tracks – a necessary and useful technology in the field of user-controlled identity management – new problems arise by introducing delegates to such systems that must be addressed by a cooperation of legal and technical experts.

Delegation will be valuable and necessary for firstly the ageing population because in the older age the need for support in many areas of life grows. Secondly, common ways of delegation in the working life, like representing a company or covering for a colleague, should consider privacy-relevant matters when being implemented in technology. Thirdly, delegation issues affect the young generation and their parents very much in daily life – with or without a proper implementation in identity management.

Acknowledgments. The authors are thankful for the constructive and very valuable comments of the anonymous reviewers and the vivid discussion among the participants at the Summer School 2009 concerning this topic.

References

1. Clauß, S., Hansen, M., Pfitzmann, A., Raguse, M., Steinbrecher, S.: Tackling the Challenge of Lifelong Privacy. In: Cunningham, P., Cunningham, M. (eds.) Proceedings of eChallenges 2009 (2009)
2. Storf, K., Hansen, M., Raguse, M. (eds.): Requirements and Concepts for Identity Management throughout Life. Deliverable H1.3.5 of the FP7 project PrimeLife, Zurich/Kiel 2009 (2009), http://www.primelife.eu/results/documents/
3. Pham, Q., Reid, J., McCullagh, A., Dawson, E.: On a Taxonomy of Delegation. In: Gritzalis, D., Lopez, J. (eds.) SEC 2009, IFIP International Federation for Information Processing. IFIP AICT, vol. 297, pp. 353–363. Springer, Boston (2009)
4. Crispo, B.: Delegation of Responsibilities. In: Christianson, B., Crispo, B., Harbison, W.S., Roe, M. (eds.) Security Protocols 1998. LNCS, vol. 1550, pp. 118–124. Springer, Heidelberg (1999)
5. Hansen, M., Pfitzmann, A., Steinbrecher, S.: Identity Management throughout One's Whole Life. Information Security Technical Report 13, 2 (May 2008), pp. 83–94 (2008)

6. Hansen, M., Fischer-Hübner, S., Pettersson, J.S., Bergmann, M.: Transparency Tools for User-Controlled Identity Management. In: Cunningham, P., Cunningham, M. (eds.) Expanding the Knowledge Economy: Issues, Applications, Case Studies – Proceedings of eChallenges 2007, pp. 1360–1367. IOS Press, Amsterdam (2007)
7. Leenes, R., Schallaböck, J., Hansen, M.: PRIME White Paper V3 – Privacy and Identity Management for Europe (2008),
   https://www.prime-project.eu/prime_products/whitepaper/
8. O'Gorman, L.: Comparing Passwords, Tokens, and Biometrics for User Authentication. Proceedings of the IEEE 91(12), 2019–2040 (2003)
9. Leenes, R. (ed.): ID-related Crime: Towards a Common Ground for Interdisciplinary Research. FIDIS Deliverable D5.2b, Frankfurt, Germany (2006),
   http://www.fidis.net/fileadmin/fidis/deliverables/
   fidis-wp5-del5.2b.ID-related_crime.pdf
10. Article 29 Data Protection Working Party: Opinion 5/2009 on Online Social Networking. Working Paper 163. 01189/09/EN, adopted on June 12, 2009, Brussels, Belgium (2009),
    http://ec.europa.eu/justice_home/fsj/privacy/docs/wpdocs/
    2009/wp163_en.pdf
11. Article 29 Data Protection Working Party: Opinion 2/2009 on the Protection of Children's Personal Data (General Guidelines and the Special Case of Schools). Working Paper 160, 398/09/EN, adopted on February 11, 2009. Brussels, Belgium (2009),
    http://ec.europa.eu/justice_home/fsj/privacy/docs/wpdocs/
    2009/wp160_en.pdf
12. Peeters, R., Simoens, K., De Cock, D., Preneel, B.: Cross-Context Delegation through Identity Federation. In: Brömme, A., Busch, C., Hühnlein, D. (eds.) BIOSIG 2008. LNI, vol. 137, pp. 79–92. GI, Köllen Verlag, Bonn, Germany (2008)
13. Joint Proposal for a Draft of International Standards on the Protection of Privacy with regard to the processing of Personal Data. Madrid Resolution of the 31st International Conference of the Data Protection and Privacy Commissioners, adopted on November 5 (2009),
    https://www.agpd.es/portalweb/canaldocumentacion/
    conferencias/common/pdfs/31_conferencia_internacional/
    estandares_resolucion_madrid_en.pdf
14. Gomi, H., Hatakeyama, M., Hosono, S., Fujita, S.: A Delegation Framework for Federated Identity Management. In: Proceedings of the ACM CCS 2005 Workshop on Digital Identity Management, New York, NY, USA, pp. 94–103 (2005)
15. Alrodhan, W., Mitchell, C.J.: A Delegation Framework for Liberty. In: Haggerty, J., Merabti, M. (eds.) Proceedings of the 3rd Conference on Advances in Computer Security and Forensics (ACSF 2008), Liverpool, UK, pp. 67–73 (2008)
16. Wohlgemuth, S., Müller, G.: Privacy with Delegation of Rights by Identity Management. In: Müller, G. (ed.) ETRICS 2006. LNCS, vol. 3995, pp. 175–190. Springer, Heidelberg (2006)
17. Wohlgemuth, S.: Privatsphäre durch die Delegation von Rechten. Vieweg+Teubner, Wiesbaden, Germany (2008)

Saving On-Line Privacy

Jan Camenisch and Gregory Neven

IBM Research – Zurich
{jca,nev}@zurich.ibm.com

Abstract. With the increasing use of electronic media for our daily transactions, we widely distribute our personal information. Once released, controlling the dispersal of these information is virtually impossible. Privacy-enhancing technologies can help to minimize the amount of information that needs to be revealed in transactions, on the one hand, and to limit the dispersal, on the other hand. Unfortunately, these technologies are hardly used today. In this paper we aim to foster the adoption by providing a summary of what such technologies can achieve. We hope that by this, policy makers, system architects, and security practitioners will be able to employ privacy-enhancing technologies.

1 Introduction

The number of professional and personal interactions we are conducting by electronic means is raising daily. These on-line transactions range from reading articles, searching information, buying music, and booking trips, to peer-to-peer interactions on social networks. Thereby we reveal a plethora of personal information not only to our direct communication partners but also to many other parties of which we are often not even aware. At the same time, electronic identification and authentication devices are becoming more and more widespread. They range from electronic tickets, toll systems, to eID cards and often get used across different applications.

It has become virtually impossible to control where data about us are stored and how they are used. This is aggravated as storage becomes ever cheaper and the fact that the increasingly sophisticated data mining technologies allow for all of these data to be used in many ways that we can not even imagine today.

It is thus of paramount importance to enable individuals to protect their electronic privacy. Luckily, there exists a wide range of privacy enhancing technologies available that can be used to this end. These range from privacy-aware access control and policy languages to anonymous communication protocols and anonymous credential systems. The PRIME (Privacy-Enhancing Identity Management for Europe) project [pria] has shown that these technologies can indeed be used together to build a trust and identity management systems that allows for protecting one's on-line privacy and that they are ready to be applied in practice. The PrimeLife project [prib] has taken these research results up and is concerned with bridging the gap from research to practice.

Let us, however, note that while technology can help, the users also need to learn about the perils our digital world and how to guard their privacy. Of

M. Bezzi et al. (Eds.): Privacy and Identity, IFIP AICT 320, pp. 34–47, 2010.

course, ICT systems must to this end provide sufficient information to the users about what is happening with their data.

It seems that making use of privacy-enhancing technologies is harder than for other security technologies. One reason for this might be that the properties that they achieve are often counter intuitive, in particular in case of cryptographic building blocks. In an attempt to foster the adoption of privacy-enhancing technologies (PETs), we overview in this paper the most important cryptographic PETs and summarize what they achieve. We also give references for technical details of them. Finally, we explain how these technologies can be embedding into larger systems.

2   Cryptography to the Aid

There is a large body of research on specific cryptographic mechanisms that can be used to protect one's privacy. Some of them are theoretical constructs, but many are actually completely practical and can be readily applied in practice. We here concentrate on the latter ones.

The oldest privacy-protecting cryptography are of course encryption schemes by themselves: they allow one to protect information from access by third parties when data is stored or when sent to a communication partner. There are, however, a number of variants or extension of such basic encryption that have surprising properties that can offer better protection in many use cases as we shall see. Apart from encrypting, one often needs to authenticate information. Typically, this is done by using a cryptographic signature scheme. The traditional signature schemes typically provide too much authentication in the sense that they are used in a ways that reveals a lot of unnecessary contextual information. The cure here is offered by so-called anonymous credential schemes and their extensions which we will present. Finally, we briefly discuss a number of cryptographic applications such as electronic voting schemes and privacy-enhanced access control schemes.

2.1   Private Credentials, Their Extensions, and Applications

Certified credentials form the cornerstones of trust in our modern society. Citizens identify themselves at the voting booth with national identity cards, motorists demonstrate their right to drive cars with driver licenses, customers pay for their groceries with credit cards, airline passengers board planes with their passports and boarding passes, and sport enthusiasts make their way into the gym using their membership cards. Often such credentials are used in contexts beyond what was originally intended: for example, identity cards are also used to prove eligibility for certain social benefits, or to demonstrate to be of legal age when entering a bar.

Each of these credentials contains attributes that describe the owner of the credential (e.g., name and date of birth), the rights granted to the owner (e.g., vehicle class, flight and seat number), or the credential itself (e.g., expiration date). The information in the credentials is trusted because it is certified by an issuer (e.g., the government, a bank) who on its turn is trusted.

There is a number of different ways how such credentials can be technically realized. Depending on their realization, they offer more or less protection of the user's privacy. For instance, they are often realized by an LDAP directory maintained by the issuer. That means that the user wants to use a credential with some party (the verifier), the user will have to authenticate, typically with a username and password towards the verifier who will then look up the user's credentials in the LDAP directory. While this realization might satisfy the security requirement of the verifier and the issuer, it offers virtually not protection to the users. Apart from username/password being a rather insecure authentication mechanism, the user has 1) no control which information the verifier request from the issuer and 2) the issuer learns with which verifier the user is communicating.

A better realization of credentials is with certificate with so-called attribute extensions [CSF+08]. Here, the user chooses a public/secret key pair and then obtains a certificate from the issuer on her public key. The certificate includes all statements that the issuer vouches for about the user. The user can then send this certificate to the verifier together with a cryptographic proof of ownership of the secret key. The user knows which data is revealed to the verifier by the certificate, but has to reveal all of the included attributes so that the verifier can check the issuer's signature. Moreover, if the verifier and the issuer compare their records, they can link the user's visit to the issuing of the credential by simply comparing the issuer's signature.

Anonymous credentials [Cha81, Bra99, CL01] (often also called private credentials or minimal disclosure tokens) solve all these problems and indeed offer the best privacy protection possible while offering the same cryptographic security. They work quite similarly to attribute certificate, the difference being that they allow the user to "transform" the certificate into a new one containing only a subset of the attributes of the original certificate. This feature is often called *selective disclosure*. The issuer's signature is also transformed in such a way that the signature in the new certificate cannot be linked to the original signature; this is usually called *unlinkability* in the literature.

Extended Functionalities. Apart from the basic features of selective disclosure and unlinkability sketched above, many anonymous credential systems offer additional features that can be very useful in practical use cases. In the following, we discuss the most important of these features.

Attribute Properties. Rather than revealing the complete value of an attribute, some credential systems allow the user in the transformation to apply any (mathematical) function to the original attribute value. For instance, if the original certificate contains a birthdate, the transformed attribute could contain only the decade in which the user was born. As a special case, the function could be boolean (meaning, having as output "true" or "false"), so that only the truth of a statement about the attribute is revealed. For instance, based on the birthdate in a certificate, the user could prove that she is between 12 and 14 years old. The schemes also allow for logical AND and OR combinations of such boolean expressions [CDS94].

Verifiable Encryption. This feature allows one to prove that a ciphertext encrypts a value that is contained in a credential. For instance, a service provider could offer its service to anonymous users provided that they encrypt their name and address as contained in their identity card under the public key of a trusted third party, such as a judge. The cryptography ensures that the service provider cannot decrypt the name and address himself, but can rest assured that the ciphertext contains the correct value. In case of misuse of the service, the service provider or a law enforcement agency can then request the third party to decrypt the user's name and address from the ciphertext. Note that it can be decided at the time of showing the credential whether or not any information in the credential should be verifiably encrypted, i.e., this need not be fixed at the time the credential is issued and can be different each time a credential is shown.

An essential feature that we require in this setting from an encryption scheme is that of a label [CS03]. A label is a public string that one can attach to a ciphertext such that without the correct label, the ciphertext cannot be decrypted. The most common usage for the label in our setting is to bind the conditions and context under which the trusted third party is supposed to decrypt (or not decrypt) a given ciphertext.

In principle, one can use any public encryption scheme for verifiable encryption [CD00]; the most efficient way to do so however is probably using the Paillier encryption scheme [Pai99] for which efficient proof protocols and an variant secure against chosen-ciphertext attacks exist [CS03]. Security against chosen-ciphertext attacks is actually crucial in this setting: the thrusted third party's jobs is essentially a decryption oracle and hence semantic security would not be sufficient.

Revocation of Credentials. There can be many reasons to revoke a credential. For example, the credential and the related secret keys may have been compromised, or the user may have lost her right to carry a credential. Also, sometimes a credential might only need to be partially revoked. For instance, an expired European passport can still be used to travel with Europe, or a driver's license revoked because of speeding could still be valid to prove the user's age or address.

Possible solutions to revocation in the case of non-anonymous credentials is to "blacklist" all serial numbers of revoked credentials in a so-called *certificate revocation list* [CSF+08] that can be queried on- or off-line, or to limit the lifetime of issued credentials by means of an expiration date and periodically re-issue non-revoked credentials. The latter solution works for anonymous credential as well, even though re-issuing may be more expensive than for ordinary credentials. The former solution as such does not work, as revealing a unique serial number of a credential would destroy the unlinkability property. However, the general principle of publishing a list of all valid (or invalid) serial numbers can still work if, rather than revealing their serial number, users leverage the attribute property feature to prove that it is among the list of valid serial numbers, that it is not among the invalid ones. A number of protocols that are work along these lines have been proposed [BS04, BDD07, NFHF09] where the solution by Nakansihi et al. [NFHF09] seems to be the most elegant one.

Another solution inspired by revocation lists is the use of so-called dynamic accumulators [CL02, CKS09]. Here, all valid serial numbers are accumulated (i.e., compressed) into a single value that is then published. In addition, dynamic accumulators provide a mechanism that allows the user to prove that the serial number of her credential is contained in the accumulated value. Whenever a credential is revoked, a new accumulator value is published that no longer contains the revoked serial number. The schemes require, however, that users keeps track of the changes to the accumulator to be able to execute their validity proofs.

We observe that enabling revocation brings along the risk that the authority in control of the revocation list (or accumulator value) modifies the list to trace transactions of honest users. For instance, the authority could fraudulently include the serial number of an honest user in the revocation list and then check whether the suspected user succeeds in proving that her credential is not on the list. Such a behavior could of course be noted by, e.g., a consumer organization monitoring changes to the public revocation values.

One idea to lessen the trust that one has to put into such a third party is by using threshold cryptography, i.e., by distributing the power to update the revocation list over multiple entities such that a majority of them is needed to perform an update.

Limited-use credentials. Some credentials, such as entrance tickets, coupons, or cash money, can only be used a limited number of times. A very basic example of such credentials in the digital world is anonymous e-cash, but there are many other scenarios. For instance, in an anonymous opinion poll one might have to (anonymously) prove ownership of an identity credential, but each credential can only be used once for each poll. Another example might be an anonymous subscription for an on-line game, where one might want to prevent that the subscription credential is used more than once simultaneously, so that if you want to play the game with your friends, each friend has to get their own subscription [CHK+06].

When implementing a mechanism to control the number of times that the same credential can be used, it is important that one can define the scope of the usage restriction. For instance, in the opinion poll example, the scope is the specific poll that the user is participating in, so that participating in one poll does not affect his ability to participate in another one. For electronic cash, on the other hand, the scope is global, so that the user cannot spend the same electronic coin at two different merchants. Overspending occurs when the same credential is used more than specified by the usage limit within the same scope. Possible sanctions on overspending could be that the user is simply denied access to the service, or that some further attributes from the user's credential are revealed [CHL06, CHK+06].

With limited-use credentials one can prevent users from sharing and redistributing their credentials to a large extent. Another means of sharing prevention is the so-called all-or-nothing sharing mechanism [CL01]. This mechanism ensures that if a user shares one credential with another user (which requires revealing the other user the secret key material of that credential) then the other user can also use all the other credential (because they are based on the same secret key material). In this case sharing a single credential would mean to share one's whole digital identity, e.g., including access to one's bank account, which people probably are not prepared to do. If, however, one wishes to make sharing of credentials infeasible, then they need to be protected by tamper-resistant hardware, which we discuss next.

Hardware Protection. Being digital, anonymous credentials are easily copied and distributed. One the one hand, this is a threat to verifiers as they cannot be sure whether the person presenting a credential is the one to whom it was issued. On the other hand, this is also a threat to users as it makes their credentials vulnerable to theft, e.g., by malware.

One means to counter these threats is to protect a credential by tamper-resistant hardware device such as a smart cards, i.e., to perform all operations with the credential on the device itself. A straightforward way of doing so in a privacy-friendly way would be to embed the same signing key in all issued smart cards. The disadvantage of this approach is that if the key of one card is compromised, all smart cards have to be revoked.

A more realistic approach is to implement the Camenisch-Lysyanskaya credential system on a standards Java card [BCGS09]. However, depending on the type of smart card, it might only be possible to process a single credential on the device. In this case, one could still bind other credentials to the device by including in each credential an identifier as an attribute that is unique to the user [Cam06]. All of a user's credentials should include the same identifier. (The issuing of these credentials can even be done without having to reveal this identifier.) When an external credential (i.e., a credential that is not embedded in the smart card) is shown, the verifier requires the user to not only show the external credential but also the credential on the smart card, together with a proof that both credentials contain the same identifier as a smart card. Using the attribute properties feature, users can prove that both credentials contain the same identifier without revealing the identifier.

More Privacy-Enhancing Authentication Mechanisms. There are a number of primitives that are related to anonymous credentials. Some of them are special cases of anonymous credentials while others can be seen as building blocks or share the same cryptographic techniques to achieve anonymity.

Blind Signatures. A blind signature scheme [Cha83] allows a user to get a signature from the signer without the signer being aware of the message nor the resulting signatures. Thus, when the signer at some later point is presented with a valid signature on a message, he is not able to link it back to the signing session that produced the signature. Blind signature schemes are a widely used building block for schemes to achieve anonymity. Examples include anonymous electronic voting [Cha83, FOO91] and electronic cash [Cha83], which we discuss below. A large number of different blind signature schemes have been proposed in the literature based on various cryptographic assumptions; there are too many to be listed here.

The main feature of blind signatures that the signer has no control whatsoever on the message being signed. This feature can at the same time be a drawback. Typically, the signer wants to impose certain restrictions on the message that he's signing, such as the expiration date of a credential, or the denomination of a digital coin. When used in protocols, blind signatures therefore often have to be combined with inefficient "cut-and-choose" techniques, where the user prepares many blinded versions of the message to be signed, all but one of which are to be opened again, and the remaining one is used to produce the signature. A more efficient approach is to use *partially* blind signatures [AF96], where the signer determines part of the signed message himself, allowing him to include any type of information, such as the issuance or expiration date of the signature.

Electronic cash. The goal of (anonymous) electronic cash [Cha83] is to prevent fraud while achieving the same privacy guarantees as offered by cash money in the real world. In particular, when a user withdraws and electronic coin from the bank, spends it at a merchant, and the merchant deposits the electronic coin at the bank, the bank cannot link the coin back to the user. However, if either the user or the merchant try to cheat by spending or depositing the same coin twice, the identity of the fraudster is immediately revealed.

Online electronic cash, i.e., where the bank is online at the moment a coin is spent, can be built using blind signatures by having the bank blindly sign random serial numbers. After having issued the blind signature to a user, the bank charges the user's account. The user can spend the money with a merchant by giving away the random serial number and the signature. To deposit the coin, the merchant forwards the serial number and signature to the bank, who verifies the signature and checks whether the serial number has been deposited before. If not, the bank credits the merchant's account; if so, the bank instructs the merchant to decline the transaction.

In off-line electronic cash [CFN88] the bank is not involved when the coin is spent, only when it is withdrawn or deposited. The techniques described above are therefore enhanced to at the time of deposit distinguish between a cheating user and a cheating merchant, and in the former case, to reveal the identity of the cheating user. Both online and off-line electronic anonymous cash can be seen as special cases of limited-use anonymous credentials as described above, where a single scope is used for all payments. To obtain off-line electronic cash, the user is required to provide a verifiable encryption of her identity, which is only decrypted in case of fraud.

Group Signatures. A group signature scheme [CvH91] allows group members to sign messages in a revocably anonymous way, meaning that any verifier can tell that the message was signed by a group member, but not by which group member, while a dedicated opening manager can lift the anonymity of a signature and reveal the identity of the signer who created it. Group membership is controlled by a central group manager, who generates the group's public key and provides the individual members with their secret signing keys. Some schemes combine the roles of group manager and opening manager in a single entity.

Group signatures satisfy a whole range of security properties, including unforgeability (i.e., no outsider can create valid signatures in name of the group), unlinkability (i.e., signatures by the same signer cannot be linked), anonymity (i.e., nobody except the opening manager can tell which signer created a signature), traceability (i.e., any valid signature can be traced back to a signer), exculpability (i.e., no collusion of cheating signers can create a signature that opens to an honest signer), and non-frameability (i.e., not even a cheating group manager can create a signature that opens to an honest signer). Many of these properties are in fact related [BMW03, BSZ05].

The showing protocol of many anonymous credential systems follows a typical three-move structure that allows them to be easily converted into a signature scheme by means of a hash function [FS87]. The resulting signature scheme inherits all the anonymity features of the credential system. A group signature scheme can then be obtained by combining it with verifiable encryption: the issuer plays the role of group manager and issues to each group member a credential with a single attribute containing its identity. Group members do not reveal their identity attribute when signing a message, but verifiably encrypt it under the public key of the opening manager. One can take this approach even further by including more attributes and using the attribute properties feature. For example, one could create a signature that reveals that some authorized group member between 18 and 25 years old signed the message, but only the opening manager can tell who exactly did.

Ring Signatures. One possible disadvantage of group signatures is that the group manager decides on the composition of the group, and that members can only sign in name of that group. Ring signatures [RST01] are a more flexible variant of group signatures that have no group manager or opening manager. Rather, users can determine the group of "co-signers" at the time a signature is created. The co-signers' collaboration is not needed in the signing process, so in fact, they need not even be aware that they are involved in a ring signature. There is no authority to reveal the identity of the signer behind a ring signature, but some schemes allow the signer to voluntarily prove that they created a signature.

Redactable and Sanitizable Signatures. In some applications it may be necessary to hide words, sentences, or entire paragraphs of a signed document without invalidating the original signature. Redactable [JMSW02] and sanitizable [ACdMT05] signatures allow exactly that, the difference being that in the former anyone can censor a document, while in the latter only a censoring authority designated by the original signer can do so. Both primitives satisfy a privacy property implying that it is impossible to link back a censored signature to the original signature that was used to create it.

Privacy-Enchancing Encryption. While the main focus of this work is on privacy-enhancing authentication, a complete privacy-friendly infrastructure also involves special encryption mechanisms. We already touched upon verifiable encryption in relation to anonymous credentials. We discuss a selection of other privacy-relevant encryption primitives here.

Anonymous Communication. Most of the anonymous authentication mechanisms described above assume rely on an anonymous underlying communication network: cryptographic unlinkability of signatures clearly does not help if the users are identifiable by their IP address. Mix networks [Cha81] can be used to obfuscate which user communicates with which servers by routing the traffic through an encrypted network of mix nodes. The exact route that a packet follows can either be decided by the mix node or by the sender of the packet. In the latter case, the message is wrapped in several layers of encryption, one layer of which is peeled off at each node; this process is often referred to as onion routing [Cha81, GRS99, CL05]. So-called dining cryptographer networks or DC-nets [Cha88] even hide the fact whether entities are communicating at all, but they of course incur a constant stream of dummy traffic between all participants in doing so.

Homomorphic and Searchable Encryption. With current technology trends such as software as a service and cloud computing, more of our information is stored by external services. Storing the information in encrypted form is often not an option, as it ruins either the service's functionality or its business model. As the main goal of encryption is to hide the plaintext, it usually destroys any structure present in the plaintext; tampering with a ciphertext either renders it invalid, or turns the plaintext into unpredictable random garbage. Some encryption algorithms however are homomorphic, in the sense that applying certain operations on ciphertexts has the effect of applying other operations on the plaintexts. One can thereby process encrypted data without decrypting it, so that for example a server can apply data mining mechanisms directly on encrypted information [OS07]. There exist homomorphic encryption schemes that support multiplication [ElG85] and addition [Pai99] of plaintexts, and since recently, also schemes that support both at the same time [Gen09].

In similar scenarios it can be useful if a server can search through encrypted information without having to decrypt it. For example, this would enable an encrypted email hosting server to perform efficient searches on your email and transmit only the matching (encrypted) emails. Special-purpose schemes have been developed for this purpose as well, both in the symmetric [SWP00] and the asymmetric [BCOP04] setting.

Oblivious Transfer. Imagine a database containing valuable information that is not sold as a whole, but that rather charges customers per accessed record. At the same time, the list of queried records reveals sensitive information about the customers' intentions. For example, a company's search queries to a patent database or to a DNA genome database may reveal its research strategy or future product plans.

An oblivious transfer protocol [Rab81] solves this apparently deadlocked situation by letting a client and server interact in such a way that the server does not learn anything about which record the client obtained, while the client can only learn the content of a single record. The adaptive variant [NP99] of the primitive can amortize communication and computation costs over multiple queries on the same database.

2.2   Example Applications

In this section we give examples of privacy-sensitive applications for which protocols have been developed by combining some of the tools we just discussed.

Electronic Voting, Polling, and Petitions. Voting privacy is more than just a desirable feature, it is a fundamental principle for a democratic election. Electronic voting schemes have been proposed based on mix networks [Cha81], based on homomorphic encryption [CF85], and based on blind signatures [FOO92].

Direct Anonymous Attestation. How can a verifier check that a remote user is indeed using a trusted hardware module, without infringing on the privacy of the user, and without having to embed the same secret key in each module? This questions arose in the context of the Trusted Computing Group (TCG). In particular, the Trusted Platform Module (TPM) monitors the operating system and then can attest to a verifier that is pristine, e.g., free of viruses and thus safe to run an application such as e-banking. To protect privacy, the TCG has specified a scheme for this attestation that can essentially be seen as a group signature scheme without the opening functionality, so that anonymity cannot be revoked [BCC04] but with a revocation feature such that stolen keys can nevertheless be identified and rejected.

Oblivious Transfer with Access Control and Prices. The techniques described above can be combined in various way to address interesting business needs. For example, imagine that each record in a patent or DNA database as described above is protected by a different access control policy, describing the roles or attributes that a user needs to have in order to obtain it. By combining anonymous credentials with adaptive oblivious transfer protocols, solutions exist where the user can obtain the records she's entitled to, without revealing the applicable access control policy to the database, or which roles she has [CDN09]. By another combination of such techniques, the database can attach different prices for each record, and let users only download as many records as their prepaid balance allows, all while remaining completely anonymous [CDN10].

3   Conclusion

Even though a large number of very advanced privacy-enhancing cryptographic primitives have been proposed in the literature, their way to broad-scale deployment in the real world presents still a number of challenges.

One is the design of user interfaces that capture the core concepts of the underlying cryptography, while hiding the details.

Another challenge is the integration of the cryptographic primitives in the overall (authentication and access control) infrastructure. For instance, to deploy anonymous credentials, one needs proper policy languages to express and communicate the access control requirements in a way that supports, e.g., selective revealing of attributes, or proving properties of attributes. Too often do such languages implicitly assume that the user reveals all of her attributes by default. Moreover, since credential attributes are often sensitive information, these policy languages have to be integrated with privacy policy languages in which servers can express how the revealed information will be treated, and for users to express to whom and under which circumstances they are willing to reveal it. Privacy policy languages such as P3P [W3C06] are a first step, but are often not fine-grained enough, and lack the tight integration with access control policies. These and other challenges are currently being addressed as part of the PrimeLife project [prib, CMN+10].

From a cryptographic perspective there are still many open problems to be addressed. Researchers are searching for more efficient primitives, as in many applications the incurred overhead is still prohibitive. Also, dedicated protocols for advanced applications like social networks or location-based services would be desirable. From a theoretical point of view, an important challenge is how existing primitives can be securely and efficiently composed to build new, more complex primitives. Finally, most of the above primitives currently still lack proper key management infrastructures so that keys can be securely stored, authenticated, and revoked.

Acknowledgements

The authors enjoyed many exciting discussions with the participants of the PrimeLife project, some of them leading us to write this overview. Thank you all! This work was supported in part by the European Community through the Seventh Framework Programme (FP7/2007-2013) project PrimeLife (grant agreement no. 216483).

References

[ACdMT05]   Ateniese, G., Chou, D.H., de Medeiros, B., Tsudik, G.: Sanitizable signatures. In: di Vimercati, S.d.C., Syverson, P.F., Gollmann, D. (eds.) ESORICS 2005. LNCS, vol. 3679, pp. 159–177. Springer, Heidelberg (2005)

[AF96]   Abe, M., Fujisaki, E.: How to date blind signatures. In: Kim, K.-c.,
            Matsumoto, T. (eds.) ASIACRYPT 1996. LNCS, vol. 1163, pp. 244–251.
            Springer, Heidelberg (1996)

[BCC04]   Brickell, E., Camenisch, J., Chen, L.: Direct anonymous attestation. In:
            Proc. 11th ACM Conference on Computer and Communications Security,
            pp. 225–234. ACM Press, New York (2004)

[BCGS09]   Bichsel, P., Camenisch, J., Groß, T., Shoup, V.: Anonymous credentials
            on a standard Java Card. In: ACM Conference on Computer and Com-
            munications Security (2009) (to appear)

[BCOP04]   Boneh, D., Di Crescenzo, G., Ostrovsky, R., Persiano, G.: Public key
            encryption with keyword search. In: Cachin, C., Camenisch, J.L. (eds.)
            EUROCRYPT 2004. LNCS, vol. 3027, pp. 506–522. Springer, Heidelberg
            (2004)

[BDD07]   Brands, S., Demuynck, L., De Decker, B.: A practical system for globally
            revoking the unlinkable pseudonyms of unknown users. In: Pieprzyk, J.,
            Ghodosi, H., Dawson, E. (eds.) ACISP 2007. LNCS, vol. 4586, pp. 400–
            415. Springer, Heidelberg (2007)

[BMW03]   Bellare, M., Micciancio, D., Warinschi, B.: Foundations of group sig-
            natures: Formal definitions, simplified requirements, and a construction
            based on general assumptions. In: Biham, E. (ed.) EUROCRYPT 2003.
            LNCS, vol. 2656, pp. 614–629. Springer, Heidelberg (2003)

[Bra99]   Brands, S.: Rethinking Public Key Infrastructure and Digital
            Certificates— Building in Privacy. PhD thesis, Eindhoven Institute of
            Technology, Eindhoven, The Netherlands (1999)

[BS04]   Boneh, D., Shacham, H.: Group signatures with verifier-local revocation.
            In: Atluri, V., Pfitzmann, B., McDaniel, P. (eds.) ACM CCS 2004, pp.
            168–177. ACM, New York (2004)

[BSZ05]   Bellare, M., Shi, H., Zhang, C.: Foundations of group signatures: The
            case of dynamic groups. In: Menezes, A. (ed.) CT-RSA 2005. LNCS,
            vol. 3376, pp. 136–153. Springer, Heidelberg (2005)

[Cam06]   Camenisch, J.: Protecting (anonymous) credentials with the trusted
            computing group's tpm v1.2. In: Fischer-Hübner, S., Rannenberg,
            K., Yngström, L., Lindskog, S. (eds.) SEC. IFIP, vol. 201, pp. 135–147.
            Springer, Heidelberg (2006)

[CD00]   Camenisch, J., Damgård, I.: Verifiable encryption, group encryption, and
            their applications to group signatures and signature sharing schemes. In:
            Okamoto, T. (ed.) ASIACRYPT 2000. LNCS, vol. 1976, pp. 331–345.
            Springer, Heidelberg (2000)

[CDN09]   Camenisch, J., Dubovitskaya, M., Neven, G.: Oblivious transfer with
            access control. In: Al-Shaer, E., Jha, S., Keromytis, A.D. (eds.) ACM
            Conference on Computer and Communications Security, pp. 131–140.
            ACM, New York (2009)

[CDN10]   Camenisch, J., Dubovitskaya, M., Neven, G.: Unlinkable priced oblivi-
            ous transfer with rechargeable wallets. In: Financial Cryptography 2010
            (2010)

[CDS94]   Cramer, R., Damgård, I., Schoenmakers, B.: Proofs of partial knowl-
            edge and simplified design of witness hiding protocols. In: Desmedt, Y.G.
            (ed.) CRYPTO 1994. LNCS, vol. 839, pp. 174–187. Springer, Heidelberg
            (1994)

[CF85]   Cohen, J.D., Fischer, M.J.: A robust and verifiable cryptographically
              secure election scheme (extended abstract). In: FOCS 1985, pp. 372–382.
              IEEE, Los Alamitos (1985)
[CFN88]   Chaum, D., Fiat, A., Naor, M.: Untraceable electronic cash. In: Gold-
              wasser, S. (ed.) CRYPTO 1988. LNCS, vol. 403, pp. 319–327. Springer,
              Heidelberg (1990)
[Cha81]   Chaum, D.: Untraceable electronic mail, return addresses, and digital
              pseudonyms. Communications of the ACM 24(2), 84–88 (1981)
[Cha83]   Chaum, D.: Blind signatures for untraceable payments. In: Chaum, D.,
              Rivest, R.L., Sherman, A.T. (eds.) Advances in Cryptology — Proceed-
              ings of CRYPTO 1982, pp. 199–203. Plenum Press, New York (1983)
[Cha88]   Chaum, D.: The dining cryptographers problem: Unconditional sender
              and recipient untraceability. Journal of Cryptology 1, 65–75 (1988)
[CHK+06]   Camenisch, J., Hohenberger, S., Kohlweiss, M., Lysyanskaya, A.,
              Meyerovich, M.: How to win the clonewars: efficient periodic n-times
              anonymous authentication. In: ACM Conference on Computer and Com-
              munications Security, pp. 201–210 (2006)
[CHL06]   Camenisch, J., Hohenberger, S., Lysyanskaya, A.: Balancing accountabil-
              ity and privacy using e-cash (extended abstract). In: De Prisco, R., Yung,
              M. (eds.) SCN 2006. LNCS, vol. 4116, pp. 141–155. Springer, Heidelberg
              (2006)
[CKS09]   Camenisch, J., Kohlweiss, M., Soriente, C.: An accumulator based on
              bilinear maps and efficient revocation for anonymous credentials. In:
              Jarecki, S., Tsudik, G. (eds.) PKC 2009. LNCS, vol. 5443, pp. 481–500.
              Springer, Heidelberg (2009)
[CL01]   Camenisch, J., Lysyanskaya, A.: Efficient non-transferable anonymous
              multi-show credential system with optional anonymity revocation. In:
              Pfitzmann, B. (ed.) EUROCRYPT 2001. LNCS, vol. 2045, pp. 93–118.
              Springer, Heidelberg (2001)
[CL02]   Camenisch, J., Lysyanskaya, A.: Dynamic accumulators and applica-
              tion to efficient revocation of anonymous credentials. In: Yung, M. (ed.)
              CRYPTO 2002. LNCS, vol. 2442, pp. 61–76. Springer, Heidelberg (2002)
[CL05]   Camenisch, J., Lysyanskaya, A.: A formal treatment of onion routing. In:
              Shoup, V. (ed.) CRYPTO 2005. LNCS, vol. 3621, pp. 169–187. Springer,
              Heidelberg (2005)
[CMN+10]   Camenisch, J., Mödersheim, S., Neven, G., Preiss, F.-S., Sommer, D.: A
              language enabling privacy-preserving access control. In: SACMAT 2010.
              ACM, New York (2010)
[CS03]   Camenisch, J., Shoup, V.: Practical verifiable encryption and decryp-
              tion of discrete logarithms. In: Boneh, D. (ed.) CRYPTO 2003. LNCS,
              vol. 2729, pp. 126–144. Springer, Heidelberg (2003)
[CSF+08]   Cooper, D., Santesson, S., Farrell, S., Boeyen, S., Housley, R., Polk,
              W.: Internet X.509 Public Key Infrastructure Certificate and Certificate
              Revocation List (CRL) Profile. RFC 5280 (Proposed Standard) (May
              2008)
[CvH91]   Chaum, D., van Heyst, E.: Group signatures. In: Davies, D.W. (ed.)
              EUROCRYPT 1991. LNCS, vol. 547, pp. 257–265. Springer, Heidelberg
              (1991)
[ElG85]   ElGamal, T.: A public key cryptosystem and a signature scheme based
              on discrete logarithms. In: Blakely, G.R., Chaum, D. (eds.) CRYPTO
              1984. LNCS, vol. 196, pp. 10–18. Springer, Heidelberg (1985)

[FOO91]   Fujioka, A., Okamoto, T., Ohta, K.: Interactive bi-proof systems and un-
           deniable signature schemes. In: Davies, D.W. (ed.) EUROCRYPT 1991.
           LNCS, vol. 547, pp. 243–256. Springer, Heidelberg (1991)
[FOO92]   Fujioka, A., Okamoto, T., Ohta, K.: A practical secret voting scheme for
           large scale elections. In: Zheng, Y., Seberry, J. (eds.) AUSCRYPT 1992.
           LNCS, vol. 718, pp. 244–251. Springer, Heidelberg (1993)
[FS87]   Fiat, A., Shamir, A.: How to prove yourself: Practical solutions to identi-
           fication and signature problems. In: Odlyzko, A.M. (ed.) CRYPTO 1986.
           LNCS, vol. 263, pp. 186–194. Springer, Heidelberg (1987)
[Gen09]   Gentry, C.: Fully homomorphic encryption using ideal lattices. In:
           Mitzenmacher, M. (ed.) 41st Annual ACM Symposium on Theory of
           Computing (STOC 2009), pp. 169–178. ACM, New York (2009)
[GRS99]   Goldschlag, D.M., Reed, M.G., Syverson, P.F.: Onion routing for
           anonymous and private internet connections. Communications of the
           ACM 42(2), 84–88 (1999)
[JMSW02]   Johnson, R., Molnar, D., Song, D.X., Wagner, D.: Homomorphic signa-
           ture schemes. In: Preneel, B. (ed.) CT-RSA 2002. LNCS, vol. 2271, pp.
           244–262. Springer, Heidelberg (2002)
[NFHF09]   Nakanishi, T., Fujii, H., Hira, Y., Funabiki, N.: Revocable group signa-
           ture schemes with constant costs for signing and verifying. In: Jarecki,
           S., Tsudik, G. (eds.) PKC 2009. LNCS, vol. 5443, pp. 463–480. Springer,
           Heidelberg (2009)
[NP99]   Naor, M., Pinkas, B.: Oblivious transfer with adaptive queries. In:
           Wiener, M. (ed.) CRYPTO 1999. LNCS, vol. 1666, pp. 573–590. Springer,
           Heidelberg (1999)
[OS07]   Ostrovsky, R., Skeith III, W.E.: Private searching on streaming data.
           Journal of Cryptology 20(4), 397–430 (2007)
[Pai99]   Paillier, P.: Public-key cryptosystems based on composite residuosity
           classes. In: Stern, J. (ed.) EUROCRYPT 1999. LNCS, vol. 1592, pp.
           223–239. Springer, Heidelberg (1999)
[pria]   PRIME project, http://www.prime-project.eu
[prib]   PrimeLife project, www.primelife.eu
[Rab81]   Rabin, M.O.: How to exchange secrets by oblivious transfer. Technical
           Report TR-81, Harvard Aiken Computation Laboratory (1981)
[RST01]   Rivest, R.L., Shamir, A., Tauman, Y.: How to leak a secret. In: Boyd,
           C. (ed.) ASIACRYPT 2001. LNCS, vol. 2248, pp. 552–565. Springer,
           Heidelberg (2001)
[SWP00]   Song, D.X., Wagner, D., Perrig, A.: Practical techniques for searches on
           encrypted data. In: IEEE Symposium on Security and Privacy, pp. 44–55
           (2000)
[W3C06]   W3C. The Platform for Privacy Preferences 1.1 (P3P1.1) Specification
           (2006), http://www.w3.org/TR/P3P11/

Context Is Everything
Sociality and Privacy in Online Social Network Sites

Ronald Leenes

TILT – Tilburg Institute for Law, Technology, and Society, Tilburg University,
The Netherlands
r.e.leenes@tilburguniversity.nl

Abstract. Social Network Sites (SNSs) pose many privacy issues. Apart from the fact that privacy in an online social network site may sound like an oxymoron, significant privacy issues are caused by the way social structures are currently handled in SNSs. Conceptually different social groups are generally conflated into the singular notion of 'friend'. This chapter argues that attention should be paid to the social dynamics of SNSs and the way people handle social contexts. It shows that SNS technology can be designed to support audience segregation, which should mitigate at least some of the privacy issues in Social Network Sites.

1 A Devilish Dilemma?

The satirical weekly the Onion featured[1] an interview with e-mom Gloria Bianco who explained how she as a modern mother copes with her teenage son. The 'interview' shows some of the interesting tensions of current social software:

"Today now!: Now we've all heard the term Facebook, but we may not know that you may use it to keep tabs on your childrens' personal lives even when they're far away from home. E-mom Gloria Bianco: "You can. You're gone love this. It's so easy, all you do is create this profile and search for your son or daughter's name and add them to your list of friends. Within minutes you can be writing on their wall. ... I look through all of my son Jeffrey's photo's every single day. ... Now I can see here he is with this young women with the low cut shirt showing a lot of skin. [interviewer: looks like he has a lot of fun] Girls like that like to have fun. ... By this feature called tagging I can find out the girl's name. ... Facebook won't allow me to see her entire profile, but I can get a good enough idea what she's like by looking at this trampy picture. ... You can see pictures posted by any of their other friends....".

Although the accompanying footage is amusing, the text itself is hardly satirical because it very much reflect current practice on social network sites. The quote illustrates one of the prominent issues of social software, the difficulty of separating audiences online. Information disclosed to friends, can just as easily be seen by moms, teachers, and bosses, which is certainly not always what the author intended.

---

[1] The Onion is a satirical weekly published on the net. The Facebook episode can be found here: http://www.theonion.com/content/video/facebook_twitter_revolutionizing

M. Bezzi et al. (Eds.): Privacy and Identity, IFIP AICT 320, pp. 48–65, 2010.

With this enormous rise in possibilities for social interaction offered by online social network sites, also serious privacy issues have risen. People are judged by the
image they paint of themselves on their profile page (and on those of others) and by
what others contribute to their profile by means of comments, tags, media uploads,
etc. The consequences of these judgments may be serious. Students have been ex-
pelled from universities, employees have been fired[2], and even people have been
killed[3] as a result of the information disclosed by themselves and others on their
profile pages.

Information that is suitable in one context may be entirely unsuitable in the next.
This is what causes a devilish dilemma. One may prevent many of the privacy issues
promulgated by online social networks by abstaining from using them, but this goes at
the expense of sociability; it may become lonely when not engaging with friends
online. On the other hand, choosing for a rich social online life currently seems to
introduce a set of serious privacy issues that most people would rather live without.
How should we cope with this dilemma? Do we have to choose between privacy and
sociality, or is there a middle ground?

We believe that privacy and sociality can be reconciled in the sense that some of
the privacy issues, namely decontextualisation, can (partially) be resolved. Doing so
requires understanding of the social dynamics of online social network sites. James
Grimmelmann [1] has argued that many policy options, including technical controls,
won't work to restore the privacy imbalances in social network sites. In this chapter, I
will argue that, although Grimmelmann gets it right regarding the social dynamics and
reasons why users engage in online social networks sites, he may underestimate the
potential of technology to mitigate privacy risks.

This chapter is organised as follows. First, I will set the stage by introducing the
main features of social network sites and describe some of the prominent privacy
issues in social network sites. Next, I will explore some of the reasons why users are
on social network sites despite these issues. Then I will illustrate how, in our view,
technical controls can help reconcile sociability and privacy. Finally, I will draw some
conclusions and propose suggestions for further work.

2   Why Bother about Social Network Sites: Privacy Issues

Social network sites inhabit the world of web 2.0 applications. A common definition
of social network, or networking, sites is provided by danah boyd and Nicole Ellison
[2] who describe them as:

> web-based services that allow individuals to (1) construct a public or semi-public profile
> within a bounded system, (2) articulate a list of other users with whom they share a
> connection, and (3) view and traverse their list of connections and those made by others
> within the system. The nature and nomenclature of these connections may vary from site to
> site.

As Grimmelmann [1] points out, this definition highlights three important aspects of
social networks: identity, relationship, and community. Apart from these characteristics,

---

[2] See for instance, http://www.theregister.co.uk/2009/02/26/facebook_comment
[3] See for instance http://news.bbc.co.uk/2/hi/uk_news/wales/8232250.stm

there is a huge variety in goals, functionality, and appearance of the different applications that span the SNS universe. Some networks target a professional context, such as LinkedIn, while others, such as Myspace or Facebook, primarily aim at leisurely contacts. Some focus on text based interactions and blogging (e.g., Livejournal.com), others tend towards multimedia (e.g., Flickr.com). Some networks are geared to maintaining existing ties (e.g., Classmates.com, Sixdegrees,com. See also the chapter by Isabelle Oomen in this volume), others facilitate finding new contacts (e.g., Match.com) and creating new networks. More and more SNSs move away from a profile centered application towards a general gathering ground for networks of related individuals (friends) [3], combining the functionalities of different kinds of social software, such as blogs, twitter, and rss-feeds. Web 2.0 has supplemented, and in some places replaced, 'real world' interactions.

Online social networks and other social software have conquered the Internet in a relatively short time. Modern profile based social networks followed in the footsteps of Classmates.com which was founded in 1995. In November 2009, Facebook passed the 300 million user bar and the social networks combined easily have more than a billion users, each of whom spends a considerable amount of time maintaining their online presence and interacting with their friends (e.g., Myspace, Hyves, StudiVz, Facebook) and professional contacts (e.g., LinkedIn). In PEW study conducted in late 2006, they found that 55% of online teens aged 12-17 have created profiles on social network sites with 64% of teens 15-17[4]. Hyves, the major Dutch SNS has about 9.5 million users (on a population of 16 million), StudiVZ, a popular German SNS for students (in a broad sense), claims to have over 15 million users.

These data provide a flattered image of the size of the networks, because many networks do not provide a way to completely terminate an account. A reason for this is that bigger networks are attractive for both potential users and advertisers. SNS providers therefore have an interest to keep accounts in their system.

Users of Social Network Sites spend a fair amount of their time online nurturing their profile and keeping in touch with their network. It is well known that many SNS users are very frank and open on their profiles and in their communication, to the point that many 'adults' wonder whether these teens have completely lost it. Consequently, there is extensive literature on the (privacy) risks associated to Social Network Sites, coming from both academics, such as [1, 4-6], and policy makers and advisory bodies, such as [7-9].

In PrimeLife heartbeat 1.2.5 [10], we have collected some 30 privacy and security issues in social network sites based on sources such as the ones mentioned in [1, 4-6] and [7-9]. Many of the issues can be understood as emanating from the underlying properties of mediating technologies [11]:

"1 Persistence: Unlike the ephemeral quality of speech in unmediated publics, networked communications are recorded for posterity. This enables asynchronous communication but it also extends the period of existence of any speech act.

2 Searchability: Because expressions are recorded and identity is established through text, search and discovery tools help people find like minds. While people cannot currently

---

[4] As reported in [11]. The study itself is: Lenhart, Amanda. 2007. "Social Networking Websites and Teens: An Overview." PEW Internet and the American Life Project, January 7.

acquire the geographical coordinates of any person in unmediated spaces, finding one's digital body online is just a matter of keystrokes.

3 Replicability: Hearsay can be deflected as misinterpretation, but networked public expressions can be copied from one place to another verbatim such that there is no way to distinguish the "original" from the "copy."[5]

4 Invisible audiences: While we can visually detect most people who can overhear our speech in unmediated spaces, it is virtually impossible to ascertain all those who might run across our expressions in networked publics. This is further complicated by the other three properties, since our expression may be heard at a different time and place from when and where we originally spoke." [11]

These properties are certainly at play in social network sites. Let me briefly explore some of the specifics of these properties in the light of social network sites. Although SNS users have control over their own profile, it is generally difficult to eradicate their online existence entirely because in many cases it is difficult to delete their profile entirely[6]. This means that information contributed to social network sites has a high degree of persistence.

Searchability provides an interesting issue because of the privacy–sociality tradeoff that is inevitable in social network sites. SNS profiles consist of a public part which is available to non SNS-members, as well as a part that can be restricted to a designated audience, typically consisting of the user's contacts labelled as 'friend'. Basically anyone can observe a public profile, provided one knows where to look. Google does not provide much help here, because it is blocked from indexing many SNS sites. In that sense, SNS's seem to have limited searchability and hence taken steps to mitigate a common privacy issue on the Internet at large. In practice this is not much of a problem because some SNS providers, such as Facebook and Hyves, require their users to register by their real names. In general there is an incentive for SNS users to be searchable; they want to attract (their) friends within a particular SNS. By choosing to make their profile non-public, users can limit access to their profiles. This prevents 'non-authorised' others (parents, teachers, bosses, etc.) from accessing their profile, but this comes at the expense of potential peers and friends being unable to find them, which clearly interferes with the social nature of the network.

The most important issue, however, seems to be the invisibility of audiences. Do SNS users have a thorough understanding of their audience? A study by Ralph Gross and Alessandro Acquisti [12] among Facebook users (in 2005) revealed that many users generously provide personal data in their profile, while hardly limiting access to their profiles. From their study it is unclear whether users don't understand their potential audience, or simply think that the benefits of disclosing their data outweigh the risks [12] (See also Oomen's contribution in this volume). Their later study [6] revealed that a large proportion of their sample is aware of the visibility of their profile,

---

[5] See Negroponte, Nicholas. 1996. Being Digital. New York: Vintage.

[6] For instance, the Canadian Privacy Commissioner in a study on 6 popular SNS's in Canada observed that 'Facebook, LinkedIn and MySpace all require more than a click of a button to delete an account – Facebook and LinkedIn require the user to email the site requesting deletion (LinkedIn guarantees a response within 5 days) while MySpace allows the user to click to request cancellation, but then sends information on how to delete the account via the email address provided at registration." [23]

although a significant minority is not. Perhaps due to media attention, users appear to change their behaviour. SNS users are increasingly locking their profiles and culling their friends list (which lead to the new terms defriending/unfriending)[7].

Given the persistence of information disclosed online, a culminating effect on top of the issue of opaque current audiences, is that also future audiences are unclear. Add to this that contexts may blur, and undesired and unexpected effects are guaranteed. What may seem appropriate information to put up for a particular audience on a profile page now, may be inappropriate information later on in a different context. Tufecki provides an example of this:

> "For example, a person may act in a way that is appropriate at a friend's birthday party, but the photograph taken by someone with a cell phone camera and uploaded to MySpace is not appropriate for a job interview, nor is it necessarily representative of that person. Yet that picture and that job interview may now intersect."[13]

Judith Donath and danah boyd provide another example of why decontextualisation may be undesirable. One of the respondents in their study says:

> 'My issue with Tribe is that the boundaries between personal and professional are TOO fuzzy. I want to get to the person, rather than to the pitch. On the other hand, I really DON'T want to know that the person I'm getting ready to do business with is in an open marriage and into kinky redheads. I don't want to see half-naked pictures of them from Burning Man. It's not that I'm a prude, or offended by that stuff in general, it's just not stuff that I want to have pushed on me when I'm talking business'.[14]

A significant problem is that social networks invite or even encourage snooping. In fact, as Joinson [15] and Lampe et al. [16] show, surveillance and social browsing are important reasons for users to spend time on the social networks. And hence, the networks facilitate content decontextualisation.

We will return to this central issue of audience segregation and contextual integrity later. First we need some understanding of why a large proportion of contemporary teenagers engage in online social network sites when it is apparent that these provide privacy risks. The short answer is: People have compelling social reasons to use SNSs and those same social factors lead them to badly misunderstand the privacy risks involved.

3 If You're Not on Myspace, You Don't Exist

For a more extensive answer to the question why on earth teenagers behave exhibitionistic online, we have to look at the social dynamics of social networks. One of the prominent researchers of 'teen sociality' in the information society is danah boyd. In her PhD thesis [17] and elsewhere [5, 11, 18] she has extensively described what moves teenagers to participate in online social network sites. A prominent reason is "because, that's where my friends are" [11]. Large scale online presence of teenagers is a network effect. The value of the network lies in its size and hence they become more attractive as they grow, and conversely, when people flock the network in large numbers the decline will progress non-linear.

---

[7] See for instance, http://www.nytimes.com/2009/01/29/fashion/29facebook.html

There is more to it than just the network effect. The three primary characteristics of Social network sites: identity, relationship, and community [1, 11] are really at play. Teenagers are in a phase in their lives where they are particularly busy with constructing their identity. Identity construction involves playing roles: theatrical performances [19]. In their performances, individuals consciously present themselves to others (information given), but also provide unconscious signals (information given off). Identity in Goffman's analysis is constructed by the roles people play and the "front" they uphold. The front consists of the "setting", objects, furniture, backdrop, but also consists of a more personal side: clothing, social position, age, gender, body language etc. Maintaining a profile on a social network site is part of this identity construction. The users "write themselves literally into being" as Jenny Sundén expresses it [20]. The users adapt their identity and their profiles on the basis of the reactions of their peers. This process of performance, interpretation, and adjustment is what Goffman calls impression management [19]. Note that impression management is not only done by teens who are in their early stages of identity development, but is an important aspect of everyday social life for all of us, albeit that identity is more stable in later stages of life for most of us[8].

The SNS platforms contain different mechanisms to provoke active identity construction. For instance, many sites facilitate the users to customise significant aspects of the 'experience' by allowing them to change the backgrounds of their profile, and modify the CSS stylesheets employed on their pages. Simply browsing through the public profiles on any site will reveal a multitude of different styles, backgrounds etc; many may look utterly horrible, but so do many teenager bedrooms. In any case these customised backgrounds are individual expressions and hardly ever accidental. There are also other ways in which SNS platform providers promote activity on the profile pages. Most SNS platforms allow other users to post comments on a profile page. On Facebook this is called 'the wall'. These postings create communication between the profile owner and visitors because generally the owner will respond to the comments, for instance by updating or chancing the page. Facebook holds several patents, some of which are related to inducing users to actively nurture their pages and interact with other users[9].

The second important feature of social network sites that explains why SNS' attract (teenage) users is relationship. SNSs allow their users to attract others on a one-to-one basis; they can invite others to become their friend, for instance. Although the act of adding someone as a contact is a multivalent act [1] because it can mean anything from "I am your friend" to "I don't even know you(, but still want to be associated to you)", it signals a link between two individuals and shows that people care about each other. Therefore even simple communication between users, such as writing on someone's wall "I'm saying something to you on your comments so that you'll feel loved"[10] gives people the idea that they are appreciated. Profiles are also used to get into contact with potential soulmates, also for, or maybe even especially for those

---

[8] Popular culture types, such as Madonna and Prince are famous exceptions. They reinvent themselves every couple of years, with success.

[9] For instance, Facebook holds US patent 7,117,254 'Method of inducing content uploads in a social network'.

[10] Posting dated 18 Feb 2008 12:41 AM by "Night of Fungi" on Facebook.

who are not the centre of attention in the offline world. danah boyd quotes a typical example of this:

> "I'm in the 7th grade. I'm 13. I'm not a cheerleader. I'm not the president of the student body. Or captain of the debate team. I'm not the prettiest girl in my class. I'm not the most popular girl in my class. I'm just a kid. I'm a little shy. And it's really hard in this school to impress people enough to be your friend if you're not any of those things. But I go on these really great vacations with my parents between Christmas and New Year's every year. And I take pictures of places we go. And I write about those places. And I post this on my Xanga. Because I think if kids in school read what I have to say and how I say it, they'll want to be my friend." – Vivien, 13, to Parry Aftab during a "Teen Angels" meeting, taken from [11]

The networks provide shy teenagers a platform to advertise themselves in a relatively safe way. They have control over their own page and can shield themselves (and remove) from insults more easily than in the real world.

The third characteristic that helps attract users to social network sites is community. Community is about doing things together and sharing thoughts and ideas with a group, but it is also about social position and social capital. The size of one's network, for instance, is clearly visible to outsiders and provides a marker of how well connected one is, and maybe how popular one is. The importance of a sizeable community is not absolute though. On Friendster the urge by some users to collect as many friends as possible has inspired the notion of "Friendster whore" [14], which carries a connotation of undesirable social behaviour. On the other end of the spectrum there is the careful pruning of networks, "defriending"[11], to only include contacts that are valuable as social capital. Within one's network there are also all sorts of subtle processes. Some sites, such as Myspace, allow their users to list their top 8 friends. This represents clear indicators of the social position of people within one's network and inspires wall postings such as "Hey ZOE!!! WHAT THE HELL!!! Why aren't I on your top friends?"[12]

The wall also functions in delineating social positions. At first glance, wall postings are awkward ways of communicating between individuals because they show only one side of a two-way communication channel. The reader, unless she has access to the profile page of the poster too, only gets to see the communication posted by the poster, not the responses by the profile owner. Email, or MSN, at first glance seems a more appropriate communication channel for such bilateral communication. However, on closer inspection, the wall – as its name already suggests –, has a social function that extends beyond the two primary actors in the communication. A wall post communicates certain content to the profile owner (and others who have access to the page), but it also shows others the author's affection to the profile owner and therefore provides a public display of this affection. Wall posting consequently are signals of one's social position within a network. The name "Wall" also reinforces the idea that social network sites are closed-off spaces, thus encouraging openness. Interestingly walls have two sides, an interior side and an exterior one. On the one hand the users may feel themselves enclosed, and hence safe, by the wall. One may also consider the wall to be the outside of a profile and writing on the wall something that

---

[11] See for instance: http://www.nytimes.com/2009/01/29/fashion/29facebook.html
[12] Post by "The Trickster" on someone's wall in Facebook dated Dec 13 2007 6:45 AM.

happens on the exterior wall, much like spray painting graffiti (with its own cultural references and customs)[13].

Online social networks provide their users the tools for online identity construction and socialisation. As danah boyd wrote in a recent blog post:

"Many youth spend little to no time in unstructured social settings, otherwise known as 'hanging out.' The practice of hanging out is consistently demonized by educationally-minded folks as a waste of time. Yet, it is in that space where youth learn to navigate social situations, make sense of impression management, and develop the social skills necessary to be productive adults. Social media has created an interesting rupture in the landscape. Youth turn to it to reclaim unstructured social encounters, to create a public space that allows them to simply hang out with their friends, peers, and cohort. The flirting, gossiping, and joking around that takes place is not proof that social media is useless, but proof that it's extremely valuable. Without other spaces in which to gather, youth have developed their own."[14]

Apart from being relevant for socialisation, SNSs feature both explicit and subtle mechanisms that attract users to participate, and since social networks sites are about sharing thoughts, experiences, ideas, media, etc, their users will disclose information.

4 None of This Is Real

That users have to share information on social network sites does not explain why they share so much information. Just as different SNS users will have different reasons for joining an SNS, there are different reasons why they may over-expose themselves. One obvious reason is that SNS users may underestimate and misunderstand the risks. Grimmelmann [1] lists a couple of heuristics that guide people in detecting harms that do not seem to work properly in online social networks. For example, users adhere to "safety in numbers"; they feel safe in the crowd and ask themselves why anyone would be interested in (harming) them specifically? The chances that their personal indiscretions will make it to the headlines of the newspapers indeed are limited, but there are sufficient numbers of people interested in them and especially in their behaviour, such as parents, teachers, and later their employers. And as already mentioned, given the fact that many subscribe under their real name, finding them in the crowd is not that hard.

Several studies have pointed out that users do not have an accurate risk perception of the privacy risks. Ralph Gross and Allesandro Acquisti, for instance, in two studies among Facebook users [6, 12] found that although a relative majority of their sample (4000 students at a US academic institution) are aware of the visibility of their profile, a significant minority is not. Their sample also turns out to be highly ignorant of Facebook's treatment of personal data. Zeynep Tufekci [13] found that non SNS users only have slightly higher levels of privacy concerns than users (average score 2.98 resp. 2.73 on a scale from 1 = not concerned at all to 4 = very concerned). The perceived likelihood that future employers, government, corporations, or romantic

---

[13] This is how the wall is depicted on the satirical sketch by the Idiots of Ants for the BBC, where someone sprays graffiti on the outside wall of the victim in the sketches' house. See http://laughingsquid.com/facebook-in-real-life-by-idiots-of-ants/

[14] http://www.zephoria.org/thoughts/archives/2009/11/30/sociality_is_le.html

partners would see their profile did not affect the actual visibility of their profiles. The students in the samples did not find any of those scenarios very likely, except for future romantic partners. Although these latter findings do not suggest that the respondents underestimate the risks (as we do not know the actual risks very precisely), the fact that they consider "others" not interested in their profiles us telling in the light of news paper reports to the contrary (see the examples quoted in the introduction).

A common advise to counter the relative ignorance of the SNS users is to raise their awareness. This advice can be found in many policy recommendations, such as [7-9].

"Recommendation SN.1 Encourage awareness-raising and educational campaigns: as well as face-to-face awareness-raising campaigns on the sensible usage of SNSs, SNSs themselves should, where possible, use contextual information to educate people in 'real-time'. Additional awareness-raising campaigns should also be directed at software developers to encourage security- conscious development practices and corporate policy."[7]

Sound as this advise may be, it is only part of the solution and may even address the wrong issue. This becomes clear when the social dynamics of the networks is scrutinized more closely. Not all SNS users are the same and hence their behaviour, although superficially equal, makes a difference when assessing it against privacy risks. One of the interesting conclusions that is drawn by various researchers, including [11, 18], is that SNS users that are aware of the fact that they operate in public space claim privacy in this public space. SNS users are not addressing the whole audience that has access to the information they publish, but rather they address their "friends" and implicitly expect others to stay out. As one kid in a kids' panel on the Revealed "I" conference 2007 in Ottawa formulated it: "Parents are not allowed in. It's my conversation". This idea may sound counter intuitive, after all is there privacy in a public space anywhere?[15] But when compared with secret diaries which are also not supposed to be read by curious parents, this call for privacy is not at all odd. Although enforcement of a ban on unsolicited observing (public) profiles is untenable, promoting a social norm that also on social network sites it is inappropriate to overhear other people's conversation may make sense.

A final phenomenon to keep in mind when addressing privacy on social networks is that not everything is what it seems. Computers and the internet are ideal places where people can experiment with their identities and explore the boundaries of their personality [21], and this is even more so in social network sites as we have argued above. In actual practice many online profiles are fairly close to the offline identities of their creators. In other words, identity experiments are limited. There is, however, a group of SNS users that takes experimenting with their identities to the extreme. The most outspoken in this category are the Friendster Fakesters [18].

"From the earliest days, participants took advantage of the flexibility of the system to craft 'Fakesters,' or nonbiographical profiles. Fakesters were created for famous people, fictional characters, objects, places and locations, identity markers, concepts, animals, and

---

[15] In fact there is. Even under the US notion of reasonable expectations of privacy as developed in Katz v. United States, 389 US 347, 348 (1967), constitutionally protected may be what a man seeks to preserve as private, even in an area accessible to the public.

communities. Angelina Jolie was there, as were Homer Simpson, Giant Squid, New Jersey, FemSex, Pure Evil, Rex, and Space Cowboys." [18]

Fakesters create profiles that are totally unlike themselves for different reasons and their story makes an interesting read, but the point I want to make is that not everything in SNS profiles is real and therefore not all information provides privacy risks in the same way. Since for Fakesters it is all a game, they may disclose an abundant amount of personal information and not seem to care about privacy at all. We, outside observers, may think that the information is real, whereas in their view it is a scam and the dark sides of information (mis)use by others may not affect them. An issue of course is that judgments are made irrespective of whether the information is accurate and therefore also fake profiles may have real consequences for their creators.

5 Sociality or Privacy?

I have provided a glance of why people, and especially teenagers, populate online social network sites and outlined some of the risks of exposing personal information on these sites. I want to use the remainder of this chapter to explore whether we have to choose between sociality and privacy, or whether we can have both. One of the key privacy issues on social network sites is the way social structures are handled. Whereas in real life we have family, friends, best friends, colleagues, team mates, lovers, ex-lovers, etc, most online social networks only recognise a very shallow sub-set. Linked-in only recognises professional contacts. Other networks, such as Facebook, Myspace, and Hyves, divide the world into "Friends", "Friends of friends" and the "rest", although admittedly they are all implementing more fine grained models. On the relationship level, most share similar model of interpersonal links – they are mutual, public, unnuanced, and decontextualised [14] which does not really go well with the nuances of relations in the real world. In social network sites, links are

- unnuanced, i.e., "there is no distinction made between a close relative and a near stranger";
- decontextualised, i.e., "there is no way of showing only a portion of one's network and content to some people";
- mutual, i.e., "if A shows B as a connection, then B has also agreed to show A as a connection"; and
- public, i.e., "they are permanently on display for others to see"

One way of improving on this is by facilitating "audience segregation" in social network sites. The concept of 'audience segregation' was coined by Canadian sociologist Erving Goffman [19]. As we have seen above, Goffman casts the process of identity construction in a stage metaphor. The social actor plays different roles for different audiences and chooses stage, props, and costume to perform for these audiences. Individuals aim to present consistent and coherent "faces" in the different contexts. Authors such as Goffman [19] and Rachels [22] have extensively argued that people need to be able to keep audiences apart in order to develop themselves and engage in meaningful relations. Part of keeping audiences apart is revealing only part of oneself in a specific context and hence show different faces in different contexts.

Goffman describes "audience segregation" implies "... that the individuals who witness him in one of his roles will not be the individuals who witness him in another of his roles" [19, p. 137]. One of the reasons for this need is the possibility to maintain different roles, e.g., spouse/parent; employed professional/spokesperson for a professional, teacher/student, scout-master and spy. This aspect of control over one's image or presentation corresponds to Goffman's notion of information given (versus information given off). Individuals often maintain or are assigned different partial identities for specific contexts (e-government, e-commerce, social networks, et cetera) and roles (citizen, consumer, friend, relative, employee, student, et cetera). Audience segregation prevents their image to be contaminated by information from other roles performed in other situations before other audiences, particularly by information that may discredit a convincing performance in the current situation [19, p. 137].

The simplistic social model implemented in most online social network sites totally neglects this crucial social mechanism and accounts for many of the privacy issues in social network sites. The information that causes many of the real world issues was simply not intended for the audience that caused the problems.

Not only does the lack of possibilities to keep audiences apart lead to privacy issues, it also in the longer run changes people's behaviour that undermines having meaningful social relations. It leads to 'flat characters', users who in their aim to be acceptable to all audiences leave out the "interesting" stuff. This is what danah boyd calls social convergence.

> "Social convergence occurs when disparate social contexts are collapsed into one. Even in public settings, people are accustomed to maintaining discrete social contexts separated by space. How one behaves is typically dependent on the norms in a given social context. How one behaves in a pub differs from how one behaves in a family park, even though both are ostensibly public. Social convergence requires people to handle disparate audiences simultaneously without a social script. While social convergence allows information to be spread more efficiently, this is not always what people desire. As with other forms of convergence, control is lost with social convergence. [23, p. 18]

If we can re-introduce the notion of audience segregation into online social network sites, we may be able to reconcile privacy and sociality, provided that users maintain their presences on the social network sites and are capable and willing to disclose information to the proper audiences.

6 Technologically Assisted Sociality

The idea of implementing audience segregation into social network sites is not new. For instance, Donath and boyd already in 2004 proposed:

> "A more promising design solution is the ability to define a set of categories and designate each person as a member of one or more of these categories. One could then set which sections of one's profile or people in one's network were for viewing by particular acquaintances. Thus, to close friends one might still show everything, but one could have a category of 'work colleagues' who would see only work related information, and not be made aware of the more outrageous connections. This faceting of profile and network would not be apparent to anyone unless two people sat down and compared what each could see of

a third; that is analogous to real world situations in which two people discuss a third whom they each know in a different context." [14, p. 78]

Others are less optimistic about this idea. Grimmelmann, for instance writes:

"The fact is, there's a deep, probably irreconcilable tension between the desire for reliable control over one's information and the desire for unplanned social interaction. It's deeply alien to the human mind to manage privacy using rigid ex ante rules. We think about privacy in terms of social rules and social roles, not in terms of access-control lists and file permissions. … The deeper problems are social. There are no ideal technical controls for the use of information in social software. The very idea is an oxymoron; "social" and "technical" are incompatible adjectives here. Adding "FriendYouDontLike" to a controlled vocabulary will not make it socially complete; there's still "FriendYouDidntUsedToLike." As long as there are social nuances that aren't captured in the rules of the network (i.e., always), the network will be unable to prevent them from sparking privacy blowups. [1, pp. 1185-1186]

This is where we disagree with Grimmelmann, although we agree with him on the general principle that regulating social behaviour by technology is problematic. Having said that, let us outline how we try to implement audience segregation, or technologically assisted sociality, in social network sites in the EU funded PrimeLife project.

Grimmelmann seems to assume that technological controls by definition are complex and that there is no context at all which would require a very fine granularity, which "can also make problems of disagreement worse." [1, p. 1087], and defaults will not help either":

"If I want to share information about myself—and since I'm using a social network site, it's all but certain that I do—anything that makes it harder for me to share is a bug, not a feature. Users will disable any feature that protects their privacy too much. The defaults problem nicely illustrates this point. Lillian Edwards and Ian Brown flirt with the idea that default "privacy settings be set at the most privacy-friendly setting when a profile is first set up," only to recognize that "this is not a desirable start state for social networking." If Facebook profiles started off hidden by default, the next thing each user would do after creating it would be to turn off the invisibility." [1, p. 1087]

We come from a different direction. We start from the assumption that mechanisms used in everyday off-line life can be implemented to assist people in their online life provided that the concepts are 'intuitive' to the user and the interface does not hamper them in their social activities. Additionally, we think we can 'Nudge' SNS users to act in a privacy savvy way without undermining sociality. This is done by [24] taking Thaler and Sunstein's Nudge 'methodology' into account: provide iNcentives, Understand mappings, Defaults, Give feedback, Expect error, Structure complex choices. The prototype application that implements our ideas is called Clique and is built on the open source SNS platform Elgg[16].

Our work builds on a number of premises. The first is that every user operates in different social contexts with distinct members. These contexts have a social meaning and can hence be labelled. For instance, I might want to distinguish between family, colleagues, professional acquaintances, and friends, whereas the reader might want to

---

[16] See http://elgg.org/. The Clique prototype can be found here: http://clique.primelife.eu/

distinguish entirely different categories, depending on their personal goals and uses of a particular social network. We call these social groups "collections". Each of the collections consists of a number of known contacts of the profile owner.

The notion of labelled social group is not uncontested. Grimmelman cites the RELATIONSHIP project which aims to provide a "vocabulary for describing relationships between people", using terms like "lostContactWith", and "apprenticeTo" [1]. He cites Clay Shirky who argued the fundamental flaws of such enterprises because it is very hard to represent the enormous complexity of social relationships (where, for instance is "closePersonalFriendOf", or "usedToSleepWith") and Facebook's inability to represent this social complexity. Our point is that the platform provider certainly can not provide the entire social complexity; there is no need for them to do this in the first place. Individuals are fully capable of representing whatever works for them. They can decide on the necessary granularity as well as on the labels they want to stick to their social categories.

While users should be able to define their own audiences within the SNS, others should not be able to inspect how a user has compartementalised their world. I may call a certain collection "idiots", but there is no need that the members of this collection are aware that they are considered idiots. Users should also be capable of deciding which of their contacts belong to the different collections. Of course this is not static, but we expect changes in the overall structure to be relatively scarce.

Fig. 1. The author's contact collections and default collection (TILT colleagues)

Maintaining ones network by no longer involving ex-lovers into all communication is something that is done in the real world as well. Figure one, shows the collections that the author has defined for one of his identities (labelled Ronald Leenes) within the PrimeLife Clique prototype. Collections can be managed by dragging contacts in or out a particular collection. Figure one also shows another feature of the prototype, the possibility to maintain different faces within the same SNS. The picture shows my professional face, one in which my real name is known. It also shows two contexts in which I operate under pseudonyms (Romix and DepronDave). These two identities represent me in my hobbies. Clique allows me to maintain my different spheres within the same software environment. This allows the user to manage a single address book and easily share data between these different spheres while still being able to control linkability.

Our second assumption is that we presume that each SNS user has a core audience in the SNS which basically reflects the primary reason for being present in the SNS. For a majority of SNS users, their core audience will consist of their immediate friends (Facebook, Hyves), for some networks, the core will more likely consist of professional contacts (Linked-in). This allows us to make assumptions about the users' behaviour. A sensible default is to assume that the user primarily wants to disclose information to this core audience, and if so, no special action should be required. This is implemented as follows. Posting information on the SNS requires the user to press the [publish] button. Subsequently a save information dialogue appears such as shown in figure 2. By default, custom will be selected and within custom the default collection – the user's core audience – will be pre-selected (as shown in figure 3). Under most circumstances this represents what the user wants to do, so pressing [submit] will do to publish the information on the SNS. Showing the user the currently selected audience (as in figure 3) will help prevent accidental data spills.

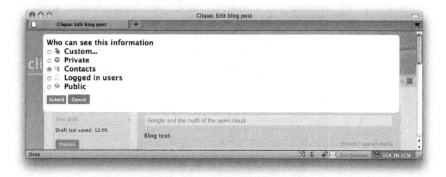

Fig. 2. Save information dialogue

This publication mechanism applies whenever the user creates or modifies any 'blob' of information on the SNS, such as posting a comment, writing a blog entry, or modifying a profile attribute. The save information dialogue allows the user to customise the audience by either selecting private, their own contacts, logged-in users, public, or make more fine grained choices in the Custom panel where they can drag contacts and collections in or out the audience for the particular blob of information (see figure 3). The mechanism as implemented nudges the user to disclose information to their

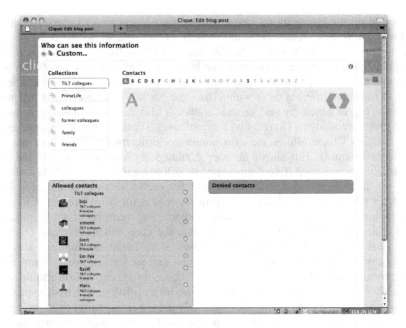

Fig. 3. Default audience pre-selected in custom target audience dialogue panel

Fig. 4. Visual audience indicators

likely intended audience (their preferred collection)without hindering making different choices.

The third assumption is that access control policies should be set on on all data disclosed in the SNS and should be as easy as possible. These policies should be as simple as possible. The access control mechanism in Clique allows the user to specify which collection and/or individuals have access to certain information. In the case of collections it should be able to exclude individual members from certain information. For instance, I may want to exclude a particular friend from discussions about a birthday present in order to maintain an element of surprise during her birthday party, something we also do in real life.

All information in the SNS contains visual indicators of the current audience. Figure 4 shows that the Google blog entry is open to the public at large (green globe icon), while the "Not for the faint of heart" post is restricted to a collection (two figures icon), in this case the PrimeLife members, minus "Hans". Each item on the SNS can be assigned its own access control policy (see figure 5 for an example of the profile page).

Fig. 5. Profile with access control policies on each attribute

One can also view one's own profile from the perspective of another user (figure 6). Contact icons feature a contextual menu (activated by mousing over the bottom-right corner of the icon) which, apart from options such as remove from my contact list, contains an option 'view my profile as this user'). These visual indicators should help the user to determine whether the image of themselves they think they project conforms to what others within the SNS actually see of them. This helps them maintain control over their audiences.

Fig. 6. Contextual menu for contacts

7 Conclusion

Context is a central concept in the disclosure of information. What is appropriate in one context is not in another. We have argued that most current online social network sites have a very simplistic model of social structures which creates many privacy issues. In our view, technology can be adopted to help users maintain different partial identities en control who can access their data even in social networks. We have developed a prototype that implements the core ideas. At the time of writing large online social network sites, such as Facebook and Hyves are clearly migrating to similar ideas, albeit currently less developed.

Whether or not SNS users can and will use the mechanisms provided remains to be seen. To test whether they do, we have set up an experimental site consisting of the Clique prototype (http://clique.primelife.eu). During 2010 we will try to attract real SNS users to use the platform in order to test the concepts and further improve the notions.

Acknowledgments. Part of the research leading to these results has received funding from the European Community's Seventh Framework Programme (FP7/2007-2013) under grant agreement No. 216483. The author wants to thank Joeri de Ruiter who did a tremendous job of implementing the ideas of the author and Bibi van den Berg into the Clique application.

References

1. Grimmelmann, J.T.: Saving Facebook. NYLS Legal Studies Research Paper No. 08/09-7 (2008)
2. boyd, d.m., Ellison, N.: Social Network Sites: Definition, History, and Scholarship. J. Computer-Mediated Comm. art. 11, 13 (2007)

3. Berg, B.v.d., Beato, F.: H1.2.6 – Audience segregation in social network sites (SNSs). PrimeLife Consortium (2009)
4. boyd, d.: Social Network Sites: Public, Private, or What? Knowledge Tree 13 (2007)
5. boyd, d.: Reflections on Friendster, Trust and Intimacy. In: Ubicomp 2003, Workshop application for the Intimate Ubiquitous Computing Workshop, Seattle, WA (2003)
6. Acquisti, A., Gross, R.: Imagined Communities: Awareness, Information Sharing, and Privacy on the Facebook. In: Danezis, G., Golle, P. (eds.) PET 2006. LNCS, vol. 4258, pp. 36–58. Springer, Heidelberg (2006)
7. Hogben, G.e.: Security Issues and Recommendations for Online Social Networks. ENISA, Heraklion (2007)
8. Liz, P.r.: Draft opinion of the Section for Transport, Energy, Infrastructure and the Information Society on The impact of social networking sites on citizens/consumers, Brussels (2009)
9. 29WP, A.: Opinion 5/2009 on online social networking. Article 29 Data Protection Working Party Brussels (2009)
10. Pekárek, M., Pötzsch, S.: H1.2.5 – Requirements and concepts for privacy- enhancing access control in social networks and collaborative workspaces. PrimeLife Consortium (2009)
11. boyd, d.: Why Youth (Heart) Social Network Sites: The Role of Networked Publics in Teenage Social Life. In: Buckingham, D. (ed.) MacArthur Foundation Series on Digital Learning – Youth, Identity, and Digital Media. MIT Press, Cambridge (2007)
12. Acquisti, A., Gross, R.: Information Revelation and Privacy in Online Social Networks (The Facebook case). In: ACM Workshop on Privacy in the Electronic Society (WPES). ACM, Alexandria (2005)
13. Tufekci, Z.: Can You See Me Now? Audience and Disclosure Regulation in Online Social Network Sites. Bulletin of Science, Technology & Society 28, 20–36 (2008)
14. Donath, J., boyd, d.: Public displays of connection. BT Technology Journal 22, 71–82 (2004)
15. Joinson, A.N.: 'Looking at', 'Looking up', or 'Keeping up with' People? Motives and Uses of Facebook. In: CHI 2008, Florence, Italy (2008)
16. Lampe, C., Ellison, N., Steinfield, C.A.: A Face(book) in the Crowd: Social Searching vs. Social Browsing. In: ACM Special Interest Group on Computer-Supported Cooperative Work, pp. 167–170. ACM Press, New York (2006)
17. boyd, d.: Taken Out of Context American Teen Sociality in Networked Publics (PhD thesis), Berkeley (2008)
18. boyd, d.: None of this is Real. In: Karaganis, J. (ed.) Structures of Participation (2007)
19. Goffman, E.: The presentation of self in everyday life. University of Edinburgh, Edinburgh (1956)
20. Sundén, J.: Material Virtualities. Peter Lang Publishing, New York (2003)
21. Turkle, S.: Life on Screen. Phoenix, London (1997)
22. Rachels, J.: Why privacy is important. Philosophy and Public Affairs, 323–333 (1975)
23. Barriger, J.: Social Network Sites: A comparative analysis of six sites. In: The Office of the Privacy Commissioner of Canada Ottawa (2009)
24. Thaler, R., Sunstein, C.: Nudge – Improving decisions about health, wealth and happiness. Yale University Press, Boston (2008)

The Freddi Staurs of Social Networking – A Legal Approach

Eleni Kosta

Interdisciplinary Centre for Law & ICT (ICRI)
Kathtolieke Universiteit Leuven
Sint-Michielsstraat 6, 3000 Leuven, Belgium
eleni.kosta@law.kuleuven.be

Abstract. One of the most remarkable cultural phenomena that blossomed in the Web 2.0 era are the social networking sites, such as Facebook, MySpace, Friendster, Bebo, Netlog or LinkedIn. The introduction of new communication channels facilitates interactive information sharing and collaboration between various actors over social networking sites. These actors, i.e. the providers and the users, do not always fit in the traditional communications models. In this paper we are going to examine how the new reality, realised via social networking sites, fits in the existing European legal framework on data protection. We are further going to discuss some specific data protection issues, focusing on the role of the relevant actors, using the example of photo tagging.

Keywords: Privacy, social networking, data controller, privacy settings.

1 Introduction

The developments in the field of information and communication technologies have always influenced -and have respectively been influenced by- social relationships. The emergence of a new generation of participatory and collaborative network technologies that provide individuals with a platform for sophisticated online (or mobile) social interaction is already a reality. An increasing number of applications and services are transforming the way in which people communicate and relate to others and to some extent are shaping society itself. Social networking sites[1], such as Facebook, MySpace, Friendster, Bebo, LinkedIn, Twitter, Netlog, Plaxo Pulse, count a growing population of users.

Boyd and Ellison define social network sites as "web-based services that allow individuals to (1) construct a public or semi-public profile within a bounded system, (2) articulate a list of other users with whom they share connection, and (3) view and traverse their list of connections and those made by others within the system. The nature and nomenclature of these connections may vary from site to site" [1]. Social networking sites are very popular among adolescents and young people, but they also

---

[1] Several other terms are used interchangeably, such as social network sites, online social networking etc.

M. Bezzi et al. (Eds.): Privacy and Identity, IFIP AICT 320, pp. 66–74, 2010.

attract the attention of users of an older age. The latter prefer however more profession-related social networking sites, such as LinkedIn [2].

The introduction of new communication channels facilitates interactive information sharing and collaboration between users over social networking sites. At the same time social networking sites serve as platforms for the exchange of vast amounts of personal information to a potentially public audience, as the profiles of the users are not always restricted to be visible only by their friends. Privacy and security considerations have been raised parallel to the great success of social networking. The privacy settings of the service can be used as a tool for the users to protect their privacy. Via the privacy settings they can restrict the access to their account or distinct parts of it only to specific contacts or categories of contacts. However not many users change the default privacy settings, which means that the privacy of the users is to a large extent in the hands of the providers of the social networking services. Recently Facebook changed the default privacy settings of all user accounts, so that specific information, such as their list of friends, photos or the pages they are fan of, are visible to everyone[2]. The Electronic Privacy Information Center (EPIC) subsequently filed a complaint with the Federal Trade Commission (FTC), urging the FTC to open an investigation into the revised privacy settings of Facebook.[3]

2 Freddi Staurs

News items on social networking sites are part of everyday reality and various reports are being published examining social networking from different perspectives. Despite the attempts at awareness raising with regard to the privacy and security risks arising from the use of social networking sites, several studies reveal that a great number of users still believe that revealing private information on a social networking site is not dangerous for their privacy and security [3, 6]. The vast expansion of social networking sites demonstrates a tendency of the users to acquire as many contacts as possible, accompanied by their eagerness to reveal personal information.

Several popular social networking sites, such as Facebook and MySpace, use the term "friend" for every contact added to the network of the user. In the off-line world, the term "friend" implies a close relation between the two parties that claim to be "friends", which in many cases does not correspond to the social networking reality. Therefore the term "friend" in social networking shall have a different connotation, as users add people to their networks for numerous reasons [4]. Most users of social networking sites "tend to list [as friend] anyone who they know and do not actively dislike" [5]. Moreover social networking sites do not allow for an indication of the intimacy between "friends", but are rather based on simplistic binary relations: friend or not friend [5, 6].

Studies have also revealed that users add to their network people they don't even know. Indicative is the experiment that was organized by the information security company Sophos in 2007, which wished to increase user awareness on the dangers of social networking in the early dawn of the phenomenon. Sophos created a Facebook

---

[2] Facebook press release, 9 December 2009,
   http://www.facebook.com/press/releases.php?p=133917
[3] http://epic.org/privacy/inrefacebook/EPIC-FacebookComplaint.pdf

account for the user "Freddi Staur" (an anagram of "ID Fraudster"). The account was represented by a small green plastic frog who divulged minimal personal information about himself. 200 friend requests were sent out in order to collect information regarding the response of the users and the degree of personal information they were willing to reveal. 87 of the 200 Facebook users contacted responded to Freddi, with 82 leaking personal information (41% of those approached), while 72% of respondents divulged one or more email address and 78% of respondents listed their current address or location[4].

3   The Reaction of European and International Privacy Bodies

The ease with which users reveal personal information in social networking sites, as well as the simultaneous lack of awareness and understanding regarding the threats and dangers lurking in such disclosure of personal information, alarmed International and European agencies, data protection and privacy advisory bodies. The European Network and Information Security Agency (ENISA) published in 2007 a position paper providing information on security issues relating to social networking services and giving recommendations regarding their use [7]. The International Working Group on Data Protection in Telecommunications (IWGDPT) adopted a report and guidance on Social Network Services, commonly known as "Rome Memorandum" [8]. The Working Group made recommendations for regulators, providers of social networking services and users, in an attempt to raise awareness on privacy issues in social networking services. The Rome Memorandum was followed by a Resolution on Privacy Protection in Social Network Services that was adopted by the 30th International Conference of Data Protection and Privacy Commissioners in 2008, which also contained recommendations for users and providers of social networking services [9]. In response to the heated debate on the protection of the privacy of the European users of social networking sites, the Article 29 Data Protection Working Party (or simply Article 29 Working Party)[5] adopted in June 2009 an opinion on social networking sites, in which it included, among others, key recommendations on the obligations of providers of social networking sites, so that they comply with the European regulatory framework on the protection of personal data [10].

4   The EU Data Protection Legislation in Front of Social Networking Challenges

A major issue arises with regard to the safeguarding of EU citizens' privacy rights and the applicability of the European data protection legal framework on providers of

---

[4] http://www.sophos.com/pressoffice/news/articles/2007/08/facebook.html
[5] Under Article 29 of the Data Protection Directive, a Working Party on the Protection of Individuals with regard to the Processing of Personal Data is established, made up of the Data Protection Commissioners from the Member States together with a representative of the European Commission. The Working Party is independent and acts in an advisory capacity. The Working Party seeks to harmonize the application of data protection rules throughout the EU, and publishes opinions and recommendations on various data protection topics.

social networking services established outside the European Union. This issue is very important as the European data protection framework sets high standards with regard to the protection of individuals relating to the processing of their personal data and imposes strict obligations to entities that process personal data. The Article 29 Working Party is of the opinion that the provisions of the Data Protection Directive[6] apply to the providers of social networking sites "in most cases", even if they are located outside the European Union [10]. The Article 29 Working Party sees two potential bases for the applicability of the Data Protection Directive: (i) the social networking service provider has an establishment in the territory of an EU Member State or (ii) although the social networking service provider does not have an establishment within the EU, he makes use of equipment situated on an EU Member State[7] [11]. In this paper, we make the assumption that the Data Protection Directive applies to providers of social networking sites, whose headquarters are established outside the European Union.

4.1 The Actors in Social Networking

The Data Protection Directive defines two basic categories of parties, which are relevant to be identified in the context of social networking services. On the one hand there is the data subject, who is the individual to whom the personal data relate: in the case of social networking the users of the sites. According to the Data Protection Directive, the individual must be identified or at least identifiable in order for data to qualify as personal data. Anonymous individuals do not qualify as data subjects under the European legal data protection framework. On the other hand there is the data controller, who is a person (natural or legal), which alone or jointly with others "determines the purposes and means of the processing of personal data"[8]. The Data Protection Directive foresees specific obligations for the data controllers regarding the processing of personal data, the respect of the rights of the users and their responsibility in case of breach of the law. The classification of a person as 'data controller' is of great importance, as he exercises the decision making both on the purposes for which personal data are collected and processed, as well as on the means to be used for a specific processing.

The definition of the data controller in social networking is a very complicated and heavily debated issue. The introduction of new communication channels in the Web 2.0 era facilitates interactive information sharing and collaboration between various actors over social networking sites, who do not always fit in the traditional communications models.

According to the Article 29 Working Party the providers of the social networking services are the ones who determine the means for the processing of the user data, as

---

[6] Directive 1995/46/EC of the European Parliament and of the Council of 24 October 1995 on the protection of individuals with regard to the processing of personal data and on the free movement of such data, hereinafter the 'data protection directive', O.J. L 281/31, 23.11.1995.

[7] The issue of applicability of the European data protection legislation to social networking services located outside the EU is dealt with extensively in this volume by A. Kuczerawy. For an analysis of the applicability of the Data Protection Directive in the context of search engine providers with similar argumentation applicable to social networking sites providers, see [12].

[8] Article 2 (d) Data Protection Directive.

they provide the social networking platform and all the basic tools regarding the user management, such as the registration and the deletion of the user accounts. The providers of social networking services also determine some of the purposes for which the data will be used, especially for advertising and marketing purposes [10]. It shall also be noted that the providers of social networking services define the functionalities of the service and in this way they also broadly determine the purposes for which users can process their data and the data of their contacts and friends. But what about the users of social networking services? Don't they bear any responsibility for their actions and interactions in these services?

4.2 Users of Social Networking Sites as Data Controllers

The users of social networking sites have a substantial degree of choice regarding the information they disclose. They share their personal information with their contacts and friends but often they share also information of other individuals. They are not merely passive actors whose data are being processed by the provider of the social networking service, but they are also actively processing information of other users. Users may usually decide on the specific application they use in order to reveal this information in a social networking site.

Before examining if the users of social networking services may serve as data controllers and if they must fulfil the obligations that are foreseen by the Directive for data controllers, it must be studied whether their actions fall within the scope of the Data Protection Directive. Even when processing of personal data takes place, the Directive does not apply, when the processing is done by a natural person in the course of a purely personal or household activity (commonly known as "household exemption")[9]. It must be thus first examined whether the users of social networking sites can justify that they process personal data for a purely personal activity. Recital 12 of the Data Protection Directive clarifies that such activities shall be "exclusively personal or domestic" and mentions as examples the private correspondence or the holding of records of addresses. The European Court of Justice (ECJ) in its ruling on the Lindqvist case took a position on the household exemption and the way it should be interpreted. The ECJ expressed the opinion that the household exemption "must […] be interpreted as relating only to activities which are carried out in the course of private or family life of individuals, which is clearly not the case with the processing of personal data consisting in publication on the internet so that those data are made accessible to an indefinite number of people" [14].

The ECJ considered the publication on the internet as not falling under the household exemption, as the data are made accessible to an indefinite number of people. Legal scholars have also come to the conclusion that it is unlikely for the household exemption to apply in the case of users of social networking sites [15, 16]. In the context of social networking, the Article 29 Working Party considered the status of a user account as private or public as a very important element in order to determine the applicability of the Data Protection Directive to the processing of personal data by the users of social networking services. More specifically, the Article 29 Working Party considered that when the information of a user profile can be

---

[9] Art. 3(2) 2nd indent Data Protection Directive.

accessed by all members of a social networking site or when the data can be indexed by search engines, then the user does not benefit from the household exemption. According to the Article 29 Working Party the same shall be the approach when the user makes no selection in accepting contacts and connects to people regardless of any possible link to them [10]. If the "household exemption" does not apply with regard to the users of social networking services, the user could in principle be considered a data controller at least "with regards to the content he chooses to provide and the processing operations he initiates" [13].

The decisive criterion for the Article 29 Working Party is the access to the user account. A user with a private account that is visible only to self-selected contacts will fall under the household exemption and shall not be considered as data controller when processing information of his friends on the social networking service. To the contrary, a user that has a public profile, accessible to the rest of the social networking community, who accepts contacts regardless of the connection they have, or whose profile (and the relevant information) is indexable by search engines, is not covered by the household exemption and shall be considered as a data controller.

Consequently, according to the argumentation of the Article 29 Working Party, a user with a private profile is not a data controller, while a user with a public one is. What if the user who has a private account opens up his profile to the public? Pursuant to the opinion of the Article 29 Working Party, he becomes a controller. But what if this user decides to make his profile private again. Does he stop being a controller? What about users who make only partial information from their profile public? Are they covered by the household exemption or are they data controllers and need to comply with the relevant obligations? The Article 29 Working Party attempted to clarify the situation regarding the applicability fo the Data Protection Directive to social networking servies. However it seems too arbitrary to consider as the key criterion in order to decide on the applicability of the Data Protection Directive the mere choice of a user to make his account public or his wish to accept as many friends as possible [13]. The opinion of the Article 29 Working Party did not manage to shed enough light on the problem of the applicability of the Data Protection Directive to the processing of personal information by the users of social networking services and there is still a need for clear and practically viable solutions.

4.3 The Example of Photo Tagging

If the "household exemption" does not apply to the users of social networking services, besides enjoying their rights as data subjects, the users become responsible for ensuring compliance with the obligations that are defined in the Data Protection Directive.[10] More specifically the users shall become responsible for ensuring, inter alia, that the processing is fair and lawful; that only the data which is necessary and relevant to the purposes will be processed, that the data are kept accurate and if needed updated; that the data shall not be kept longer than necessary for the fulfilment of the purposes, that the right of the data subject regarding the processing of the personal data are respected (right of access, rectification, erasure or blocking); that the data are kept in a secure way [13, 18].

---

[10] For a comprehensive analysis of the obligations of the data controller see Kuner, 2007.

A user that wishes to publish information about other individuals on his profile is allowed to do it only based on a legitimate ground for processing personal data, such as the consent of the person concerned. The user must, for instance, obtain the unambiguous consent of the relevant persons before posting any information about them and shall remove any information relating to them upon their request.

Let us take a closer look into the popular function of tagging photos (tagging). Tagging allows users to "tag" a person that appears on a photo uploaded to a social networking site indicating the name of the person and possibly also his email address. If the tagged person is also user of the specific social networking site, he is normally allowed to remove the tag, but he is not allowed to remove the photo. However, if the person is not a registered member of the social networking site, he will not even have the possibility of deleting the tag. The situation becomes even more complicated if we take into account that any other user of the social networking site has the possibility to "tag" faces that appear on other users' photos. The user that uploads the photo and the one that ads the tag to it, shall base their action on a legitimate ground, such as the consent of the person concerned. In this case, the person who appears on a photo shall give his prior consent not only for the tagging, but also for the uploading of his photo. This means that before uploading a photo and eventually adding tags to it, a user shall acquire the consent of the persons that appear on the photo. Failure to do so would be interpreted as violation of the obligations of the data controller under the European data protection legislation.

The negative implications for the user are obvious from such an approach. The users are not realising that they are breaching the data protection legislation when they upload the photos from a party they attended and they tag their friends. Currently social networking sites allow the dissemination of information about other individuals without their consent, which is problematic in various cases. From the example of photo uploading and tagging it becomes obvious that there is a need for further refinement of the legal obligations and rights of the users of social networking services.

5 Concluding Thoughts

The development of the Internet and the emergence of Web 2.0 introduced a new era in the communication of the Internet users and the exchange of user-generated content. One of the most remarkable cultural phenomena that blossomed in the Web 2.0 era are the social networking sites, such as Facebook, MySpace, Friendster, Bebo, Netlog, LinkedIn to name just a few. Social networks enable the connection of users and they facilitate the exchange of information among them. However the users reveal vast amounts of personal information over social networking sites, without realising the privacy and security risks arising from their actions. The European Data Protection legislation could be used as a means for protecting the users against the unlawful processing of their personal information, although a number of problems arising regarding its applicability. However, the whole *rationale* behind social networking service is exactly the revealing and sharing of user personal information. There is therefore a need for further refinement of the legal obligations and rights of the users of social networking services.

The European Commission set up in April 2008 a European Social Networking Task Force in the context of its Safer Internet Programme[11]. Main goal of this Task Force was the development of guidelines for the use of social networking sites by children [19]. These guidelines are currently voluntarily adopted by 17 leading social networking sites, such as Facebook, Bebo and MySpace[12] and will be evaluated a year after their adoption, i.e. in February 2010. In this way the European Commission promoted a solution of self-regulation in a first attempt to protect the minor users of social networking sites.

Acknowledgment. The research leading to these results has received funding from the European Community's Seventh Framework Programme (FP7/2007-2011) under the PICOS project (Grant Agreement no. 215056).

References

1. boyd, d., Ellison, N.: Social Networks Sites: Definition, History, and Scholarship. Journal of Computer-Mediated Communication article 11, 13(1) (2007)
2. Anderson Analytics: Social Network Service (SNS) A&U Profiler, provided to eMarketer on July 13 (2009), http://www.emarketer.com
3. boyd, d.: Taken Out of Context – American Teen Sociality in Networked Publics. PhD dissertation, University of California, Berkeley (2008)
4. boyd, d.: Friends, Friendsters, and MySpace Top8: Writing Community Into Being on Social Network Sites. First Monday 11(12) (2006)
5. boyd, d.: Friendster and Publicly Articulated Social Networks. In: Conference on Human Factors and Computing Systems (CHI 2004), April 24-29. ACM, Vienna (2004)
6. Gross, R., Acquisti, A.: Information Revelation and Privacy in Online Social Networks (The Facebook case). In: Proceedings of the 2005 ACM workshop on Privacy in the electronic society, pp. 71–80 (2005)
7. ENISA: Security Issues and Recommendations for Online Social Networks (2007)
8. International Working Group on Data Protection in Telecommunications (IWGDPT): Report and guidance on Social Network Services ("Rome Memorandum") (2008)
9. Data Protection and Privacy Commissioners: Resolution on Privacy Protection in Social Network Services. In: 30th International Conference of Data Protection ad Privacy Commissioners (October 2008)
10. Article 29 Data Protection Working Party: Opinion 5/2009 on online social networking (WP 163) (June 12, 2009)
11. Article 29 Data Protection Working Party: Opinion on data protection issues related to search engines (WP 148) (April 4, 2008)
12. Kosta, E., Kalloniatis, C., Mitrou, L., Kavakli, E.: Search engines: gateway to a new "Panopticon"? In: Fischer-Hübner, S., Lambrinoudakis, C., Pernul, G. (eds.) TrustBus 2009. LNCS, vol. 5695, pp. 11–21. Springer, Heidelberg (2009)
13. Van Alsenoy, B., Ballet, J., Kuczerawy, A., Dumortier, J.: Social networks and web 2.0: are users also bound by data protection regulations? IDIS Journal (2009), doi:10.1007/s12394-009-0017-3
14. Case C-101/01, Bodil Lindqvist I-12971 (2003)

---

[11] http://ec.europa.eu/information_society/activities/sip/index_en.htm

[12] A full list of the signatories and their self-declarations are available online at http://ec.europa.eu/information_society/activities/social_networking/eu_action/selfreg/index_en.htm#self_decl

15. Wong, R., Savirimuthu, J.: All or nothing: this is the question? The application of Art. 3(2) Data Protection Directive 95/46/C to the Internet. The John Marshall Journal of Computer & Information Law 25 (2008)
16. Wong, R.: Social Networking: Anybody is a Data Controller!
    http://papers.ssrn.com/sol3/papers.cfm?abstract_id=1271668
    (revised version October 2008)
17. Kuner, C.: European Data Protection Law – Corporate Compliance and Regulation, 2nd edn. Oxford University Press, Oxford (2007)
18. Edwards, L., Brown, I.: Data Control and Social Networking: Irreconcilable Ideas? In: Matwyshyn Andrea Harboring Data, pp. 202–227. Stanford University Press, Stanford (2009)
19. European Social Networking Task Force: Safer Social Networking Principles for the EU (February 10, 2009),
    http://ec.europa.eu/information_society/activities/social_ne
    tworking/docs/sn_principles.pdf

Facebook and Its EU Users – Applicability of the EU Data Protection Law to US Based SNS[*]

Aleksandra Kuczerawy

Interdisciplinary Centre for Law & ICT (ICRI) – K.U.Leuven
Sint-Michielsstraat 6, 3000 Leuven, Belgium
aleksandra.kuczerawy@law.kuleuven.be

Abstract. The present paper examines the problem of applicable data protection law in a relationship between EU users and non-EU based Social Networking Site (SNS). The analysis will be conducted on the example of Facebook, which is one of the most popular SNS. The goal of the paper is to examine whether European users of Facebook can rely on their national data protection legislations in case of a privacy infringement by the SNS. The 95/46/EC Directive on Data Protection provides several options to protect EU residents in such relation. The paper will analyze whether Facebook's participation in the Safe Harbor Program means that it is a subject to the regulation of the Data Protection Directive. Then, the paper will discuss if data processing activities of Facebook fall under the scope of the Data Protection Directive at all.

Keywords: Social Networking Sites, data protection, applicable law, cookies, transfer of data to third countries.

1 Introduction

Social Networking Sites (SNS) are a phenomenon of social interactions that became part of our lives faster than anybody could have imagined. Widely accessible platforms where people share data became very popular worldwide and have a constantly growing number of users. In Europe, many SNS have developed targeting the audience of the country where they are based. Each European country has a preferential SNS (Hyves in the Netherlands, StudiVZ in Germany, NetLog in Belgium or NaszaKlasa in Poland). Additionally, there is also a number of SNS originating from the USA that have users throughout the whole of Europe. Whereas the European

---

[*] Part of the research leading to these results has received funding from the European Community's Seventh Framework Program (FP7/2007-2013) under grant agreement n° 216483. The information in this document is provided "as is", and no guarantee or warranty is given that the information is fit for any particular purpose. The above referenced consortium members shall have no liability for damages of any kind including without limitation direct, special, indirect, or consequential damages that may result from the use of these materials subject to any liability which is mandatory due to applicable law.

M. Bezzi et al. (Eds.): Privacy and Identity, IFIP AICT 320, pp. 75–85, 2010.

based SNS are without any doubt subject to their national privacy laws, the situation of US based SNS is not that clear. Insofar as US based SNS are providing a service from the US, although directed to users worldwide, the applicability of the European privacy regime as defined by the Data Protection Directive (hereinafter DPD or the Directive)[1], is being debated. The apparent similarity of EU based and US based websites, which provide the service in the native language of the user, could mislead their users and make them believe they could enjoy the same level of protection. It is thus crucial to define the situation of such foreign based SNS regarding the applicable data protection law when dealing with European users. In order to find an answer to the complex issue of applicable law this article will rely on the example of Facebook as one of the most popular SNS in both the USA and Europe.

The problem of determining the applicable law for online interactions is not a new one. With the advent of the Internet it became immediately clear that one of its main characteristics is a lack of territorial borders. In a traditional setting, the national borders help to indicate an appropriate national law to be applied. With the absence of that factor alternative solutions had to be found to adjust to the new situation. Concerns have risen in particular in Business to Business (B2B) and Business to Consumer (B2C) online contracting with regard to the applicable contract law and consumer law. The question is now being raised for the applicability of data protection laws.

First concerns have emerged with regard to the applicability of the EU regime to data processing activities of search engines. The Article 29 Working Party[1] in this case stated that the EU data protection law applies if a non EU based search engine makes use of cookies on the territory of the EU. The question however pops up again with regard to SNS as they are called to process a large amount of personal data of their users. But can the same solution, as the one used for search engines, be relied on when it comes to SNS? This article will discuss such possibility analysing the specific situation of the US based SNS Facebook because of its popularity among European users. It will first highlight Facebook's participation in the Safe Harbor program. The article will focus on the very specific issue of the applicability of data protection law for EU users of a non-EU based Social Network. It will exclusively focus on the relation between the SNS providers and its users, not entering into other concerns that could arise with regard to the applicable regime to relations between users of SNS[2].

2   Situation of Facebook

Facebook is a non-EU based social networking site. Its main place of establishment is Palo Alto in California, USA which makes it a subject to the US law [3]. Facebook offers its services all over the world, and a substantial proportion of its users are based in the EU.

---

[1] Under Article 29 of the Data Protection Directive, a Working Party on the Protection of Individuals with regard to the Processing of Personal Data is established, made up of the Data Protection Commissioners from the Member States together with a representative of the European Commission. The Working Party is independent and acts as an advisory body. The Working Party seeks to harmonize the application of data protection rules throughout the EU, and publishes opinions and recommendations on various data protection issues.

[2] For the applicability of the Data Protection Directive to users of SNS see [2].

First of all, it should be clarified that the services offered by Facebook as a SNS provider constitute 'data processing' in the light of the DPD. 'Data processing' is defined as any operation or set of operations which is performed upon personal data, whether or not by automatic means, such as collection, recording, organization, storage, adaptation or alteration, retrieval, consultation, use, disclosure by transmission, dissemination or otherwise making available, alignment or combination, blocking, erasure or destruction [1]. As the definition is very broad, it undoubtedly covers activities performed by providers of SNS who, at least, collect and store data of their users.

Furthermore, Facebook is in the position of data controller, as an entity which alone or jointly with others determines the purposes and means of the processing of personal data [1]. As expressed in several opinions, by providing the technical side of the service, in other words by making it possible to actually process data on the website, the provider determines the purposes and means of the data processing [4]. Due to these circumstances, Facebook can be described as a US based data controller involved in the processing of personal data of European individuals.

3   First Hope: Facebook as a Member of Safe Harbor

3.1   Safe Harbor Program

When looking at Facebook's privacy policy [5], one can see that the company is a member of the EU Safe Harbor Privacy Framework [6]. The Safe Harbor program was developed by the US Department of Commerce in consultation with the European Commission. It was introduced to solve the problem created by the new regime regulating transfers of personal data established by the Directive. Such transfers are prohibited whenever the country where the data is imported does not guarantee an adequate level of protection – like the USA where the data protection is based on self-regulatory approach.

The Directive provides a series of derogations to the prohibition of transfers of data to third countries if adequate safeguards of protection are guaranteed, e.g. through contractual agreements [7]. Such possibility has been introduced in art. 25.6 of the Directive. The Safe Harbor renders data transfers possible on condition that companies importing personal data commit themselves to a set of privacy principles negotiated by the US Department of Commerce and the Commission. Such commitment is established through a voluntary subscription to the Safe Harbor program.

The Department of Commerce provides a list of requirements that have to be fulfilled by the company in order to be able to join. The list of necessary steps consists of: company's self-assessment whether it is eligible for participation in the program; determination of dispute resolution and enforcement mechanisms; submission of a written certificate to the Department of Commerce; disclosure of the company's commitment to the Safe Harbor principles; implementation of the Safe Harbor principles in practice; and reaffirmation of the membership on annual basis [8]. Companies that are eligible to participate in the program are those that are subject to the jurisdiction of the Federal Trade Commission (FTC) or the Department of the Transportation (DOT). Once a company fulfils these criteria it is signed up to the program. It is not however within the scope of competence of the Department of Commerce to examine a company's situation with regard to the EU data protection law as long as such companies remain subject to US law for the processing of personal data on US territory.

As a consequence of a subscription, data collected in the EU can be transferred to the US for further processing. Once in the US, the data are deemed to be protected under principles similar to those of the DPD [9]. For the European data subject this means, apart from the guarantee of the adequate protection, that any claims brought by the European residents against US companies will be heard in the US, in accordance to the US law [10].

3.2 Transfer or Not?

Undoubtedly, it was very cautious of Facebook to subscribe to such program. However, was it necessary? From a legal perspective, only if Facebook is being transferred personal data collected in the EU, would it need to join the program.

First of all, it should be noted that provisions of art. 25 DPD are addressed to the controller based in the EU. The concept of data transfer to third countries refers to the situation when there is a data controller on the territory of the EU who collects the data of the EU individuals and exports them to another controller (or a processor) outside of the EU. It means that two different actors are necessary to participate, both of them acting as separate data controllers or as a controller and a processor[3]. Moreover, in case the data transfer occurs, there is an obligation of compliance with the law of the location in which the data is collected, before it is sent outside of the EU [11]. It is normally a responsibility of the data exporter, i.e. the controller in the EU. It would imply that an entity collecting data for Facebook in the EU, such as a local branch of the company, is under such obligation.

According to the information provided on the website of Facebook, its headquarters are based exclusively in the US. When feeding Facebook with their data, users are thus sending them directly to the US. There is no EU-based intermediary in the processing of these data. We should then consider, in such case, that there is a lack of one (transferring) party because the US company does not act as an EU controller. Therefore, it is not really a transfer of data in the understanding of the Directive [12]. In absence of EU based controller, the provisions of article 25 and 26 DPD, do not apply to this situation. For that reason, the US company does not need to comply with the restrictions for data transfers [11].

It is thus surprising that Facebook has opted for subscribing to the Safe Harbor program. In practice, even though the 'real' transfer does not occur, the US Department of Commerce accepts Safe Harbor subscriptions from US based companies that only process the personal data of European users from their US websites [11].

Facebook was of course free to do so, as the Safe Harbor is a voluntary program. However, such decision does not mean that it committed to comply with the EU Data Protection law. It only means that it committed to a US voluntary program improving

---

[3] 'Data controller' means the natural or legal person, public authority, agency or any other body which alone or jointly with others determines the purposes and means of the processing of personal data (art. 2(d)DPD). 'Data processor' means a natural or legal person, public authority, agency or any other body which processes personal data on behalf of the controller (art. 2 (e)DPD).

the level of protection of their users' data with regards to the protection as provided in the US.

As shown above, as long as the user sends his data directly to the US without any intermediary in Europe, the regime of international transfers of personal data cannot apply. This leads to a more fundamental question whether the processing of European users' data by a US based SNS could fall under the provisions of the EU Directive. To that effect, it is necessary to determine whether art. 4 of the DPD, which defines the rule of choice of law, applies.

An important hint regarding the relation between art. 4 DPD and art. 25 DPD was given by Art. 29 WP. In its Opinion about the level of protection provided by the Safe Harbor it stated that the program does not affect the application of Article 4 of the Directive [13]. This means that the Principles of Safe Harbor were not intended to substitute the national provisions implementing the Directive in situations where those national provisions apply. The following section will hence analyse the applicability of the national data protection regulations.

4 The Specific Rule of Choice of Law of Art. 4: Towards a Solution?

Art. 4 of the Data Protection Directive addresses the problem of applicability of national data protection laws of the Member States. Despite the complexity of the issue, due to its international character, art. 4 has not been extensively analyzed so far [14]. This is quite remarkable, considering the possible broad impact of the provision.

Art. 4 prescribes the application of the national data protection laws of the EU Member States when a) the processing is carried out in the context of the activities of an establishment of the controller on the territory of that Member State, when b) the processing is carried out on the territory where the law of a Member State applies, and c) when the controller is located outside of the EU but it uses equipment on the territory of a Member State. Art. 4.1(a) could apply if European offices of Facebook were involved in processing of the European users' data. However, information about the exact nature of the activities of the offices located in Europe and, most important, whether they are involved in data processing is very difficult to obtain[4]. For this reason the analysis will focus on the 'equipment criterion' of art. 4.1 (c).

4.1 Use of Equipment

Article 4.1(c) of the DPD states that each Member State shall apply the national provisions it adopts pursuant to this Directive to the processing of personal data where the controller is not established on Community territory and, for purposes of processing personal data makes use of equipment, automated or otherwise, situated on the territory of the said Member State, unless such equipment is used only for purposes of transit through the territory of the Community [1]. This means that EU countries can directly apply their national data protection legislations to non-EU based websites whenever they would make use of equipment located on the territory of the said countries (but not when the equipment is used solely for the transit purposes).

---

[4] Questions sent to Facebook through the Privacy Help Center were left unanswered.

Does this apply to Facebook then? Here, it is necessary to enter into a discussion about the interpretation of the term 'equipment'. According to the Art. 29 Working Party it is a decisive factor for the application of the European data protection law. Such 'equipment' should be at the disposal of the controller for the processing of personal data [15]. However, it does not have to be a full control but it is sufficient that the controller determines which data are collected, stored, transferred, altered etc., in which way and for which purpose [15].

It is a strong opinion of the Art. 29 Working Party that the user's PC constitute exactly the type of equipment described in the working document [15]. To apply this criterion, it is sufficient for the controller to make use of the users' PC by placing cookies on the hard disk. The national law of Member State where the user's personal computer is located would then apply to the question under what conditions user's personal data may be collected by placing cookies on his hard disk [15]. Such is the case of Facebook [5]. It follows that Facebook users' national law of EU Member State would be applicable to the processing.

This position has been confirmed by the Art. 29 WP opinion on search engines [16], and a recent opinion on online social networking [17]. Such an approach, however, might have very severe effects. It could lead in fact to a direct application of the Directive, and consequently of the national data protection laws of all EU countries to every non-EU based website using cookies with users on the territory of the EU [18]. So basically, it could apply to the entire Internet [11].

On the one hand, it seems to shield European users in case of any processing of their data as it puts them under the full protection of the European data protection law. Such an extent of protection would be satisfying and definitely enough, from the DPD point of view, to protect the privacy of European residents. Hence, it could end the discussion at this point. On the other hand, it makes the situation of all non-EU based data controllers involved in the processing of data of European users extremely complicated. When applying such interpretation to the analyzed case, the result would be that Facebook has to simultaneously comply with data protection legislations of each EU country where the users enjoy the service (so practically all 27 Member States). Such requirement is in many views not pragmatic. Moreover, it is described by some authors as an 'impossible burden' [11].

Here it should be mentioned that in the traditional, off-line setting any company doing business in another country has to do so in compliance with the local law, and there is nothing unusual about it. Moreover, it refers to all areas of law, including data protection law. Sometimes the need of compliance is even taken to a higher level when the weaker party is given a special amount of protection. A perfect example of such regulation is consumer law. It provides the protection of the local law of the consumer irrespectively of the location of the seller [19]. Moreover, this principle cannot be ruled out through a choice of law clause in the contract. Maybe it would be worth considering whether data subjects, who undoubtedly are the weaker party, should not be granted protection embedded in the similar idea. However interesting the question is, it is beyond the scope of this article. But it shows that the requirement of compliance with the local law of the user is not an extravagant concept. So is the situation of Facebook so much different to see such a requirement as an impossible burden?

Currently, the broad scope of application of art. 4.1 c DPD is a result of the Art. 29 WP's interpretation of the term 'equipment' and not of the wording of the Directive. This broad effect seems to be going further then originally designed back in 1995 when the use of technologies like cookies was not so common[5]. These are the reasons why this provision causes heated discussions and is often criticized. Defining such a broad scope of art. 4.1.c in the Directive itself would undoubtedly provide stronger legal basis to effectively protect EU data subjects in relations with non-EU data controllers. This is definitely one of the issues that could be clarified during the next revision of the Directive.

4.2 Limits of the "Cookies" Solution

In many ways the "cookies" criterion appears insufficient to provide a satisfying answer to the problem at stake. The artificial nature of such construction is even more striking when we look into the E-privacy Directive [21]. The former wording of the article 5.3 of the 2002 E-privacy Directive prescribed that the use of cookies should be only allowed when the user is informed about it, in a clear and comprehensive way, in accordance with the DPD, and is offered the right to object to such processing by the data controller [21]. The recent amendments to the Telecoms package, introduced at the end of 2009, modified the wording of this provision and now it requires the user's prior consent before the installation of cookies on his computer [22]. This change has attracted lot of attention from the industry but it is still unclear how will it influence the discussed problem.

The user must be notified when the cookie is installed on his computer. If he doesn't agree to that, a paradoxical situation could occur. The user, wishing to protect his privacy by refusing the cookies would in fact deprive himself of the protection by his national data protection law. This would happen because art. 4.1 (c) DPD applies only if the data controller uses equipment, so the user's computer, on the territory of the Member State, through the cookie. This situation would however not occur in case of user's objection to the use of cookie. Thus, there would be no ground to apply art. 4.1 (c) DPD.

The whole situation is spiced up by the fact that most of the time the user refuses the cookie in a belief that he is protecting his own privacy. However, many services are not possible to enjoy without accepting the cookies, and Facebook is no exception here. It is undeniable that the problem of the protection of the collected data would disappear if the service could not be provided without the use of cookies. In the former version of the Facebook 's Privacy Policy, users were informed that "[they could] remove or block this [persistent] cookie using the settings in [their] browser if [they] want[ed] to disable this convenience feature". In the new Privacy Policy, in life since November 2009, users are however informed that opting for the removal or blocking of cookies "may impact [their] ability to use Facebook"[5]. Therefore it seems not possible to enjoy the full service without having previously accepted the use of cookies. Although this seems to simplify the problem of the privacy protection, it however raises questions about a real possibility of users to object to the use of cookies in practice.

---

[5] Cookies technology was developed in 1994, see more in [20].

The arguments above create an inevitable impression that 'the cookie construction' from art. 4.1(c), although designed to provide a basis for the protection of the European residents' data, is in fact an artificial rule that may be too weak to provide an efficient protection in practice. Such a conclusion can be drawn especially in light of the obligation installed by art. 5.3 of the E-privacy Directive to require users' consent for the use of cookies. The shield provided by art. 4.1 (c) DPD can be easily removed by the user acting in a good faith. An inevitable impression is created that cookie construction does not provide a workable solution and, in fact, when put into practice can lead to more questions than answers. For this reason it can only be considered as a temporary solution which should be reconsidered with the next revision of the Data Protection Directive.

4.3 An Illusory Protection

Another aspect of the problem is related to the most often heard criticism of art. 4.1(c): the difficult enforceability of the provision. The assumed power of an EU Member State to apply its national data protection legislation to a non-EU website processing data of its citizens by means of cookies is not synonymous with that Member State's ability to enforce such judgment [11].

The Article 29 WP was fully aware of that difference. For that reason, it called for caution in applying art. 4.1(c) to concrete cases. The objective of the rule is to ensure that individuals receive protection of their national data protection laws in those cases where it is necessary, where it makes sense and where there is a reasonable degree of enforceability having regard to the cross-frontier situation involved [15]. At the same time, the Working Party believes that many third countries will recognize and enforce such judgment [15]. Moreover, it presents an opinion that in third countries where data protection rules and authorities are in place, enforcement will not be a problem [15]. This however is not a common opinion. According to Kuner, enforcement in this case seems very unlikely. In his view, every unsuccessful attempt of enforcement would only lead to undermining of the general respect for data protection law [11]. He also recalls the even stronger opinion of Mann who calls a similar attempt a violation of international law [11]. It is considered that an idea of any State trying to enforce its own law on foreign actors outside its borders is simply against commonsense and the present international order [23].

Given these arguments, an additional observation can be made. It has to be emphasized that applicable law, jurisdiction and enforcement are three related, but separate questions. For each one of them there are specific rules. Therefore, the weak chance of enforcement should in general not be a reason to disregard a correctly determined applicable law.

5 Conclusion

The situation of the European users of Facebook, regarding the issue of the applicable data protection law is neither clear nor easy to solve.

First unclarity stems from Facebook's participation in the Safe Harbor program. A lack of controller in Europe, participating in the process, point to the fact that there is no transfer of data. It means that there is no addressee of art. 25 DPD and the special restrictions for data transfers to third countries do not apply to the situation under discussion. The fact that Facebook has decided to join the Safe Harbor program is in any case beneficial for EU users as it improves the level of protection of their data in the US. However, as shown in this article, this does not mean that Facebook complies with the DPD. Additionally, it could mislead its users with regards to the real level of protection ensured.

In order to determine whether Data Protection Directive is applicable one should look into art. 4.1(c) which is directed to the non-EU based data controllers who use equipment in the EU. The Art. 29 WP has recently clearly stated that the provisions of the Data Protection Directive apply to SNS providers in most cases, even if their headquarters are located outside of the EEA [17]. It reached this conclusion by acknowledging 'cookies' as a way of making use of equipment (in the form of user's computer) on the territory of the Member States. So, it seems that the processing of users' data would be regulated directly by the European data protection law, and consequently by the user's national law.

This approach, however, is heavily criticized, for several reasons. One of them refers to weak chances of enforcement of a decision taken on the basis of this rule. Moreover, an obligation to comply with the national data protection laws of the EU countries, because of use of cookies, is often considered as a burden too heavy for the providers of services from outside of the EU. Furthermore, there is a risk that for any service allowing its users to enjoy it with disabled cookies, the protection spread over the EU individuals with the 'cookie provision' could be easily eliminated by the users themselves, in an attempt to protect their privacy. All these critical arguments, thus, create an impression that art. 4.1 (c), in its current form, does not provide a basis strong enough to ensure the protection of the European data subjects in the context of SNS.

It can be clearly concluded that the current situation provides no legal certainty. It undoubtedly calls either for another solution, or for a stronger legal basis for the existing one. Unfortunately, until now there is no case law that would help to find criteria of interpretation.

The Art. 29 WP, in order to make the situation clearer, could maybe enter into discussions on this specific problem with Facebook. Such idea is based on the precedent of the discussions initiated with Google. In 2008 an attempt to address and seek industry perspectives on data protection issues related to search engines was made through an invitation to an open discussion placed in the Opinion 148. The 'call for opinion' was answered by Google which replied through an official 'Response to the Article 29 Working Party Opinion on Search Engines' [24] published on its website. In this document Google addressed problematic issues of data protection related to search engines and presented its point of view on the subject. The reply was undeniably a contribution to the discussion which could be repeated now.

Another example of openly addressing a service provider is a recent action of the Canadian Data Protection Authority which issued a report criticizing some points of Facebook's Privacy Policy and pointing out that such policy was not compliant with the Canadian Data Protection Law [25]. Quite surprisingly to most observers Facebook replied almost immediately organizing a set of meetings and promising to fix the controversial points which have not been solved immediately [26]. It will of course take some time to see how serious the promise was, however, the first step has been made and the dialogue has been started. What is the most important aspect here is the fact that the action of the Canadian DPA was not ignored by Facebook. In these circumstances maybe it is time for the Art. 29 WP to follow the Canadian example in taking more dynamic steps and more actively target Facebook, as the US based SNS with the biggest number of users in Europe. There are more issues than only applicable law that could be discussed and hopefully solved that way.[6]

Acknowledgments. The author would like to thank Brendan Van Alsenoy, Fanny Coudert, Eleni Kosta and Karel Wouters for their support with legal and technical knowledge and their critical review of the solutions proposed.

References

1. Directive 95/46/EC of the European Parliament and of the Council of 24.10.1995, on the protection of individuals with regard to the processing of personal data and on the free movement of such data (Data Protection Directive) (OJ L 281, 23.11.1995)
2. Van Alsenoy, B., Ballet, J., Kuczerawy, A., Dumortier, J.: Social networks and web 2.0: are users also bound by data protection regulations? In: Identity in the Information Society (IDIS), Special issue on Social Web and Identity (2009), doi:10.1007/s12394-009-0017-3, http://www.springerlink.com/content/u11161037506t68n/
3. Facebook Factsheet, http://www.facebook.com/press/info.php?factsheet
4. Wong, R., Savirimuthu, J.: All or nothing: this is the question?: The Application of Art. 3(2) Data Protection Directive 95/46/EC to the Internet
5. Facebook Privacy Policy, http://www.facebook.com/policy.php?ref=pf
6. Safe Harbor list of companies, http://web.ita.doc.gov/safeharbor/SHList.nsf/f6cff20f4d3b8a3 185256966006f7cde/1c51b941879c2e87852572d700734dc1?OpenDocum ent&Highlight=2,Facebook
7. Safe Harbor, U.S. Department of Commerce, http://www.export.gov/safeharbor/index.asp
8. Helpful Hints Prior to Self-Certifying to the Safe Harbor, http://www.export.gov/safeharbor/eu/eg_main_018495.asp
9. Safe Harbor Principles and FAQ, http://www.export.gov/safeharbor/SH_Overview.asp, http://www.export.gov/safeharbor/SH_FAQ8.asp
10. Safe Harbor, U.S. Department of Commerce, http://www.export.gov/safeharbor/eg_main_018236.asp
11. Kuner, C.: European data protection law: corporate compliance and regulation, 2nd edn., New York (2007)

---

[6] In the Report Canadian DPA addressed the following issues: collection of date of birth, default privacy settings, Facebook advertising, Third-Party applications, new uses of Personal Information, collection of Personal Information from sources other than Facebook, account deactivation and deletion, accounts of deceased users, Personal Information of Non-Users, Facebook Mobile and Safeguards, monitoring for anomalous activity, deception and misrepresentation.

12. De Terwangne, C., Louveaux, S.: Data Protection and Online networks. Computer Law and Security Report 13(4), 234–246 (1997)

13. Opinion 4/2000 on the level of protection provided by the Safe Harbor Principles, WP 32 adopted on May 16 (2000), http://ec.europa.eu/justice_home/fsj/privacy/docs/wpdocs/2000/wp32en.pdf

14. Veronica, P.A.M.: International aspects of personal data protection *Quo vadis* EU? In: Veronica, P.A.M., Pablo, P. (eds.) Challenges of privacy and data protection law, Bruxelles, pp. 383–413 (2008)

15. Art. 29 Data Protection Working Party, Working document on determining the international application of EU data protection law to personal data processing on the Internet by non-EU based web sites, WP 56 (adopted on May 30, 2002)

16. Art. 29 Data Protection Working Party, Opinion 1/2008 on data protection issues related to search engines, WP 148 (adopted on April 4, 2008)

17. Art. 29 Data Protection Working Party, Opinion 5/2009 on online social networking, WP 163 (adopted on June 12, 2009)

18. Terstegge, J.: In: Bullesbach, A., Poullet, Y., Prins, C. (eds.) Concise European IT Law, Alphen aan den Rijn (2005)

19. Art. 12 of the Directive 97/7/EC of the European Parliament and of the Council of 20 May 1997 on the protection of consumers in respect of distance contracts (OJ L 144) (June 4, 1997)

20. Schwartz, J.: Giving Web a Memory Cost Its Users Privacy, September 4. New York Times (2001)

21. Directive 2002/58/EC of the European Parliament and of the Council of 12 July 2002 concerning the processing of personal data and the protection of privacy in the electronic communications sector (e-Privacy Directive), (OJ L 201) (July 31, 2002)

22. Directive 2009/136/EC of the European Parliament and of the Council of 25 November 2009 amending Directive 2002/22/EC on universal service and users' rights relating to electronic communications networks and services, Directive 2002/58/EC concerning the processing of personal data and the protection of privacy in the electronic communications sector and Regulation (EC) No 2006/2004 on cooperation between national authorities responsible for the enforcement of consumer protection laws (OJ L 337) (December 18, 2009)

23. Mann, F.A.: The Doctrine of Jurisdiction in International Law, 1964, 111 Recueil des Cours 9, 145-146. In: Kuner, C. (ed.) European data protection law: corporate compliance and regulation, 2nd edn., New York (2007)

24. Google's Response to the Article 29 Working Party Opinion on Search Engines, http://blogs.taz.de/ctrl/files/2008/09/google.pdf

25. Report of Findings into the Complaint Filed by the Canadian Internet Policy and Public Interest Clinic (CIPPIC) against Facebook Inc. Under the Personal Information Protection and Electronic Documents Act,
http://www.priv.gc.ca/cf-dc/2009/2009_008_0716_e.cfm

26. Facebook Announces Privacy Improvements in Response to Recommendations by Canadian Privacy Commissioner,
http://www.facebook.com/press/releases.php?p=118816

On the Security and Feasibility of Safebook: A Distributed Privacy-Preserving Online Social Network*

Leucio Antonio Cutillo[1], Refik Molva[1], and Thorsten Strufe[2]

[1] EURECOM, Sophia-Antipolis, France
[2] TU Darmstadt, Darmstadt, Germany
{cutillo,molva}@eurecom.fr, strufe@cs.tu-darmstadt.de

Abstract. Safebook tackles the security and privacy problems of on-line social networks. It puts a special emphasis on the privacy of users with respect to the application provider and provides defenses against intruders or malicious users. In order to assure privacy in the face of potential violations by the provider, Safebook is designed in a decentralized architecture. It relies on the cooperation among the independent parties that represent the users of the online social network at the same time. Safebook addresses the problem of building secure and privacy-preserving data storage and communication mechanisms in a peer-to-peer system by leveraging trust relationships akin to social networks in real life. This paper resumes the contributions of [7,9,8], and extends the first performance and security evaluation of Safebook.

1   Introduction

Having started as a recreational facility, Online Social Networks, like *facebook*, *LinkedIn*, or *Xing* are becoming a predominant player in the global information processing realm both for personal and professional purposes. Catering for a broad range of users of all ages, and a vast difference in social, educational, and national background, they allow even users with limited technical skills to publish personal information and to communicate with one another. The ease of access and increased information dissemination that are inherent features of Online Social Networks (OSN) on the other hand raise new security and privacy concerns for people and companies alike. As the surge of unprecedented network-based security problems that accompanied the global spread of the Internet in the 1990's, the unlimited dissemination of private data through the OSN seems to pave the way for unprecedented data security and privacy exposures. Data and relationships that were strictly confined to the private realm of individuals or organizations are made available to a huge and often unlimited set of parties thanks to the facilities of OSN. Access to private data of individuals

---

* This work has been supported by the SOCIALNETS project, grant no 217141, funded by the EC FP7-ICT-2007-8.2 for Pervasive Adaptation.

M. Bezzi et al. (Eds.): Privacy and Identity, IFIP AICT 320, pp. 86–101, 2010.

or organizations becomes much easier for malevolent intruders or simply curious parties either through the lack of restriction by a majority of naive users, the lack of awareness or some breeches in the access control mechanisms of OSN.

Analyzing the OSN with respect to their security properties and the privacy of their users, some obvious threats become apparent. Generally, a wealth of personal data on the participants is stored at the providers, especially in the case of OSN targeting non-professional purposes. This data is either visible to the public, or, if the user is aware of privacy issues and able to use the settings of the respective Social Networking Services (SNS), to a somewhat selected group of other users. As profiles are attributed to presumably known persons from the real world, they are implicitly valued with the same trust as the assumed owner of the profile. Furthermore, any actions and interactions coupled to a profile are again attributed to the assumed owner of this profile, as well. Different studies have shown that the participants clearly represent the weak link for security in OSN and that they are vulnerable to several types of social engineering attacks [12,4,14]. This partially is caused by a lack of awareness to the consequences of simple and presumably private actions, like accepting contact requests, tagging pictures, or acts of communication like commenting on profiles or leaving wall posts. However, the usability of privacy controls offered by the SNS, and finally and most importantly, inherent assumptions about other participants and trust in other profiles, which are actually a desired characteristic, certainly add to the problem. However, analyzing the privacy problems in current OSN, it becomes apparent that even if all participants were aware and competent in the use of SNS, and even if a comprehensive set of privacy measures were deployed, the OSN would still be exposed to potential privacy violations by the omniscient service provider: the complete data, directly or indirectly supplied by all participants, is collected and stored permanently at the databases of the providing company, which potentially becomes a big brother capable of exploiting this data in many ways that can violate the privacy of individual users or user groups. The importance of this privacy exposure is underlined by the market capitalization of these providers, of which estimations range from 580m $US, in the case of myspace, to 15bn $US for Facebook Inc. [1]. In consequence, we consider the protection of private data in OSN a pressing topic, which current providers are not likely to address.

In this paper we suggest a SNS called Safebook that is specifically designed to prevent privacy violations by intruders, malicious users, and OSN providers alike. Safebook is mainly characterized by a decentralized architecture relying on the cooperation among the peers, in order to prevent potential privacy violations due to centralized control.

2   Security in OSN

In order to analyse the security objectives of OSN we first introduce a model to provide a suitable framework for a discussion on their security.

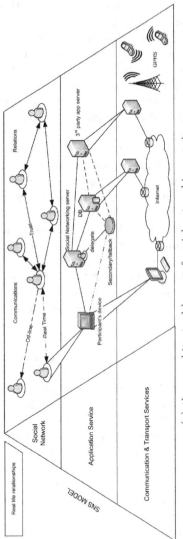

(a) three architectural layers of social networking services

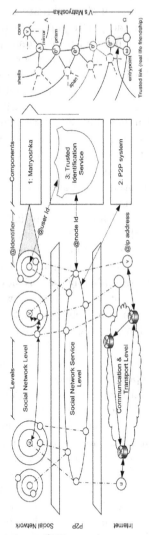

(b) Overlays of Safebook (left), main components (center) and matryoshka structure (right).

Fig. 1. On the top: a model for OSN; on the bottom: an overview of Safebook's architecture

2.1   SNS Model

Social Network Services can be represented by a layered model (cmp. fig. 2), featuring three levels as follows:

- the *Social Network* (SN) level, digitally representing all the users and their relationships;
- the *Application Services* (AS) level, hosting the SN application infrastructure;
- the *Communication & Transport* (CT) level, providing the classical networking services.

The **SN** level offers a set of functions to the users that are corresponding to interactions in real life, like, e.g., searching for friends, retrieving profile information, displaying information, and giving comments. It typically consists of the actual users and their social interactions provided by advanced services that are based on the SNS infrastructure.

The **AS** level consists of the SNS platform and server that implements the SN functionality as a combination of lower layer mechanisms like, e.g., data storage and retrieval, access control, join and leave management, and is under control of the SNS provider. Various approaches characterized by redundancy and delegation strategies enhance availability to contrast service failures (e.g., redirection of requests to secondary servers in case of high load or server failures). Another part of the AS level are the third party applications that are increasingly made available through the SNS.

The **CT** level finally represents the transport and internetworking protocols and communication infrastructures that provide the basic digital communication facilities.

Based on this model, we define an *internal* attacker as a misbehaving legitimate party, e.g., a malicious user in the SN level, a malicious service provider in the SNS level, or a party that has access to the infrastructure at the CT level, like an eavesdropper with a local-, or a malicious ISP with a global view of the network. An *external* attacker on the other hand is an intruder that tries to violate security at one or more levels (cmp. fig. 2) without the privileges of internal attackers.

2.2   Security Objectives in OSN

Existing threats on OSN raise the three major security requirements of privacy, integrity and availability.

Privacy encompasses a variety of objectives ranging from basic confidentiality, preventing the disclosure of secrets, to the controlled disclosure of sensitive personal data through countering even sophisticated inference techniques that aim at deriving any type of information. Protecting sensitive personal information is especially important in OSN. Privacy threats in OSN include direct information theft by breach of access control schemes or staged attacks, like, e.g., cloning or phishing, that aim at capturing user credentials in order to further disclose private data. Beyond simple prevention of disclosure, the OSN needs to provide control of the degree at which personal information is disclosed to selected other parties.

The privacy objective often is further detailed into communication unobservability, unlinkability, and untraceability, all of which have to be met, in OSN, too. Unobservability in this case demands that no entity, which is not directly part of the communication can gather any information on request, sender or receiver; unlinkability demands that obtaining two messages, no third party may be able to determine if both messages were sent by the same sender, or to the same receiver; and untraceability finally demands that, given a target user, it should be impossible to list his actions in the system.

Integrity aims at preventing unauthorized modification of information and integrity in OSN focuses on the protection of stored user records against tampering by unauthorized parties, ranging from external intruders to potential internal attackers like maliciously behaving legitimate users. OSN require both the integrity of the data stored in user accounts as well as integrity and authentication as part of the account management. Thus, attacks like profile modification or tampering with data have to be prevented as well as impersonation of legitimate users or cloning of their accounts.

Availability is a global security concern for OSN and aims at assuring the operation of the SNS in the face of malicious or erroneous behavior, preventing users from getting access to the service. The main concern of availability are DoS attacks, but other integrity threats like data pollution and cloning also impair the availability of SNS by affecting the quality of the service perceived by the users.

While privacy has to address broad assumptions regarding adverse parties, including the SNS and application providers as well as external attackers and malicious legitimate users, both integrity and availability primarily address the latter, since the former have an inherent interest that they are met.

3   Decentalized OSN

The architecture of Safebook consists of two overlays, as shown in fig.2. Each Safebook node is thus part of the Internet, the peer-to-peer overlay and the social network overlay. The components of Safebook (cmp. fig.2) are:

1. several *matryoshkas*
2. a *peer to peer substrate*
3. a *trusted identification service* (TIS)

Matryoshkas are particular structures providing end-to-end confidentiality and distributed data storage with privacy. They leverage on existing trust of OSN members in real life. The Peer-to-peer substrate provides a decentralized global data access. The trusted identification service guarantees authentication and provides unique addresses to each member of Safebook. It can be provided offline and may be implemented in a distributed fashion.

Matryoshkas. The Matryoshka of a user (cmp. 2 on the right) is a structure composed by various nodes surrounding the user's node in concentric shells. The user's node is thus the *core* of his matryoshka and can also be part of some other users' matryoshkas. Every core is associated to a unambiguous *user identifier* computed and certified by the TIS. User identifiers are used to route requests through the matryoshkas. The inner shell of a matryoshka consists of nodes belonging to the trusted contacts of the user. The second shell consists of nodes that are trusted contacts of nodes in the inner shell and so on. It is important to note that nodes on the same shell do not necessarily share trust relationships between themselves, except for the inner shell, which all share their relation to the core node.

The nodes on the inner shell cache the data for the core and are thus called *mirrors*, they serve requests if the core is offline. A data request message reaches a node in the inner shell from a node in the outer shell through a path that provides hop-by-hop trust. The reply follows the same path in the reverse direction. As they act as a gateway for every request to the matryoshka's core, the nodes in the outermost shell are called *entrypoints*. All the nodes between the mirrors and the entrypoints are called *prisms* and extend the hop-by-hop trusted paths. Based on this, the matryoshkas assure cooperation enforcement in our OSN. We point out that the trust relationship between nodes is not used in a transitive fashion, as none of the nodes on a path, other than the direct neighbors, needs to be trusted by any user.

Peer-to-peer substrate. The peer-to-peer substrate consists of all the nodes and provides data lookup services. Currently, a DHT derived from KAD[13] is used as the P2P substrate. Nodes are arranged according to their *node identifiers* and lookup keys correspond both to members' user identifiers and to the hash of their attributes, like full names or the likes. All nodes that belong to the outer shell of a user's matryoshka register themselves as entrypoints for this matryoshka with the nodes that are responsible for the respective lookup keys. The identity of a peer is revealed only to his trusted contacts since they are the only ones that can link his IP address to his user identifier.

Trusted identification service. The trusted identification service (TIS) guarantees resistance against sybil and impersonation attacks by providing each node with a unique node- and user- identifier, and the related certificates. The existence of the TIS does not contrast our goal of privacy preservation through decentralization since the TIS is not involved in any data management activity and it is used only to prevent impersonation and a free selection of a node identifier and hence their position in the DHT. Moreover the TIS can be implemented in a decentralized fashion and does not have to be constantly online.

3.1   Operations

The most important operations of our OSN are the matryoshka creation, the profile publication and the data retrieval.

Matryoshka creation. In order to join Safebook a member $\mathcal{V}$ has to be invited by another member $\mathcal{A}$. After this phase, having obtained the necessary credentials from the TIS, $\mathcal{V}$ can start building his matryoshka. $\mathcal{V}$'s final goal is to register in the DHT his user id and a particular set of lookup keys associated to his identity, as e.g. a hash of his full name[1]. At the beginning $\mathcal{V}$ has only $\mathcal{A}$ in his contact list, so he sends $\mathcal{A}$ a signed registration request containing the lookup key(s) he wants to register, his certificate associated to his user id signed by the TIS, and a time-to-live (ttl) counter. This first message presents the user id of the sender instead of his node identifier. This prevents the node in the DHT responsible for $\mathcal{V}$'s lookup key from linking that key with $\mathcal{V}$'s node identifier.

Once $\mathcal{A}$ receives the registration message it decreases the ttl counter, chooses one (or several) of his trusted contacts, called $\mathcal{B}$, as a next step and sends $\mathcal{B}$ the request message signed with his node identifier. This will prevent the registering node in the DHT from retrieving the social relationships between the OSN members constituing $\mathcal{V}$'s matryoshka. It is important to note that no assumption is held about social relationship between $\mathcal{V}$ and $\mathcal{B}$. This process runs until the ttl counter expires, when $\mathcal{V}$'s lookup key is registered in the DHT. The node responsible for that key, hereafter called **_dock_**, maintains a reference table associating the key with the ip addresses of the entrypoints of $\mathcal{V}$'s matryoshka.

The number of contacts each node chooses to forward the registration request is determined by the **_spanning factor_**. It defines the branching of the tree through the matryoshka whose root are the mirrors and whose leaves are the nodes in the outer shell, starting from the core's direct connections. The higher the spanning factor, the higher is the number of nodes composing the tree, and the higher is thus the probability to have a _valid path_ through the tree, i.e. a path where all the nodes are online. The spanning factor and the number of inner shell nodes each core should have is fundamental to guarantee data availability and will be investigated in section 4.

Profile publication. A user's data can be public, protected or private and its publication takes place at the contacts' nodes being in the inner shell of the user's matryoshka. All the published data is signed by the owner and encrypted using a simple group-based encryption scheme.

Each node can manage the profile information, the trusted contact relations and the messages. The profile information consists of the data a member wants to publish in the OSN and is organized in atomic attributes. The trusted contact relations represent the _friend list_ of the user and associate each contact with a particular trust level. Real time communication messages can be exchanged by each member of the OSN, in this case the communication doesn't stop at the first matryoshka shell but reaches the core.

Data retrieval. The requests are routed according to the P2P protocol until they reach a dock. Unlike the common KAD approach, the requests are routed in a recursive way to hide the real requester's node identifier. The dock sends back

---

[1] $\mathcal{V}$ can of course choose to register different lookup keys, in addition to his user id, to increase his visibility.

the list of all the entrypoints of the target user's matryoshka. The requesting node then sends its request (or delegates a trusted contact to do that) to a subset of the entrypoints of the target matryoshka. The requests are forwarded through the matryoshka to the mirrors, who serve it and send a response along the inverse path. See figure 3(a) for more details.

4 Feasibility

In this section we will analyze the feasibility of our approach with respect to data availability and delays.

We will focus on:

- the minimum number of contacts a node needs to have in order to guarantee the availability of his data;
- the minimum number of hops in the matryoshkas to provide anonymity;
- the expected delay for data retrieval.

Data availability. One can see each mirror as a root of a tree whose leaves lie in the outer shell. Let nop be the probability of each node being online, $span$ the spanning factor of the tree passing through a user $\mathcal{V}$'s matryoshka and $shell$ its shells number, i.e. the number of hops between $\mathcal{V}$ and whichever node in the outer shell. Let Λ be the mirror set and $\|\Lambda\|$ its cardinality. Thanks to a simple geometric law (1) it is possible to compute the probability ov_{shell} that at least one inner shell node can be reached, i.e. the probability that $\mathcal{V}$'s data is accessible.

$$
\begin{aligned}
ov_0 &= nop \\
ov_j &= nop\left(1 - (1 - ov_{j-1})^{span}\right), j \in [1 \ldots shell - 1] \\
ov_{shell} &= \left(1 - (1 - ov_{shell-1})^{\|\Lambda\|}\right)
\end{aligned}
\tag{1}
$$

Let the probability to have at least one valid path through a user's matryoshka be as high as 90% as a requirement. We refer to a valid path as a path where each node is on-line. Assuming that $span = 1$, this goal is achieved with different values of $shell$, nop, and number of contacts in the inner shell, as shown in figure 2(a).

According to a recent work on Skype[2][10] we can assume nop to be at least as high as 0.3. We rely on this data since Skype, as Safebook, enhances users' interactions by providing messaging services such as chat.

As one can see in figure 2(a), the number of mirrors λ that is needed with $shell = 3$ and $nop = 0.3$ is 85. With $shell = 4$ the number of mirrors increases to 290. By selecting a spanning factor of $span = 2$, the same availability is achieved with 13 to 23 mirrors, respectively with $shell = 3$ and $shell = 4$ (see figure 2(b)). This amount of contacts is much more likely to be reached. From previous studies we have access to the graph of Xing[3] and could show that the average number η of a member's contacts in that application is 24.

---

[2] http://www.skype.com
[3] http://xing.com

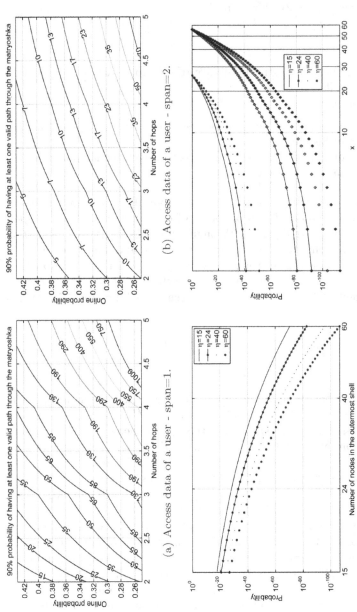

(a) Access data of a user - span=1.

(b) Access data of a user - span=2.

(c) Disclosure probability over the number of entrypoints with span=1 (left), and over x (right, logscale, the attacker knowing 50%+x of the entrypoints' contact lists), span=2, for $\|\Omega\| = 50$ (top, with points) and $\|\Omega\| = 110$ (bottom, with diamonds).

Fig. 2. On the top: required number of mirrors to guarantee a reachability of 90% for different number of shells (x axis) and online probabilities (y axis); on the bottom: disclosure probability for the identities of the nodes on the first hidden shell

Data lookup. The overall data lookup time T_{dr} can be seen as the sum of the DHT lookup time T_{DHT} and the round trip time in the matryoshka T_M: the first one depends above all on the DHT, while the second one depends above all on the availability of nodes constituing the matryoshka itself.

The choice of the P2P substrate plays an essential role in our OSN performances since it determines T_{DHT}. We use a DHT similar to Kademlia [13] called S2S. Unlike Kademlia, in S2S lookups are performed in a recursive way and message confidentiality is assured with hop-by-hop signature and encription operations.

The round trip time in the matryoshka T_M can be seen as twice the time required to reach a mirror from an entrypoint. As we have shown in the previous sections, a number of hops between three and four reasonably guarantees to each member both anonimity and data availability. This number of hops is comparable with that one encountered, on average, for a successful lookup in KAD[4].

Starting from a CDF representing a one-hop RTT distribution computed from real measurements [16], assuming to find at least one path in S2S where all the nodes are online, we derived the CDF distribution of the total delay for a profile data retrieval in Safebook, taking into account 4 hops for a successful lookup in S2S, 4 hops to cross the matryoshka and one additional hop in case the real data requester delegates the data request to a trusted contact (cmp fig.3(b)). Results show the 90% of profile data lookup succeed in about 10 seconds if no off-line node is met along the path.

Assuming the entrypoint list of the target user's matryoshka is cached, only 5 hops are required and the 90% of future profile data lookup will succeed in about 6 seconds.

Overall data lookup time T_{dr} is thus likely to be on the order of 6-10 seconds, without taking into account that the social proximity can correspond to the geographical one.

5   Security and Privacy

The following section discusses Safebook's properties with respect to the privacy, integrity and availability goals we introduced in the first part of this work.

5.1   Separation of Identifiers

In order to protect the privacy, users need to have control over the disclosure of their data to only trusted users. However, to provide the P2P functionality, node ID and IP address of all nodes need to be public and can not be hidden from other participants. Safebook in consequence seperates these two identifiers. While the node ID is used as an address in the P2P overlay, and the node ID public keys are used for hop-by-hop message encryption, the user ID is used to address the users in the social network layer and the user ID public keys in consequence are

---

[4] According to recent studies [16] conducted on KAD as implemented in aMule, 90% of the lookups succeed in less than four hops.

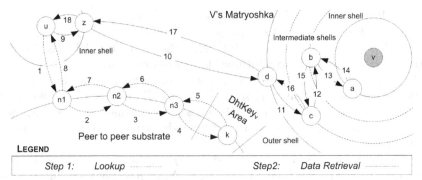

(a) Profile data retrieval with delegation: user $\mathcal{U}$ retrieves $\mathcal{D}$'s reference from the DHT and delegates $\mathcal{V}$'s profile data request to his trusted contact $\mathcal{Z}$.

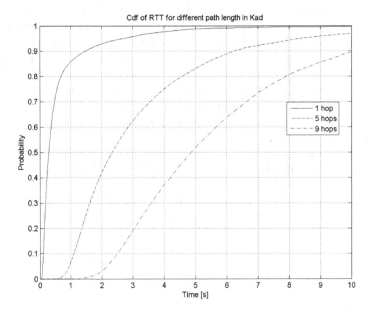

(b) Estimated RTT for data retrieval in 9 hops (first retrieval) and 5 hops (future retrieval).

Fig. 3. Profile data retrieval and estimated RTT assuming a successful DHT lookup in 4 hops, a matryoshka with 4 shells and request delegation

used for end-to-end encryption of messages between communicating users. Only trusted contacts of a node are able to link these two identifiers, as they serve as mirrors and in consequence know both.

Furthermore, due to the recursive nature of the Safebook protocols, no node inside or outside the matryoshka can trace the trusted connections between two users that span the matryoshka.

5.2   Trusted Identification

A wide range of attacks on P2P systems and online social networks are possible due to the lack of trusted identification of participans. Safebook harnesses the concept of an identification service to this end: The TIS and the certification policy play an essential role in preventing malicious users from manipulating identifiers and performing attacks such as profile cloning, profile porting, identity theft, DoS by aimed placing of nodes in the DHT, sybil and man-in-the-middle.

5.3   Separation of Identification and Communication

The only party in Safebook that is able to link the user ID and node ID of users other than their own trusted acquaintances on the SN level is the TIS. Considering correlated compromise of a TIS by an attacker, which due to misconfiguration logs all registration requests, this ability could potentially be used to break the privacy of Safebook users, by disclosing their participation in Safebook or retrieving their set of trusted contacts. However, the TIS does not possess the keypairs of the user- and node ID and in consequence retrieving profile information does not lead to any information being disclosed, as it is encrypted for trusted users. It is unable to compromise integrity by tampering with messages for the same reason.

Another possibility for disclosure is monitoring the communication relations of nodes. However, the TIS does not participate in any of the communication protocols other than the identity creation and in consequence can not obtain any information as an insider. Analysing the OSN model in section 2, another possibility for monitoring becomes apparent: a collusion of the TIS with the service provider on the CT level would circumvent the concept of separation. However, this attack is only successful if the ISP controls the access to all users of Safebook, as only the privacy of users using the directly monitored Internet connections can be disclosed. Entirely protecting the privacy on the CT level is only possible when leveraging much more complex concepts of anonymization, which for the sake of efficiency is refrained of. Safebook indeed does not provide anonymous communications on the network level.

5.4   Communication Indirection and Cooperation Incentives

Matryoshkas provide the basic OSN services like profile data storage and communication obfuscation, as described in section 3. The caching of profile information is necessary for reasons of availability, and selecting trusted users for this services leads to an inherent cooperation enforcement. It causes the need to obfuscate who is serving a profile information request, in order to protect the trust relation between the source and the caching node, though. For this reason, several shells of indirection obfuscate the connections and communication between users. Friendship relations between nodes on adjacent shells build hop-by-hop trusted paths for anonymization. The trust in each hop additionally provides cooperation enforcement for the service of forwarding messages, as dropping messages potentially harms the service of a trusted acquaintance.

5.5 Matryoshka Analysis

Considering that the matryoshkas are created based on trusted links, and considering further that humans tend to accept friendship requests and disclose their contact lists more freely than they should [4], it seems feasible to obtain the wealth of relationship information that is innate to the matryoshkas.

Let θ_i^j be the i-th node in the j-th shell of a user $\mathcal{V}$'s matryoshka $\Theta_{\mathcal{V}}$, with M representing the outermost shell. Let $\{NId_{\theta_i^j}\}$ be its node identifier and $\{UId_{\theta_i^j}\}$ its user identifier. Finally, let $\Omega_{\mathcal{V}}$ be the entrypoint set of $\mathcal{V}$'s matryoshka. Assuming $\mathcal{U}$ is a malicious user that aims at guessing the relationship information from a selected matryoshka, and $\mathcal{A}$ is a direct contact of this matryoshkas's core $\mathcal{V}$, Safebook is required to hide the information about the relationship between $\mathcal{A}$ and $\mathcal{V}$. The multitude of layered shells prevents $\mathcal{U}$ from directly disclosing another user $\mathcal{A}$'s identity and, as a consequence, $\mathcal{A}$'s friendship with $\mathcal{V}$, as described above. However, $\mathcal{U}$ could try to guess the identity of the nodes and access their contact lists by befriending them from the outer layer through to the core consecutively. Assuming $\mathcal{U}$ retrieves $\Theta_{\mathcal{V}}$'s entrypoint list $\{NId_{\theta_i^M}\}, \theta_i^M \in \Omega_{\mathcal{V}}$, $M = Maxshell$, further assuming $\mathcal{U}$ was by chance able to derive all user IDs of the containing nodes, and finally assuming $\mathcal{U}$ gathers that $\Theta_{\mathcal{V}}$ has $Span = 1$. In this unlikely case the probability for $\mathcal{U}$ to disclose the identity of the prisms $\{UId_{\theta_k^{M-1}}\}$ based on $\{NId_{\theta_i^M}\}$ and by accessing all contact lists of the θ_i^M would be: $(\frac{1}{\eta})^{\|\Omega\|}$ where η represents the average number of contacts of every user. Figure 2(c) (left) plots this probability over the number of entrypoints, showing that it is negligible even for very small values of η.

The task of guessing for an attacker is a little easier when $Span = 2$. In this case, two nodes on a shell share the same predecessor, and $\mathcal{U}$ could derive the cut set of contact lists it obtained, thus generating a good estimate for some of the nodes on the next shell. $\mathcal{U}$ hence needs access to valid contact lists of at least one half of the entrypoints, only, while every additional friend list will improve the chance for correct guesses. If $\mathcal{U}$ can obtain contact lists from $50\% + x$ of the entrypoints, it can compute the intersection between ω_i's and ω_j's friendlists, and, in the worst case that both nodes only share one common contact, derive the identity of one node θ_k^{M-1} with certainty. The probability for the full disclosure of the identities of all predecessors is:

$$\left[1 - \left(1 - \frac{2^{\frac{\|\Omega\|}{2}}}{\binom{\|\Omega\|}{\frac{\|\Omega\|}{2}}} \right)^{\binom{\frac{\|\Omega\|}{2}}{\frac{\|\Omega\|}{2}+n}} \right] \left(\frac{1}{\eta} \right)^{\left(\frac{\|\Omega\|}{2} - x \right)}$$

Assuming that, in the case of $x = \frac{\|\Omega\|}{2}$, $\mathcal{U}$ has access to all the entrypoint's contact lists, and further assuming the worst case in which the intersections always contain a single node only, $\mathcal{U}$ would thus derive $\left\{ UId_{\theta_k^{M-1}} \right\}$ with certainty. Figure 2(c) (right) shows the probability of guessing $\{UId_{\theta^{M-1}}\}$ as a function over x in case $\|\Omega\| = 50$ (top) and $\|\Omega\| = 110$ (bottom), always considering the worst case of atomic intersections. While for low x the probability again is quite low, it unsurprisingly increases to a possibility of 1 with x growing to $\frac{||\Omega||}{2}$.

However, in Safebook neither the number of shells nor the span value are fixed, as the nodes in the registration paths decrease $TtlMatr$ by 1 or more. They additionally can select, according to their characteristics, a number of next hops that slightly differs from $Span$. As finally the barrier for the attacker, which has to obtain both the user ID of the entrypoints and their contact lists are quite high, and as the probability is only valid for the worst case of seperate, atomic intersections between all pairs of contact lists of these users, we consider this vulnerability as negligible.

6   Related Work

The fact that OSN pose as a serious threat to the security of their users has been shown in multiple studies[12,4,14]. t has sparked a plethora or ideas on how to solve this problem at the same time.

NOYB[11] is an approach that tries to mitigate the existing problems by cryptographic means. Applying substitutions according to secret dictionaries, it renders the managed public profiles, which still may be stored in centralized OSN, useless to anybody lacking access to the dictionaries. While protecting some of the content of the profiles, it does not protect the relation between users, be it an accpted friendship or message exchange.

Yeung et al.[17] propose to use a Friend-of-a-Friend as an OSN: storing contact list information in addition to conventional content at a common webserver, which is maintained by the respective user itself, they provide a framework to create relations between the managed sites, thus indirectly offering OSN functionality. To somehow protect the content partially, they propose some access control based on an existing language for the definition of AC policies. Unlike Safebook, the system does not protect the identity of its users.

Persona [2] is an approach to combine attribute-based crypto with traditional public-key cryptography, to offer a more flexible and fine-grained access control. Persona users are identified by public keys and they store their encrypted data with their own storage service. In order to create an OSN link, they exchange their public key and storage service location out of band. While better protecting the identity of users, the complete privacy that Safebook offers is still not given.

The related work closest to Safebook is probably PeerSon [5]. Buchegger et al. propose to use an existing, external system, OpenDHT, to store the profile information, and encryption to prevent unauthorized access. While PeerSon represents a fully distributed OSN with a much lighter architecture, the privacy protection of Safebook is by far more comprehensive.

An entirely different family of systems is based on a different history, but similar to Safebook: Darknets and related P2P systems[15,6,3] aim at anonymizing the communication between their users completely. They follow concepts similar to Safebook: they establish connections between trusted users only and apply hop-by-hop anonymization. However, they typically suffer from delays that are far beyond acceptable for an OSN, are unable to guarantee the availability of less popular content, and do not provide means for any kind of social networking services.

7   Conclusions and Future Work

This paper studies the privacy problems that users of current Online Social Networks (OSN) are facing. It defines a layered model to illustrate different parts of a typical OSN infrastructure, the different roles of the participating stakeholders, and possible points of intereference. The model then is used to define security and privacy objectives that Social Networking Services (SNS) are expected to meet.

Since current OSN do not comply to these objectives, which, due to the deviating interest of their stakeholders is not likely to change any time soon, the paper subsequently introduces Safebook, a new approach for privacy preserving online social networking. Safebook is based on the two main ideas of decentralization and leveraging trust from real world relationships. It integrates the three core concepts of the matryoshka, a group of nodes per user, which collaboratively stores the profile information and serves for communication anonymization, a peer-to-peer substrate for the location of the users and their published content, and trusted identification service to guarantee the authenticity of credentials.

In order to evaluate the privacy protection provided by Safebook, it's security properties are subsequently analyzed and discussed in detail. The evaluation shows that Safebook is able to preserve the privacy of its users, even in terms of communication unobservability, untraceability and unlinkability. Additionally it is demonstrated, that Safebook provides integrity and availability.

The decentralized design of Safebook, and the introduction of additional indirection for reasons of communication anonymization through the matryoshka are challenging when considering performance requirements. After performing a preliminary feasibility study, we currently analyze the performance of Safebook in appropriate detail, while being in the process of conducting a comprehensive simulation study to both validate the performance and parametrize the protocols at the same time. In parallel, we already have built a prototype of Safebook, which currently is in the stage of early testing and shall be available for download soon. For the purpose of enhancing the authentication of Safebook, we are planning to put a stronger focus on the possibilities to better leverage the knowledge from existing trust relationships, quite possibly by applying secret matching schemes and secret handshakes, and to study the interdependency when introducing a reputation scheme into Safebook. The last point promises to be especially interesting, as the assumption of anchoring the participants and their connections in the real world and the relationship between the users significantly changes the setting for decentralized reputation systems.

References

1. Modelling the Real Market Value of Social Networks (2008),
   http://www.techcrunch.com/2008/06/23/modeling-the-real-market-value-of-social-networks/
2. Baden, R., Bender, A., Starin, D., Spring, N., Bhattacharjee, B.: Persona: An online social network with user-defined privacy. In: ACM SIGCOMM, Barcelona, Spain (August 2009)
3. Bennett, K., Grotho, C.: GAP - Practical Anonymous Networking. In: Dingledine, R. (ed.) PET 2003. LNCS, vol. 2760, pp. 141–160. Springer, Heidelberg (2003)
4. Bilge, L., Strufe, T., Balzarotti, D., Kirda, E.: All Your Contacts Are Belong to Us: Automated Identity Theft Attacks on Social Networks. In: 18th Intl. World Wide Web Conference (2009)
5. Buchegger, S., Schiöberg, D., Vu, L.H., Datta, A.: PeerSoN: P2P Social Networking. In: Social Network Systems (2009)
6. Clarke, I., Sandberg, O., Wiley, B., Hong, T.W.: Freenet: A Distributed Anonymous Information Storage and Retrieval System. In: Federrath, H. (ed.) Anonymity 2000. LNCS, vol. 2009, pp. 46–66. Springer, Heidelberg (2001)
7. Cutillo, L.-A., Molva, R., Strufe, T.: Privacy preserving social networking through decentralization. In: IEEE WONS (2009)
8. Cutillo, L.A., Molva, R., Strufe, T.: Safebook: a privacy preserving online social network leveraging on real-life trust (2009)
9. Cutillo, L.-A., Molva, R., Strufe, T.: Safebook: Feasibility of Transitive Cooperation for Privacy on a Decentralized Social Network. In: World of Wireless, Mobile and Multimedia Networks (2009)
10. Guha, S., Daswani, N., Jain, R.: An Experimental Study of the Skype Peer-to-Peer VoIP System. In: Peer-to-Peer Systems
11. Guha, S., Tang, K., Francis, P.: NOYB: Privacy in Online Social Networks. In: Online Social Networks, pp. 49–54 (2008)
12. Jagatic, T.N., Johnson, N.A., Jakobsson, M., Menczer, F.: Social phishing. Communications of the ACM, 94–100 (2007)
13. Maymounkov, P., Mazieres, D.: Kademlia: A Peer-to-Peer Information System Based on the XOR Metric. In: P2P-Systems. LNCS (2002)
14. Moyer, S., Hamiel, N.: Satan is on My Friends List (2008),
    http://www.blackhat.com/html/bh-usa-08/bh-usa-08-archive.html
15. Rogers, M., Bhatti, S.: How to Disappear Completely: A Survey of Private Peer-to-Peer Networks (2007)
16. Steiner, M., Carra, D., Biersack, E.W.: Faster content access in KAD. In: Peer-to-Peer Computing (September 2008)
17. Yeung, C.M.A., Liccardi, I., Lu, K., Seneviratne, O., Berners-Lee, T.: Decentralization: The Future of Online Social Networking. In: Future of Social Networking (2009)

Privacy-Respecting Access Control in Collaborative Workspaces

Stefanie Pötzsch and Katrin Borcea-Pfitzmann

Technische Universität Dresden, Faculty of Computer Science
D-01062 Dresden, Germany
{stefanie.poetzsch,katrin.borcea}@tu-dresden.de

Abstract. In these days' information society, people share their life with others not only in their direct, personal environment, but also on the Internet by using social software such as collaborative workspaces. In this context, an important issue is maintaining control over personal data, i.e., who is able to access which information. In this paper, we argue why traditional access control mechanisms are inappropriate for collaborative workspaces in general and present a concept for privacy-respecting access control in a web forum as an instance of collaborative workspaces.

Keywords: Access Control, Collaborative Workspaces, Personal Data, Privacy, Web Forum.

1   Introduction

The social life of these days' information society of the twenty-first century is altered in fundamental ways by technological developments. This includes the possibilities of social software to support users in sharing their life with others. In this context, two important issues are the promotion of a greater awareness for privacy among users of social software and enabling them to maintain control over personal data, i.e., to determine and enforce who is able to access which information. While there is research going on addressing the first problem [Pöt09a], [Pöt09b], in this paper we focus on the second point. As emphasized by [RI07], sharing of information is an important feature of social software, however not everything is intended to be shared with everyone. Typically, collaborative workspaces, which are in the focus of this paper, implement access control mechanisms that impart users only minimal freedom of decision in this regard. Users can only choose from a small set of "user groups", which are predefined by the administrator of the system, at the best. Hence, in order to enhance users' privacy in collaborative workspaces, there is a need for user-controlled and fine-grained access control to the content and meta-data generated by users during communication.

The paper is organised as follows: In the next section we introduce the basics of collaborative workspaces and highlight the role of personal data in this type of application. In Section 3 we argue why traditional access control mechanisms

M. Bezzi et al. (Eds.): Privacy and Identity, IFIP AICT 320, pp. 102–111, 2010.

are inappropriate for collaborative workspaces in general. Section 4 presents a concept for privacy-respecting access control in a web forum whereby the web forum represents one instance of collaborative workspaces. We conclude the paper with a brief summary and the indication of interesting points for further theoretical and practical research.

2   Collaborative Workspaces and Personal Data

Collaborative workspaces are infrastructures and platforms that enable users to work together, e.g., gathering information or creating contents in a collaborative manner or simply sharing data between each other, e.g., in a wiki, web forum or chat. The main feature of this type of social software is the collaborative creation and modification of content. Thus, the focus is on artifacts produced by a number of users. In addition, another type of social software are social networking sites, where the main focus is on user profiles and traversable connections between these profiles [PP09]. Figure 1 shows a graphical representation of the classification.

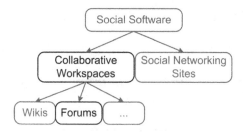

Fig. 1. Classification of social software

For this working paper we focus on collaborative workspaces, and, to be more specific, on web forums as a particular instance of collaborative workspaces. Web forums allow users to discuss particular topics by posting their opinions, experiences, or questions via a web form to a central data storage on the Internet. Several posts that refer to the same subject are grouped into a "thread". Figure 2 provides an overview of the hierarchical structure of content elements in a forum.

Contributions to a forum can contain *personal data* in terms of personal information, expression of thoughts and feelings of the writer. As pointed out by Adams [Ada99], it is important what is deemed sensitive or intimate in the perception of the individual rather than if it can be evaluated by third parties (e.g., lawyers, computer specialists). This argument emphasizes the need for user control with regard to the access control mechanisms implemented in collaborative workspaces. From a privacy perspective, the disclosure of personal data in collaborative workspaces is not target-aimed. Besides all the positive aspects that users of web forums experience, sharing personal data with possibly millions of

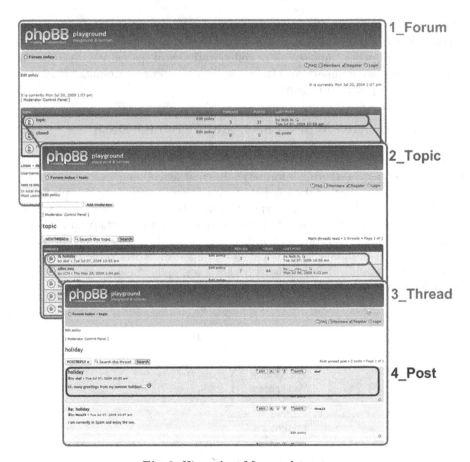

Fig. 2. Hierarchy of forum elements

strangers on the Internet may result also in negative consequences, e.g., identity theft, surveillance, harassment, bullying or cyber stalking [PP09], [KWM+08], [Wor09]. Yet, from a social perspective, revelation to an intended audience is necessary for two reasons: First, the exchange of information, both personal and non-personal, is the major feature of the application and the motivation why people use it. Second, the exchange of implicit and explicit personal data allows users of collaborative workspaces to get an impression of the potential interaction partners and their situations. In this sense, the disclosure of personal data contributes to the success of social interactions and the forming of communities [Cut95].

Our approach for privacy-respecting access control works for all kinds of forums: for those that require a registration with an e-mail address and password or that allow users by other means to contribute under a unique pseudonym as well as for forums that let users post completely anonymously. Usually, the users of a forum do not possess extensive member profiles stored with the forum service. However, different posts from the same user are still linkable by a nickname.

Especially in the case of linkability between different posts from the same writer, privacy-aware users have an interest to restrict access to their contributions in order to limit the risk of being continually monitored by any third party.

3   Related Work on Access Control

Access control mechanisms allow to restrict the access to specified resources. A fair amount of currently available web forums are open to the public, at least with regard to read access. Thus, users of these forums disclose personal data potentially to the "whole world". Even if options for more selective access control are provided by the forum software, still only the technical administrator has the possibility to predefine different access rights on behalf of all users without being able to know about their individual preferences. The most common access control mechanisms used in social and collaborative software are:

- **Access Matrix Model** [Lam71]. The access control matrix is a table, which lists all users of the system in rows and all resources in columns. Each element $e_{u,r}$ of the table specifies the access rights that user u has on resource r. Reading the access control matrix column-by-column provides tuples of rights and user names for each resource, called access control lists (ACLs). Reading the table line-by-line results in a capability list (CL), i.e., for each user it is indicated what access rights she is granted to which resources.

- **Role-Based Access Control** [SCFY96]. Role-based access control mechanisms are similar to ACLs, with this difference: user names are assigned to one or more fixed roles and for each resource it is defined which role is allowed to perform which action.

- **Team-Based or Group-Based Access Control** [Tho97]. For this approach, user names are grouped in teams or groups, e.g., according to their current context of work. Access rights to resources are assigned to these teams or groups, respectively.

A detailed comparison of advantages and disadvantages of these mechanisms with regard to their applicability in the area of social software can be found in [TAPH05], [FWBBP06] and [RI07].

All of the mechanisms indicated above are based on the idea of the existence of an administrative party (e.g. the provider) that defines lists, roles, or groups and assigns the names of all users of the system to these lists, roles, or groups in order to enable the management of access to resources. Even if this management task would not depend on a single administrative party, but could be set by each user for her own contributions as for instance suggested by Razavi and Iversion [RI08] in their approach for social networking sites, another problem remains. In order to assign a user name to a list, role, or group, it would still be necessary to know about the existence of the user name. The author of a contribution and the user who is to be granted access need at least to meet once - in the physical world or virtually. However, in a public forum for instance, the author of a post is potentially looking for new contacts, who fulfill specified requirements, e.g., live in the same city or are a member of the same fitness centre. This is, the author is not able in any case to specify the names of all other users who should have access to the contribution. Both requirements, namely (i) the existence of an administrative party who decides about access control settings and (ii) that user names are known, are our strongest points of criticism and the reason why we do not consider the introduced approaches as applicable for user-controlled and privacy-respecting access control in collaborative workspaces.

4   Concept for User-Controlled and Privacy-Respecting Access Control

We suggest to enhance the access control features available in the forum software by a finer grained and privacy-respecting approach. This implies that access control policies should be possible to specify not only for the whole forum or for topics, but additionally also for threads and particular posts. The policies need to be set by the user being the owner of the personal data instead of by an administrative party. Furthermore, to respect the privacy of readers, our access control concept for collaborative workspaces must not rely on user names. Instead, according access rules should indicate which properties or certificates someone has to prove to get access to the corresponding resource. Forum platforms typically provide the roles "adminstrator" for addressing technical issues and "moderator" for content-related moderation of topics. Our approach should allow to keep both roles. Hence, we have to consider the following requirements for user-controlled and privacy-respecting access control in a forum whereby these are easily generalisable to further kinds of collaborative workspaces:

- No administrative party, but each user should be able to define and modify access rules to her contributions, i.e., personal information, expression of personal thoughts and feelings.
- Other persons, who should or should not be able to access the personal data are not necessarily known by the user.
- These other persons also have an interest to protect their privacy.
- User-controlled and privacy-respecting access control can be applied to different levels of content granularity (e.g. forum, topic, thread, post).
- An administrator of the forum should be able to address technical issues of the platform, but should not necessarily have access to content data.
- Moderators should be able to moderate particular topics.
- The owner of a resource is always able to have access on it.

To address these points, we propose to let the user define access control policies together with her contributions indicating the attributes a reader has to possess and to prove. In order to protect the privacy also of the other persons, properties or attributes should be presentable in an anonymous way and not linkable when repeatedly used. This requirement can be fulfilled using the concept of *anonymous credentials* proposed by Chaum in 1985 [Cha85] and technically realised in the Identity Mixer (short: Idemix) system [CvH02]. The idea of access control based on anonymous credentials and policies is not new in general and was demonstrated in selected use cases for user - service provider - scenarios in the project PRIME ([ACK+09], [HBPP05]). We build on the results of PRIME and investigate the applicability of the concept and the implementation in collaborative scenarios between a number of users, where all parties have an interest to protect their privacy on the one hand, but to engage in social interaction on the other hand. Whereas [FWBBP06] started from scratch and did a prototypical implementation of an e-Learning application that was specifically designed to work with PRIME technology, this paper devotes to enhancing existing forum software (phpBB). It demonstrates the feasibility of maintaining existing concepts of the platform and integrating new privacy-enhancing functionality at the same time.

All proofs for attributes including the proof for possessing a particular role (that may be required by an access control policy) can be realised by showing the appropriate credential. This implies that the process of creating a new resource includes that the originator of that resource receives the corresponding credential (`cred:Owner-`*Thread-ID* or `cred:Owner-`*Post-ID*) from the forum platform and stores it on the local device. The roles *administrator* and *moderator* can be realised with help of the credential-based access control approach as well, i.e., the according credentials (`cred:Admin-Forum` and `cred:Moderator-`*Topic-ID*) are issued to the corresponding persons. Together with a new resource, default access control policies are created, which ensure that users who show the administrator credential or moderator credential get the required access granted to fulfill their roles. The owner of a resource possessing the owner credential always has access to that resource and can modify the access control policies to, e.g., allow further other users with certain provable properties read and maybe also write access to the resource.

In general, credentials are offered by particular organisations, so called *credential issuers*. Credential issuers need to be known to the public, so that everybody has a chance to get credentials certifying attributes of the user. In the course of this paper, we need to assume an existing infrastructure of credential issuers. Regarding the question which credentials can be used in the access control policies, there are two possibilities: Either a set of all possible credentials needs to be globally defined or a generally accepted standard for defining new credentials is required. Certainly, both alternatives have advantages and disadvantages. The efforts and costs of determining a globally defined set of credentials are comparable with the assumption of knowing all user names. Yet, having knowledge of all credentials instead of all user names offers an improvement in terms of privacy. More flexibility in the definition of credentials and, connected to this, also in the definition of access control policies, can be provided if a general standard of credential definition would exist. Originators of resources could apply this standard to specify the possession of which attributes a resource requester has to prove. If someone tries to access a resource and that user does not possess the corresponding newly defined credential, which is requested by the access control policy, she needs to be able to get information which credential is required and how to get it. A detailed analysis of possible attacks on privacy and the requested trust structures for both of the sketched alternatives lies beyond the scope of this paper, however it indicates an interesting point for further research.

The following example scenario serves as demonstration how access control based on credentials and access control policies in a web forum should work:

Assuming someone – let's call him Hannes – posts a message to the thread "Fit for summer" in a publicly accessible forum. The access control policy of the thread is derived from the parent topic, which is set to be open for reading and writing exclusively for people who have proven to be male. Hannes additionally restricts access to his post to allow only men being member of the same fitness centre, which Hannes attends.

Table 1. Example of an Access Control Policy

(1) Forum: [(cred:Admin-Forum) OR (everybody*[default]*)] AND
(2) Topic: [(cred:Moderator-SportsAndCars) OR (everybody*[default]*)] AND
(3) Thread: [(cred:Moderator-SportsAndCars)   OR   (cred:Owner-FitForSummer) OR (cred:male)] AND
(4) Post: [(cred:Moderator-SportsAndCars) OR (cred:Owner-PostFromHannes) OR (cred:memberOfFitnessCentreXYZ)]

Whenever someone requests access to Hannes' post, the access control policy is evaluated according to the hierarchical order of content elements of the forum (cf. Table 1). In our example, step (1) ensures that authorised users are either an administrator of the forum or – since we have chosen a public forum for the example – any regular user. Step (2) specifies that users are allowed to read the topic "Sports and Cars" if they are a moderator of this topic or anybody else. The latter applies since the example does not specify any restriction on topic level as well. Step (3) ensures that only users who are either moderator of the topic "Sports and Cars" or who are owner of the thread or who are male get read access to the thread "Fit for summer". At last, step (4) determines that only users who are either moderator of the topic "Sports and Cars", owner of the post, or a member of the fitness centre XYZ can read the post created by Hannes. Accordingly, read access to Hannes' post is only granted if the whole policy (steps 1 – 4) is evaluated to be "true". Similar to this example for *read access*, further policies need to be defined in order to specify *add, edit* or *delete* rights of a resource. All users who add a post to a particular thread have the opportunity to further restrict access to their own contribution. Obviously, it is not possible for them to overwrite access control policies of parent elements (or any other element) for which they do not possess the corresponding credentials.

If the presented access control concept is used in a very restrictive way, forum users will experience a high level of privacy but a low amount of interactions. Vice versa, if the access control is handled very open users could lose much of their privacy. Certainly, it would be inappropriate to use the proposed privacy extension for every contribution in a forum. However, having this feature at disposal may encourage privacy-aware users to discuss issues, which they would not address in public forums, or to state unpopular and uncensored opinions to a specified audience. In order to practically test the approach in real-life scenarios and to collect data aiming at determining and study the compromises between privacy and social interaction that different types of forum users make, we currently work on the implementation of the presented concept.

5   Conclusions and Future Work

In the paper, we showed that traditional access control mechanisms are inappropriate for privacy-respecting access control in collaborative workspaces. Further, we elaborated requirements on user-controlled and privacy-respecting access control in a web forum as an instance of collaborative workspaces. We presented a concept of enhancing existing features of a forum with access control mechanism based on anonymous credentials and access control policies. These can be individually specified by each user for her contributions on a fine-grained level. This way, the requirements outlined in Section 4 can be fulfilled.

Hence, specifying individual access control rules on content items represents a useful privacy enhancement of the application, but it also requires additional effort from the users. Further research is needed to investigate whether and how users become able to understand their benefit from this additional effort. The concept for privacy-respecting access control in collaborative workspaces described in this paper is currently being implemented by extending the access control component of the popular forum software *phpBB*. This is, we will be able to conduct experiments with end users in the near future and report about the practical applicability of our approach.

So far, the privacy enhancement is completely based on advances of the access control mechanism of the forum. In the future we want to elaborate on questions related to the management of different predefined access control settings and pseudonyms in collaborative scenarios. Building on technical solutions for scenarios where the user interacts with a single provider, which are already developed within PRIME, we want to point out that interactions between an arbitrary number of users are expected to be more dynamic with regard to access control preferences and the use of pseudonyms. For instance, Alice has used a pseudonym A_B to communicate with Bob and a pseudonym A_H when talking to Hannes. In case Alice starts an interaction, which involves both Bob and Hannes, she needs to decide which pseudonym to chose for this communication. Thus, existing mechanisms need to be extended and to proof their suitability for real life in our setting.

Another interesting point that needs detailed discussion and elaboration is the question of credential-issuing and revoking of credentials in case the certified claim is no longer valid, e.g., a person no longer attends the indicated fitness centre or is no longer moderator of a topic in the forum.

Acknowledgments. We thank Rainer Böhme, Stefan Köpsell, and our anonymous reviewers for their helpful comments as well as Hagen Wahrig for working on the practical realisation of the concept. The research leading to these results has received funding from the European Community's Seventh Framework Programme (FP7/2007-2013) under grant agreement no. 216483.

References

[ACK⁺09]   Ardagna, C.A., Camenisch, J., Kohlweiss, M., Leenes, R., Neven, G., Priem, B., Samarati, P., Sommer, D., Verdicchio, M.: Exploiting Cryptography for Privacy-Enhanced Access Control: A result of the PRIME Project. Journal of Computer Security, JCS (2009) (to appear)

[Ada99]   Adams, A.: The implications of users' privacy perception on communication and information privacy policies. In: Proceedings of Telecommunications Policy Research Conference, Washington, DC (1999)

[Cha85]   Chaum, D.: Security without identification: Transaction systems to make big brother obsolete. Communications of the ACM 28, 1030–1044 (1985)

[Cut95]   Cutler, R.H.: Distributed presence and community in cyberspace. Interpersonal Computer and Technology 3(2), 12–32 (1995)

[CvH02]   Camenisch, J., van Herreweghen, E.: Design and implementation of the idemix anonymous credential system. In: Proceedings of the 9th ACM conference on Computer and communications security, pp. 21–30 (2002)

[FWBBP06]   Franz, E., Wahrig, H., Böttcher, A., Borcea-Pfitzmann, K.: Access Control in A Privacy-Aware eLearning Environment. In: First International Conference on Availability, Reliability and Security, pp. 879–886 (2006)

[HBPP05]   Hansen, M., Borcea-Pfitzmann, K., Pfitzmann, A.: PRIME - Ein europäisches Projekt für nutzerbestimmtes Identitätsmanagement. It - Information Technology, Oldenbourg 6(47), 352–359 (2005)

[KWM⁺08]   Kao, D.-Y., Wang, S.-J., Mathur, K., Jain, S., Huang, F.F.-Y.: Privacy Concealments: Detective Strategies Unveiling Cyberstalking on Internet. In: APSCC 2008: Proceedings of the 2008 IEEE Asia-Pacific Services Computing Conference, Washington, DC, USA, pp. 1364–1368. IEEE Computer Society, Los Alamitos (2008)

[Lam71]   Lampson, B.: Protection. In: 5th Princeton Symposium on Information Science and Systems, pp. 437–443 (1971)

[Pöt09a]   Pötzsch, S.: Privacy Awareness: A Means to Solve the Privacy Paradox? In: IFIP Advances in Information and Communication Technology, vol. 298, pp. 226–236. Springer, Boston (2009)

[Pöt09b]   Pötzsch, S.: Untersuchung des Einflusses von wahrgenommener Privatsphäre und Anonymität auf die Kommunikation in einer Online-Community. In: Fischer, S., Maehle, E., Reischuk, R. (eds.) Informatik 2009, Im Fokus das Leben, Lübeck, Bonn, September 28-October 2. LNI, vol. 154, pp. 2152–2165. Gesellschaft fr Informatik (2009)

[PP09]   Pekárek, M., Pötzsch, S.: A comparison of privacy issues in collaborative workspaces and social networks. In: Identity in the Information Society, Special Issue on Social Web and Identity (2009)

[RI07]   Razavi, M.N., Iverson, L.: Towards usable privacy for social software. Technical Report LERSSE-TR-2007-03, University of British Columbia (2007)

[RI08]   Razavi, M.N., Iverson, L.: Supporting selective information sharing with
                people-tagging. In: Proceedings of the ACM CHI 2008 Extended Ab-
                stracts on Human Factors in Computing Systems, Florence, Italy (April
                2008)
[SCFY96]   Sandhu, R.S., Coyne, E.J., Feinstein, H.L., Youman, C.E.: Role-based
                access control models. IEEE Computer 29(2), 38–47 (1996)
[TAPH05]   Tolone, W., Ahn, G.-J., Pai, T., Hong, S.-P.: Access control in collabo-
                rative systems. ACM Comput. Surv. 37(1), 29–41 (2005)
[Tho97]   Thomas, R.K.: Team-based access control (TMAC): a primitive for
                applying role-based access controls in collaborative environments. In:
                RBAC 1997: Proceedings of the second ACM workshop on Role-based
                access control, pp. 13–19. ACM, New York (1997)
[Wor09]   Online harassment and cyberstalking cumulative statistics for the years
                2000-2008 (2009),
                http://www.haltabuse.org/resources/stats/
                Cumulative2000-2008.pdf

A Three-Dimensional Framework to Analyse the Governance of Population Registers

José Formaz and Olivier Glassey

Swiss Graduate School of Public Administration (IDHEAP)
Swiss Public Administration Network (SPAN)
Route de la Maladière 21
1022 Lausanne, Switzerland

Abstract. In June 2006, the Swiss Parliament made two important decisions with regards to public registers' governance and individuals' identification. It adopted a new law on the harmonisation of population registers in order to simplify statistical data collection and data exchange from around 4'000 decentralized registers, and it also approved the introduction of a Unique Person Identifier (UPI). The law is rather vague about the implementation of this harmonisation and even though many projects are currently being undertaken in this domain, most of them are quite technical. We believe there is a need for analysis tools and therefore we propose a conceptual framework based on three pillars (Privacy, Identity and Governance) to analyse the requirements in terms of data management for population registers.

Keywords: governance, population registers, identity, privacy, Unique Person Identifier (UPI).

1 Introduction

The increasing use of Information and Communication Technologies (ICT) has gradually permeated almost every domain of our daily life. The rise of this information or network society [1] generates a fast-growing volume of electronic records, reconfiguring among other things the way governments manage their population registers. Relying increasingly on the aggregation of data about individuals, such registers tend to integrate a Unique Person Identifier (UPI).

In Switzerland, the Parliament made in June 2006 two important decisions with regards to public registers' governance and individuals' identification. It adopted a new law on population registers[1] aimed at simplifying data collection and exchange of personal data between registers, and it also approved the introduction of a new old-age and survivors' insurance[2] number [2]. Both decisions are closely related, as the

---

[1] The Federal Act on the Harmonisation of the Register of Residents and of other Official Registers of Persons. www.admin.ch/ch/e/rs/4/431.02.en.pdf

[2] The Old Age and Survivors' Insurance (OASI) is the main Swiss social security insurance which provides pensions for retired persons, widows/ widowers and orphans. This insurance covers all individuals who live or are gainfully employed in Switzerland and is compulsory for foreign nationals too.

M. Bezzi et al. (Eds.): Privacy and Identity, IFIP AICT 320, pp. 112–121, 2010.

law on the harmonisation of registers intends to use the new social insurance number to uniquely identify individuals in the official registers of persons.

The structure of this paper is as follows. First we present the recent changes in the Swiss law affecting public registers and personal identification. Then we outline the notions of governance, identity management and privacy. On the basis of these concepts, we propose a three-dimensional framework to study population registers' governance. We conclude by giving some insight into future work we intend to undertake.

2 The Swiss Public Registers

According to the United Nation Statistics Division [4], the main administrative function of public registers is to provide reliable information for the various purposes of government. This encompasses program planning, budgeting and taxation; the issuing of unique personal identification numbers; the establishment of the eligibility of individuals for voting, education, health, military service, social insurance scheme; and for police and judicial references.

2.1 Recent Evolution of Swiss Public Registers[3]

So far public registers are very fragmented in Switzerland. Until 2004 vital records (births, deaths, weddings, and adoptions) were held on paper registers by 1750 Cantonal offices throughout the country. Since then the Federal Department of Justice and Police provides Cantons with a centralized database called Infostar. In addition to these cantonal registers there are more than 2500 disconnected communal registers of residents. In the Canton of Bern alone, 392 communes use 26 different software solutions to manage residents' data [5].

Beside these "stricto sensu" population registers, there are several other registers that store data on citizens: fiscal register, foreigners' register, building and housing register, and so on. Other databases that are not directly considered as registers are also connected to the official registers and store records on education, social welfare services, military, etc.

As long as the thousands of Swiss public registers were paper-based or not interconnected, there was little need to study the governance of these registers' data. The situation has evolved with the Federal Act on the Harmonisation of the Registers (FAHR). Approved in June 2006 and enacted in January 2008, its purpose is twofold: first, to simplify the statistical use of data contained in the registers of persons, and secondly to foster data exchange between these registers, namely:

- the computerised civil status register (Infostar) maintained by the cantons and operated by the Federal Office of Justice;

- the Central Migration Information System (ZEMIS) of the Federal Office for Migration;

---

[3] By public register, we mean any register maintained by law, regulation, or practice, by or on behalf of a unit of Federal, cantonal, or local government, that contains information that can be linked to a specific individual. No inference should be drawn by the use of the term that any type of information identified as a public register is or is not publicly available [3].

- the information system for diplomats and international civil servants (Ordipro) of the Federal Department of Foreign Affairs;

- the matriculation register maintained by the Swiss diplomatic and consular representations abroad for the networked administration of data and for the Swiss Abroad (VERA) maintained by the Federal Department of Foreign Affairs;

- the Central Register of Insured Persons, the Central Pensions Register and the Register of Benefits-in-Kind of the Central Compensation Office.

- the cantonal and communal registers of residents as well as electoral registers

Research in the domain of public registers' data governance is scarce, as many countries do not have decentralized registers as they exist in Switzerland (they are maintained at a central level, e.g. Ministries), while some countries do not have population registers at all. Furthermore, as long as public registers were paper-based or not interoperable, the control of these registers was made de facto as reproduction or search of an entire database was difficult or impossible [6]. With the spread of computers into government records keeping, new capabilities allow access at multiple locations, research and sorting by different criteria, and inexpensive reproduction of complete databases. This challenges older policies established while data were kept on paper registers.

2.2 The Necessity of a Unique Person Identifier

The next Federal Census planned for 2010 should use data provided by these various population registers (previous censuses were based on questionnaires and interviews). In order to collect and aggregate data automatically, a UPI is required for each Swiss resident. Thus, the FAHR approved by the Parliament in 2006 allows the use of the new old-age and survivors' insurance number as a UPI. Although it guarantees the complete anonymity of insured persons[4], the use of this number as a UPI in official registers raises some questions in terms of privacy and identity management.

Indeed, despite consultation procedures launched by the Federal Council during the years 2003-2004, three successive UPI projects have been rejected by interested parties, mainly for data protection issues [7]. Following a first proposal to introduce a UPI for all public registers, a second project envisaged to establish six sector ID numbers for population, social security, tax, defence, justice and statistics. Supposed to insulate data and to protect citizen's privacy, neither this proposal nor a third one providing a UPI limited to the domains of residents, civil status, foreigners and refugees found favour with circles close to data protection.

Given the difficulties of finding a consensus on a new law aimed at providing a univocal number to identify individuals in public registers, the Federal Council chose as a UPI the new old-age and survivors' insurance number which was one among other amendments to the OASI law. Approved by the Parliament in 2006, together with the FAHR, this decision bothered several actors with whom we have discussed

---

[4] The previous number had data informing about the date of birth, the sex, the first letters of the surname, and the Swiss or foreign nationality.

(politicians, data protection commissioners and other civil servants) for the lack of discussion surrounding the imposition of this UPI.

Far from being a Swiss particularity, these last ten years have seen a growing tendency toward the usage of UPI within European countries [8]. Nevertheless, some countries are explicitly against the implementation of such numbers for data protection concerns. In Germany for instance, "it is already certain that there will be no universal personal identifier, [...] because this would be hardly justifiable under data protection law"[5]. This is the only country of the fifteen original EU members to be explicitly against an UPI for the future.

3 Conceptual Insights

To study the Swiss public registers, we selected three concepts that need to be defined more precisely: governance, identity management and privacy.

3.1 From Governance to e-Governance?

One of the main areas of research we want to look into is the elaboration of rules and the decision processes that govern the management of the registers' personal data, especially with the new possibilities provided by the information society. In order to achieve this goal, we will first define more precisely what the concepts of governance and e-governance encompass.

Governance is such an elusive concept that some consider "there are almost as many ideas of governance as there are researchers in the field" [9]. According to the United Nations Development Programme which published a policy paper on governance for sustainable human development [10], governance is the exercise of economic, political and administrative authority to manage a country's affairs at all levels. It is participatory, consensus oriented, accountable, transparent, responsive, effective and efficient, equitable and follows the rule of law.

Incorporating the elements of the UNDP definition, Kauzya further defines governance as a multifaceted compound situation of institutions, systems, structures, processes, procedures, practices, relationships, and leadership behaviour in the exercise of social, political, economic, and managerial/administrative authority in the running of public or private affairs [11].

Except by referring to *kybernan*, the Greek root of governance meaning "to steer" (a ship or a chariot), any consensus on a definition of governance is hard to achieve. However, there are two domains that are well defined and widely accepted: political governance (whether global, local or territorial) and corporate governance. Both share a common approach based on decision processes and stakeholders' participation (shareholders, executives, political leaders, citizens, interest groups or any other organisation). As we want to study the governance of public registers, it is clearly the political governance that we are interested in.

Widely used and discussed both in the public and private sectors, the governance approach emerges together with the computerisation of the society. Some writers

---

[5] www.deutschland-online.de/DOL_en_Internet/broker.jsp?uMen=3ec0071d-6f2a-2114-fbf1-b1ac0c 2f214a

speak about information and governance revolutions, and estimate that e-governance lies at the heart of these two global shifts [12]. In a recent article, Dawes describes e-governance as a dynamic and open socio-technical system where social elements and technical aspects are continually evolving on their own while continuously interacting with each other in ways that cannot be controlled [13]. This system is made up of six dimensions: societal trends, human elements, interaction and complexity, information management, purpose and role of government, and changing technologies. Each dimension includes a number of factors, among them privacy, identity and trust for the human elements. These factors have also been identified as the first research fields in a project funded by the European Commission which aims at sketching e-government in 2020 [14].

Data governance has a specific meaning in the field of Information Systems. Encompassing the people, processes and technology, it refers to the overall management of the consistency, accessibility, usability, integrity, and security of the data employed in an organization.

3.2   Identity Management and Privacy

Lying at the heart of many forms of government service delivery, personal identification[6] was based until recently on manual form filling and paper-based authentication processes, with then a storage (and most of the time oblivion) of the form. With the digitalization of registers and their use to provide specific information for an administrative procedure, these identification mechanisms are not sufficient anymore. There is also a qualitative difference between the granting of online access to information and its provision in paper form [16].

If the extensive use of ICT to gather, process, share and store personal data brings about real enhancements with regard to public services, it generates tensions and debates as well. By implementing a UPI within public registers, the FAHR makes the multiple identities citizens have when dealing with different parts of the public sector (as individual, elector, taxpayer, student, unemployed person, soldier, patient, prisoner, and so on) interoperable.

However this paper is not about a technical approach of eIdentity management (user name, password, personal identification numbers, smart cards, PKI, fingerprint readers, mobile phone, and so on). We are interested in the legal-normative approach of identity management, answering to questions such as how does the law on public registers' harmonisation fit together with data protection legislation? Furthermore the Swiss Confederation and many Cantons have a law on transparency stating that all public documents and information must be publicly available, with exceptions for national security, trade secrets and citizen's privacy [17].

Privacy issues are closely linked with the *interoperability*[7] between registers, both domains being presented as key tensions at the launch of the new journal *Identity in the Information Society* [19]. The link between the privacy of personal information

---

[6] To get a better understanding of concepts like identity, identification and authentication, see [15].

[7] Interoperability refers to the ability of information and communication technology systems and of the business processes they support to exchange data and to enable sharing of information and knowledge [18].

and the use of ICT by public authorities was already tackled by the U.S. Office of Technology Assessment in the eighties [20]. Since then, while the extent of privacy infringement depends on the definition we have of this elusive concept, concerns regarding data profiling and data mining[8] are often expressed. Another well-known phenomenon in database management is the re-purposing [21], also named data creep [22] or function creep [23], [24], [25], and defined as the gradual use of personal data for a purpose other than that originally declared. Without explicit legal grounds, these unanticipated or secondary uses are illegal.

So far we have portrayed general dimensions of governance, identity management and privacy. We still need to specify sets of requirements that will define our three-dimensional framework. By following this framework, this should allow us to analyse governance processes of population registers' data, considering privacy and identity management dimensions and allowing us to formalise relationships between actors, processes and data.

4   A Three-Dimensional Framework

Our framework explores the potential of three approaches to the analysis of Swiss population registers. These three approaches are:

a)   on governance, the COBIT model

b)   on identity management, the laws of identity developed by Cameron

c)   on privacy, a set of criteria from the Swiss and European data protection laws.

4.1   The COBIT Model

To specify the set of requirements in terms of data governance, we will use the information criteria of CoBIT [26]. This framework for IT governance consists of a set of good practices ensuring that IT is aligned with the business and enables business processes. It also provides resources for risk and performance management. The data requirements (or information criteria) defined by CoBIT are:

- *Effectiveness*: relevant, correct, consistent, usable and timely information.

- *Efficiency*: provision of information through the optimal use of resources.

- *Confidentiality*: protection of sensitive information from unauthorised disclosure.

- *Integrity*: accuracy, validity and completeness of information.

- *Availability*: information is available when required.

- *Compliance*: information use is complying with the laws, regulations and internal policies.

- *Reliability*: information can be trusted.

---

[8] Data profiling is the process of examining the data available in an existing data source and collecting statistics and information about that data. Data mining is the process of extracting hidden patterns from data. Source: www.wikipedia.org

4.2 The Seven Laws of Identity

Apart from this governance dimension, an identity layer must be added to our framework. Cameron defines digital identity as a set of claims made by one digital subject about itself of another digital subject, with a digital subject being a person or a thing and a claim being an assertion of the truth of something, e.g. "I am Paul and I am over 18", "I am Mary and I am married to John" [27]. Cameron furthermore defines seven laws of identity that are now widely used:

- *User control and consent*: digital ID systems must only reveal information identifying a user with the user's consent.

- *Minimal disclosure for a constrained use*: the solution which discloses the least amount of identifying information and best limits its use is the most stable long term solution.

- *Justifiable parties*: digital ID systems must be designed so that the disclosure of identifying information is limited to parties having a necessary and justifiable place in a given identity relationship.

- *Directed identity*: a universal ID system must support both "omnidirectional" identifiers for use by public entities and "unidirectional" identifiers for private entities, thus facilitating discovery while preventing unnecessary release of correlation handles.

- *Pluralism of operators*: a universal ID system must channel and enable the interworking of multiple identity technologies run by multiple identity providers.

- *Human integration*: the universal ID metasystem must define the human user as a component integrated through protected and unambiguous human-machine communications.

- *Consistent experience across contexts*: a unifying ID metasystem must guarantee its users a simple, consistent experience while enabling separation of contexts through multiple operators and technologies.

According to his own words, Cameron defined these laws with the goal of "giving Internet users a deep sense of safety, privacy and certainty about who they are relating to in cyberspace". The context of population registers managed by the public sector is different, but these laws are still very relevant, even if they need to be adapted in some cases.

4.3 Criteria from the Swiss and European Data Protection Legislation

The third dimension of our framework relates to privacy. Referring both to the Swiss Federal Act on Data Protection [28] and to the European Directive on the protection of individuals with regard to the processing of personal data [29], we can put forward the following key principles:

- *Lawfulness:* personal data must be processed lawfully.

- *Purpose:* personal data must be collected for specific and legitimate purposes.

- *Proportionality:* personal data must be proportionate with the purposes for which they are collected and/or further processed.
- *Accuracy:* personal data must be accurate and up-to-date. Inaccurate or incomplete data should be erased or rectified.
- *Anonymity:* personal data must be preserved in a form which permits identification of data subjects for no longer than required for the purposes for which the data are stored or further processed.
- *Obviousness:* the collection of personal data and especially the purpose of its processing must be evident to the data subject

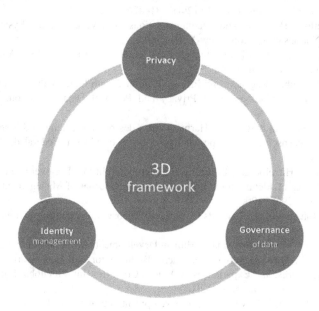

Fig. 1. The three-dimensional framework

5 Conclusion

The pace of technological change that characterizes today's networked society brings about many risks and opportunities. Population registers are no exception, but our framework enables us to consider the action of governments with respect to its data governance. This should help to set up an approach that identifies citizens in ways that respect their personal privacy and builds confidence in government services, while allowing the sharing of relevant data in order to deliver more personalized and interconnected services.

In order to launch a broad study on population registers, we are currently in discussion with various stakeholders: Cantons, communes, Swiss Federal Statistics Office, and other research centres. We will use our framework to analyse needs and requirements of these various stakeholders in terms of data exchange and of registers' harmonisation. We believe this project will offer a very interesting field of experimentation and validation for the approach described in this paper.

References

1. Castells, M.: The Rise of the Network Society. In: The Information Age, vol. 1. Blackwell, Oxford (1996)
2. Walter, J.-P.: Vers une société sous surveillance? La problématique du nouveau numéro AVS. Flash Informatique SP, EPFL (2006)
3. Gellman, R.: Public Records-Access, Privacy, and Public Policy: A Discussion Paper. Government Information Quarterly 12(4), 391–426 (1995)
4. United Nations: Principles and Recommendations for a Vital Statistics System, Revision 2. United Nations publication, New-York (2001)
5. Glassey, O.: Swiss Population Registers and eIdentity Issues. In: 13th Annual IRSPM Conference, Copenhagen (2009)
6. Gellman, R.: Public Registers and Privacy: Conflicts with Other Values and Interests. In: 21st International Conference on Privacy and Personal Data Protection, Hong Kong (1999)
7. Office Fédéral de la Statistique: Harmonisation des registres, numéro d'identification de personne et recensement de la population: décision du Conseil Fédéral du 10 juin 2005 (2005)
8. Otjacques, B., Hitzelberger, P., Feltz, F.: Interoperability of E-Government Information Systems: Issues of Identification and Data Sharing. Journal of Management Information Systems 23(4), 29–51 (2007)
9. Björk, P., Johansson, H.: Towards Governance Theory: In Search for a Common Ground. IPSA Papers (2001)
10. UNDP: Governance for Sustainable Human Development. A UNDP Policy Paper (1997)
11. Kauzya, J.-M.: Local Governance Capacity Building for Full range Participation: Concepts, Frameworks, and Experiences in African Countries. In: 4th Global Forum on Reinventing Government, Marrakech (2002)
12. Heeks, R.: Building e-Governance for Development: a Framework for National and Donor Action. i-Government working paper no. 12 (2001)
13. Dawes, S.: Governance in the digital age: A research and action framework for an uncertain future. Government Information Quarterly 26(2), 257–264 (2009)
14. Codagnone, C., Wimmer, M.A.: Roadmapping eGovernment Research: Visions and Measures towards Innovative Governments in 2020. MY Print snc di Guerinoni Marco & C., Clusone (2007)
15. Clarke, R.: Human Identification in Information Systems: Management Challenges and Public Policy Issues. Information Technology & People 7(4), 6–37 (1994)
16. McDonagh, M.: The protection of personal information in public registers: the case of urban planning information in Ireland. Information & Communications Technology Law 18(1), 19–38 (2009)
17. Glassey, O.: A Framework to Analyze Data Governance of Swiss Population Registers. In: 8th International EGOV Conference, Linz (2009)
18. IDABC: European Interoperability Framework for Pan-European eGovernment Services, Version 1.0. European Communities, Luxemburg (2004)
19. Halperin, R., Backhouse, J.: A roadmap for research on identity in the information society. Identity in the information society 1(1) (2008)

20. Regan, P.: Privacy, Government Information, and Technology. Public Administration Review 46(6), 629–634 (1986)
21. Wright, D., Gutwirth, S., Friedewald, M., De Hert, P., Langheinrich, M., Moscibroda, A.: Privacy, trust and policy-making: Challenges and responses. Computer Law & Security Report 25(1), 69–83 (2009)
22. Beynon-Davies, P.: Personal identity management and electronic government: The case of the national identity card in the UK. Journal of Enterprise Information Management 20(3), 244–270 (2007)
23. Clarke, R.: Privacy and Public Registers. In: IIR Conference on Data Protection and Privacy, Sydney (1997)
24. Rundle, M.C.: E-Infrastructures for Identity Management and Data Sharing: Perspectives Across the Public Sector. OII Forum Discussion Paper no 12 (2007)
25. Taylor, J.A., Lips, M., Organ, J.: Identification practices in government: citizen surveillance and the quest for public service improvement. Identity in the Information Society 1(1) (2008)
26. IT Governance Institute, COBIT 4.1 (2007), http://itgi.org/cobit
27. Cameron, K.: The Laws of Identity (2005), http://www.identityblog.com/stories/2005/05/13/TheLawsOfIdentity.pdf
28. Federal Assembly of the Swiss Confederation: Federal Act on Data Protection (1992), http://www.admin.ch/ch/e/rs/235_1/index.html
29. European Parliament and Council: Directive 95/46/EC on the protection of individuals with regard to the processing of personal data and on the free movement of such data. OJ L 281, p. 31 (1995),
    http://www.edps.europa.eu/EDPSWEB/webdav/site/mySite/shared/Documents/EDPS/DataProt/Legislation/Dir_1995_46_EN.pdf

Use of ePassport for Identity Management in Network-Based Citizen-Life Processes

Pravir Chawdhry and Ioannis Vakalis

Institute for the Protection and Security of the Citizen
Joint Research Centre, 21027 Ispra (VA) Italy
{Pravir.Chawdhry,Ioannis.Vakalis}@jrc.ec.europa.eu

Abstract. Digital identity management (IdM) for citizen-life processes requires trusted relationship among the service providers and users. Current IdM systems tend to lack the trust component in particular for online transactions. We propose the use of ePassport as a globally interoperable trust token to bridge the gap between offline and online environments. The paper analyses trust attributes of the ePassport and recognizes the extensions required to its deployment in an online IdM for high-value transactions. An architecture is proposed for a network-based IdM system to support three categories of life processes: eGovernment services, high value private services, and eCommerce. The solution is compatible with privacy-enhancing technologies while at the same time creating trusted digital identities and offering users convenience.

Keywords: identity management, online services, trusted identity, privacy.

1 Introduction

Citizens engage in a variety of life processes, managed by public and private sectors, where there is need to provide a proof of identity to participate in the process. In some cases the proof of identity is required only once, in other cases it may be asked repeatedly. Examples of such processes are: banking, social security, international travel, staying in hotels, high-value purchases, car rental, use of credit card, joining private clubs, admission to a school or university, seeking employment, health services, etc.

There are numerous types of identity documents: national identity card, passports, social security card, health insurance card, employer's card, banker's card, driving license, etc. Most of the identity documents, with the exception of the national identity card, are function-specific and context-dependent, even though in practice they may be accepted in other contexts.

The kind of identity-related information offered by identity documents also varies: ranging from facial identity linked to the name of a person, it may also include signatures, date of birth, address, citizenship, medical information, and other personal and biographic data. With the advent of smart cards in the past decade, the ambition of storing a variety of information has suddenly taken a leap. The idea of a multi-function identity card has been mooted but reservations remain due to the privacy risks involved.

M. Bezzi et al. (Eds.): Privacy and Identity, IFIP AICT 320, pp. 122–133, 2010.

Passports are official identity documents intended to facilitate international travel of citizens. However, due to their official status and universality passports are also used and accepted as identity documents with photo-Id in various citizen-based processes other than travel. This is particularly true in the countries where national identity cards are not mandatory, such as Ireland and the United Kingdom.

Electronic passports (or, ePassports) were introduced in the EU in August 2006 as a means of strong authentication for border control. The ePassports store certain biometric data of the bearer on a chip embedded within the passport booklet. In the EU, the biometric data stored on the chip is digital image of the face and from mid-2009, it will also include the fingerprint.

Only authorized readers at EU border control points can access the fingerprint image stored on the chip whereas the facial image and biographical data may be read by any ePassport reader available commercially. With the diffusion of ePassports and related technology, it is quite feasible that in the near future various citizen-service outlets will be equipped with the devices to read and store the biographical data and facial biometric.

In face-to-face interaction, the printed biographic data page of the ePassport can still be used as a photo-Id like the traditional passport. However, to provide a function for network-based identity, it needs to be augmented so that a whole range of trust-based services may be offered in a convenient and uniform manner. This will avoid the need to create a separate electronic identity, detached from the physical realm.

The idea of using governmental tokens as the basis for identity services has been investigated in some countries, with the recent introduction of eIDs. Questions have been raised if eIDs are more appropriate tokens for eCommerce in comparison to ePassport with privacy issues already pointed out.

This paper investigates key issues of trust in a network-based identity infrastructure based on ePassports. The paper is organized as follows. Section 2 presents a brief overview of trust mechanisms in the ePassport infrastructure. In Section 3 we examine key approaches to network-based IdM and identify key requirements for a network-based IdM system. In Section 4 we propose an IdM architecture for deploying ePassports in network-based citizen-life processes characterized by varying degree of risk. We conclude with a discussion of key challenges in Section 5.

2   Trust Mechanisms in the ePassport Infrastructure

There are two types of definition of trust one is social/legislative and the other type is quantitative/mathematical. So the definitions for trust of the first type refer to qualities [11] that the trusted party should possess:

- predictability of the trusted party,
- completion of transactions even in the absence of full knowledge,
- immediate payback of any type is not a strict requirement,
- exposed vulnerabilities are not exploited,
- reputation

Table 1. Trust relationships and constraints in ePassport infrastructure

Infrastructure Perspective	Roles & Constraints		
	Passport Holder	**Issuing State**	**Border Control Post**
IdM role	principal	identity provider	service provider
Trust relationship boot up.	Provides pre-requisites (e.g. feeder documents on his identity) to the issuing authorities.	Establishes the pre-requisites to the trust relationship with the principal.	Establishes the pre-requisites to the trust relationship with the issuing authorities.
Legacy function.	Presents the passport as a traditional booklet to authenticate himself. Doesn't know how the scanned MRZ data is used, shared and retained.	Provides identity through a photo and biographic data on a printed page.	Uses the visual inspection means to check the authenticity of the passport and match the printed photo with the live subject.
BAC minimum scope.	In addition to the printed biographical data, also provides primary biometrics[1] (live facial image) to authenticate himself. Agrees tacitly to allow access his biometric data for the purpose of border control.	Provides facial biometric on a contactless smartcard chip, embedded in the passport booklet. Permits passive authentication to anyone with a suitable ePassport reader. Through ICAO membership, implicitly authorizes other ICAO members right to read their chips.	Uses the MRZ data on the printed page to enable access to the facial biometric on chip. May use visual means or image recognition to do the match between the facial biometric and the subject.
BAC max scope.	No additional action required.	Separately provides a digital certificate to authorized service providers for active authentication of chip data. These digital certificates are not highly protected.	Global scope – Needs certificate of the issuing country to authenticate the validity of data on the ePassport chip.
EAC.	Also provides his secondary biometrics (fingerprints) to authenticate himself. Agrees tacitly to allow access his biometric data for the purpose of border control.	Provides certificates in a hierarchy of identity providers and service providers. Explicit authorization provided only to other EU countries.	Terminal authentication needed: Requires terminals with explicit authority from identity providers via secret cryptographic keys to enable reading of the secondary biometrics.
Organizational model.	National passports / travel documents are recognized internationally as trusted credentials for identity.	National passport issuers as identity providers; implicit authorization to all ICAO states for BAC level trust; explicit authorization to the other EU States for EAC level trust.	No specific steps are required to operate at BAC level; at EAC level, the protection of private cryptographic keys is a major responsibility. Mutual recognition of passports as trusted identity.

---

[1] According to the EU passport specification [9] ace is the primary biometric, fingerprint and iris are secondary.

In the quantitative models of trust, a special category of logic representing belief is used as a base [12] and the trust levels are expressed in terms (e.g. high, medium, low) or in number scales (e.g. 1-5).

The European ePassport infrastructure is specific to border control applications and is designed for wide-scale interoperability. It consists of two trust levels. Level 1 trust is built in a mechanism known as Basic Access Control (BAC) designed to offer global interoperability and specified by ICAO. Level 2 trust is built at an enhanced level, known as Extended Access Control (EAC) and is based on additional specification for EU-wide interoperability. Trust in the context of border control can be defined between three parties: (a) principal – the entity holding the passport as an identity token; (b) identity provider – the passport issuing State; (c) the service provider – a border control post in the same or another State. Table 1 shows trust relationships and constraints between the three parties.

As Table 1 shows, the ePassport infrastructure is based on federated trust. It has been developed on top of the legacy passport infrastructure. It grants right to access basic identity information to all ICAO members through the BAC mechanism.

There is no explicit provision of privacy policy of the (border control) service providers nor is there option for privacy preferences by the holder. The basic as well as advanced functions of the ePassport (EAC and eVisa) assume implicit consent of the holder in all usages by service providers (i.e. the border control). For advanced functions, however, only a targeted subset of federation members are authorized to access privileged information (i.e. the secondary biometrics).

However, ePassport infrastructure is designed for identity verification in face-to-face mode. Feasibility of its deployment in the networked environment will be examined in Section 4.

3   Network-Based Identity Management

3.1   Current Approaches

Currently there are two main approaches to network-based identity management: centralized and distributed. In the centralized approach, a single entity acts as the identity provider (IdP) in the context of several service providers (SPs). The centralized IdP may offer an option to use pseudonyms as well as creating several service groups which require similar set of personal data. An example of centralized IdP is *Microsoft Passport*. In the decentralized approach several IdPs may form a federation mutually to recognize each other's user sets as well as services. Examples of federated systems are Liberty Alliance and OpenID. Whereas both of these approaches have put considerable emphasis on privacy protection and user convenience, neither of them is particularly strong in mandating trust mechanisms either on the part of the service providers or the end users. Instead they tend to rely on mechanisms such as reputation. Moreover, OpenID lacks the trust model and Liberty Alliance lacks an end-to-end implementation.

Practical implementations of IdM by several commercial vendors are geared towards large enterprises who would have various data services and a large number of users spread around several locations and/or departments with different roles and privileges. This latter is generally termed as a Centralized Authentication Service (CAS). Although this last category is interesting in its own right due to its practical commercial relevance, it is not so much relevant for multi-organizational services directed to citizen-life processes, spanning eGov services, banking, healthcare, e-shopping, education, edutainment and social networks.

The proposed scenario assumes that both the IdPs and the SPs organizations are trustworthy and they follow the legislation regarding the personal data protection and they have clear privacy policies.

For citizen-oriented services, in recent years there have been national initiatives to issue government-certified electronic identity (eID) e.g. in the form of X.509 certificates. Both card-based and file-based schemes have been proposed, however there is a lack of consensus on technical standards thus the interoperability remains a challenge [5][7]. Furthermore, in case of X.509 certificates, the certification authority needs the proof of identity at the time of issuance and since the certificates are possession based tokens, a loss of the storage medium would lead to the risk of impersonation or identity theft.

3.2 Main Requirements of eID

Whereas in face-to-face identity verification scenario human decision is often combined with the technical mechanisms to deliver an acceptable degree of trust in the claimed identity, network-based identity verification needs to rely on technical means only. We identify the following requirements of digital identity management in relation to citizen-life processes for network-based interaction:

(a) Trust
   a.   Trusted credentials of the service providers
   b.   Trust credentials of the identity provider
   c.   Trusted credentials of the consumers (end users)
(b) Privacy and data protection
   a.   Data protection as required by law
      o   By the IdP
      o   By the SP
   b.   Common Criteria[10]
      o   Anonymity
      o   Pseudonymity
   c.   Data Avoidance[10]
      o   Unlinkability
      o   Unobservability
(c) Security
   a.   Communication security – confidentiality, integrity, availability, non-repudiation
   b.   IdM infrastructure security
   c.   Protection against identity fraud (protection of identity)

      i. Authenticity of breeder documents (proof of identity at the time of enrolment)

     ii. Binding between the user with trust credential at the time of authentication

(d) Interoperability
    a. Between diverse identity providers
    b. Between identity providers and service providers
    c. Between the IdM system and the user environment (context)

(e) Usability
    a. Ease of use
    b. Accessibility
    c. Efficiency
    d. Adaptable to widest range of users, use cases, life processes

From a brief inspection of the above list, it becomes quite obvious that an IdM solution would have to make design trade-offs between the diverse requirements based on the priorities, cost, state of the art technology and scalability of alternative options for the underlying IdM architecture. Alternative solutions can still be evaluated in terms of the above requirements.

3.3 Risk-Based Authentication

In relation to security and trust, a key issue is the binding mechanism between the claimed identity and the claimant in a scheme. The strength of binding during authentication should be appropriate enough to mitigate the risks involved in the transaction as well as the limitations or possible circumventions of different types of identity tokens (biometrics, digital certificates, password, etc). The scheme can be based on *possession, knowledge* or *personal traits* of the subject. NIST has proposed four levels of authentication[13] which we extend as shown in Table 2. In many applications, multi-factor authentication may also be a practical option leading to a combination among password, biometric, hardware token and digital certificate.

Table 2. Risk-based Authentication Options

Authentication Level	Risk assessment by Service Provider	Registration Policy of the Identity Provider	Means of User Authentication	Examples	Primary Concern
0	No risk – no damages	No proof of identity required; self-certification; unlimited period of enrolment	None or Userid / password; password strength not enforced	Chat rooms, email services; shopbot search; blog hosts	Privacy; Usability
1	Low – small damages	Weak proof of identity: by referral of a trusted token or trusted identifier; implicit identity verification through an online payment gateway; unlimited fixed period of enrolment	Userid / password password strength may be enforced; repeated authentication attempts blocked	Online shopping; low-value social networks	Data protection; usability; security

Table 2. (*Continued*)

Authentication Level	Risk assessment by Service Provider	Registration Policy of the Identity Provider	Means of User Authentication	Examples	Primary Concern
2	Medium – significant damages	Remote enrolment accepted; online validation of identity; offline validation Periodic re-validation of identity and privileges	Identity tokens (software or hardware); biometrics	Online tax filing and other eGov services; high-value social networks	Trust; Security; data protection; usability
3	High – considerable damages	Personal presence and/or verification of claimed identity through multiple sources; security vetting; periodic re-validation of identity and privileges	Biometrics; hardware or software tokens; secure access; cards with hard crypto	Banking; eHealth services; access to sensitive data	Trust; security
4	Very high – unacceptable level of damages	Personal presence of the applicant is required; verification of breeder documents; security vetting; limited time enrolment; periodic re-validation of identity, privileges and security vetting	Cards with hard crypto; multi-factor authentication; access to service only within supervised premises with physical access control; two-person authentication	National security; commercial secrets; services for high-value persons	Trust; security

4 Proposed Architecture

4.1 Federation of Trusted Identities

As outlined in Section 3, the main requirements of a user-based IdM system are trust, privacy, security, interoperability and usability.

We adopt the federated model where ePassport as the primary identity token to ensure trust and convenience whereas a SAML-2 based federation technology ensures security and interoperability [14].

A separation of the identity providers from the service providers will in itself enhance privacy protection. User demand for privacy protection and the multi-vendor based competing solutions would further encourage adoption of the most powerful privacy-enhancing technologies by the identity providers and service providers.

Figure 1 shows the proposed model where users are enroled with a trusted identity provider of their choice, based on trusted credentials. When using trusted networked services, the relevant identity provider verifies the user's identity and furnishes the user information required for service provision.

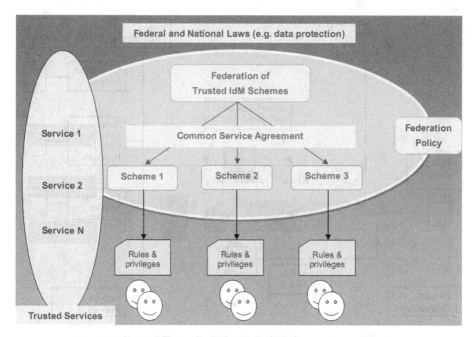

Fig. 1. Federation of Trusted Identities based on common trust policy

4.2 Services for Trusted Identities

A trusted identity management architecture based on ePassport is proposed in Figure 2. The diagram represents the use of the three main risk categories of services utilizing e-passport based identity verification.

(a) **Public / eGov services:** For the government online services the IdP can use passport as a base document for identity enrolment. When providing entitled services in a trusted kiosk-based environment, the ePassport can be used for real-time biometric authentication. In this case, the user is in control of his passport and the eGov service provider is in control of the trusted kiosk incorporating passport reader and biometric scanner (e.g. digital camera). Use of fingerprint is not foreseen for services unrelated to border control. Accessibility to the national passport database may not be needed if the kiosk can do the chip authentication.

(b) **High-value private services:** Trusted organizations (banks, hospitals) offering high-value services often use own identity management, thus acting both as identity provider and service provider. However, this type of IdM can be simplified by deriving core identity from the ePassport and supplementing it with relevant demography data for health services and/or financial services. Registration would require the physical presence of the user. The identity provider will be responsible for releasing only the relevant data depending on the service requested. Facial biometric verification with ePassport as a reference token may be done for security or convenience, depending the service. The Service provider will be in control of the ePassport reader terminal which in some cases may include a

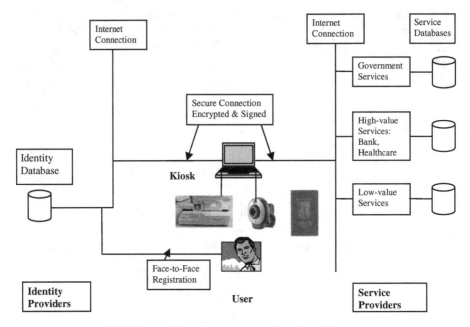

Fig. 2. Trusted identity management based on ePassport

webcam for face recognition. This will avoid the need for creating private biometric databases for authentication by private sector.

(c) **Low-value private services**: A multitude of private service providers (e-shops,
social networks) do not need to verify the precise and full identity of the user,
rather only a partial identity yet still more than just the self-declared pseudonyms
to have sufficient trust in the user. The trust level of the service provider is also a
very important requirement. They may find it adequate for service provision to
have, for instance, a pseudonym with a genuine age and password verified by an
IdP who could ensure the pseudonymity and trust in the user at the same time. No
biometric verification would be needed for such services even though the enrolment with the IdP was based on ePassport and biometrics.

With the three categories of use scenario above, it is technically feasible for a single
IdP to serve all three types of service providers if the end-user so prefers whereas it is
also feasible for a user to have more than one IdP. The IdPs will need to demonstrate
their capability for privacy-enhancing features such as anonymization and unlinkability to satisfy user demands and compete openly based on value-added benefits for
trust, privacy, and risk minimization for the end users as well as the service providers.

4.3   The Scheme - Two Remote Identification Schemes Binding to e-Passport
Information

A major question that arises in such a scheme is how to bind the passport to the holder
in a remote environment. There are two emerging categories of technical implementations that we can distinguish in the literature for this type of services:

(a) **Direct model.** Based on a trusted device concept, which can provide real-time identity verification directly using ePassport. This is particularly relevant for the eGov services based on multi-service kiosks. Figure 3 shows the communication between the user and the IdP in this scenario.

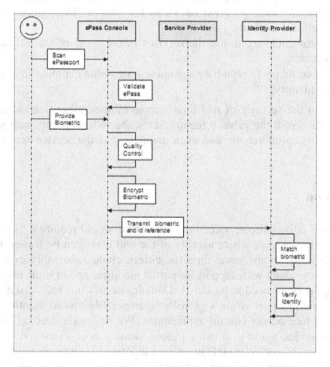

Fig. 3. ePassport-based remote identity verification by the IdP

(b) **Indirect Model.** The Identity Provider (IdP) supplies an e-security token (smart-card, certificate etc.). The IdP operates under regulations (national or international). The token is provided after an enrolment phase based on the information that exists on the ePassport and may include additional information, the IdP may consider as generally required by the high-value service providers.

The indirect model requires an enrolment phase where the client is providing his passport information to the IdP and in return he receives a customer card (smart-card) to which the e-passport information is tied to. Every time the client requests a service from a service provider (also referring as Relying Party) he uses his e-security token. In the smart card there is no passport information is stored only an identification number which is read during a transaction with a local smart card reader. For multi-factor authentication, the user could also use a password in conjunction with the smart card to identify himself.

On the other hand the direct model does not use an additional e-security token. Only the passport data is used for verification by face biometric. A futuristic implementation of the direct model may obviate the need for the use of an IdP where user becomes his own IdP through the use of a certified personal trusted device which are sealed tamper-resistant mobile devices. These devices can be thought of as extended mobile devices (PDA, mobile phones) employed with a passport reader (even with biometric reader). However, they are not yet in the consumer market arena.

There are two main risks regarding the above methods in common with any authentication scheme based on possession and knowledge. This applies to both the direct and the indirect methods.

1. An impostor could try to use the services in the name of the holder using the passport information.

2. the holder could try to repudiate a genuine transaction claiming that an impostor used his online identity.

Advancement in the security of real-time remote biometric verification could minimize these risks. From the privacy requirements, the federated approach already admits unlinkability, pseudonyms and even anonymity if the service provider admits this property.

5 Discussion

An ensemble of citizen-life services in online world would require a trusted identity management infrastructure where identity of the end users can be trusted by the service providers while at the same time the citizen could reasonably expect to have respect of privacy, along with support for partial identities and in some cases anonymity. These requirements need to be satisfied simultaneously in a balanced manner.

The electronic passport offers a globally interoperable trusted identity infrastructure for face-to-face border control applications. We have examined its feasibility to be used in the online world to provide trusted identity as an extension. This will require introduction of certain new features in a federated identity management system to bridge the gap between online and offline identities.

There are several challenges that remain in the realm of research and technical advances continue to be made. It seems evident that the binding between the end user and the network-based enrolment and authentication processes is the key challenge for electronic identity management. The extent to which biometrics can be used for trusted remote authentication is fast becoming a reality and banking services are already running trials of such systems around the world. As more experience is gathered in managing risks in such scenarios, routine deployment will follow.

Another issue is about who should be in control of the authentication devices (ePassport reader, smart card readers etc)? Ideally, in a two-party transaction, both parties should be able to exert an equitable degree of control to maintain the required amount of trust in the transactional relationship. The kiosk environment is state of the art in offering self-services to citizens while ensuring trust as well as secure transaction.

The schemes proposed in this paper are amenable to the adoption of privacy-enhancing technologies by the identity providers as well as service providers. The framework allows the citizens to exert a value-based preference on the market offerings in terms of convenience, security, privacy and trust thereby promoting innovation in identity management for online environment.

References

1. Hansen, M., Krasemann, H., Krause, C., Rost, M.: Identity management systems, IMS: identification and comparison study (2003)
2. Hansen, M., Pfitzmann, A., Steinbrecher, S.: Identity management throughout one's whole life. Information Security Technical Report 13(2), 83–94 (2008)
3. ICAO, MRTD specifications Technical document 9303, Machine Readable Travel Document (2006), http://www2.icao.int/en/mrtd/Pages/default.aspx
4. Ostdjk, M.: Using the ePassport for online authentication, Telematica Institute, Report TI/RS/2009/002 (2009), http://www.telin.nl
5. Bruegger, B.P., Huehnlein, D., Schwenk, J.: TLS federation – a secure and relying party-friendly approach for federated identity management. In: BIOSIG 2008, pp. 93–106 (2008)
6. Bottoni, A., Dini, G.: Improving authentication of remote card transactions with mobile personal trusted devices. Computer Communications 30, 1697–1712 (2007)
7. Bruegger, B.P.: eID interoperability scenario,
   http://www.vrk.fi/vrk/fineid/files.nsf/files/
   71D771700F919761C22573EC00293FAC/file/10-scenarios-8.pdf
8. Arora, S.: National eID card schemes – a European overview. Information Security Technical Report 13(2), 46–53 (2008)
9. EU passport specification Working document (EN) (28/06/2006)
10. Anonymity Terminology,
    http://dud.inf.tu-dresden.de/literatur/
    Anon_Terminology_v0.18.pdf
11. Abdul-Rahman, A., Hailes, S.: Supporting trust in virtual communities. In: Proceedings of the 33rd Hawaii International Conference on System Sciences, vol. 6, p. 6007 (2000)
12. Josang, A.: Prospectives for Modelling Trust in Information Security. In: Mu, Y., Pieprzyk, J.P., Varadharajan, V. (eds.) ACISP 1997. LNCS, vol. 1270, pp. 114–125. Springer, Heidelberg (1997)
13. NIST Electronic Authentication Guideline,
    http://csrc.nist.gov/publications/nistpubs/800-63/
    SP800-63V1_0_2.pdf
14. Ragouzis, N., et al.: Security Assertion Markup Language (SAML) V2.0 Technical Overview. OASIS Committee Draft (March 2008), Document ID sstc-saml-tech-overview-2.0-cd-02, http://www.oasis-open.org/committees/download.php/27819/
    sstc-saml-tech-overview-2.0-cd-02.pdf

The Use of Privacy Enhancing Technologies for Biometric Systems Analysed from a Legal Perspective

Els J. Kindt

Abstract. The deployment of biometric systems could have serious life long implications for the privacy and data protection rights of individuals. The use of
appropriate biometric technologies permitting the creation of multiple trusted
revocable protected biometric identities may present a response to this challenge.
The paper presents a review from a legal perspective of these privacy enhancing
technologies which are being developed in the 7th framework EU project
TURBINE. It is argued that if privacy considerations are taken into account in
the design and technology of biometric systems, this will have a positive influence on the review of the proportionality of the use of biometric systems.

Introduction

Biometric technologies are increasingly applied in identity management systems as a
more secure solution for identity verification, for example for access control in a
company or for online applications. However, because of the unique link with a person, the use of biometric characteristics has also caused many serious concerns. These
include the potential use of the biometric data for linking information about persons
within or across various information sources and the undesired re-use of biometric
information for purposes which were not initially envisaged at the collection of the
data, for example for profiling or surveillance purposes. Moreover, biometric data
may reveal sensitive information, and last but not least, the biometric characteristics
used remain in principle persistent over years and cannot be re-issued if compromised. In case of abuse of biometric data (e.g., for identity theft purposes), this will
render the life of the victim quite burdensome in proving that he or she has not committed the offences or crimes whereby his or her 'stolen' biometric data were used, if
not impossible.

Many of these privacy and data protection issues have been identified and discussed by national Data Protection Authorities and in the Article 29 Data Protection
Working Party document on biometrics of August 2003.[1] The Working Party in this
document called upon the industry to develop biometric systems that are privacy and
data protection compliant.

In this paper, it will be discussed whether and under which conditions the local
storage of biometric characteristics on an object under the control of the data subject
is effective in enhancing the privacy protection. In addition, other features and aspects
of biometric identity management systems are particularly relevant for making systems data protection compliant 'by design'. Some of these features will be further

---

[1] Article 29 Data Protection Working Party, *Working document on biometrics, WP 80*, 1 August
2003, 12 p.

M. Bezzi et al. (Eds.): Privacy and Identity, IFIP AICT 320, pp. 134–145, 2010.

described. This will primarily be done by means of discussing the research and the developments in the 7th framework EU project TURBINE, which focuses on the development of trusted revocable protected biometric identities.[2] It is argued that where the privacy is included in the design, this will influence the review of the risks of the use of biometric characteristics as compared with the benefits, also referred to as the proportionality issue. Finally, the features discussed could lead to the formulation of best practices in the use of biometric characteristics for the enhancement of identity management systems and certification.

1 Biometric Data under the Control of the Data Subject

The concept of control by the data subject has been put forward at regular times as an important element of privacy. Alan F. Westin defined in 1967 privacy as 'the claim of individuals, groups or institutions to determine for themselves when, how, and to what extent information about themselves is communicated to others.[3] Westin therefore sees privacy as a form of autonomy, in particular, the ability to control the flow of information about oneself. Arthur R. Miller wrote in 1971 that 'the basic attribute of an effective right to privacy [is] the individual's ability to control the flow of information concerning or describing him'.[4]

The Convention No. 108 for the Protection of Individuals with regard to Automatic Processing of Personal Data and the Data Protection Directive 95/46/EC, however, gave a far more limited role to control over personal data or to applications controlled by the users. These legal instruments attempted to reconcile the demand for a free flow of personal data with the right to privacy of individuals. Because of the type of processing of personal data, at the time of enactment of the Convention and the Directive mainly by mainframe computers, the articles did not provide for an express right for the data subject to control his or her personal data, but rather for information rights (transparency) and access and correction rights. Some countries, however, in particular Germany, provide for a constitutional right to informational self-determination. The German Federal Constitutional Court has, based on the 'general right of personality' of the Constitution[5], recognized various expressions of this right, including the right to respect for

---

[2] TrUsted Revocable Biometric IdeNtitiEs project (TURBINE), EU project no. 216339 (2008-2011), www.turbine-project.eu .See also J. Breebaart, C. Bush, J. Grave and E. Kindt, 'A reference architecture for biometric template protection based on pseudo identities', in A. Brömme (ed.), *Proceedings of the Special Interest Group on Biometrics and Electronic Signatures*, Bonn, Gesellschaft für Informatik, 2008, pp. 25-37.

[3] A. Westin, *Privacy and Freedom*, New York, Atheneum, 1967.

[4] A. Miller published in 1971 in the United States the book 'The Assault on Privacy', in which he examined the effect of the technological revolution (of that time) on individual privacy. He made various proposals to reconcile technology with society values, which aroused discussion and controversy. See A. Miller, *The Assault on Privacy: Computers, Data Bases and Dossiers*, Ann Arbor, University of Michigan press, 1971.

[5] The German Federal Constitution of 23 May 1949 contains two articles which are important to understand the 'general right of personality', specific for Germany : Article 1 (1) which establishes the fundamental right of protection of human dignity and Article 2 (1) which states the fundamental right to develop freely one's personality.

privacy in 1970, and the right of informational self-determination in 1983.[6] This right to informational self-determination is important for the data protection legislation in Germany. Partly due to the changes in the use of computers, applications and the worldwide network infrastructure, the concept of individual control gains more and more attention and support, also in other countries of the European Union. At the same time, it should be admitted that control over information, including over personal data, remains on the conceptual level problematic[7].

Privacy thought of as *the right to decide over and to control personal information* is of particular importance for biometrics. The Data Protection Directive 95/46/EC, however, does not contain any specific provisions supporting individual control. It lacks, for instance specific requirements relating to the place of storage of personal data, which is a central issue regarding biometric data. In case of central storage of biometric characteristics, use of the characteristics for identification without knowledge of the data subject and re-use for other purposes are amongst the fears and risks which are put forward.[8] Local storage on an object under the control of the individual has been therefore suggested[9] and may be one of the most important methods to protect biometric data because it allows the data subject to control the use of the biometric characteristics and serve as protection against attacks of central databases.

Individual control over biometric data has almost become a requirement for privacy compliance by some national Data Protection Authorities (DPAs).

In 2000, The French DPA, the CNIL, rendered several opinions with regard to the use of fingerprints in the private sector and which were (to be) centrally stored for a variety of purposes. The CNIL underlined that that fingerprints were not only mainly

---

[6] BVerfG, 15 December 1983, *BVerfGE* 65, 1. This right to informational self-determination heavily determines and weights upon the interpretation of the data protection legislation. See also G . Hornung and Ch. Schnabel, 'Data protection in Germany I : The population census decision and the right to informational self-determination', *Computer Law & Security Review*, 2009, pp. 84-88.

[7] Many legal scholars reject the idea of ownership rights in information and/or data. Some maintain that only intellectual property rights could govern any rights in relation to information. Questions remain as to the enforceability of a right to control and protect information, not only against contracting parties but also against third parties. Ownership over data in databases however may become more accepted. See also E. Kindt, 'Ownership of Information and Database Protection', in J. Dumortier, F. Robben and M. Taeymands (eds.), *A Decade of Research @ the Crossroads of Law and ICT*, Gent, Larcier, 2001, pp. 145 – 160.

[8] Biometric data is increasingly stored in central databases, not only in the private sector, but also for government use. In the Netherlands, for example, the Passport Act, which was modified further to Regulation 2252/2004, now provides for the central storage of fingerprints upon application for a travel document (see Art. 4a paragraph 2b of the Act of 26 September 1991 containing the rules for the issuance of travel documents, as modified by the Act of 11 June 2009 modifying the Passport Act relating to the modification of the travel document administration, the latter published in *Stb.* 2009, 252, also available at https://zoek.officielebekend makingen.nl/stb-2009-252.html).

[9] See for example, the Dutch DPA in its report At Face value : R. Hes, T. Hooghiemstra and J. Borking, *At Face Value. On Biometrical Identification and Privacy,* Achtergrond Studies en Verkenningen 15, The Hague, Registratiekamer, September 1999, p. 52 ('At Face Value Report'). Shortly before, the Dutch DPA had stressed the use of privacy-enhancing technologies in its other report by R. Hes and J. Borking e.a. (eds.), *Privacy-enhancing technologies : the path to anonymity,* Den Haag, Registratiekamer, 1999.

used by the police in the past, but that a database with fingerprints is likely to be used by the police in the future as well, and is to become 'a new instrument of the police', irrespective of the original purposes of the processing.[10] The CNIL has thereupon developed a position on the use of biometric identifiers (in particular fingerprints) which shall in principle not be stored centrally for the reasons set out above, but which shall be stored locally, on an object in the possession and/or under the control of the data subject (for example, on a smart card or a token). Other DPAs are following this position and have also given advice and guidelines not to store biometric data centrally.[11] The central storage has also been considered a major element for the decision on the infringement of the fundamental right to respect for privacy in case law of the European Court of Human Rights.[12] At this point, what is clear is that besides centralized or federated identity management systems, user-centric identity management, where the user can make choices, comes into view. New models 'involve (...) the users in the management of their personal information and how that information is used, rather than to presume that an enterprise or commercial entity holds *all* the data'.[13]

The local storage of biometric characteristics, in particular fingerprint, is one of the aspects researched in the 7th framework programme research project TURBINE. It proposes a user-centric IdM system model, which allows the data subject to manage its identities and the personal information released. TURBINE's research concentrates on the transformation of fingerprints of an individual into several unlinkable 'pseudo-identities' for different applications based on the same fingerprint. Various architectures are presented and reviewed in the project. After elaborating the various options, the local storage of the biometric characteristics such as on a token under the control of the data subject or on secured hardware with a 'match-on-card' functionality, is further researched and tested because of its privacy-enhancing potential.

Control by the data subject, however, *is not limited* to *physical control* over the object on which the biometric characteristics are stored. Control also requires that there are tools provided for the data subject to obtain information about the process in which his or her characteristics are used for identity verification or authorization (output), and to provide instructions (input).[14] Such input could, in case the application provides for multiple identities, for example, be the selection of one of the identities.[15] TURBINE, for example, for its demonstrators has defined a user interface, which is a component that can be integrated and which will enable the data subject to provide/receive such in- and output. Any data transfer from or to the on-token data storage may be controlled (by means of the 'pseudo identity selector' implemented on the

---

[10] CNIL, *21e rapport d'activité 2000*, Paris, CNIL, p.108.

[11] For example, the DPAs of Greece and Belgium.

[12] See ECHR, *S. and Marper v. U.K.*, nos. 30562/04 and 30566/04, 4 December 2008.

[13] Prime, *Prime White paper*, 2008, v.3.0, p. 2, available at https://www.prime-project.eu/prime_products/white_paper/PRIME-Whitepaper-V3.pdf ('Prime White paper ') The text was cited from the *Liberty Alliance Project Whitepaper : Personal Identity*, 23 March 2006, available at http://www.projectliberty.org/liberty/content/view/full/ 340/(offset)/30 .

[14] Compare with the Prime-console, intended to allow the data subjects to manage their personal data (see Prime White paper, pp. 8-9).

[15] See also the so-called 'Identity protector (IP)' mentioned by the Dutch DPA which shall be seen 'as a part of the system that controls the exchange of the user's identity within the information system'. See At Face Value report, p. 62.

token[16]) and needs to be approved by the user through this interface. The interface would also provide for an opportunity to implement a multi-layered information notice to the data subject, enriched with additional information that is required to make the biometric system transparent for the person concerned. A multi-layered information notice is referred to by the Article 29 Working Party in an Opinion on harmonized information provisions in 2004.[17] It would essentially allow controllers to employ a simplified short notice in their user interface, as long as the latter is integrated in a multi-layered information structure, where more detailed information is available, and the total sum of the layers meets national requirements.[18] The additional information could include information about the biometric process, such as confirmation of the use of the verification functionality, the place of storage, error rates, the deletion of copies of biometric characteristics, security measures, and about alternative means in case of failure of the system.

The improved control by the data subject in the TURBINE project, however, would not imply that the data subject can access the protected biometric identity. There is only a 'partial access control' by the data subject: the data subject *holds* the token, *induces* the verification based on the biometric characteristic by presenting the life sample and also because the data subject may *select* an identity.[19]

Various architectures and technical solutions with a user-centric approach other than TURBINE have been developed, tested and used as well.[20]

Other means for control over personal data by the data subject have been suggested. For example, the central storage of biometric data, which can only be accessed after input by the data subject of username with PIN.[21]

---

[16] The token does not merely provide data storage, but also implements intelligent access control for the stored data.

[17] The Article 29 Working Party, Opinion on More Harmonised Information Provisions, 25 November 2004, available at http://ec.europa.eu/justice_home/fsj/privacy/_docs/wpdocs/2004/wp100_en.pdf

[18] More specifically, the Article 29 Working Party envisages that there could be up to three layers of information: (i) the *short notice*, which provides the essential information (and, in view of the circumstances, any additional information necessary to ensure fair processing); (ii) the *condensed notice*, which includes all relevant information required under the Data Protection Directive; and (iii) the *full notice*, which includes all national legal requirements and specificities.

[19] Some also refer to a so-called 'divided control model' when the biometric data and the usage of the device is controlled by the data subject, while the processing itself is controlled by an organisation acting as controller. See E. Kindt and L. Müller (eds.), *D.3.10. Biometrics in identity management*, Frankfurt, Fidis, 2007, 130 p., available at www.fidis.net

[20] For example, Priv-ID, see http://www.priv-id.com/; see also the proof of concept of 'encapsulated biometrics' of the AXS Internet Passport, described in L. Müller and E. Kindt (eds.), D3.14 Model implementation for a user controlled biometric authentication, Frankfurt, Fidis, August 2009, 57 p., available at www.fidis.net

[21] See R. Van Kralingen, C.Prins and J. Grijpink, 'Het lichaam als sleutel', *National Programma Informatietechnologie en Recht*, 8, Alphen aan den Rijn/Diegem, Samsom BedrijfsInformatie Bv, 1997, p. 20. See also e.g., Biermann, H., Bromba, M., Busch, C., Hornung, G. ,Meints, M. and Quiring-Kock, G. (eds.) *White Paper zum Datenschutz in der Biometrie,* 2008, available at http://teletrust.de/fileadmin/files/ag6/Datenschutz-in-der-Biometrie-080521.pdf

In any case, the conditions of a local biometric storage under which the control of the data subject may be effective remain important and need to be reviewed and evaluated on a case by case basis. These conditions are not always clearly specified by the various national Data Protection Authorities[22] and advocates of privacy enhanced biometrics systems who stress the importance of the concept of control by the data subject. Some opinions of the DPAs on same or similar issues are even divergent. At least, one will note that some opinions contain far more detailed requirements in setting out the conditions for the processing of biometric characteristics than others.

2 Other Elements by Design Which Enhance Privacy

Other features, such as the transformation of the data[23], in addition to control by the data subject, however, are also important and needed to protect one's privacy. These elements are in most cases not specified as such in data protection legislation. In order to be effective, the features shall be embedded from the start in the architecture of the biometric system. It is interesting to note that discussions about privacy in the architecture and design of a system in fact refer to a more technical understanding of privacy, such as preventing unintended leakage of information. Particular privacy threats in systems which are mentioned include surveillance (i.e., the monitoring of electronic communications and transactions), the aggregation of information (i.e., the linking of information as related to each other or to a particular subject) and use for profiling, and identification (i.e., connecting information to a person). Privacy protecting concepts in an architecture from a more technical point of view and which are crucial for privacy thus include unlinkability, unobservability, anonymity and pseudonymity.[24] Below, we discuss some of the privacy enhancing technologies developed in TURBINE that supplement control by the data subject.

Issuance of multiple identities and limitation of the ability to link - In theory, a unique human characteristic will give a very similar digital presentation each time the characteristic is used (provided some conditions are fulfilled, such as, for example, the use of the same algorithms and methods). As a result, information from databases which use the same characteristic (and provided the same technologies are used) can be related to one and the same person and can be combined.[25] A privacy-enhancing requirement for biometric systems is therefore the transformation and manipulation of the biometric

---

[22] However, compare with the N°AU-019 of the French DPA, the CNIL, which, in addition to the general legal security requirement, contains supplementary and detailed requirements relating to security for the Unique Authorization (UA) for vein of fingers analysis (Article 6).

[23] Such transformation would not only protect the data but could for example also permit the issuance of multiple revocable identities, as will be discussed below.

[24] See A. Pfitzmann and M. Hansen, Anonymity, Unlinkability, Undetectability, Unobservability, Pseudonymity, and Identity Management – A Consolidated Proposal for Terminology (Version v.0.31 Febr. 15, 2008), available at http://dud.inf.tudresden.de/literatur/Anon_Terminology_v0.31.pdf

[25] This issue is also referred to as the use of biometric data as unique identifiers.

data such that different identities can be issued.[26] The possibility to issue multiple identities is important because it is essential for protecting the privacy of the individuals involved upon the use of their unique human characteristics. This, far from being a trivial requirement is a main topic of research in the TURBINE project.

In addition, further manipulation of biometric data is needed to limit the ability to link identities and the related personal data from different databases. TURBINE develops technology and methods for the limitation of the use of a protected biometric identity *in a specific situation or for a specific service* whilst ensuring that these different identities (and the personal data linked with a specific biometric identity) cannot be linked to each other (excluding the risk of cross-linking). This is done by combining the protected binary identity derived from the captured biometric sample with a service identifier which limits the use of the biometric identity to a specific service context. In this way, and with help of cryptographic techniques, the pseudo identity based on the biometric characteristics is meaningless outside the service context.

Deletion of image and unprotected template - A further privacy enhancement can be achieved by not storing the original image of the biometric characteristic or any intermediate data between the extraction steps and the protected template. The source data and the unprotected template should *always be deleted* after the extraction process for enrolment or comparison. Such deletion does not only apply to the local device (such as e.g., the biometric scanner), but also to all other components of the biometric system. This could also be confirmed to the data subject during the process. Only under this condition can the possible misuse of the image or template, such as the use as a unique identifier for combining all information linked with a specific biometric identity or the use of possible sensitive information contained in the image or template be prevented.

Revocation and re-issuance - Another important feature is the possibility to re-issue a protected biometric identity, in case a previously issued protected biometric identity would be compromised or lost (possibility to revoke). The fact that the biometric characteristics of a person are unique and persistent and can in principle not be changed in case of abuse has always been one major concern for biometric systems. This concern can be overcome if an identity provider could issue more than one biometric identity which can be revoked. This has been researched for some years [27] and several methods for such 'revocable biometrics' have been proposed now. The possibility to revoke a biometric identity is equally tested and demonstrated in TURBINE. For this purpose, the template protection process includes means for the generation of multiple independent protected biometric identities from the same biometric characteristics. The process of generating multiple independent protected identities from the same biometric characteristics is referred to as 'diversification'. The technology developed in TURBINE provides the individual with the option to revoke an identity for

---

[26] Multiple identities combined with accountability is also proposed as a requirement in the Prime White paper for identity management systems in general. See Prime White paper, p. 11. Accountability refers to the possibility to make the link back to the individual if needed.

[27] See, for one of the first publications, N. Ratha, J. Connell, and R. Bolle, 'Enhancing security and privacy in biometrics-based authentication systems' IBM systems Journal, vol. 40, 2001, pp. 614-634.

a given application in case of need. Various privacy advocates and some DPAs have pointed to this important privacy-enhancing aspect for biometric systems.[28]

Protected templates – The biometric identities which satisfy the aforementioned requirements, during storage, transmission and comparison operations, are in TURBINE referred to as 'protected biometric templates' or 'protected templates'.[29] From such templates, it should also *be impossible to reverse engineer (i.e., retrieve or recode)* the original biometric image, features or template, or any derivatives that reveal 'sensitive' information from the biometric sample (such as health related data). A further feature of protected templates is that they allow for the use of pseudonymous identities without revealing the 'real' (in particular, 'civil') identity of the data subject. For this to work on a larger scale, some forms of standardization are required. Efforts to achieve such standardization of some aspects of protected templates are under way.[30]

'Anonymous' access control mechanisms - While biometric characteristics facilitate in essence the identification of person or the verification of an identity or pseudonym, it is not always required that the biometric data are used in such a way. If there is no need for identification or verification of the identity or pseudonym, *'anonymous' access control mechanisms* deploying biometric characteristics stored on the token may be used to manage the authorization of a given person to an area or place.[31] A scheme based on group signatures and encryption allows access for a data subject without verification of the identity. The biometric data stored on the token or card and a local on-card or off-card matching of biometric data allow the cryptographic keys and computational mechanisms stored on the smartcard to be unlocked. The service provider can thus verify whether the anonymous user who accesses the service or place belongs to a group of authorized data subjects. The biometric characteristics are in this case hence not used for the authentication, i.e., the verification of the correct user, but only for the authorization check. Some DPAs have pointed to the need to deploy such mechanisms in case there is no need to check or verify the identity of a person. The Belgian DPA, for example, stated that this way of access control is important in the evaluation of the proportionality of a system.[32] The scheme as

---

[28] See A. Cavoukian and A. Stoianov, Biometric encryption : a positive-sum technology that achieves strong authentication, security and privacy, Privacy Commissioner Ontario, 2007, available at www.ipc.on.ca

[29] About the concept of protected templates, see also U. Korte, J. Merkle, M. Niesing, 'Datenschutzfreundliche Authentisierung mit Fingerabdrücken. Konzeption und Implementierung eines Template Protection Verfahrens – ein Erfahrungsbericht', Datenschutz und Datensicherheit 2009, pp. 289 – 294.

[30] See J. Breebaart, B. Yang, I.Buhan-Dulman, Ch. Busch, 'Biometric Template Protection. The need for open standards' in Datenschutz und Datensicherheit 2009, pp. 299-304.

[31] Compare with the use of anonymous credentials, as set forth in Prime White paper, pp. 10-11.

[32] Commission for the Protection of Privacy, Opinion upon own initiative concerning the processing of biometric data in the framework of the authentication of persons, Opinion N° 17/2008 of 9 April 2008, p. 19.

developed in TURBINE, allows for de-anonymization in case of need (semi-anonymous access control).

Identity management organisation – The overall organisation of a privacy enhanced biometric identity management system is an important topic. First, the roles of the identity and service providers should be clearly defined. It shall also be specified for which components of the biometric system, data and data flows they bear responsibility. This responsibility shall relate in the first place to data protection and compliance in general, including data breach. The access control regarding agents and personnel of the identity provider and service provider to the information stored in the biometric system is therefore an important requirement. Moreover, identity and service providers shall also be responsible for the functioning of the specific components of the biometric system and possible failure. For this reason, they will have an interest to obtain representations and warranties from the manufacturers of the systems.

Another central issue is how the identity or the credentials of an individual shall be established prior to enrolment. The promised enhanced security of biometric systems is only guaranteed if clear agreements are made between the stake holders involved on how individuals need to prove their identity or the necessary credentials. This is especially important in case the biometric identity would be used for authenticating the civil identity.

3 The Proportionality Issue

An important question regarding the legality of the use of biometric systems is whether such a system is proportionate to its purposes. The proportionality requirement refers to a general principle of law, which has its origin in mainly public law.[33] In general, the principle requires a fair balance and reasonable relationship between the means used and the objective(s) sought. To the extent that a chosen application would present privacy and data protection risks for the data subject, the proportionality test requires that the risks of the application do not outweigh the interests and benefits sought by the controller. The proportionality principle is reflected in various articles of the Directive 95/46/EC, including in the provision that states that personal data must be 'adequate, relevant and not excessive in relation to the purposes for which they are collected and/or further processed' (Article 6.1 (c)). If a biometric system allows the deletion of the original image and the unprotected templates and uses protected templates, from which it is in principle not possible to reverse engineer the original biometric image or template, and which do not permit the linkage of data from different databases but allow the issuance of multiple identities, such biometric system is using best efforts for meeting the aforementioned requirement that the system shall use data which are not excessive.

Article 7 of the Directive 95/46/EC contains as a ground for making the data processing legitimate that the processing is necessary for the legitimate interests pursued

---

[33] In public law, the proportionality principle lays some fundamental rules for justifying state interference with the fundamental rights and freedoms of individuals. On the proportionality of biometric systems, see also E. Kindt, 'Biometric applications and the data protection legislation', *Datenschutz und Datensicherheit (DuD)* 2007, pp. 166-170.

by the controller except where such interests are overridden by the interests for fundamental rights and freedoms of the data subject. The risks of using unique identifying human characteristics in automated applications have been described at length in many reports.[34] These risks include the cross-linking of information, the re-use of information for other purposes than those initially envisaged, the use of sensitive information contained in biometric data and the impossibility to re-issue biometric characteristics. If the technological design and subsequent implementation is able to limit (or exclude) most or some of these risks associated with the use of biometric characteristics, the use of such biometric systems for particular objectives will be in a better balance with the aims that are sought. Limiting the risks by one or more 'privacy by design' elements which enhance the privacy of the data subject as described above, could therefore have a positive influence on the evaluation of the interests of the data subject who may have fewer objections against the use by the controller of biometric data for legitimate interests. Finally, the Directive 95/46/EC requires that the processing shall be lawful (Articles 5 and 6.1(a)). The latter implies that the system shall not only comply with the specific data protection requirements, but also that, in conformity with Article 8 of the European Convention on Human Rights and Article 7 and 8 of the Union Charter, it shall be reviewed whether the processing is interfering with the *fundamental rights* to respect for privacy and data protection. If interference remains, it shall be 'necessary in a democratic society'.[35] The necessity can only be proven if one can show that there is a 'pressing social need' to use a biometric system, that the system is 'relevant and sufficient' and that the processing of biometric data is proportional with the legitimate aim. Using privacy enhancing technologies will in our view reduce the interference with fundamental rights and improve the required proportional use. The DPAs who have reviewed biometric systems sometimes require that the security reasons for deploying a biometric system shall be of a more important general nature[36] than the security needs of the controller alone. On the other hand, DPAs have imposed no stringent requirements as to the need to show that a biometric system is relevant and sufficient. With regard to the proportionality review, 'privacy by design' is taken into account by various DPAs in so far that the DPAs have a clear preference that biometric data are not stored in a central data base, but on an object under the control of the data subject. However, many other technical specifications as to how such data which are locally stored may be used, are not provided by most DPAs. The local storage of biometric data on an object under the control of the data subject will in our opinion only be effective if other conditions are fulfilled. These conditions include that even if the biometric data are locally stored, biometric data shall not be copied during enrolment or later comparison in a central database. In addition, the use of protected templates which exclude the possibility of

---

[34] See, for example, J. Goldstein, R. Angeletti, M. Holzbach, D. Konrad, M. Snijder, *Large-scale Biometrics Deployment in Europe : Identifying Challenges and Threats*, P. Rotter (ed.), JRC Scientific and Technical Reports, European Commission JRC – IPTS, Seville, 2008, 135 p ; see also E. Kindt and L. Müller (eds.), *D.3.10. Biometrics in identity management*, Frankfurt, FIDIS, 2007, 130 p.

[35] This comes in addition to the need of some basis in domestic law (which is accessible and foreseeable) and a legitimate aim. These requirements will not be further analysed herein.

[36] For example, the need to secure access to a nuclear power plant is of a more general (public) interest than the interest of the controller alone.

linking information and which permit the issuance of several biometric identities based on the same characteristics should also be considered. Clear information and transparency on how the biometric data is used and processed is also essential, while in some cases more control over the biometric identities should be given to the data subject. Choosing a biometric system whereby the privacy is included in the design combining the discussed privacy-enhancing technologies and features will have a positive effect on the requirement of the proportional use of biometric applications.

Conclusion: Towards Best Practices

The discussion above should further induce the discussion and the formulation of best practices for the privacy friendly processing of biometric data. Best practices are a way of self-regulation which is often promoted by stakeholders of a particular sector. In the past, there have been initiatives promulgating best practices for biometrics, such as the Privacy Best Practices in Deployment of Biometric Systems of the BioVision project.[37] These proposed best practices however need to be reviewed in the light of the advancements of the biometric techniques and should aim in the first place to counter or limit as much as possible the most serious risks involved in the processing of biometric data and which relate to the special nature of biometric data.

The best practices in relation to the development and deployment of a biometric system will in general always depend upon compliance with data protection provisions, including the need for legitimate purposes and interests of the controller to use such system. The processing of biometric data, however, requires further 'best practices'. They would include, from a more general perspective, the deployment of irreversible and unlinkable templates which allow the deletion of the biometric images and unprotected templates. In addition, multiple biometric identities which can be revoked in case of misuse or any other need should be deployed. Moreover, only the verification function of a biometric should be used and the biometric data should be stored in a decentralized way. Additional specific security measures, including deploying cryptographic methods, limited access to any biometric data and a clear deletion policy, should be described as well. With regard to the enhanced rights for the data subjects, data subjects should be entitled to pseudonymity[38] and 'anonymity'[39] upon the use of a biometric system as much as possible. From an organizational and legal point of view, there should be a strict limitation of the use of a biometric system to either a private sector use or a governmental use. Furthermore, the functioning of the biometric system should be transparent for the data subject. This would imply extending the information provision to the data subjects and increasing control rights. They should also receive additional information about the most essential properties of the comparison system and the alternative procedures in case of failure of the system.

---

[37] BioVision, *Privacy Best Practices in Deployment of Biometric Systems,* August 2003, 49 p.

[38] Pseudonymity would in this context mean the right for the data subject to choose a pseudonym biometric identifier which does not allow to identify the data subject directly.

[39] 'Anonymity' in this context would be 'anonymous' comparison whereby the identity of the data subject is not stored or revealed.

Because biometric products and systems are difficult to evaluate as to their technical operation and effects by non-technical persons, such biometric products and systems may need to be reviewed by experts, both IT-experts but also legal experts. This would lead to the certification of the biometric products and systems relating to its privacy-enhancing characteristics and privacy-compliance in a certification program which also take the privacy regulations in a consistent way into account.[40]

Such best practices in combination with certification could render the application of the (sometimes complex) legal regulation more clear. The European Privacy and Data Protection Authorities have called for legislation that will encourage the development and adoption of best practices, including privacy by design.[41] These efforts could finally result in a responsible use of one's biometric data in systems throughout one's life.

Acknowledgements. This paper is based on research in the 7th framework EU project TURBINE supported and funded by the EU Commission and is made possible because of the contributions by all partners to the project (see http://www.turbine-project.eu). The author thanks Koen Simoens of K.U.Leuven, COSIC, Belgium for the review of this paper and his valuable comments. The paper is representing only the author's view and is not binding on TURBINE partners or the European Commission.

---

[40] An example of a European wide certification scheme which provides a privacy trust mark for end-users (but which is not typical for biometric systems) is EuroPriSe. See EuroPriSe, EuroPriSe Criteria, v.1.0, available at https://www.europeanprivacyseal.eu/criteria/ EuroPriSe%20Criteria%20Catalogue%20 public%20version%201.0.pdf

[41] European Privacy and Data Protection Commissioners, Declaration on leadership and the future of data protection in Europe, Edinburgh, 23-24 April 2009, 1 p.

Assuring Privacy of Medical Records in an Open Collaborative Environment - A Case Study of Walloon Region's eHealth Platform

Syed Naqvi, Gautier Dallons, Arnaud Michot, and Christophe Ponsard

Centre of Excellence in Information and Communication Technologies, Belgium
{syed.naqvi,gautier.dallons,arnaud.michot,christophe.ponsard}@cetic.be

Abstract. In many European countries, elderly citizens constitute a growing part of the population. In some countries like Belgium, it is expected to be as high as one third of the population by 2060. Non-traditional high-tech healthcare solutions are therefore indispensable to cope with the shortage of medical and paramedical staff in the future. In this context, several eHealth projects are launched to modernise the public healthcare system and to address the challenges of declining active workforce in the medical domain. The Walloon Region of Belgium is sponsoring an eHealth Platform for the deployment of internet-based technologies for monitoring of patients and exchange of medical records between hospitals and general practitioners. In this paper, we provide an overview of this eHealth platform and report on-going design activities on managing privacy-sensitive medical data by using a context-aware access control model.

Keywords: eHealth, medical records privacy, access control, open collaborative environments, medical ethics.

1 Introduction

Provision of adequate healthcare services to the increasing elderly population in the coming decades has emerged as a great challenge for the policy makers and healthcare professionals. The current ageing trends depict significant increase in the proportion of elderly population worldwide [1]. The situation in Walloon region of Belgium is not different than the rest of the world. According to the estimation of the Belgian National Statistical Institute, the elderly citizens of Walloon region will constitute almost a third of its population by the early second half of the current century [2]. In order to cope with the resulting demographic realities especially the declining active workforce in the medical domain, several technology-based healthcare projects are launched in the country so as to modernise the public healthcare system. In the same context, Walloon regional government is sponsoring an eHealth Platform *Les TIC au Service des Patients* (ICT for Patient Care) for the deployment of internet-based technologies for monitoring of patients and exchange of medical records between hospitals and general practitioners [3]. This paper provides an overview of this platform and

M. Bezzi et al. (Eds.): Privacy and Identity, IFIP AICT 320, pp. 146–159, 2010.

elaborates our work on managing privacy-sensitive medical data over the eHealth platform by using a context-aware access control model.

The set of legal requirements for collecting, storing, and processing of human data is provided in the section 2. Salient features of the eHealth platform are described in the section 3. Section 4 presents a pragmatic analysis of different access control models and evaluation of their suitability for assuring privacy of medical records in the specific context of the eHealth platform. This analysis yields that OrBAC (Organisation-based Access Control) model [4] is the most suitable for deriving access control decisions. The strength of the OrBAC model is therefore highlighted through a real life scenario in the section 5 where access to a patient's medical record is presented in different situations such as a routine visit to general practitioner, medical treatment at a different clinic, and emergency situations. Those also include potential conflict situations and show how to reason in such a situation both at an abstract level (at design time, using model-checking technology) and at a concrete level (at run-time and instance level). This scenario is deployed on an existing OrBAC engine. We show that organisation-based access control policy assures privacy of digital records by granting access to various actors of the eHealth ecosystem. A number of limitations about the design of scalable set of rules are also highlighted.

2 Legal Requirements for Medical Records Confidentiality

Regulations on the processing of personal data assure the legally enforceable rights for data subjects and obligations for those who process personal data. They also set forth penalties for offenders. This legal coverage spans any information (including health related information) concerning an identified or identifiable person. It is extremely important for the technology-based healthcare solutions to fully comply with these regulations as any shortcomings in the design and/or development phases may lead to legal prosecutions.

2.1 European Union Directive 95/46/EC

This directive on the protection of individuals with regard to the processing of personal data and on the free movement of such data [5] sets the foundations of confidentiality as fundamental principles applicable to all forms of electronic communications. Among others, it imposes conditions of *transparency, legitimacy* and *proportionality* for the processing of personal data.

Article 29 Data Protection Working Party. This article defines *working party* on the protection of individuals with regard to the processing of personal data; and recommends specific legislation in member states to regulate the electronic records.

European Union directives are legal bindings on Member States. Their adoption on the Member State level is required for their transposition into national legislation. Following sub-section describes the Belgian law that implements European directive 95/46/EC.

2.2 Belgian Law of 11 December 1998 on Privacy Protection

Article 22 of the Belgian Constitution already guarantees the right of privacy and private communications. Belgium promulgated its Data Protection Act in 1992 to regulate the processing and use of personal information. This legislation was subsequently modified to make it coherent with the European directive 95/46/EC. The definition of *processing* is extended in the new law so as to enlarge the scope of its application to determine the possible processing of special categories of data and to reinforce data subjects' rights.

The collection, storing, and processing of data over the eHealth Platform requires strict adherence to these legislations. The project consortium includes interdisciplinary experts of IT laws to assure the compliance of legal and regulatory issues. Two main requirements are emerging from this law:

1. The access must be compliant with the finality of the collected private data
2. The collected data must be proportional to the finality

Concretely, it means that the access must be as restrictive as possible depending on the access finality. So, the access context has to be considered in order to determine the finality. The context has a direct impact on rights.

3   Walloon Region's eHealth Platform

Walloon region's eHealth Platform *Les TIC au Service des Patients* (ICT for Patient Care) is an ambitious project that aims to deploy state of the art telemedicine technologies and to advance the existing scientific endeavours to better address the imminent future needs of secure distance healthcare systems. First demonstrator of this platform is planned for the first trimester of 2010 whereas the final prototype of this platform is anticipated for 2012. The salient features of this platform include:

- Multi-platforms and multi-modal interfaces and tailored to users' needs. This research area will explore and develop adaptive human machine interfaces. These interfaces will be adaptive to the context of their use and patient's profile.
- Tangible interface adapted to special users. A new mode of interaction with tangible communicating objects will be studied.
- Inference and composition of services. Different types of mechanisms for services composition will be studied, analyzed and enhanced to meet the needs of the eHealth services.
- Communication protocol for medical equipment. Standard communication protocol for the medical equipment will be defined.

- Security Model for medical data. Technical solutions necessary to ensure the protection of personal data such as medical data will be examined.
- Services certification model. The ways and means of ensuring the overall safety of the platform will be investigated.
- Data mining and integration of medical data. Necessary mechanisms will be developed to achieve interoperability of medical data.
- Review of legal constraints. Analysis of legal constraints on data protection and compliance requirements will be conducted.

Figure 1 gives an overview of the various stakeholders of the eHealth platform. The eHealth project aims to provide medical care to different kinds of elderly patients at home. Initially there are three groups of direct beneficiaries of this project. However, this platform can be easily adapted for other types of

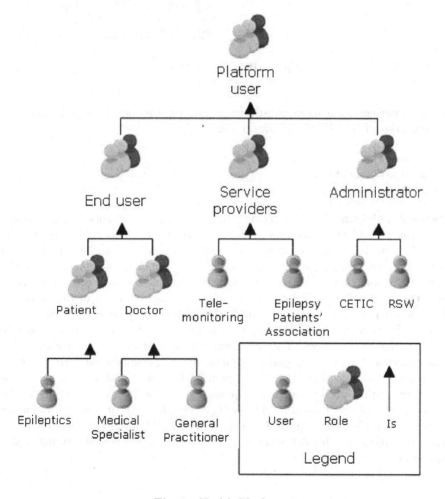

Fig. 1. eHealth Platform

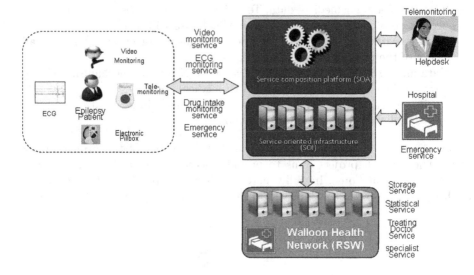

Fig. 2. eHealth Infrastructure

diseases/patients that require distance medical care at their homes. The current beneficiaries of the eHealth platform are:

- Elderly citizens
- Epilepsy patients
- Parkinson patients

Figure 2 highlights the fundamental architectural components of the eHealth platform. This platform will ensure patient care at home through its monitoring of various medical parameters and will provide prevention and adequate intervention on the basis of available medical information of the patient in care. The data generator (such as hospitals) will be responsible for data protection; however they will not be accountable for the security architecture of the platform. The delegation of the security will be bound by the contractual agreements among the participants of the platform in accordance with the compliance to the existing privacy laws. This platform will also ensure better coordination among medical actors (e.g. general practitioners, specialists, laboratories, etc.) paramedics (nurses, physiotherapists, pharmacists, etc.) and nonmedical (dieticians, remote health monitoring companies, etc.) who play specific roles in the management of the patient at home. This eHealth platform will also enable Walloon region's technological SMEs to develop and test new products and services through eHealth pilot scenarios and then at a larger scale by using this platform.

4   State of the Art

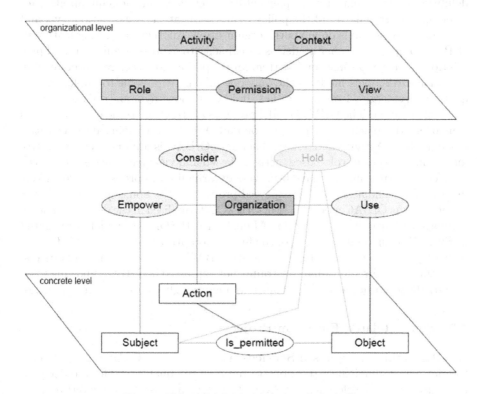

Fig. 3. The OrBAC Model (taken from [16])

4.1   Access Control Models

Access control models are often classified into two broad categories namely Discretionary Access Control (DAC) [6] and Mandatory Access Control (MAC) [7]. Some common implementations of these models include *access control lists (ACLs)* that are considered as the most common mechanism for implementing DAC policies [8]; *Bell-La Padula model* [9] that focuses on data confidentiality and access to classified information; *Chinese wall security policy* [10] that keeps information from one client separated from persons or teams which are working on projects or tasks for a competitor of first client; and *Role-based Access Control (RBAC)* [11].

RBAC is increasingly becoming the de facto access control model for highly scalable networked systems due to its simplified management of authorisation with flexibility in specifying and enforcing enterprise-specific security policies. In the RBAC model, access permissions are administratively associated with roles, and users are administratively made members of appropriate roles. Roles can be granted new permissions as new applications and actions are incorporated, and permissions can be revoked from roles as needed.

We use OrBAC for deriving access control decisions as it allows security policy definition independent of its implementation details by introducing an abstract level [4]. The granularity of the policy definition is at the organisation level and therefore abstraction is done via the organisation. Another interesting feature of OrBAC compared to other models is its capacity to express permissions and prohibitions relative to some context (temporal, spatial, user-declared, prerequisite, provisional)[12]. This model is the only one making it possible to implement requirements emerging from privacy law. Indeed, it allows dynamic right depending on access context. The OrBAC model provides abstraction to the classical access control entities (such as Subject, Action and Object) into organisational entities (such as Role, Activity and View). Therefore OrBAC is a unified access control model that integrates role-based, activity-based and view-based access controls.

Access controls models have been widely formalised in order to perform verification and validation of their expected properties [13]. Some specific work was devoted to the OrBAC model. In [14], OrBAC is formalised in the description logic language with default and exception ALde. In [15], the OrBAC model is translated in Event-B using refinement steps: the first step captures the abstract part of the security policy, the second step introduces OrBAC subjects, actions and objects, and a third step for additional constraints not expressed in OrBAC, allowing to go beyond the limits of the model to cope with increasingly complex security policies.

4.2   Some Related European Projects

OLDES: Older people's e-Services at home. The OLDES project aims to offer new technological solutions to improve the quality of life of older people, through the development of a very low cost and easy to use entertainment and health care platform. OLDES is creating an infrastructure of channels. The project is considering three main categories for care:

1. entertainment and companionship;
2. clinical monitoring;
3. domestic monitoring.

The first category does not correspond with the objectives of the eHealth project; however, the last two categories are inline with the eHealth objectives. We participate in the OLDES project as a consortium member; and the experience gained through this project is a valuable asset for our participation in the eHealth platform.

EPSOS: European Patients Smart Open Services. The EPSOS project is a large scale pilot project with the goal of establishing an interoperable environment for electronic exchange of health information. EPSOS is not a development project in its own right rather it is an implementation quest that aims to facilitate the existing national solutions to communicate with each other enabling secure access to patient health information, particularly with respect to basic patient summaries and ePrescriptions between different European healthcare systems.

EPSOS has the potential of providing an established framework for the integration of our eHealth platform into a European eHealthcare infrastructure where medical records can be securely accessed for treating a Walloon resident travelling abroad or seeking expert opinion of nonlocal medical expert for a medical case study.

CALLIOPE: Call for Interoperability. The Calliope is a European thematic network for eHealth interoperability that aims to create an open forum to support the implementation of interoperable eHealth infrastructures and services across Europe. The network is focusing on a defined set of *Priority Areas* and is already collaborating with the EPSOS project. It is therefore as significant for our eHealth platform as the EPSOS project is.

5 Designing the Access Control Model

5.1 Experimentation Scenario

This scenario illustrates dynamic rights depending on the access finality and context. Figure 4 gives an overview of the case study conceptual model.

- As a general rule, doctors only have access to their speciality if they take care of the patient except in specific contexts.
- In consultations, only physicians who are responsible have access to the relevant part of the record (a cardiologist, the cardiac record, etc.)

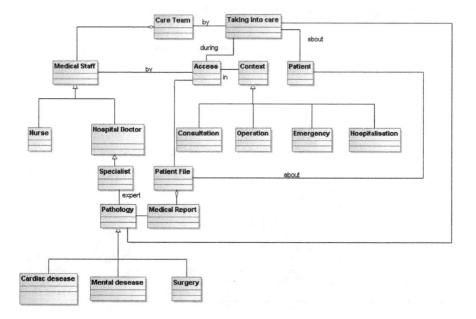

Fig. 4. Conceptual model of the case study

- In operations, the entire care team (including nurses) has access to the record except psychiatric records.
- In any emergency, the whole support team has access to everything.
- In the hospital, only doctors directly involved have access to the entire medical record, except the psychiatric parts.

The invariants, which must be satisfied during the life of the system implementing this scenario, are:

- All medical staff have access to health records in emergency situations.
- The psychiatric record is accessible only to the psychiatrist who takes care of the patient except in an emergency situation.
- The nurses never have access to medical records except in emergency situations or in the operating theatre where doctors are already present.
- Only the doctor who is treating a patient has access to the patient's medical records (partial or total depending on the situation).

5.2 MotOrBAC Implementation

The use case example scenario is implemented by using MotOrBAC [17] as the experimentation engine. The access control policy is expressed in OrBAC. The policy rules are implemented by using separation of constraints and hierarchies. The policy rules contains subjects (medical and paramedical staff); objects (patients records); and actions (read, write).

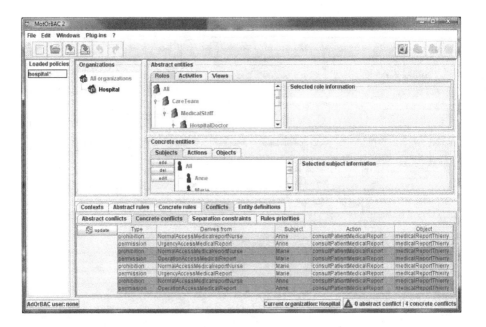

Fig. 5. Implementation of use case scenario in MotOrBAC

MotOrBAC engine identifies the conflicts among the policy rules. In our use case scenario these conflicts are mainly raised due to the expression of both positive and negative privileges in the same set of policy rules. Managing such conflict at the abstract level is advised because it reduces the occurrence of conflict to be dealt with at the concrete level. It will reduce the need of adding several resolution rules at a concrete level which can make the model difficult to maintain in the long term, i.e. when the number of instances grows.

In order to produce an OrBAC model with no or well-identified conflict, we defined a conflict detection and resolution process based on a model formalisation and checks using Alloy.

5.3   Conflict Detection

A conflict occurs when a subject is both permitted and prohibited to carry out a specific action on a particular object in the same context of an organisation. It is especially critical to detect and resolve conflicts at design time to ensure that the behaviour of the policy is adequate. For instance, to ensure that in an emergency situation, medical staff will have access to the necessary information such as surgical information that is not accessible to them in other contexts.

MotOrBAC distinguishes between abstract and concrete conflicts. Abstract conflicts occur between rules, while concrete conflicts involve concrete instances and reflect a concrete situation where the abstract conflict will occur, with reference to particular instances of subjects, objects, roles, context, etc. MotOrBAC is also able to detect abstract conflicts through syntactic analysis, by examining the permission obligation and prohibition of each rule. Abstract conflicts can be made concrete through SAT-solving, through tools such as Alloy [18].

The following model snippet shows a partial formalisation of the medical domain.

```
sig Pathology{}                 // pathology

abstract sig MedicalStaff{}      // medical staff
sig GP, Nurse extends MedicalStaff {}
sig Specialist extends MedicalStaff {
    pathology:Pathology
}
sig Surgeon extends Specialist{}

abstract sig Context{            // context
    team: set MedicalStaff,
    patient: Patient
}
sig Consultation, Emergency extends Context{}

sig Record {}                    // medical records
sig Patient{                     // patient information
    file:Pathology -> lone Record
}
```

```
sig OrbacRule {                    // OrBAC rule
    staff:MedicalStaff,
    patient:Patient,
    context:Context,
    records: set Record
}
```

Some contextual rules are formalised here after for an access in a consultation context and in an emergency context. Additionally, it is also stated that nurses normally have no access.

```
// consultation: only GP or Specialist
fact consultation_staff {
    all c:Consultation, s:c.team | s in GP || s in Specialist
}

// all medical staff have access in emergency situation
fact emergency {
    all c:Emergency, s:MedicalStaff | s in c.team =>
        (one rule:OrbacRule | rule.staff=s && rule.patient=c.patient
                && rule.context=c && rule.records=ran[c.patient.file])
}

// nurse has no access to medical file
fact nurse {
    all n:Nurse | no rule:OrbacRule | rule.context=Consultation && n in rule.staff
}
```

The following consistency check on the model can be run using the tool and will fail to find any model instance due to a conflict. By relaxing the predicate, it appears that the problem is related to the presence of nurse in the team. Actually, in the above formalisation nurses are not allowed to access any patient information.

```
// access in Operation context
pred surgery(p:Patient, c:Operation){
    c.patient=p && some s:Surgeon| s in c.team && some n:Nurse| n in c.team
}
// running the related check
run surgery for 5 but 1 Patient, 1 Operation, 1 Context
```

5.4 Conflict Resolution

Once a conflict is detected, several resolution techniques can be applied:

- OrBAC supports the notion of priority, to denote that one rule has higher importance than another one, and that the later one might be violated in a situation where these two rules conflict with each other.
- Another technique is to weaken one of the conflicting rules to ensure that the precondition of the rule cannot be true at the same time

– The last one is to ensure that the situation that makes the rule conflicting cannot occur, typically by modifying other parts of the model. For instance, one could imagine forbidding administrative staff and medical staff to intersect in order to prevent a conflict between a privacy protecting rule against administrative staff and a medical rule giving access to data to medical staff [19].

To solve the abovementioned conflict, we apply the weakening by explicitly allowing nurse to access in the *Operation* context. The corrected formalisation is the following.

```
fact nurse {
    all n:Nurse | no rule:OrbacRule |  n in rule.staff && rule.context=Consultation
}
```

5.5   Resulting OrBAC Model

OrBAC rules can be directly inferred from the previous model. Some representative rules are the following:

– *Prohibition NormalAccessMedicalreportNurse* for role=*Nurse*, activity=*ConsultMedicalReport*, context=*defaultContext*
– *Permission OperationAccessMedicalReport* for role=*Nurse*, activity=*ConsultMedicalReport*, context=*Operation*
– *Permission ConsultationAccessMedicalReport* for role=*HospitalDoctor*, activity=*ConsultMedicalReport*, context=*Consultation*

The resulting model can then easily be deployed. We can also encode it in the MotOrBAC tool to check about the conflicts at concrete level.

6   Conclusions and Perspectives

Technology-based healthcare solutions such as telemedicine have already been striving for some comprehensible solutions for assuring the privacy of personal data due to the fact that any breach of personal data privacy inflicts irreversible consequences. The emerging technology-based public healthcare systems offer the promising feature of ensuring needful healthcare facilities to the population especially to the increasing proportion of society's elderly population. However, these systems have to be equipped with the adequate security features that can provide privacy assurances to comply with legal obligations.

The eHealth project of the Walloon region of Belgium is an ambitious initiative that aims to address the growing needs of contemporary healthcare practices. In this paper, we presented our proposed solution for assuring privacy of medical records in an internet-based open environment that can handle both routine medical practices and emergency situations.

The current use case scenario does not analyse the privacy concerns of electronic prescribing; however, it is an important area that requires thoughtful consideration especially to assure secure interoperability of the eHealth medical records with its counterparts in other countries/regions. We also plan to work out the security requirements for assuring overall privacy in the advent of integrating the eHealth platform into a European or into some other international Healthcare infrastructure (such as Health-Grid). We also need to investigate the privacy concerns associated with the use of smart devices in the eHealth platform. The security and privacy concerns are exacerbated when these gadgets are deployed in the open networking architectures. The term *internet of things* is recently coined for this paradigm. Our future directions include research on privacy assurance solutions for the eHealth platform composed over the internet of things.

Acknowledgment

The work presented in this paper is carried out in the context of an eHealth project of the Walloon Region, supported by the FEDER - European Union and the Walloon Region under the terms defined in the Convention ECV12020022296F. Part of the underlying research has also received funding from the European Union's seventh framework programme (FP7 2007-2013) Project RESERVOIR under grant agreement number 215605.

References

1. Kinsella, K., He, W.: An Aging World: 2008 - Int. Population Reports (P95/09-01) (June 2009)
2. Belgian National Statistical Institute, http://www.statbel.fgov.be
3. Réseau Santé Wallon, http://www.reseausantewallon.be
4. Abou El Kalam, A., El Baida, R., Balbiani, P., Benferhat, S., Cuppens, F., Deswarte, Y., Miège, A., Saurel, C., Trouessin, G.: Organization Based Access Control. In: Proceedings of the 4th IEEE International Workshop on Policies for Distributed Systems and Networks (Policy 2003), Como, Italia (June 2003)
5. Directive 95/46/EC of the European Parliament and of the Council of October 24, 1995 on the protection of individuals with regard to the processing of personal data and on the free movement of such data, CELEX number 31995L0046, Official Journal L 281, November 23, pp. 0031 - 0050 (1995)
6. Lampson, B.W.: Protection. ACM SIGOPS Operating System Review 8(1), 18–24 (1974)
7. United States Department of Defense, Trusted Computer System Evaluation Criteria (TCSEC), Deaprtment of Defense Standard CSC-STD-00l-83 (August 1983)
8. Ferraiolo, D., Kuhn, D.R., Hu, V.C.: Assessment of Access Control Systems, Technical Report NISTIR 7316, National Institute of Standards and Technology, US Department of Commerce (2006)
9. Bell, D.E., La Padula, L.J.: Secure Computer Systems: Mathematical Foundations, MITRE Corporation Technical Report (1973)
10. Brewer, D.F.C., Nash, M.J.: The Chinese Wall Security Policy. In: IEEE Symposium on Security and Privacy, pp. 206–214 (1989)
11. Sandhu, R.S., Coyne, E.J., Feinstein, H.L., Youman, C.E.: Role-Based Access Control Models. IEEE Computer 29(2), 38–47 (1996)

12. Cuppens, F., Cuppens-Boulahia, N.: Modeling contextual security policies. International Journal of Information Security (IJIS) 7(4) (August 2008)
13. Habib, L., Jaume, M., Morisset, C.: Formal definition and comparison of access control models. Journal of Information Assurance and Security (JIAS), Special Issue on Access Control and Protocols 4(4) , 372–381 (2009)
14. Boustia, N., Mokhtari, A.: Representation and Reasoning on ORBAC: Description Logic with Defaults and Exceptions Approach. In: Proceedings of the 2008 Third international Conference on Availability, Reliability and Security (March 2008)
15. Benaïssa, N., Méry, D.: Proof-based design patterns, final report of the RIMEL project (ANR-06-SETI-015) (August 2008)
16. Miege, A.: Definition d'un environnement formel d'expression de politiques de securite. Modele Or-BAC et extensions' PhD Dissertation in IT Security, Networks and Computer Science Department of ENST Paris (2005)
17. MotOrBAC: An open source implementation of the OrBAC model,
    http://motorbac.sourceforge.net
18. Jackson, D.: Software Abstractions Logic, Language, and Analysis. MIT Press, Cambridge (2006)
19. van Lamsweerde, A., Darimont, R., Letier, E.: Managing Conflicts in Goal-Driven Requirements Engineering. IEEE Transactions on Software Engineering, Special Issue on Managing Inconsistency in Software Development, 908–926 (November 1998)

Goal-Oriented Access Control Model for Ambient Assisted Living

Fabio Massacci and Viet Hung Nguyen

University of Trento, Italy
{fabio.massacci,vhnguyen}@unitn.it

Abstract. Ambient assisted living is a new interdisciplinary field aiming at supporting senior citizens in their home by means of embedded technologies. This domain offer an interesting challenge for providing dependability and security in a privacy-respecting way: in order to provide services in an emergency we cannot monitor on a second-by-second base a senior citizen. Beside being immoral, it would be illegal (at least in Europe). At the same time if we do not get notified of an emergency, the entire system would be useless.

In this paper we present an access control model for this domain that extends RBAC with the notion of organizational model, goals and dependencies. In this model we can associate permission to the objectives that have been assigned to the users of the system and solve the trade-off between security and dependability.

1 Introduction

Ambient assisted living (AAL) [25,24,7] is a home environment enhanced with embedded technologies (sensors, cameras, and similar electronics devices) in order to support elderly people's daily tasks. This raises numerous challenges related not only to technology i.e., interaction between human and smart devices [32,28], but also to the safety and security [22] of the human living in such environments.

From a privacy and security perspective, two kinds of challenges are identified:

- *Dependability*: The life of the elderly people will be at risk if important data are not accessible at the right time;
- *Privacy*: Private data are being delegated from system to system so the privacy of the person is at risk as well.

To protect data privacy, when sensitive data are being processed, the access should be justified by a certain purpose requiring the disclosure of the data. So the authorization to access certain resources is not only based on the entitlement to use a resource, but also on the purpose for which the resources are being used. Such principle is summarized with the phrase: *no purpose, no data*.

In the domain of database this is well understood. In fact, the protection of customer privacy is a legal requirement that any enterprise information system

M. Bezzi et al. (Eds.): Privacy and Identity, IFIP AICT 320, pp. 160–173, 2010.

has to fulfill and enforce. Not surprisingly, many research efforts have proposed new privacy-aware technologies. Among them, Hippocratic databases offer mechanisms for enforcing privacy rules in database systems for inter-organizational business processes [1]. In [20], Massacci et al. extend those mechanisms in order to implement hierarchical purposes, distributed authorizations and minimal disclosure supporting the business processes of virtual organizations. The proposed framework uses a goal-oriented approach to analyze privacy policies of the enterprises involved in a business process.

In contrast, we do not find an equally large number of comprehensive security solutions in the domain of Ambient Assisted Living addressing the issue of purpose. Indeed the solution on the US side is the exact opposite of what EU legislation would mandate: collect all data and the identify sophisticated rules for access control [31]. We could define sum this policy as *collect and protect.* Beside being illegal in the EU this approach has two major scalability problems: at first the complexity of managing the security policies and second and foremost the complexity of managing the actual data.

In general the collection of sensitive data without a specific purpose is illegal in Europe. Data about video surveillance is subject to even stricter regulations. Of course, a company in charge of a smart-home maintenance might try to cover itself by collecting blanket privacy give-aways by its customers but such attempts would be struck down and heavily sanctioned by the privacy commissioner if legally challenged.

As an example in Italy (which has a weaker legislation than Germany) distance monitoring of workers is strictly forbidden and patient monitoring in hospitals is only allowed in special wards (rianimation) and anyhow subject to preliminary approval (Garante della privacy ruling in 2004 [13]):

"Video surveillance equipment should only be activated if other measures (alarm systems, sensors, etc.) are considered to be insufficient and/or unfeasible following a careful analysis. [. . .] Supervision of medical facilities and monitoring of patients hospitalised in certain departments and/or units such as resuscitation units should be limited to the cases in which this is absolutely indispensable on account of the sensitive nature of many data to be possibly collected in this way, by limiting the scope of surveillance to certain premises and well-defined time ranges. "

As it is immediately clear that if even in a resuscitation unit you cannot run a 24/7 monitoring by humans the idea of remote day-by-day monitoring in a home is far beyond what is legally possible, no matter how much consent forms you collect (in the same way that you can't collect signatures of people accepting to be sold in slavery).

Consider just the issue of video monitoring. Even the local provider for elderly and public housing in Trento, a sparsely populated Italian province, has well over 1000 houses, scattered among valleys and mountains (which explains why they are interested in AAL solutions). The cost for getting connectivity, storage, and security protection measures for the wealth of sensor and video streaming of all collectible data would largely exceed the cost of hiring a personal nurse for each of the elderly people in question.

1.1 Contributions of This Paper

We introduce a formal access control model extending RBAC which is called Goal-oriented role based access control (GoRBAC for short). And based on it, we are aiming at limiting the issued authorizations to the permissions needed to fulfil the current goal of the involved actors or sub-systems.

This access control model has been fully implemented and demonstrated in a real smart-home. We present here only the formal aspects of the model and refer to [21] for the details of the demonstration scenario. A video representing the real system is also available on the web (`http:\\www.disi.unitn.it\~massacci`).

In the rest of the paper we present our case study on Ambient Assisted Living (§2). Then we present the formal notion of Organizational Model (§3) and notion of Goal-Oriented Access Control (§4) and its dynamics. Finally we discuss related work (§5) and conclude the paper (§6).

2 The Ambient Assisted Living Scenario

For the demonstration purpose, in our work we consider a typical *eHealth* application where an old man living alone in his smart-house. The house is embedded with different smart-devices (oximeter, camera, and so on) to monitor the person 24/7. It is also able to detect whether he is endangered and sends an emergency alert to the Monitoring and Emergency Response Center (MERC).

In particular, there are three scenarios of the *eHealth* application are taking into account as follows.

Normal Operation: It is the normal situations with usual daily activities.

Emergency: In the second one, the patient feels dizzy and falls down in the kitchen. Moreover, the oximeter reports that his heart rate is too high. According predefined detection rules, it is recognized as an emergency. The smart-home security manager sends an alert message to MERC. MERC access to smart-home (whose security manager has changed the right of access following a suitable pattern) to retrieve his medical data and the snapshot at the falling time as well. When the emergency is confirmed, MERC setups a rescue team and sends it to smart-home. When the rescue team arrives, the smart-home's WSN detects their identity and the security manager send it to MERC for authorization. The rescue team then are correctly authorized by MERC, afterward the smart-home security manager sends a one-time password to MERC who in turn forward it to the rescue team i.e., by SMS. The rescue team use this password to open the smart-home.

Social worker: In the final scenario, the patient is recovered, but he still need some medicine treatment. The medicine are delivered to smart-home by a social worker from the hospital.

These scenarios show a challenge to the smart-home security manager: MERC should be able to collect medical data from his smart house (and also other smart houses). In the meanwhile, to comply with the privacy law, the security

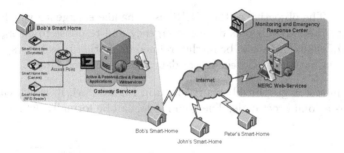

Fig. 1. E-health system infrastructure

Table 1. Security challenges in the scenarios

No.	Scenario	Security challenges
1	Normal Operation	The patient should be monitored 24/7 even if one monitoring device fail. The collected information should not be accessed from outside even the MERC. No one could not enter the house with out the patient's agreement.
2	Emergency	MERC should be able to access the sensors' data. The rescue team are allowed to open the door and accessed medical data for a proper pre-treatment. These permissions are temporarily granted, and should be revoked when the emergency ends.
3	Social worker	The social worker can open the door if the patient could not do this, but the social worker should not be able to access patient's medical information when he is in the house.

manager should not not let data out until it serves some purposes. These security challenges are summarized in Table 1. The basic infrastructure of a such system is depicted in Figure 1.

3   A Goal-Oriented Organizational Model

The organizational model proposed here is based on the security-requirements engineering methodologies presented in [14] for socio-technical systems. The original model has been simplified by restricting it to functional goals and adapting it to the security notion of roles instead of using the notion of actors. Simplification was necessary also because the original work was focussing on requirements engineering where a rich set of construct is a feature while here we need to make extremely fast run-time decisions.

A *goal model* consists of a set of *goals* and their relationships. Goals are recursively decomposed until they arrive to concrete *operational goals* (*operations* for short) which could be directly assigned to human or software components to in order to be achieved. We consider a simple way to decompose goals which is the *means-end* decomposition. This relationship shows that the *end goal* is obtained if the *means goals* are achieved.

Example 1. The objective of the MERC is to handle emergency which is can be refined into the two subgoals detect emergency and response to emergency. The detection of emergencies can be further refined in another possible ways to detect the urgent situations as Collect sensor data, Analyze sensor data.

The goal model is graphically represented in Figure 2(a), in which each goal is denoted as a round rectangle. The goal model can be formally defined as follow.

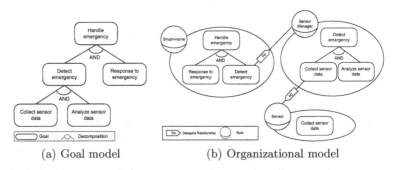

(a) Goal model   (b) Organizational model

Fig. 2. A portion of goal model (a) and corresponding organizational model (b) of the case study

Definition 1. *A goal model is a triplet* $\langle G, Dc, OP \rangle$, *in which G: is a set of goals representing stakeholder objectives and requirements.* $Dc \subseteq G \times 2^G$: *is a set of one-to-many Means-End-decompositions which constitutes an acyclic relations.* $OP \subset G$: *is a set of operational goals which can be fulfilled directly by actors.*

In comparison with the original goal model in [14] the notion of AND-decomposition of goals has been collapsed into the means end-decomposition, and we do not explicitly represent OR-decomposition as it is captured by different means-end decomposition of the same goal.

While this might be strictly less precise (as decomposition it is not the same as means-end), it greatly simplifies the cognitive overhead of policy writers and the run-time efficiency of enforcement.

An *organizational model* is constructed by adding to a goal model, a set of roles, the hierarchy among roles and the assignments of goals to roles. Loosely speaking a role is an abstract characterization of the behavior of a socio-technical actor within the domain. Loosely speaking GoRBAC roles corresponds to RBAC roles with goals on top. The assignment schemes include the goals-to-roles assignments and the goals' decompositions to roles assignments.

Example 2. We add three roles to the goal model described in Figure 2(a): Smart-Home, Sensor Manager, Sensor. The goal-to-role assignment and delegation relationship are depicted in Figure 2(b).

Definition 2. *An organizational model,* $\mathcal{M}$, *is tuple of* $\langle \mathcal{M}^G, R, \mathcal{A}_{G \times R}, \mathcal{A}_{Dc \times R}, De \rangle$, *where* $\mathcal{M}^G$: *is a goal model. R: is a set of role.* $\mathcal{A}_{G \times R} \subseteq G \times R$: *is an assignment of* *goals to roles.* $\mathcal{A}_{Dc \times R} \subseteq Dc \times R$: *is an assignment of goal decompositions to roles.* $De \subseteq \{R \times G \times R\}$: *is set of dependency relations in which one role can depend on another role to fulfill certain goal.*

The assignment of goals to roles is an obligation, that means the agent playing that role must satisfy all its assigned goals. A goal can be assigned to different roles and vice versa. Once a role is in charge of a certain goal, it can satisfy this goal if this goal is a concrete operation, or decompose this goal into other subgoals, or delegate it to another role. Different roles might choose different way to fulfill and thus refine the goals. This explains why we needed to associate the particular assignment of goal decompositions to roles.

  Goals, goal decompositions assigned to a particular role and available delegation relations that originate from this role are called *role model.*

Definition 3. *Given a role r, a role model is the tuple* $\langle \mathcal{A}^r_{G \times R}, \mathcal{A}^r_{Dc \times R}, De^r \rangle$ *where* $\mathcal{A}^r_{G \times R}, \mathcal{A}^r_{Dc \times R}$ *and* De^r *are, respectively, set of goals, set of decompositions and set of delegation assigned to r.*

Goals can be decomposed in many ways but we must be sure that agents in charge of their fulfillment can actually do something in order to achieve them. In other words, the human or the the system playing a role can decide either to satisfy the goal itself, or delegate some subtask to other role.

Definition 4. *An organizational model,* $\mathcal{M}$ *and a role r and a goal g assigned to r the goal g is* actionable *for r if*

- $g \in OP$ *is a concrete operation, or*
- *there exists* $\langle g, S_G \rangle \in \mathcal{A}^r_{Dc \times R}$ *and for all goals* $g' \in S_G$, *either* g' *is actionable or there exists a role r' and a delegation* $\langle r, g', r' \rangle \in De^r$ *such that* g' *is actionable for r'.*

Example 3. In Figure 2(b), the role configuration of **Sensor Manager** includes three goals, one decomposition and one delegation. **Analyze sensor data** is a concrete operation performed by **Sensor Manager**, and **Collect sensor data** is delegated to **Sensor**. Thus, these two goals are actionable, and **Detect emergency** is actionable as well. Therefore, this role configuration is actionable.

Since roles are not physical entities, goals are actually satisfied by *agents* (or principals) which are actors with concrete, physical manifestation such as human individuals or machines.

Remark 1. We prefer to use the notion of agents rather then the common term *users* because the intuitive understanding of users in this scenario is that they corresponds to human beings. Agents in this setting can be either human or software agents in the same sense that Alice and Bob in security protocols are often just dramatis personae for actual software processes running the protocols.

The configuration also defines the assignment of agents to each role.

Definition 5. *Given an organizational model $\mathcal{M}$, an organizational configuration $\mathcal{M}^C$ is a tuple of $\langle \mathcal{A}^c_{G \times R}, \mathcal{A}^c_{Dc \times R}, De^c, A, \mathcal{A}_{A \times R} \rangle$, where $\mathcal{A}^c_{G \times R}$ is an assignment of goals to roles, $\mathcal{A}^c_{Dc \times R}$ is an assignment of decompositions to roles, De^c is set of delegation among actors, A is a set of agents, $\mathcal{A}_{A \times R}$ is an assignment of agents to roles. The following properties hold:*

1. $\mathcal{A}^c_{G \times R} \in \mathcal{A}_{G \times R}$, $\mathcal{A}^c_{Dc \times R} \in \mathcal{A}_{Dc \times R}$, $De^c \in De$, $\mathcal{A}_{A \times R} \subseteq A \times R$;
2. *For each role $r \in R$, r has an actionable configuration within $\mathcal{M}^C$.*

In other words we require that the current assignments of roles to agents is such that all goals can be fulfilled. So an agent playing a certain role r might delegate something to another role r' but the system must be sure that there is actually some agent that can play the latter role r'.

This is only a necessary and not a sufficient condition for success: operations might fail in practice or other agents might fail to deliver. Upon notification of failures or successful achievements, the run-time system must make sure that the appropriate configurations are selected.

An organizational model can have many configurations. The one currently considered by the run-time system is the *active configuration*.

4   Goal Oriented RBAC

So far we have only defined the functional goals of the system and not yet introduced the notion of permissions. The main idea behind GoRBAC is to strengthen (and weaken at the same time) a traditional RBAC access control decision using the organizational model. In fact, the grant of a permission to access an object is not an end per se but it is a mean to achieve a goal.

As in traditional RBAC, we want to ensure that only authorized users are allowed to access the resources. However, different strategies can be used for defining when and how these authorizations are issued.

- *Privacy*: the main issue for the privacy strategy is to ensure that the *privacy-critical resources* are accessed only by authorized agents when needed. This strategy implements the principle "no purpose no data". The definition 6 clarifies the meaning of the purpose of an operation in our model.
- *Dependability*: in a dependability context, the system aims to maximize the probability of successful fulfillment of the critical goals. The derived permissions are generated once the user is authorized the fulfillment the top-level goal. In particular, if a service have different decompositions, we derive permissions for all of them in order to increase the availability of the service.

Definition 6. *Given an organizational model $\mathcal{M}$ and its active configuration $\mathcal{M}^C$, the purpose of an operation is a set of goals which satisfy follows:*

$$Purpose(op) = \{op\} \cup \{g \in G \,|\, \exists g_1 \in Purpose(op), \exists S_G \subset 2^G, \exists r \in R$$
$$\langle \langle g_1, S_G \rangle, r \rangle \in \mathcal{A}'_{Dc \times R} \wedge g \in S_G\}$$

We give a simplified version of the traditional RBAC as defined in [26].

Definition 7. *RBAC model is a tuple* $\langle U, R, OP, P, \mathcal{A}_{U \times R}, \mathcal{A}_{P \times R} \rangle$ *where A is a set of agents, R is set of roles,* $\mathcal{A}_{A \times R}$ *is a agent-to-role assignment,* $P \subseteq OP$ *is a set of permissible operations (or permissions).* $\mathcal{A}_{P \times R} \subseteq P \times R$ *is a many-to-many permission-to-role assignment relation.*

The traditional RBAC distinguishes between operations and objects, and then pairs them into permissions. In the AAL setting such distinction is not always useful. There are operations that requires simultaneous access to a number of objects and can be better understood by users if explained at this level of details.

Example 4. Access to patient data requires to have access to the positioning information of the camera and the oximeter readings. Turning-on the camera is a simple operation from the point of view of the user but at the software level is a complex operation that requires access to a number of objects starting from the IP address to the camera.

This definition can be extended as usual with hierarchies and sessions(see[26]).

The set of authorizations which constraints whether an user u is able to do an operation op is defined as follows:

$$\mathcal{A}_{RBAC} = \{\langle u, op \rangle \mid \exists r \in R. \langle u, r \rangle \in \mathcal{A}_{A \times R} \wedge \langle op, r \rangle \in \mathcal{A}_{P \times R}\} \qquad (1)$$

We define the GoRBAC as an extension of RBAC as follows.

Definition 8. *A GoRBAC Model is a tuple* $\langle RBAC, \mathcal{M}, \mathcal{G}, \mathcal{M}^c, \mathcal{P} \rangle$, *where RBAC is the RBAC model,* $\mathcal{M}$ *is the organizational model,* $\mathcal{G} \subset G$ *is a set of critical goals and* $\mathcal{P} \subset P$ *is a set of privacy sensitives permissions,* $\mathcal{M}^c$ *is the active configuration of the organizational model.*

The following property must also hold: For each $\langle g, r \rangle \in \mathcal{A}_{G \times R}$, *if an operation op has a purpose g then it is assigned to r.*

The permission of performing an operation op is granted to an agent a if:

1. if the operation op serves for the satisfaction of a critical goal a is fulfilling.
2. else if the secure object is privacy sensitive then this operation should serves for the satisfaction of a goal which a is fulfilling and a is authorized to access this object regard to the security policy in RBAC model.
3. else a is authorized regard to the security policy in RBAC model.

To this end, beside the GoRBAC model, the runtime security management maintains a record describing the active agents and their fulfilling goals at runtime. We call this record *runtime configuration* defined as follow:

Definition 9. *Given an active configuration,* $\mathcal{M}^c$, *of a system. The runtime configuration of the system is defined as a triplet* $\langle \mathcal{A}^*_{A \times R}, \mathcal{A}^*_{G \times A}, De^* \rangle$, *where*

- $\mathcal{A}^*_{A \times R} \subseteq \mathcal{A}^c_{A \times R}$ *is an active agent-to-role assignment,*
- $\mathcal{A}^*_{G \times A} \subseteq \mathcal{A}^c_{G \times A}$ *is an active goal-to-agent assignment,*

Table 2. List of basic events updating the runtime configuration

Event	Actions
$Add\_agent(a)$	–
$Activate\_role(a,r)$	**CHECK** $\langle a,r \rangle \in \mathcal{A}^c_{A \times R}$ **DO** $\mathcal{A}^*_{A \times R} \leftarrow \mathcal{A}^*_{A \times R} \cup \{\langle a,r \rangle\}$
$Activate\_goal(a,g)$	**CHECK** $\exists r \in R. \langle g,r \rangle \in \mathcal{A}^c_{G \times R} \wedge \langle g,r \rangle$ *is able to activate* $\wedge$ $\{a,r\} \in \mathcal{A}^*_{A \times R}$ **DO** $\mathcal{A}^*_{G \times A} \leftarrow \mathcal{A}^*_{G \times A} \cup \{\langle g,a \rangle\}$
$Delegate(a_1,g,a_2)$	**CHECK** $\exists r_1, r_2 \in R. \langle a_1, r_1 \rangle \in \mathcal{A}^*_{A \times R} \wedge \langle a_2, r_2 \rangle \in \mathcal{A}^*_{A \times R} \wedge$ $\langle g,a_1 \rangle \in \mathcal{A}^*_{G \times A} \wedge \langle r_1, g, r_2 \rangle \in De'$ **DO** $\mathcal{A}^*_{G \times A} \leftarrow \mathcal{A}^*_{G \times A} \cup \{\langle g,a_2 \rangle\}$ $De^* \leftarrow De^* \cup \{\langle a_1, g, a_2 \rangle\}$
$Goal\_Fulfilled(a,g)$	**CHECK** $\langle g,a \rangle \in \mathcal{A}^*_{G \times A}$ **DO** Deactivate g **DO** Propagate the fulfillment to parent goals related to g and update accordingly their fulfilment and active status.
$Goal\_Failed(a,g)$	**CHECK** $\langle g,a \rangle \in \mathcal{A}^*_{G \times A}$ **DO** Deactivate g **DO** Check the fulfillment status of the other parent goals of g in the active configuration and update accordingly their fulfilment and active status.
$Deactivate\_Role(a,r)$	**CHECK** $\langle a,r \rangle \in \mathcal{A}^*_{A \times R}$ **DO** $\mathcal{A}^*_{A \times R} \leftarrow \mathcal{A}^*_{A \times R} \setminus \{\langle a,r \rangle\}$ $\forall g \in G. \langle g,a \rangle \in \mathcal{A}^*_{G \times A} \wedge \langle g,r \rangle \in \mathcal{A}'_{G \times R}$, deactivate the child goals of g in the active configuration.
$Undelegate(a_1,g,a_2)$	**CHECK** $\langle a_1, g, a_2 \rangle \in De^* \wedge \langle g,a_1 \rangle \in \mathcal{A}^*_{G \times A} \wedge \langle g,a_2 \rangle \in \mathcal{A}^*_{G \times A}$ **DO** $De^* \leftarrow De^* \setminus \{\langle a_1, g, a_2 \rangle\}$ **DO** Deactivate g and its child goals in the active configuration. **DO** Unfulfill the child goals of g in the active configuration.

– $De^* = A \times G \times A$ *is a set of active delegation relationships among agents. The following property should be valid.*

$$\langle a_1, g, a_2 \rangle \in De^* \rightarrow \exists r_1, r_2 \in R. \{\langle a_1, r_1 \rangle, \langle a_2, r_2 \rangle\} \subseteq \mathcal{A}^c_{A \times R} \wedge \langle r_1, g, r_2 \rangle \in De^c$$

The runtime security management maintains the runtime configuration and modifies it with respect to events. The Table 2 presents the basic events that the security manager takes into account for updating the runtime configuration.

The security request $\langle a, op \rangle$ is granted if and only if:

$$\langle a, op \rangle \text{ is granted} \begin{cases} \text{if } \exists g \in \mathcal{G}.g \in Purpose(op) \text{ and } \langle g,a \rangle \in \mathcal{A}^*_{G \times A} \\ \text{elseif } ; op \in \mathcal{P} \text{ and } \langle g,a \rangle \in \mathcal{A}^*_{G \times A} \text{ and } \langle a,op \rangle \in \mathcal{A}_{RBAC} \\ \text{elseif } \langle a,op \rangle \in \mathcal{A}_{RBAC} \end{cases}$$

In this way the fulfillment of critical goals always override whatever setting of permission needed to accomplish the task at hand. This is an absolute require-ments for emergency services. For example, in many medical authorization sys-tem, a red button "Night shift", when only few doctors are present, is present to override any normal authorization process. Obviously, logging procedures might be put in place to monitor such events.

Example 5. In an emergency context, authenticating the rescue team against the smart home is considered as a critical goal. We can imagine different authentication mechanisms providing different levels of robustness. The most robust mechanism could be defined as the default one but if we are missing some resources to fulfill it, the system will activate any other available mechanism.

At the same time, if the data is privacy sensitive you do not want it to be accessed unless there is some purpose that has been actually assigned to the user requesting the permission.

Example 6. The medical data of the patient is considered as privacy sensitive resource. Therefore, the access to it is regulated by the "no purpose no data" principle. The social worker is allowed to access it only if it is playing rescue team member role during an emergency context.

For normal authorizations we fall back to the standard RBAC authorization. At this point a genuine conflict might arise: the user might be assigned by the organization a goal which he cannot fulfill. This happens frequently in daily life. However, since the goal is not critical for the organization, we can as well afford the time to let the user go back to the system administrator and solve the problem with the required care.

Example 7. During an ordinary check on the patient status, only his doctor is allowed to access his data.

5   Related Works

In our case, the security requirements of the system concern the access to the resource available in AAL environment. Traditionally, the access control policy is defined as a list of permissions that is statically defined at design time [11,26,16,4,23]. For RBAC, once a role is activated at runtime, all related permissions are also activated. Using a hierarchy of roles, we can limit the set of permissions that are activated at the same time but still any subject S playing a role R is entitled to use all the related permissions no matter if it needs them or not for its current activities.

Moyer and Abamad have proposed a Generalized access control model (G-RBAC) [23]. GRBAC introduces new concepts such as subject roles, object roles and environment roles. Subject roles are like traditional RBAC roles, object roles abstract the various properties of objects, and environment roles capture environmental information, such as time of day. All these meta-information about objects and subjects introduced through these new concepts increase the expressiveness of the RBAC model, allow a fine access control decision and a more flexible access control scheme.

RBAC constraints [2,5,8] are essentially used to enforce higher level organization security policy such as LP and SoD principles . These constraints can be related to user-role assignment, role-permission assignment or to some runtime context conditions [10,18]. In this last case, even if the user is entitled to access a certain resource, the actual authorization is given only after checking the related constraints. From an administration point of view, the usage of constraints is fundamental for enforcing higher level security or privacy requirements but it also increases complexity of maintenance related activities.

OrBAC [15] and Multi-OrBAC [16]. OrBAC introduces context as a new entity to specify the circumstances in which the organization grants permissions on objects. In Multi-OrBAC, each role and permission is valid in a specific organization. This model is more adapted to distributed and heterogeneous systems.

dRBAC (Distributed RBAC)[12] has been proposed as an access control framework for Dynamic Coalition Environments. It is intended to be decentralized trust-management and access-control mechanism for systems that span multiple administrative domains.

All these frameworks are interesting and appropriate in their application domains. However, none of them compare issued permissions against the real needs of the user from a functional point of view. This issue is fully delegated to administrators off-line. At runtime, the system checks if the request satisfies more or less sophisticated conditions of some stored permissions in order to grant the access. So any user can dispose of all their privileges even if they are not needed for the current activity they are performing.

Active security models for access control are those defining the permissions at workflows and operations level [29]. They defined Conceptual Foundations for a Model of operation-based Authorizations. The permissions in these models are associated to the activity of the system and this constraint is expressed in terms of an association between access operation and workflow activity.

T-RBAC (Temporal RBAC) has been introduced by Bertino et a. in [4]. It addresses the dynamic aspects related to periodic activations and deactivations of roles, and temporal dependencies among these actions actions.

For systems dealing with privacy sensitive data, different privacy frameworks and languages have been proposed to specify the privacy requirements and enforce them at runtime. Among work centered on the notion of purpose, LeFevre et al. [19] enhance Hippocratic databases with mechanisms enforcing queries to respect privacy policies stated by an enterprise and customer preferences. In essence, they propose to enforce the minimal disclosure principle by providing mechanisms to data owners that control who can access their personal data and for which purpose.

To support the negotiation of private information, the World Wide Web Consortium (W3C) proposed the Platform for Privacy Preferences (P3P) [9]. This standard provides mechanisms that allow customers to check web site privacy policies before they disclose their personal data to the site. Another mechanism for negotiation is presented by Tumer et al. [30]. Enterprises specify which information is mandatory for achieving a service and which is optional, while customers specify the type of access for each part of their personal information

Mechanisms for enforcements are proposed by Karjoth et al. [3,17]. The Enterprise Privacy Authorization Language (EPAL) [3] enables an enterprise to exactly formalize the privacy policies that shall be enforced within the enterprise itself. However, these proposals do not provide mechanisms for enforcing the minimal disclosure principle. In Byun et al. [6], the Role-Based Access Control model is extended by introducing the notion of purpose and a purpose management model. Similarly to our approach, they introduce purpose hierarchies in order to reason on access control. However, their hierarchies are based on the principles of generalization and specialization and are not expressive enough to support complex strategies defined by enterprises.

A policy itself may be sensitive because from the analysis of the disclosed policies an unauthorized user may infer sensitive information. Following this observation, some approaches propose to protect not only personal information, but also policies themselves [27].

We would like to evaluate GoRBAC against other RBAC based access control frameworks that have been cited in this section. We analyze the pros and cons of the cited RBAC extensions against two criteria :1) the least privilege principle and 2) AC policy management.

– Least Privilege principle: the comparison is based on the more or less constraints introduced by the new model with regard to the RBAc model.

  Example 8. For example, GoRBAC add an additional condition to be verified before grating the access. In fact, the model states that having the permission to access a resource, is a necessary but not sufficient condition. In addition the access request should be justified by the current responsibilities assigned to the requester. Thus GoRBAC enforces more the least privilege compared to RBAC.

– AC Policy management: the comparison is based on the complexity of specifying the policy rules and the granularity of the policy with regard to the real system operations.

  Example 9. In GoRBAC, the access control policy is specified at organizational level and it is based on the responsibilities assigned to the different roles inside the organization. The fine-grained access control policy related to every operations and every object in the system is derived automatically. Thus, we are clearly facilitating the tasks for the security administrators.

6   Conclusions

To sum-up this paper we have presented a novel access control model, GoRBAC, which take into account the purpose of operations. The model is based on the notion of organizational model in order to implement the notion of "no purpose, no data" behind data access. To verify to model in experiment, we also developed a prototype [21] implementing the case study discussed in section 2. In that work, we deployed the prototype in the real environment, Smart-Home at Trento, and conducted the experiments with the scenarios presented in Section2.

References

1. Agrawal, R., Kiernan, J., Srikant, R., Xu, Y.: Hippocratic Databases. In: Proc. of VLDB 2002, pp. 143–154 (2002)
2. Ahn, G.-J., Sandhu, R.: Role-based authorization constraints specification. TISSEC 3(4), 207–226 (2000)
3. Backes, M., Pfitzmann, B., Schunter, M.: A Toolkit for Managing Enterprise Privacy Policies. In: Snekkenes, E., Gollmann, D. (eds.) ESORICS 2003. LNCS, vol. 2808, pp. 162–180. Springer, Heidelberg (2003)
4. Bertino, E., Bonatti, P.A., Ferrari, E.: TRBAC: A temporal role-based access control model. TISSEC 4(3), 191–233 (2001)
5. Bertino, E., Ferrari, E., Atluri, V.: The specification and enforcement of authorization constraints in workflow management systems. TISSEC 2(1), 65–104 (1999)
6. Byun, J.-W., Bertino, E., Li, N.: Purpose Based Access Control of Complex Data for Privacy Protection. In: Proc. of SACMAT 2005, pp. 102–110. ACM Press, New York (2005)
7. Cook, D.J., Das, S.K.: How smart are our environments? an updated look at the state of the art. Pervasive Mob. Comput. 3(2), 53–73 (2007)
8. Crampton, J.: Specifying and enforcing constraints in role-based access control. In: Proc. of SACMAT 2003, pp. 43–50. ACM Press, New York (2003)
9. Cranor, L., Langheinrich, M., Marchiori, M., Reagle, J.: The Platform for Privacy Preferences 1.0 (P3P1.0) Specification. W3C Recommendation (April 2002)
10. Damiani, M.L., Bertino, E., Catania, B., Perlasca, P.: Geo-rbac: A spatially aware rbac. ACM Trans. Inf. Syst. Secur. 10(1), 2 (2007)
11. Ferraiolo, D., Kuhn, D.: Role Based Access Control. In: 15th National Computer Security Conference (1992)
12. Freudenthal, E., Pesin, T., Port, L., Keenan, E., Karamcheti, V.: dRBAC: distributed role-based access control for dynamic coalition environments. In: Proc. of ICDCS 2002, pp. 411–420. IEEE Press, Los Alamitos (2002)
13. Garante per la protezione dei dati personali. Video surveillance - the general provision adopted by the garante. Official Bullettin 49 (April 2004), http://www.garanteprivacy.it/garante/doc.jsp?ID=1116810
14. Giorgini, P., Massacci, F., Mylopoulos, J., Zannone, N.: Requirements Engineering for Trust Management: Model, Methodology, and Reasoning. Int. J. of Inform. Sec. 5(4), 257–274 (2006)
15. Kalam, A.A.E., Baida, R.E., Balbiani, P., Benfrhat, S., Cuppens, F., Deswarte, Y., Miege, A., Saurel, C., Trouessin, G.: Organization Based Access Control. In: 4th International Workshop on Policies for Distributed Systems and Networks, Policy 2003 (2003)
16. Kalam, A.A.E., Deswarte, Y.: Multi-OrBAC: a New Access Control Model for Distributed, Heterogeneous and Collaborative Systems. In: 8th IEEE International Symposium on Systems and Information Security (2006)
17. Karjoth, G., Schunter, M., Waidner, M.: Platform for Enterprise Privacy Practices: Privacy-enabled Management of Customer Data. In: Dingledine, R., Syverson, P.F. (eds.) PET 2002. LNCS, vol. 2482, pp. 69–84. Springer, Heidelberg (2003)
18. Kulkarni, D., Tripathi, A.: Context-aware role-based access control in pervasive computing systems. In: SACMAT 2008: Proceedings of the 13th ACM symposium on Access control models and technologies, pp. 113–122. ACM, New York (2008)
19. LeFevre, K., Agrawal, R., Ercegovac, V., Ramakrishnan, R., Xu, Y., DeWitt, D.J.: Limiting Disclosure in Hippocratic Databases. In: Proc. of VLDB 2004, pp. 108–119. Morgan Kaufmann, San Francisco (2004)

20. Massacci, F., Mylopoulos, J., Zannone, N.: Hierarchical Hippocratic Databases with Minimal Disclosure for Virtual Organizations. VLDB J. 15(4), 370–387 (2006)
21. Massacci, F., Nguyen, V.H., Saidane, A.: No purpose, no data: Goal-oriented access control for ambient assisted living. In: CCS 2009 Workshop on SPIMACS (2009)
22. Moncrieff, S., Venkatesh, S., West, G.: Privacy and the access of information in a smart house environment. In: Proc. 15th of MULTIMEDIA 2007, pp. 671–680. ACM, New York (2007)
23. Moyer, M., Abamad, M.: Generalized role-based access control. In: ICDCS 2001: Proceedings of the The 21st International Conference on Distributed Computing Systems, Washington, DC, USA, p. 391. IEEE Computer Society, Los Alamitos (2001)
24. Nehmer, J., Becker, M., Karshmer, A., Lamm, R.: Living assistance systems: an ambient intelligence approach. In: ICSE 2006: Proceedings of the 28th international conference on Software engineering, pp. 43–50. ACM, New York (2006)
25. Pigot, H., Mayers, A., Giroux, S.: The intelligent habitat and everyday life activity support. In: 5th Int. Conf. on Simulations in Biomedicine, pp. 507–516 (2003)
26. Sandhu, R.S., Coyne, E.J., Feinstein, H.L., Youman, C.E.: Role-based access control models. IEEE Computer 29(2), 38–47 (1996)
27. Seamons, K.E., Winslett, M., Yu, T., Yu, L., Jarvis, R.: Protecting Privacy during On-line Trust Negotiation. In: Dingledine, R., Syverson, P.F. (eds.) PET 2002. LNCS, vol. 2482, pp. 129–143. Springer, Heidelberg (2003)
28. Stelios, M.A., Nick, A.D., Effie, M.T., Dimitris, K.M., Thomopoulos, S.C.A.: An indoor localization platform for ambient assisted living using uwb. In: MoMM 2008: Proceedings of the 6th International Conference on Advances in Mobile Computing and Multimedia, pp. 178–182. ACM, New York (2008)
29. Thomas, R.K., Sandhu, R.S.: Task-based authorization controls (tbac): A family of models for active and enterprise-oriented autorization management. In: Proc. of the IFIP TC11 WG11.3 11th Int. Conf. on Database Security, London, UK, pp. 166–181. Chapman & Hall, Ltd., Boca Raton (1998)
30. Tumer, A., Dogac, A., Toroslu, H.: A Semantic based Privacy Framework for Web Services. In: Proc. of ESSW 2003 (2003)
31. Wang, Q., Shin, W., Liu, X., Zeng, Z., Oh, C., Alshebli, B.K., Caccamno, M., Gunter, C.A., Gunter, E.L., Hou, J., Karahalios, K., Sha, L.: 1-living: An open system architecture for assisted living. IEEE International Conference on Systems, Man, and Cybernetics, SMC (2006)
32. Xie, D., Yan, T., Ganesan, D., Hanson, A.: Design and implementation of a dual-camera wireless sensor network for object retrieval. In: IPSN 2008: Proceedings of the 7th international conference on Information processing in sensor networks, Washington, DC, USA, pp. 469–480. IEEE Computer Society, Los Alamitos (2008)

Privacy of Outsourced Data

Sabrina De Capitani di Vimercati and Sara Foresti

Dipartimento di Tecnologie dell'Informazione
Università degli Studi di Milano
Via Bramante 65 - 26013 Crema, Italy
firstname.lastname@unimi.it

Abstract. Data outsourced to an external storage server are usually encrypted since there is the common assumption that all data are equally
sensitive. The encrypted data however cannot be efficiently queried and
their selective release is not possible or require the application of specific
solutions. To overcome these problems, new proposals have been recently
developed, which are based on a fragmentation technique possibly combined with encryption. The main advantage of these proposals is that
they limit the use of encryption, thus improving query execution efficiency. In this paper, we describe such fragmentation-based approaches
focusing in particular on the different data fragmentation models proposed in the literature. We then conclude the paper with a discussion on
some research directions.

1 Introduction

Data outsourcing is emerging today as a successful paradigm allowing individuals and organizations to exploit external services for storing, managing, and
distributing huge collections of possibly sensitive data. Within a data outsourcing architecture, data are stored together with application front-ends at the
sites of an external server who takes full charges of their management. Although
publishing data on external servers may increase service availability, reducing
data owners' burden of managing data, it introduces new privacy and security
concerns. As a matter of fact, the outsourced data are no more under the control of their data owners and therefore their privacy as well as their integrity
may be put at risk. The protection of the privacy of the data is however of
paramount importance and is becoming an emerging problem as it is also tes-
tified by a number of recent regulations that require organizations to provide
privacy guarantees when storing, processing, and sharing sensitive information
(e.g., California Senate Bill 1386 and the Personal Data Protection code - legislative decree no. 196/2003). Existing approaches (e.g., [1,2,3,4]) for protecting
the privacy of outsourced data assume that an overlying layer of encryption is
applied on the data before outsourcing them, which implies that the outsourced
data cannot be efficiently queried and that a selective release (i.e., different pieces
of information to different parties) is either not possible or require the application of specific solutions based on two layers of encryption [5,6]. Recently, novel

M. Bezzi et al. (Eds.): Privacy and Identity, IFIP AICT 320, pp. 174–187, 2010.

proposals have been developed, where encryption is not mandatory for ensuring protection [7,8,9]. This introduces a paradigm shift that permits to address the protection issue with a different perspective, thus giving the possibility of designing novel models and techniques where the use of encryption is minimized or is absented. These proposals are based on the observation that often what is sensitive is the association among data more than the data per se. For instance, in a hospital the list of illnesses cured and the list of hospitalized patients could be made publicly available, since what is sensitive is the association of a specific illness to a patient. Although this association must be protected, it is not necessary to encrypt both the list of illnesses and the list of hospitalized patients; it is sufficient to prevent their joint visibility to non authorized users.

In this paper, we illustrate recent proposals for protecting outsourced data that are based on the use of fragmentation possibly combined with encryption. The remainder of this paper is organized as follows. Section 2 introduces the basic scenario and concepts on which all the fragmentation-based proposals rely on. Section 3 describes an approach based on the combination of fragmentation and encryption and where the outsourced data are stored at two non-communicating pair of servers. Section 4 presents an approach where again fragmentation and encryption are used in combination and where outsourced data can be fragmented among multiple unlinkable fragments. Section 5 illustrates a proposal that departs from encryption and where a small portion of the data is stored at the data owner side. Section 6 presents some open issues for the considered scenario. Finally, Section 7 concludes the paper.

2   Scenario and Basic Assumptions

We consider the problem of outsourcing data while preserving their privacy. Current approaches in the literature assume that a single relation r over relational schema $R(a_1, \ldots, a_n)$, with a_i an attribute on domain $D_i, i = 1, \ldots, n$, contains all sensitive information that needs to be protected [7,8,9]. Note however that the techniques that will be described in the following can also work with other data models. The privacy requirements are instead modeled through *confidentiality constraints*. A confidentiality constraint c over a relational schema $R(a_1, \ldots, a_n)$ is a subset of attributes in R^1 ($c \subseteq R$) meaning that for each tuple in r, the (joint) visibility of the values of the attributes in c is considered sensitive and must be protected. While simple, the definition of confidentiality constraints captures different protection requirements. In particular, depending on the attributes involved, confidentiality constraints can be classified in the following two categories.

- *Singleton constraints*. A singleton constraint states that the *values* assumed by the attribute in the constraint are considered sensitive and cannot be released (e.g., the SSN of the patients in a hospital is considered sensitive).

---

[1] When clear from the context R is used to denote either the relation schema R or the set of attributes in R.

PATIENT

SSN	Name	DoB	ZIP	Job	Illness	Physician
123-45-6789	A. Perry	75/12/22	22030	Nurse	Pneumonia	H. Daily
987-65-4321	B. Pott	71/03/18	22045	Employee	Diabetes	I. Dale
246-89-1357	C. Powal	65/06/14	22021	Manager	Hypertension	J. Dooley
135-79-2468	D. Prately	51/09/30	22030	Cook	Flu	K. Davis
753-19-8642	E. Preston	42/08/06	22041	Nurse	Gastritis	L. Denis
864-29-7531	F. Pickett	82/10/07	22020	Nurse	Flu	M. Dicks
264-81-5773	G. Pyne	68/04/24	22045	Employee	Pneumonia	N. Doe

$c_0 = \{\texttt{SSN}\}$
$c_1 = \{\texttt{Name, DoB}\}$
$c_2 = \{\texttt{Name, ZIP}\}$
$c_3 = \{\texttt{Name, Illness}\}$
$c_4 = \{\texttt{Name, Physician}\}$
$c_5 = \{\texttt{DoB, ZIP, Illness}\}$
$c_6 = \{\texttt{DoB, ZIP, Physician}\}$
$c_7 = \{\texttt{Job, Illness}\}$
$c_8 = \{\texttt{Job, Physician}\}$

(a)   (b)

Fig. 1. An example of relation (a) and of well defined constraints over it (b)

- *Association constraints.* An association constraint states that the *association* among the values of the attributes in the constraint is considered sensitive and cannot be released (e.g., the association of the name of patients with their illnesses must be protected).

Since the satisfaction of a confidentiality constraint c_i implies the satisfaction of any constraint c_j such that $c_i \subseteq c_j$, a set $\mathcal{C} = \{c_1, \ldots, c_m\}$ of confidentiality constraints is supposed to be *well defined*, that is, $\forall c_i, c_j \in \mathcal{C}, i \neq j, c_i \not\subseteq c_j$.

Example 1. Figure 1 illustrates an example of relation (PATIENT) along with a set of well defined confidentiality constraints, modeling the following privacy requirements:

- the list of SSNs of patients is considered sensitive (c_0);
- the association of patients' names with any other information in the relation but the job is considered sensitive ($c_1, \ldots, c_4$);
- attributes DoB and ZIP can work as a quasi-identifier [10] and therefore can be exploited to infer the identity of patients; their associations with both Illness and Physician are then considered sensitive (c_5 and c_6);
- the association between Job and Illness and the association between Job and Physician are considered sensitive (c_7 and c_8).

Note also that the association of patients' Name and SSN is sensitive and should be protected. However, such a constraint is redundant, because SSN has been declared sensitive (c_0): protecting SSN as an individual attribute implies automatic protection of its associations with any other attribute.

Given a relation r over schema $R(a_1, \ldots, a_n)$ and a set $\mathcal{C}$ of confidentiality constraints over R, the goal is to outsource the content of r in such a way that the sensitive associations represented as confidentiality constraints are protected. The approaches proposed in the literature for addressing such a problem are typically based on a possible combination between *fragmentation* and *encoding* techniques. Fragmentation consists in partitioning the attributes in R in different subsets (fragments), which are then outsourced in place of R. Formally, a fragment F_i of a relation R is defined as a subset of the attributes in R ($F_i \subseteq R$), while a *fragmentation* $\mathcal{F}$ is a set of fragments over R (i.e., $\mathcal{F} = \{F_1, \ldots, F_m\}$). The set of tuples of relation r over R projected on the attributes in F_i is a *fragment instance* over F_i. Intuitively, fragmentation protects sensitive associations by breaking them. Encoding means that the values of some attributes are obfuscated to make them readable only by authorized users. Although different encoding techniques can be adopted [7], we only consider *encryption* as an encoding technique. The approaches in the literature then differs in how the original relational schema R is fragmented to avoid the joint visibility of attributes involved in constraints and in how and whether encryption is used. In particular, existing approaches for enforcing confidentiality constraints can be partitioned into three different categories:

- *non-communicating pair of servers*, when R is partitioned into two fragments stored on two non-communicating servers and encryption (or another encoding technique) is used for protecting attributes when they cannot be stored in the two fragments without violating the constraints;
- *multiple fragments*, when R is partitioned into two or more disjoint fragments, possibly stored on the same server, and encryption is used within each fragment for maintaining in encrypted form all attributes not appearing in the clear;
- *departing from encryption*, when R is partitioned into two fragments, one stored at the data owner site and the other one stored at the external server. The two fragments can be joined by authorized users only and encryption is not used.

In the following, we present these three different strategies in more details. The discussion will focus on the different techniques that can be used to compute a fragmentation that satisfies the privacy requirements. The interested reader can refer to [11] for a detailed discussion on additional issues that arise in the data outsourcing scenario.

3   Non-communicating Pair of Servers

The first proposal suggesting the use of fragmentation and encryption for outsourcing data while enforcing a set of confidentiality constraints has been presented in [7]. The basic idea consists in partitioning the original relational schema R into two fragments stored on two non-communicating servers, which do not know each other, thus preventing the joint visibility of attributes in the two fragments. We now describe the data fragmentation model and briefly illustrate how to compute a fragmentation.

3.1   Data Fragmentation Model

A relational schema R is partitioned into two fragments F_1 and F_2 stored at two non-communicating servers in such a way that the attributes involved in a confidentiality constraint cannot appear all together in a fragment. An encoding technique is used whenever an attribute cannot be stored within one of the two fragments without violating a confidentiality constraint. The encoding of an attribute $a \in R$ consists in representing the values of the attribute with two different attributes a^1 and a^2 included in the two fragments F_1 and F_2, respectively. The values of attribute a can then be reconstructed only by authorized parties opportunely combining the values of the two corresponding attributes a^1 and a^2. For instance, if attribute a is encrypted, then a^1 may contain the encrypted values of a and a^2 may contain the key(s) used for encrypting the values of attribute a. A fragmentation $\mathcal{F}$ is then defined as a triple $\langle F_1, F_2, E \rangle$, where E is the set of encoded attributes stored at both servers (i.e., $E \subseteq F_1$ and $E \subseteq F_2$) and $R = F_1 \cup F_2$. A fragmentation $\mathcal{F}$ is correct if $\forall c \in \mathcal{C}$ conditions $c \nsubseteq F_1$ and $c \nsubseteq F_2$ are both satisfied. At the physical level, a fragmentation $\mathcal{F} = \langle F_1, F_2, E \rangle$, with $F_1 = \{a_{1_1}, \ldots, a_{1_n}\}$, $F_2 = \{a_{2_1}, \ldots, a_{2_m}\}$, and $E = \{a_{e_1}, \ldots, a_{e_l}\}$ translates into two physical fragments with schema $F_1^e = \{\underline{\text{tid}}, a_{e_1}^1, \ldots, a_{e_l}^1, a_{1_1}, \ldots, a_{1_n}\}$ and $F_2^e = \{\underline{\text{tid}}, a_{e_1}^2, \ldots, a_{e_l}^2, a_{2_1}, \ldots, a_{2_m}\}$, respectively. Attribute tid is the primary key of both physical fragments and guarantees the *lossless join* property. The lossless join property guarantees that the content of the original relation r over R cal always be reconstructed through the join between the fragment instances over F_1^e and F_2^e. The join operation may be performed on the common attribute tid that can be either: *1)* the key attribute of R, if it is not sensitive, or *2)* an attribute that is added to both F_1^e and F_2^e during the fragmentation process, otherwise.

With this model, singleton constraints can only be satisfied by encoding the attributes in the constraints. Association constraints can instead be satisfied either by splitting the attributes in the constraints between F_1 and F_2, or by encoding at least one of the attributes in the constraints. Note however that it is not always possible to satisfy an association constraint via fragmentation. As a matter of fact, since there are only two fragments it may happen that the attributes involved in an association constraint cannot be split between the two fragments without violating another constraint. In these cases, it is necessary to apply an encoding technique on one of the attributes involved in the constraint.

Example 2. Consider relation PATIENT in Figure 1(a) and the set of well defined constraints over it in Figure 1(b). Suppose also that encryption is used as an encoding technique. Figure 2 illustrates the fragment instances over the physical fragments corresponding to the correct fragmentation $\mathcal{F} = \langle\{$DoB, Illness, Physician$\}, \{$DoB, ZIP, Job$\}, \{$SSN, Name$\}\rangle$. For simplicity, in this figure both encrypted values and corresponding keys are represented with Greek letters. Note that attribute DoB can be replicated without violating any constraint, thus improving query performance. Singleton constraint c_0 is enforced by encrypting attribute SSN. Association constraints $c_1, \ldots, c_4$ are satisfied by encrypting attribute Name. Finally, association constraints $c_5, \ldots, c_8$ are satisfied by fragmenting the involved attributes.

3.2   Minimal Fragmentation

Given a relational schema R and a set of well defined constraints $\mathcal{C}$ over it, there may exist different correct fragmentations. For instance, a fragmentation that encodes all attributes in R is always correct. However, such a fragmentation implies a higher query evaluation cost for authorized users than a fragmentation

F_1^e | | | | | F_2^e | | | | |

tid	SSN[1]	Name[1]	DoB	Illness	Physician	tid	SSN[2]	Name[1]	DoB	ZIP	Job
1	α	ϑ	75/12/22	Pneumonia	H. Daily	1	o	τ	75/12/22	22030	Nurse
2	β	ι	71/03/18	Diabetes	I. Dale	2	π	υ	71/03/18	22045	Employee
3	γ	κ	65/06/14	Hypertension	J. Dooley	3	ϖ	ϕ	65/06/14	22021	Manager
4	δ	λ	51/09/30	Flu	K. Davis	4	ρ	φ	51/09/30	22030	Cook
5	ε	μ	42/08/06	Gastritis	L. Denis	5	ϱ	χ	42/08/06	22041	Nurse
6	ζ	ν	82/10/07	Flu	M. Dicks	6	σ	ψ	82/10/07	22020	Nurse
7	η	ξ	68/04/24	Pneumonia	N. Doe	7	ς	ω	68/04/24	22045	Employee

Fig. 2. An example of a correct fragmentation in the non-communicating pair of servers scenario

that minimizes the use of encoding and that resorts to fragmentation whenever possible. The query evaluation cost can be measured in different ways. In [7] the authors adopt an *affinity matrix*, which is a matrix with a row and a column for each attribute in R. Each entry $M[a_i, a_j]$, with $i \neq j$, represents the cost that would be paid in query execution if attributes a_i and a_j do not belong to the same fragment. Each entry $M[a_i, a_i]$, with $i = 1, \ldots, n$, represents the cost that would be paid if attribute a_i is encoded. The cost of a fragmentation $\mathcal{F}$ is then defined as the sum of the cells $M[a_i, a_j]$ in the matrix such that $a_i \in F_1$ and $a_j \in F_2$, and the cells $M[a_i, a_i]$ in the matrix such that $a_i \in E$.

The problem of computing a fragmentation with minimum cost is NP-hard since, as proved in [7], the hypergraph coloring problem [12] reduces to it. As a consequence, an algorithm that computes a fragmentation with minimum cost would operate in time exponential with the number of attributes in R. To avoid this inconvenience, in [7] the authors propose to combine known approximation algorithms used for solving the min-cut and the weighted set cover problems, obtaining three different heuristics working in polynomial time.

4   Multiple Fragments

The main problem of the approach illustrated in Section 3 is that it is based on the complete absence of communication among the storage servers (which have to be completely unaware of each other). This assumption is however difficult to enforce in practice and a collusion among the servers, or with an authorized user of the system, can breach the privacy of the data. The solution proposed in [8], and refined in [13,14], removes the need of having two non-communicating pair of servers. Like for the previous solution, we first describe the data fragmentation model and then illustrate how to compute a fragmentation.

4.1   Data Fragmentation Model

The proposal illustrated in [8] uses fragmentation and encryption for enforcing a set $\mathcal{C}$ of confidentiality constraints defined over a relational schema R and produces a set of fragments. The resulting fragments can be stored on the same server since they cannot be joined for reconstructing the content of the original relation. A fragmentation $\mathcal{F} = \{F_1 \ldots F_n\}$ is therefore considered *correct* if the following conditions hold: *1)* $\forall c \in \mathcal{C}, \forall F \in \mathcal{F}, c \not\subseteq F$; *2)* $\forall F_i, F_j \in \mathcal{F}, i \neq j$, $F_i \cap F_j = \emptyset$. Condition 1 states that a single fragment cannot contain in the clear attributes that form a confidentiality constraint. Condition 2 states that the fragments are disjoint. At the physical level, a fragmentation $\mathcal{F} = \{F_1 \ldots F_n\}$, with $F_i = \{a_{i_1}, \ldots, a_{i_m}\}$, $i = 1, \ldots, n$, translates into a set of physical fragments F_i^e, $i = 1, \ldots, n$. Each physical fragment F_i^e contains all the attributes in F_i in the clear, while all the other attributes of R are encrypted. The reason for reporting all attributes of R (in either encrypted or clear form) in each of the physical fragment is to guarantee that any query can be executed by querying a single physical fragment. Formally, the schema of a physical fragment F_i^e corresponding to fragment $F_i = \{a_{i_1}, \ldots, a_{i_m}\}$ is $F_i^e(\underline{salt}, enc, a_{i_1}, \ldots, a_{i_m})$ where:

- *salt* is the primary key of F_i^e and contains a randomly chosen value;
- *enc* contains the encryption of all the attributes of R that do not belong to the fragment (i.e. R - F_i), combined before encryption in a binary XOR ($\oplus$) with a salt;
- $a_{i_1}, \ldots, a_{i_n}$ correspond to the attributes in fragment F_i.

Note that to protect encrypted values from frequency-based attacks [15], a salt is applied on each encryption. Attribute *salt* of a physical fragment stores such values that due to their randomness can also be used as primary keys.

Singleton constraints can only be satisfied by encryption, that is, by preventing attributes in singleton constraints to appear in the clear within a fragment. Association constraints can be satisfied by storing the attributes composing the constraint in different fragments. This is always possible because if an attribute cannot be inserted in an existing fragment without violating a confidentiality constraint, then a new fragment can be created and the attribute can be inserted in it. In this way, we *maximizes the visibility* of the data since encryption is used only for protecting singleton constraints. A fragmentation $\mathcal{F}$ that satisfies all the confidentiality constraints and that maximizes data visibility is a fragmentation where each attribute that does not appear in singleton constraints belongs to *exactly* one fragment in $\mathcal{F}$. Clearly, a solution maximizing visibility permits a more efficient query evaluation.

Example 3. Consider relation PATIENT in Figure 1(a) and the set of constraints over it in Figure 1(b). An example of a correct fragmentation that maximizes visibility is $\mathcal{F} = \{\{\text{Name, Job}\}, \{\text{DoB, ZIP}\}, \{\text{Illness, Physician}\}\}$. Figure 3 illustrates the fragment instances over the physical fragments corresponding to $\mathcal{F}$. Note that only attribute SSN does not appear in the clear in the fragments since it belongs to a singleton constraint (c_0).

4.2   Minimal Fragmentation

Given a relational schema R and a set $\mathcal{C}$ of well defined constraints over it, there may exist different correct fragmentations that maximize visibility. As an example, a fragmentation $\mathcal{F}$ composed of singleton fragments, one for each attribute that does not appear in a singleton constraint is a correct fragmentation. Such

F_1^e				F_2^e				F_3^e			
salt	enc	Name	Job	salt	enc	DoB	ZIP	salt	enc	Illness	Physician
s_1^1	α	A. Perry	Nurse	s_1^2	ϑ	75/12/22	22030	s_1^3	τ	Pneumonia	H. Daily
s_2^1	β	B. Pott	Employee	s_2^2	ι	71/03/18	22045	s_2^3	υ	Diabetes	I. Dale
s_3^1	γ	C. Powal	Manager	s_3^2	κ	65/06/14	22021	s_3^3	ϕ	Hypertension	J. Dooley
s_4^1	δ	D. Prately	Cook	s_4^2	λ	51/09/30	22030	s_4^3	φ	Flu	K. Davis
s_5^1	ε	E. Preston	Nurse	s_5^2	μ	42/08/06	22041	s_5^3	χ	Gastritis	L. Denis
s_6^1	ζ	F. Pickett	Nurse	s_6^2	ν	82/10/07	22020	s_6^3	ψ	Flu	M. Dicks
s_7^1	η	G. Pyne	Employee	s_7^2	ξ	68/04/24	22045	s_7^3	ω	Pneumonia	N. Doe

Fig. 3. An example of a correct fragmentation in the multiple fragments scenario

a fragmentation however makes query execution inefficient. As a matter of fact, queries defined on more than one attribute can be executed only with the involvement of the client. Like for the non communicating pair of servers scenario, it is important to identify, among all the correct fragmentations maximizing visibility, the one that minimizes the cost of query execution for the client. To this purpose, there are different metrics that can be adopted for measuring the quality of a fragmentation. A simple metric is the *number of fragments* composing a fragmentation $\mathcal{F}$ [8]. The rationale is that a low number of fragments implies that more attributes are stored in the clear in the same fragment, thus improving the efficiency in query execution. The problem of computing a fragmentation that minimizes the number of fragments is however NP-hard (the hypergraph coloring problem [12] reduces to this problem). To the aim of efficiently computing a correct fragmentation with a limited, even if not minimum, number of fragments, in [8] the authors introduce a definition of *minimality* that is based on the representation of a correct fragmentation that maximize visibility through a *fragment vector*. Given a fragmentation $\mathcal{F}=\{F_1,\ldots,F_m\}$ of a relational schema R, the fragment vector $V_{\mathcal{F}}$ representing $\mathcal{F}$ is a vector with an element $V_{\mathcal{F}}[a]$ for each attribute a in $\bigcup_{i=1}^m F_i$, where $V_{\mathcal{F}}[a]$ is set to F if attribute a belongs to fragment F.

Example 4. Consider fragmentation $\mathcal{F}=\{\{\texttt{Name, Job}\}, \{\texttt{DoB, ZIP}\}, \{\texttt{Illness, Physician}\}\}$ in Figure 3. The fragment vector representing $\mathcal{F}$ is defined as follows.

- $V_{\mathcal{F}}[\texttt{Name}] = V_{\mathcal{F}}[\texttt{Job}] = \{\texttt{Name, Job}\}$;
- $V_{\mathcal{F}}[\texttt{DoB}] = V_{\mathcal{F}}[\texttt{ZIP}] = \{\texttt{DoB, ZIP}\}$;
- $V_{\mathcal{F}}[\texttt{Illness}] = V_{\mathcal{F}}[\texttt{Physician}] = \{\texttt{Illness, Physician}\}$.

Fragment vectors define a partial order relationship, denoted $\preceq$, among the correct fragmentations maximizing visibility of a relational schema R with respect to a set $\mathcal{C}$ of well defined constraints. In particular, a fragmentation $\mathcal{F}'$ *dominates* $\mathcal{F}$, denoted $\mathcal{F}\preceq\mathcal{F}'$, iff $V_{\mathcal{F}}[a]\subseteq V_{\mathcal{F}'}[a]$, for all attributes in R that do not belong to singleton constraints. Also, $\mathcal{F}\prec\mathcal{F}'$ iff $\mathcal{F}\preceq\mathcal{F}'$ and $\mathcal{F} \neq \mathcal{F}'$. In other words, a fragmentation $\mathcal{F}'$ dominates a fragmentation $\mathcal{F}$ if $\mathcal{F}'$ can be obtained by merging two (or more) fragments in $\mathcal{F}$.

Example 5. Consider relation PATIENT in Figure 1(a), the set of constraints over it in Figure 1(b), and the following two correct fragmentations that maximize visibility: $\mathcal{F}_1=\{\{\texttt{Name, Job}\}, \{\texttt{DoB, ZIP}\}, \{\texttt{Illness, Physician}\}\}$ and

$\mathcal{F}_2 = \{\{\texttt{Name}\}, \{\texttt{Job}\}, \{\texttt{DoB, ZIP}\}, \{\texttt{Illness, Physician}\}\}$. Since $\mathcal{F}_1$ can be obtained by merging fragments $\{\texttt{Name}\}$ and $\{\texttt{Job}\}$ in $\mathcal{F}_2$, $\mathcal{F}_2 \preceq \mathcal{F}_1$.

The problem of computing a fragmentation with a minimal number of fragments consists then in computing a fragmentation $\mathcal{F}$ that maximizes visibility and such that there is not a fragmentation $\mathcal{F}'$ maximizing visibility and correctly enforcing $\mathcal{C}$, such that $\mathcal{F} \prec \mathcal{F}'$. The algorithm proposed in [8] to solve this problem operates in $O(n^2 \cdot m)$, where n is the number of attributes in R, while m is the number of non singleton constraints in $\mathcal{C}$.

Alternative metrics that provide a more precise measure on the quality of a fragmentation are based on the use of an affinity matrix [13] or on the definition of a specific cost function that models the cost of evaluating a set of representative queries on $\mathcal{F}$ [14]. It is interesting to note that both the affinity matrix in [13] and the cost function in [14] are monotonic with respect to the dominance relationship $\preceq$. This means that the quality of a fragmentation increases with the increase of the the number of attributes represented in the clear in the fragmentation. In [14] the authors exploit this property and propose an exact algorithm for computing a fragmentation with minimum cost, which avoids to visit the whole space of solutions by exploiting relation $\preceq$ and the monotonicity of the cost function.

5   Departing from Encryption

A significant advantage of the solution based on multiple fragments is that it uses encryption only for protecting attributes involved in singleton constraints. However, the efficiency of query execution is still a problem since encryption causes a computational overhead for the client when executes a query, and for the data owner in key management. In [9,16] the authors put forward the idea of completely departing from encryption. The proposed solution is based on the assumption that the data owner is willing to store a small portion of the data to guarantee the enforcement of confidentiality constraints.

5.1   Data Fragmentation Model

The proposal illustrated in [9] assumes that a subset of the data are stored at the data owner side, while the remaining information is outsourced to an external storage server. The input of the problem is still a relational schema R and a set $\mathcal{C}$ of confidentiality constraints defined over R. The result of the fragmentation process is a pair $\mathcal{F} = \langle F_o, F_s \rangle$ of fragments, where F_o is stored at the data owner side and F_s is stored at the storage server. A fragmentation $\mathcal{F}$ is considered *correct* if fragment F_s does not violate any constraint in $\mathcal{C}$ (i.e., $\forall c \in \mathcal{C}$ condition $c \not\subseteq F_s$ is satisfied) and all attributes of R appear in at least one fragment to avoid loss of information. Note that fragment F_o could possibly violate constraints, since it is stored at the data owner side that is supposed to be trusted and accessible only by authorized users. The solution in [9] also assumes that even if the data owner is willing to store a portion of the data,

	F_o^e					F_s^e		
tid	SSN	Name	ZIP	Job	tid	DoB	Illness	Physician
1	123-45-6789	A. Perry	22030	Nurse	1	75/12/22	Pneumonia	H. Daily
2	987-65-4321	B. Pott	22045	Employee	2	71/03/18	Diabetes	I. Dale
3	246-89-1357	C. Powal	22021	Manager	3	65/06/14	Hypertension	J. Dooley
4	135-79-2468	D. Prately	22030	Cook	4	51/09/30	Flu	K. Davis
5	753-19-8642	E. Preston	22041	Nurse	5	42/08/06	Gastritis	L. Denis
6	864-29-7531	F. Pickett	22020	Nurse	6	82/10/07	Flu	M. Dicks
7	264-81-5773	G. Pyne	22045	Employee	7	68/04/24	Pneumonia	N. Doe

Fig. 4. An example of a correct fragmentation in the departing from encryption scenario

her storage capacity is limited. A first consequence of this assumption is that the information should not be replicated in the two fragments F_o and F_s. In other words, fragments F_o and F_s should be disjoint to avoid replication of attributes already stored at the server side also at the data owner side. The only attributes that the two fragments have in common is an identifier that is needed to guarantee the lossless join property. Such an identifier can correspond to the primary key of R, if it is not sensitive, or an attribute that does not belong to the relational schema R and that is added to both the fragments during the fragmentation process, otherwise. At the physical level, a fragmentation $\mathcal{F} = \langle F_o, F_s \rangle$, with $F_o = \{a_{o_1}, \ldots . a_{o_i}\}$ and $F_s = \{a_{s_1}, \ldots . a_{s_j}\}$ translates into two physical fragments $F_o^e(\underline{\mathtt{tid}}, a_{o_1}, \ldots . a_{o_i})$ and $F_s^e(\underline{\mathtt{tid}}, a_{s_1}, \ldots . a_{s_j})$, respectively, where $\mathtt{tid}$ is the common identifier.

Since data are only partially outsourced and data are not encrypted, singleton constraints can only be satisfied by storing the involved attributes at the data owner side. Also, association constraints can be satisfied only by fragmentation, that is, by storing at least one of the attributes in the constraint at the data owner side. Note that, in this case, all the constraints can be enforced by fragmentation, even if $\mathcal{F}$ is composed of two fragments only since F_o is supposed to be stored at a trusted party.

Example 6. Consider relation PATIENT in Figure 1(a) and the set of well defined constraints over it in Figure 1(b). An example of a correct fragmentation is $F_o=\{\mathtt{SSN}, \mathtt{Name}, \mathtt{ZIP}, \mathtt{Job}\}$ and $F_s=\{\mathtt{DoB}, \mathtt{Illness}, \mathtt{Physician}\}$. Figure 4 illustrates the fragment instances over the physical fragments corresponding to F_o and F_s. Constraint c_0 is satisfied by storing attribute $\mathtt{SSN}$ in F_o. Constraints $c_1, \ldots, c_4$ are satisfied by storing attribute $\mathtt{Name}$ in F_o. Constraints c_5 and c_6 are satisfied by storing attribute $\mathtt{ZIP}$ in F_o. Constraints c_7 and c_8 are satisfied by storing attribute $\mathtt{Job}$ in F_o.

5.2 Minimal Fragmentation

Similarly to previous approaches, given a relational schema R and a set of well defined constraints $\mathcal{C}$ over it, there may exist different fragmentations that are correct and non-redundant. For instance, a fragmentation where $F_o=R$ is obviously correct but it coincides with no outsourcing. Among all possible correct fragmentations, it is necessary to compute a solution that reduces either the storage at the data owner side, or the data owner's intervention in the query evaluation process (or both of them).

For computing a fragmentation that minimizes storage and computational burden for the data owner it is necessary to define a metric able to measure the cost of a fragmentation. In [9] the authors propose different metrics that depend on the resource whose consumption should be minimized (e.g., the storage space, the bandwidth capacity, the computational power) and on the information available at fragmentation time. For instance, a simple metric corresponds to the number of attributes in F_o. The minimization of the number of attributes implies a minimization of the storage space used at the data owner side as well as a minimization of the number of queries that require an involvement of the data owner. If, for example, is also available the information about the size of the attributes in R, then another possible metric consists in the total size of the attributes stored at the data owner side. More sophisticated metrics can be defined when information on the possible query workload is known.

In [9] the authors show that independently from the metric adopted to measure the cost of a fragmentation the problem of computing a fragmentation with minimum cost is NP-hard (the minimum hitting set problem [12] reduces to it in polynomial time). Therefore, in [9] the authors propose a heuristic algorithm that solves the problem in polynomial time with respect to the number of attributes in R. The main advantage of this algorithm is its flexibility, since it can be adopted with any metric.

6   Open Issues

The problem of satisfying confidentiality constraints in data outsourcing is becoming of great interest and different solutions have been proposed to the aim of maximizing the advantages of outsourcing, while preventing unauthorized accesses to sensitive information. There are however different issues that require further investigations and that we now briefly describe.

– *Multiple relations.* Most of the solutions proposed in the literature for privacy protection are based on the assumption that the sensitive information is stored in a single relation. An interesting direction that needs to be explored consists in assuming that data are represented through a set of relations that can be possibly joined.
– *Definition of confidentiality constraints.* The proposals illustrated in this paper are based on the assumption that confidentiality constraints are defined by the data owner according to her knowledge of the domain. However, the definition of a correct and complete set of confidentiality constraints is a critical and difficult task since it is necessary to consider the relationships among data. In particular, functional dependencies must be taken into account, since otherwise they could be exploited for inference attacks.
– *Data utility.* When publishing data, there are two contrasting needs that have to be taken into consideration: privacy protection and data utility. The fragmentation-based techniques described in this paper mainly focus on privacy protection and do not consider data utility. It would then be interesting to extend such proposals by exploring novel solutions that will

take into consideration not only the privacy requirements but also explicit requests for views over data. These view requirements can be expressed, for example, as associations that have to be preserved during the fragmentation process.

- *Obfuscated associations.* Whenever the association among a set of attributes is considered sensitive (and it is therefore modeled as a confidentiality constraint), it is not possible to publish the involved attributes in a fragment, even if the utility of the data would considerably increase. It would be then interesting to define a solution that allows the publication of a sanitized/obfuscated version of sensitive but useful associations. The publication method should carefully handle the tradeoff between data utility, on one side, and association confidentiality, on the other side.
- *Metrics.* The computation of a minimum fragmentation implies the definition of a metric that is used to evaluate the cost of a fragmentation. A metric needs to take into consideration different parameters, such as, the storage at the data owner side, the computational resources required to the client for query evaluation, and the bandwidth occupation necessary for interactions among parties. Also, the metric adopted should be based on information that should be available to the data owner in advance with respect to the fragmentation process and that should be easy to compute. It would then be interesting to define sophisticate metrics able to capture the different parameters that may have an impact on the cost of a fragmentation.
- *Write operations.* A common aspect of all the proposals discussed is that they only support read operations. There are however different contexts where the consideration of read operations only may be a limitation (e.g., within a multi-owner context). It would then be interesting to extend current approaches for supporting write operations.

7   Conclusions

Fragmentation has been recently investigated as a technique for guaranteeing the protection of outsourced data. In this paper, we described three different solutions presented in the literature that possibly combine fragmentation and encryption and that produce a fragmentation correct with respect to the given privacy requirements. We then concluded the paper with a discussion on some open research challenges.

Acknowledgments

The paper is based on joint work with Valentina Ciriani, Sushil Jajodia, Stefano Paraboschi, and Pierangela Samarati. The authors would like to thank Pierangela Samarati for her comments, suggestions, and discussions that helped improving the organization of the paper. This work was supported in part by the EU within the 7FP project "PrimeLife" under grant agreement 216483.

References

1. Damiani, E., De Capitani di Vimercati, S., Jajodia, S., Paraboschi, S., Samarati, P.: Balancing confidentiality and efficiency in untrusted relational DBMSs. In: Proc. of the 10th ACM Conference on Computer and Communications Security (CCS 2003), Washington, DC, USA (October 2003)
2. Ceselli, A., Damiani, E., De Capitani di Vimercati, S., Jajodia, S., Paraboschi, S., Samarati, P.: Modeling and assessing inference exposure in encrypted databases. ACM Transactions on Information and System Security (TISSEC) 8(1), 119–152 (2005)
3. Hacigümüş, H., Iyer, B., Mehrotra, S., Li, C.: Executing SQL over encrypted data in the database-service-provider model. In: Proc. of the ACM SIGMOD International Conference on Management of Data (SIGMOD 2002), Madison, WI, USA (June 2002)
4. Hacigümüş, H., Iyer, B., Mehrotra, S.: Providing database as a service. In: Proc. of 18th International Conference on Data Engineering (ICDE 2002), San Jose, California, USA (February 2002)
5. De Capitani di Vimercati, S., Foresti, S., Jajodia, S., Paraboschi, S., Samarati, P.: Over-encryption: Management of access control evolution on outsourced data. In: Proc. of the 33rd International Conference on Very Large Data Bases (VLDB 2007), Vienna, Austria (September 2007)
6. De Capitani di Vimercati, S., Foresti, S., Jajodia, S., Paraboschi, S., Samarati, P.: Encryption policies for regulating access to outsourced data. ACM Transactions on Database Systems (to appear 2010)
7. Aggarwal, G., Bawa, M., Ganesan, P., Garcia-Molina, H., Kenthapadi, K., Motwani, R., Srivastava, U., Thomas, D., Xu, Y.: Two can keep a secret: a distributed architecture for secure database services. In: Proc. of the Second Biennial Conference on Innovative Data Systems Research (CIDR 2005), Asilomar, CA, USA (January 2005)
8. Ciriani, V., De Capitani di Vimercati, S., Foresti, S., Jajodia, S., Paraboschi, S., Samarati, P.: Fragmentation and encryption to enforce privacy in data storage. In: Biskup, J., López, J. (eds.) ESORICS 2007. LNCS, vol. 4734, pp. 171–186. Springer, Heidelberg (2007)
9. Ciriani, V., De Capitani di Vimercati, S., Foresti, S., Jajodia, S., Paraboschi, S., Samarati, P.: Keep a few: Outsourcing data while maintaining confidentiality. In: Backes, M., Ning, P. (eds.) ESORICS 2009. LNCS, vol. 5789, pp. 440–455. Springer, Heidelberg (2009)
10. Samarati, P.: Protecting respondents' identities in microdata release. IEEE Transactions on Knowledge and Data Engineering 13(6), 1010–1027 (2001)
11. Samarati, P., De Capitani di Vimercati, S.: Data protection in outsourcing scenarios: Issues and directions. In: Proc. of the 5th ACM Symposium on Information, Computer and Communications Security (ASIACCS 2010), Beijing, China (April 2010)
12. Garey, M., Johnson, D.: Computers and Intractability; a Guide to the Theory of NP-Completeness. W.H. Freeman, New York (1979)
13. Ciriani, V., De Capitani di Vimercati, S., Foresti, S., Jajodia, S., Paraboschi, S., Samarati, P.: Combining fragmentation and encryption to protect privacy in data storage. ACM Transactions on Information and System Security (to appear 2010)

14. Ciriani, V., De Capitani di Vimercati, S., Foresti, S., Jajodia, S., Paraboschi, S., Samarati, P.: Fragmentation design for efficient query execution over sensitive distributed databases. In: Proc. of the 29th International Conference on Distributed Computing Systems (ICDCS 2009), Montreal, Quebec, Canada (June 2009)
15. Schneier, B.: Applied Cryptography, 2/E. John Wiley & Sons, Chichester (1996)
16. Ciriani, V., De Capitani di Vimercati, S., Foresti, S., Jajodia, S., Paraboschi, S., Samarati, P.: Enforcing confidentiality constraints on sensitive databases with lightweight trusted clients. In: Proc. of the 23rd IFIP TC-11 WG 11.3 Seventeenth Annual Working Conference on Data and Application Security (DBSec 2009), Montreal, Quebec, Canada (July 2009)

Sharing Data for Public Security

Michele Bezzi, Gilles Montagnon, Vincent Salzgeber, and Slim Trabelsi

SAP Labs, France
name.lastname@sap.com

Abstract. Data sharing is a valuable tool for improving security. It allows integrating information from multiple sources to better identify and respond to global security threats. On the other side, sharing of data is limited by privacy and confidentiality. A possible solution is removing or obfuscating part of the data before release (anonymization), and, to this scope, various masking algorithms have been proposed. However, finding the right balance between privacy and the quality of data is often difficult, and it needs a fine calibration of the anonymization process. It includes choosing the 'best' set of masking algorithms and an estimation of the risk in releasing the data. Both these processes are rather complex, especially for non-expert users. In this paper, we illustrate the typical issues in the anonymization process, and introduce a tool for assisting the user in the choice of the set of masking transformations. We also propose a caching system to speed up this process over multiple runs on similar datasets. Although, the current version has limited functionalities, and more extensive testing is needed, it is a first step in the direction of developing a user-friendly support tool for anonymization.

1 Introduction

Governmental agencies, corporates, academic and research institutions hold a huge amount of data containing information on individual people or other sensitive data. They have often to release part of these data for research purposes, data analysis or application testing. For example, sharing of log data has been proved a valuable resource for research in network security against coordinated attacks [9], and collecting these data from multiple organizations allow to analyze the emergence of worldwide threats.

However, these data contain sensitive information and organizations are hesitant to share them. To reduce the risk, data holders use masking techniques (*anonymization*) for limiting disclosure risk in releasing sensitive datasets, such as generalizing the data, i.e., recoding variables into broader classes (e.g., releasing only the first two digits of the zip code or removing the last octet of an IP address) or rounding numerical data, suppressing part of or entire records, randomly swapping some fields among original data records, permutations or perturbative masking, i.e., adding random noise to numerical data values.

These anonymization methods increases protection, lowering the disclosure risk, but, clearly, they also decrease the quality of the data and hence its utility [4]. Finding the ideal balance between risk and utility and identifying the

M. Bezzi et al. (Eds.): Privacy and Identity, IFIP AICT 320, pp. 188–197, 2010.

right set of anonymization methods, among the many possible ones, to reach this equilibrium point is the main challenge of the data masking process. To this scope, there is the need to derive some criteria to assist the user in the choice of the set of transformations to be applied. In particular, we need to set the context specific requirements that define the information that has to be preserved, and use suitable metrics to quantify the disclosure risk in releasing the data. To address the latter point, various metrics for estimating disclosure risk have been proposed so far [3,12,1,7]. They are typically based on the following attack scenario: an attacker has the knowledge about some variables, which may identify a record in the dataset. Considering the example of a medical database, the attacker may know a few attributes (age, gender, marital status) from an external public register (e.g., census data) or other source of information (e.g., knowing age and address of his neighbor). He then tries to match these variables (*keys*) with the partly altered records in the released database. In case of stochastic masking transformations, this matching may use probabilistic algorithms [14,3,8,2]. In the case of log files, an attacker may inject some information (e.g., scanning some specific ports), with the goal of later recognizing them in the anonymized logs. When a unique record matches a combination of key variables, the attacker can re-identify the masked record, assuming he is certain that the record is in the dataset. Risk metrics quantify 'how difficult' is this process of re-identification.

Ideally, such metrics/criteria should help the user to choose the appropriate set of masking methods for a specific dataset.

The goal of this paper is two fold: First, we introduce the main challenges for anonymizing data, describing two possible scenarios where data sharing may be valuable (see Sects. 2.1 and 2.2) and outlining the general requirements for the anonymization process (see Sect. 2.3). Second, we propose a model for supporting the user in the anonymization process (see Sect. 3), which includes a disclosure risk estimator and an efficient method for searching the 'best' set of anonymization methods. In Sect. 4 we will describe a prototype implementation of this model. Finally, conclusions are drawn in the last section.

2   Use Cases and Challenges

To illustrate the problem let consider two possible scenarios: data sharing of log files, and data sharing of personal identifiable information (PII).

2.1   Sharing Network Logs

Computer attacks are becoming more coordinated and addressing multiple targets at the same time, with large number of compromised hosts from many different organizations, possibly, in different countries. Detecting and reacting to these attacks may require cooperation of many institutions, and, often, a large scale analysis of network log data from all the possible targets [9]. However, organizations are often reluctant to share data, because they fear the risk of leaking sensitive information, or for privacy concerns or for not revealing the structure of their internal network, which may reveal potential weaknesses to further attackers. Consequently, to promote data sharing we need to deal with possible privacy and security concerns of data holders. To this scope, the idea is to remove or modify potential sensitive information before release using various data masking transformations . These transformations include recoding variables into classes (e.g., releasing only the last bytes of an IP address or considering just two classes for the port number), suppressing part of or entire records (also known as black marker [10]), randomly swapping some fields among original data records, one-to-one mapping on a defined random set of IP numbers or perturbative masking, i.e., adding random noise to the number of packets transmitted [5]. Clearly, in this process we have to preserve the relevant information for data analysis, thus the set of transformations used has to be calibrated to specific analytics method to be applied.

2.2 Sharing PII for Improving Public Safety

Data sharing between public agencies, and public and private organizations, can help improving public safety. For example, sharing health-care data can improve scientific research, and enable early detection of disease outbreak, as shown by the Real-Time Outbreak Detection System [13], which is a syndromic surveillance system based on health data integrated with data collected routinely for other purposes, such as absenteeism data, sales of over-the-counter health care products, etc ... . Similarly, police and fire departments could integrate multiple data sources, and share their information to optimize their capability of providing a coordinated defense.

The continuous growth of digital data may ulteriorly boost these approaches, but the the same time it raises privacy issues, and contrast with the increasing citizen awareness on privacy, and permission to use personal data is often difficult to obtain without guareenting some privacy protection. Accordingly, it is becoming crucial to develop technical methodologies to allow sharing of data without losing privacy. As in the previous example on network log data, anonymization techniques may be used to remove or obfuscate the more privacy-risky information, enabling the collection of large datasets of heterogeneous data from multiple sources.

2.3 Challenges

The major challenges in anonymization are not related to develop novel masking methods, but more to use them in a effective ways in the different contexts. In other words, there is a number of anonymization algorithms, the issue is which of them to choose to perform the anonymization balancing the conflicting privacy and utility requirements.

Utility requirements typically express what the data consumer wants to preserve. They are clearly dependent on the specific application, in particular to define what fields have to be anonymized, and how much information should be preserved. Still, some general requirements in increasing level of complexity include:

- Preserving syntax/format. A basic requirement: the syntax should be conserved. It implies that the syntactical rule for each attribute must be considered. E.g., IP addresses conventions, first vs. last digits in zip codes or credit card numbers.
- Preserving semantics. In some cases, there is the need to keep the 'meaning' of some attributes. Therefore, names should be replaced with meaningful names (possibly language-specific), diseases with diseases, ... To this scope, it may be needed, first, to have the necessary semantic information in the original dataset, then to have available databases with list of candidates for replacement.
- Preserving Relationships. Data themselves are often used as keys in relational database. In particular, unique identifiers, as Social security number, may play this role. Accordingly, in some cases, the anonymization process should mask this data in a consistent way, to avoid to lose the relationships between tables, for example hashing these values.
- Preserving the distribution of original data. E.g., the percentage of empty fields, or the distribution of diseases. This can be particularly relevant for heavy-tailed distributions, where extreme values have to be correctly sampled.
- Preserving consistency. Attributes are often correlated, so the anonymization process should be applied in a consistent way across multiple attributes. E.g., city, states, telephone numbers.

Privacy requirements are also strongly context dependent, in some cases privacy regulations impose specific constraints on the anonymization process (e.g., HIPAA safe-harbor rules for medical data), but individuals or organizations may define additional requirements.

Quantifying the privacy level is very important for all the above mentioned scenarios, it provides a metrics that supports data holder in gauging privacy risk-utility. Even if various measures have been proposed so far, they are still limited used in the real-world applications. Typical issues include:

- Performance. Most of the algorithms used for estimating privacy risk do not scale when huge amount of real data are used. E.g., shopping data can easily have the size of several gigabytes. For such application current privacy metrics are still too time consuming.
- Attacker model. To perform an estimation of the disclosure risk, we need to define the attack model, and its basic assumptions. Typically, it is assumed that a possible attacker may use some external source of information (dictionary) to match some fields (keys) in the anonymized dataset, and infer some other information (e.g., identity or the value of some attribute) that were hidden during the anonymization process. This raises various issues:
  • Definition of keys. Identifying which attributes, or combination of attributes, may be used for re-identification is sometimes a difficult task.
  • Definition/access to *dictionaries*. The basic idea in many privacy metrics definition, is trying to link the anonymized data to some external (not anonymized) data source (dictionary). Such dictionaries are often

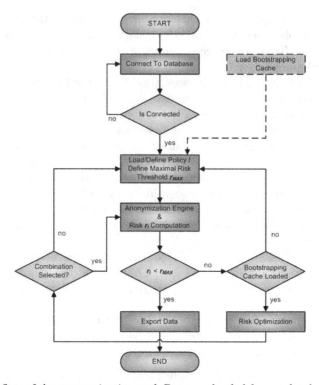

Fig. 1. The flow of the anonymization tool. Data are loaded from a database, then user selects the anonymization methods via a GUI or loading a policy file. The anonymization engine applies the masking transformation and computes the risk. If risk exceeds the the threshold r_{MAX}, the risk optimization module proposes additional masking, otherwise the anonymized dataset is exported.

difficult to identify and access for the data holder before the data are actually released. For example, the test data for the Netflix context has been, partially, de-anonymized using a different, not-expected, source of external information [6].

- Complexity. The impact of different masking transformations on the risk value is often difficult to assess, especially for not-expert user, since risk value may depend on the amount and content of data, the assumptions of the risk metrics, etc... . Accordingly, for the user it is often hard to select the optimal process to minimize the risk.

To address some of the issues above, we developed a tool that supports the user in the anonymization process. The protection model we propose here is composed by two core components (see Fig. 1):

- an Anonymization Engine, comprising a set of masking algorithms for anonymizing the original dataset and a disclosure risk estimator.
- a Risk Optimizer, which suggests the user the "best" combinations of masking transformations to decrease the risk under a pre-defined level.

3   An Anonymization Tool

These components are integrated in the following process: a user wants to share a dataset, e.g., for data analysis purpose, but he also wants to minimize the risk to reveal sensitive or private information. To this scope, the original dataset has to be anonymized before release. The user loads the original dataset, and sets the level of disclosure risk he wants to attain (r_{MAX}) using a specific metric. The user can choose a first set of masking transformations, for example in the case of datasets containing personal information, remove the social security number, generalize the postal code and age, etc. . This step can be performed by the user via a suitable user interface (see Fig. 2(Top)), or loading a predefined *anonymization policy* written by some security expert in a machine-readable language (e.g., XML [10]).

The anonymization engine applies the masking algorithms as specified by the user or by the anonymization policy and estimates the disclosure risk using a risk metrics r_i (e.g., using one of the metrics listed in Sect. 1). If the computed risk r_i is lower than the maximum acceptable risk r_{MAX}, the anonymized dataset can be released. Otherwise extra masking steps are needed. In the latter case, the user may decide to mask additional fields in the dataset or additionally downgrading data in already masked field (e.g., editing the policy or using a graphical interface to select the additional transformations). This manual work is tedious and it needs a technical understanding of the effect of the various transformations on the risk value. To optimize this process, we developed the Risk Optimizer module, which performs a search on the space of possible masking transformations, estimate the corresponding risks and, then, proposes to the user the 'closest' ones to the original transformations, which do not exceed the maximum risk value. This search space is highly-dimensional, even if we limit the masking transformations to the suppression of fields (or, equivalently, the replacement with a random value), the number of possible states to explore grows exponentially with the number of fields and the number of records in the dataset, making unfeasible to run even local search in case of large datasets. However, in many applications, the anonymization process is run on multiple instances on the same type of data-sets, so we propose a bootstrapping approach for speeding up the search. The idea is running an exhaustive search on a reduced set of records and caching the corresponding transformation set/risk values in a lookup table. The test sample can be the dataset used in the first run or, if it is too large, a random sample of it. In the following runs, the Risk Optimizer module uses the lookup table to estimate the set of transformations that can be applied to reach the risk threshold chosen by the user, and, at the same time, it is the closest to those originally selected, and proposes it to the user. The user selects one of them, and runs the Anonymization Engine to produce the masked dataset and, then, it checks to actual value of the risk. Clearly, if we change the type of dataset (e.g., medical data to log file), new lookup tables have to be created and stored.

We will show in the next section, how this approach can largely speed up the search process.

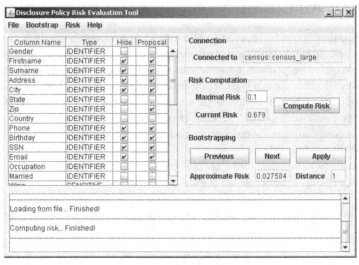

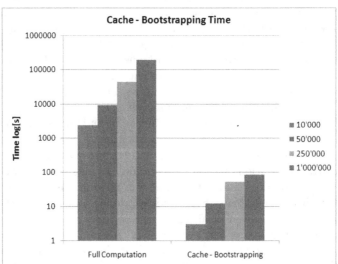

Fig. 2. Top: The Graphical User Interface. Ticking the 'Hide' box, the user can suppress or replace with random values the corresponding column in the dataset. After the first run, the Risk Optimizer suggests to suppress an additional column (the zip code in this case, see 'Proposal' column) to get to the maximum risk value allowed, as set by the user. Bottom: The runtime for using an exhaustive search (left bars) and the caching algorithm (right bars) for 4 datasets containing $10^4, 5 \times 10^4, 2.5 \times 10^5, 10^6$ records. A first dataset has been created for initialize the lookup tables. Then, using new datasets, we compute the processing time with/without using the caching system.

4   The Prototype

We implemented the anonymization tool described above[1]. The tool has a graphical user interface, see Fig. 2(Top), which allows the user to easily load the dataset by querying a SQL database or fetching data from an SAP system, then he can create manually a disclosure policy by clicking on the attributes to display and the attributes to hide, or to load a predefined XML policy file. The current version supports only one kind of masking, i.e., suppression, so the user can simply decide to remove or not a certain field (column), clicking the tick box as shown in Fig. 2(Top) or by the appropriate policy file. User can also set the maximum value for the disclosure risk that he wants to achieve at the end of the anonymization.

By clicking on the 'Compute Risk' button the tool applies the chosen masking transformation and computes the corresponding final risk. The risk value is computed, first estimating the probability of re-identifying a single record, and then deriving the total percentage of records that could be re-identified (see Refs. [2,11] for details).

If the risk exceeds the set threshold value, the user can manually set additional masking using the interface or ask to the system to search for a policy that matches the desirable risk. In this case, the bootstrapping system will propose to the user several less risky combinations that are close to his initial disclosure preferences, see Fig. 2(Top).

In Fig. 2(Bottom) we show the performance of the caching system for different size of the datasets. The caching system gives a large improvement in the performance of the system (note, the log scale for the processing time), fluctuations over multiple runs (not shown) are of the order of few percents. The testing datasets contain typical PII data: street address, city, zip code, country, gender, age, etc ... . They were randomly generated using a personal information generator [2].

5   Conclusions

Data sharing is a valuable tool for improving security, but privacy and confidentiality concerns restricts the sharing of data. Data anonymization is used to address these issues, and various masking techniques are available. However, finding the ideal trade off between privacy and utility of the data is often difficult. Quantitative estimation of the privacy risk, privacy metrics, supports the user in the selection of the best combination of anonymization transformation, but the available metrics are typically computationally intensive, and they had a limited application to real-world scenarios up to now. In addition, non-expert user may find difficult to assess the impact of the different anonymization algorithms on the risk value.

---

[1] For a detailed description of a first version of this prototype see Ref. [11].

[2] Fake Name Generator - http://www.fakenamegenerator.com/. This generator provides fake personal information with a realistic and coherent semantic meaning (e.g., valid city, state, and zip code combinations).

In this paper, we illustrated the typical issues in the anonymization process, and presented a tool for assisting the user in the choice of set of masking transformations. This tool makes easy for not-expert user to select the minimal set of anonymization methods to reach a certain level of privacy risk, addressing one of the main difficulties of the anonymization process, that is the complexity of usage.

We also introduced a caching system to speed up this process over multiple runs on similar datasets. This allows to improve the performance of the tool in most of the application scenarios, addressing the performance requirement (see Sect. 2). Although, the presented model was tested on simple test data and includes only a small set of transformations, our preliminary results show that the tool, after an initial bootstrapping, can handle a dataset with one million of records in a rather short time. Clearly, introducing new masking transformations, such as generalization, will largely increase the dimensionality of the search space and introduce new challenges in terms of preserving the semantics of the data and the relationships between attributes. This case is currently under investigation.

Acknowledgements

The research leading to these results has received funding from the European Communitys Seventh Framework Programme (FP7/2007 2013) under grant agreement No. 216483.

References

1. Benedetti, R., Franconi, L.: Statistical and technological solutions for controlled data dissemination. Pre-proceedings of New Techniques and Technologies for Statistics 1, 225–232 (1998)
2. Bezzi, M.: An entropy-based method for measuring anonymity. In: Proceedings of the IEEE/CreateNet SECOVAL Workshop on the Value of Security through Collaboration, Nice, France (September 2007)
3. Duncan, G., Lambert, D.: The risk of disclosure for microdata. Journal of Business & Economic Statistics 7, 207 (xx 1989), doi:10.2307/1391438, http://dx.doi.org/10.2307/1391438
4. Duncan, G., Keller-McNulty, S., Stokes, S.: Disclosure risk versus data utility: The RU confidentiality map. Technical paper, Los Alamos National Laboratory, Los Alamos, NM (2001)
5. Kounine, A., Bezzi, M.: Assessing disclosure risk in anonymized datasets. In: Proceedings of the FloCon Workshop (January 2009)
6. Narayanan, A., Shmatikov, V.: How to break anonymity of the netflix prize dataset (October 2006), http://arxiv.org/abs/cs/0610105
7. Samarati, P.: Protecting respondents' identities in microdata release. IEEE Trans. on Knowl. and Data Eng. 13(6), 1010–1027 (2001)
8. Skinner, C.J., Elliot, M.J.: A measure of disclosure risk for microdata. Journal of the Royal Statistical Society: Series B (Statistical Methodology) 64(4), 855–867 (2002), http://www.blackwell-synergy.com/doi/abs/10.1111/1467-9868.00365

9. Slagell, A., Yurcik, W.: Sharing computer network logs for security and privacy: A motivation for new methodologies of anonymization (2005), citeseer.ist.psu.edu/slagell05sharing.html
10. Slagell, A.J., Lakkaraju, K., Luo, K.: Flaim: A multi-level anonymization framework for computer and network logs. In: LISA, USENIX, pp. 63–77 (2006)
11. Trabelsi, S., Salzgeber, V., Bezzi, M., Montagnon, G.: Data disclosure risk evaluation. In: 2009 Fourth International Conference on Risks and Security of Internet and Systems (CRiSIS), October 2009, pp. 35–72 (2009)
12. Truta, T.M., Fotouhi, F., Barth-Jones, D.: Assessing global disclosure risk in masked microdata. In: WPES 2004: Proceedings of the 2004 ACM workshop on Privacy in the electronic society, pp. 85–93. ACM Press, New York (2004)
13. Tsui, F.C., Espino, J.U., Dato, V.M., Gesteland, P.H., Hutman, J., Wagner, M.M.: Technical Description of RODS: A Real-time Public Health Surveillance System. J. Am. Med. Inform. Assoc. 10(5), 399–408 (2003), http://www.jamia.org/cgi/content/abstract/10/5/399
14. Yancey, W.E., Winkler, W.E., Creecy, R.H.: Disclosure risk assessment in perturbative microdata protection. In: Domingo-Ferrer, J. (ed.) Inference Control in Statistical Databases. LNCS, vol. 2316, pp. 135–152. Springer, Heidelberg (2002)

An Analysis for Anonymity and Unlinkability for a VoIP Conversation

Ge Zhang

Karlstad University, Karlstad, Sweden
ge.zhang@kau.se

Abstract. With the growth of its popularity, VoIP is increasingly popular nowadays. Similarly to other Internet applications, VoIP users may desire to be unlinkable with their participated VoIP session records for privacy issues. In this paper, we explore the Items of Interests (IOIs)[1] from anonymisation aspects based on a simplified VoIP model and analyse the potential links between them. We address possible methods to break the links. Finally, we also discuss requirements for a VoIP anonymisation Service (VAS) in terms of functionality, performance and usability. Based on this, we discuss the fundamental design requirements for a VAS which we intend to subsequently implement.

1 Introduction

Voice over IP (VoIP) is a method which enables users to build voice conversation with partners at a distance by transferring encoded voice data over packet-switched networks (e.g., the Internet). Like other applications in the Internet, VoIP users may search for privacy protection, such as anonymity. For example, a caller may prefer to withhold his/her real identity to others (even a callee) for various reasons. However, to the best of our knowledge, most existing VoIP anonymity solutions are based on a single Trusted Third Party (TTP) and no detailed analysis of VoIP anonymity in terms of unlinkability has been done. Thus, we are motivated to explore this area further. Similar to the terminologies in [1], we define **caller anonymity**, which means to a potential VoIP caller, each requested VoIP conversation record is unlinkable; **callee anonymity**, which means to a potential VoIP callee, each accepted VoIP conversation record is unlinkable; **relationship anonymity**, which means for a given VoIP conversation record, its caller and callee are unlinkable. Caller/callee anonymity is a stronger property than relationship anonymity: an attacker has to break both caller anonymity and callee anonymity in order to break relationship anonymity. Thus, as long as caller/callee anonymity is achieved, relationship anonymity is achieved as well. *In this research, we focus on the caller/callee anonymity for standardized VoIP services.* First, we enumerate the Items of Interest (IOIs) based on a simplified VoIP model. Second, we depict the potential relationship among these IOIs and explain

---

[1] The IOIs in this paper refer to a piece of information which an attacker is interested to know.

M. Bezzi et al. (Eds.): Privacy and Identity, IFIP AICT 320, pp. 198–212, 2010.

how a user can be tracked by observing the relationship among the IOIs. Based on this, we suggest methods to break the relationships to make the actual user unlinkable to a VoIP session. Finally, we propose some further requirements on a VoIP anonymisation Service (VAS) which we will investigate in our future work.

The rest of this paper is organized as follows. Section 2 introduces standardized VoIP protocols. Some previous works on VoIP anonymity and their limitations are presented in Section 3. Section 4 shows our analysis of VoIP anonymity in terms of unlinkability. Section 5 proposes requirements of a VAS. We discuss our considerations on a VAS design in Section 6. Section 7 provides conclusions of this paper.

2   SIP-based VoIP

Current standards for VoIP protocols and services are standardized by the Internet Engineering Task Force (IETF). Among these protocols, three of them are essential: the Session Initiation Protocol (SIP) [2], the Session Description Protocol (SDP) [3] and the Realtime Transport Protocol (RTP) [4]. SIP is designed as a signaling protocol aiming at establishing, modifying or terminating a session between users. A SIP server[2] provides SIP clients with multiple services such as locating users, relaying SIP messages, etc. While SDP is designed for the purposes of session announcement, session invitation. A SDP message is generally contained in a SIP message as a message payload. After negotiating by using SIP and SDP messages, users can build a media session with each other. The session can comply with RTP protocol, which provides end-to-end network transport functions suitable for bidirectional transmitting encoded voice packets over network services. SIP and SDP communications are generally classified as *signaling layer* while RTP communications are characterized as *media layer*.

2.1   Signaling Layer

A SIP user needs to login to the domain of the SIP server for requesting the services. In this way, a SIP client sends the SIP server a REGISTER message including a SIP Uniform Resource Identifier (URI) and the networking location [3] of the user. The format of SIP URI is similar to an Email address, consisting of a pair of user name and domain name, (e.g., "sip:ge.zhang@kau.se"), which represents a user with username "ge.zhang" at "kau.se" domain. After receiving the REGISTER message, the SIP server will keep the mapping between the URI and its networking location. Therefore, the SIP server is able to locate and forward messages to this user later. The procedure is as follows:

1. $user \longrightarrow server : REGISTER < URI_{user}, Location_{user}, ... >$
2. $server \longrightarrow user : 200OK$

---

[2] We assume the SIP server includes all necessary service components (e.g., SIP proxy server, SIP registrar, SIP redirect server) in this paper.

[3] In most cases, the location information is denoted by the IP address and port number of a client's User Agent (UA).

After successful registering, the SIP users are able to call or to be called. Here, we describe how a VoIP session can be built by using SIP. We assume that there are three entities involved in this model: the caller, the callee and the server. The caller would like to build a conversation with the callee, so the caller knows the URI_{callee}, but does not know the $location_{callee}$. Therefore, the caller needs the server's help to setup a signaling communication to the callee. In this way, the caller first sends the server an INVITE request, including $URI_{caller}, URI_{callee}, Location_{caller}$, etc. The server should know $Location_{callee}$ if the callee has been already registered on the domain. In this way, the server can forward the INVITE message to the callee. The callee then responses a 200OK message to accept the calling request. The 200OK message, including the location of the callee, will be forwarded to the caller. Finally, the caller sends the callee an ACK message to acknowledge the calling request. Then, the conversation should be established without the participation of the server. The procedure is as follows:

1. $caller \longrightarrow server : INVITE < URI_{caller}, URI_{callee}, Location_{caller}, ... >$
2. $server \longrightarrow callee : INVITE < URI_{caller}, URI_{callee}, Location_{caller}, ... >$
3. $callee \longrightarrow server : 200OK < URI_{caller}, URI_{callee}, Location_{callee}, ... >$
4. $server \longrightarrow caller : 200OK < URI_{caller}, URI_{callee}, Location_{callee}, ... >$
5. $caller \longrightarrow callee : ACK$
6. $caller \longleftrightarrow callee$: Conversation on media layer

2.2   Media Layer

An RTP session consists of two kinds of data streams: one for the actual encoded voice data stream and another for control information, named as RTP Control Protocol (RTCP) [5]. Three features of RTP sessions are especially important for our research:

– Transmitted voice data is encoded and decoded using a special purpose speech codec algorithm (e.g., G.711 [6] and Speex [7]) negotiated in the signaling level. The codec takes the voice from users as input, which is typically sampled at either 8k samples or 16k samples per second (Hz). As a performance requirement, the inter-arrival packet time of voice stream is generally fixedly selected between 10 and 50 ms, with 20 ms being the common case. Thus, given a 8 kHz voice source, we have 160 samples per packet with 20 ms packets interval. Moreover, the size of each voice packet depends on the encoding bit rate of adapted codec. Two types of encoding bit rate can be distinguished: **Fixed Bit Rate (FBR)** and **Variable Bit Rate (VBR)**. With FBR (e.g., G.711), end points produce voice packets always with the same size. On the other hand, VBR (e.g., Speex) means that the encoding bit rate varies according to the type of voice. Therefore, end points produce voice packets with different size.
– RTP allows discontinuous transmission (**silence suppression**) [8], which is a capability of endpoints to stop sending RTP packets during silent periods of its owner. In this circumstance, additional resources (e.g., bandwidth) can be saved. However, whether to use silence suppression is usually a configuration option for users.

- Each endpoint periodically sends control packets by using RTCP to the other side [4]. The control packets contain information about the received and transmitted data rates, delay jitter and packet losses. A RTCP communication generally uses a different communication channel from voice data communication.
- The Secure Realtime Transport Protocol (SRTP) [9] specifies a new RTP profile to provide confidentiality, integrity protection and data origin authentication to the RTP and RTCP traffic. SRTP requires a key exchange mechanism to generate session keys for encrypting and decrypting the voice data traffic. The key exchange mechanisms are classified into signaling level (e.g., MIKEY [10]) and media level (e.g., ZRTP [11]), depending on whether the exchanging is taken place in signaling traffic or the media traffic.

3   Related Work

RFC3323 [12] endeavored to design a mechanism which enables SIP users to launch anonymous calls. To achieve this goal, some identity information in SIP messages (e.g., user's URI, IP address of User Agent (UA), etc) should be concealed from other subjects. The author thus proposed two kinds of privacy-enhanced mechanisms: *user-provided privacy* and *network-provided privacy*. User-provided privacy mechanism is designed for a requirement of low-level anonymity. With this mechanism, optional personal information is removed from SIP messages (e.g., a SIP message can optionally contain a URL pointing to an online photo of the caller. As an optional information, this kind of URL should be automatically stripped by a user-provided privacy). The actual VoIP call is not impacted without these optional information. However, the effect of this mechanism is rather limited: users' URI and the IP addresses of their equipments still appear in SIP messages. Without these information, the SIP servers do not know where the responses of these messages should be forwarded. Thus, RFC 3323 suggested the network-provided privacy mechanism, in which a privacy server, working as a trusted third party, constantly converts the user's URI in a SIP message to a randomized pseudonym. A privacy server also should keep the mapping state of the user's URI and the pseudonym for the routing purpose. Based on RFC 3323 [12], Charles Shen, et al., [13] proposed a more comprehensive analysis on identity leaking of SIP messages. They further represented an architecture with a privacy server, which was implemented according to the specifications of RFC 3323. However, their solutions heavily rely on a single Trusted Third Party (TTP). Nevertheless, a single TTP-based anonymisation service is insufficient to provide a high-level protection: It can be broken as long as the TTP is manipulated or compromised by attackers.

4   The Analysis of Caller/Callee Anonymity

In this section, we list potential *IOIs* with their relationships in the VoIP context based on the VoIP model in Section 2. Then, we analyse how a VoIP user can be traced by exploiting the relationships.

4.1   Item of Interest (IOIs)

Much information can be revealed during a VoIP communication. A more comprehensive analysis of personal information leaking in SIP and SDP messages has been discussed in [13]. However, personal information is supposed to be minimised if the user searches for privacy protection, which means a privacy-aware VoIP user does not provide any personal information unless they have to. Taking this condition into account, we list several potential IOIs based on the simplified VoIP model proposed in Section 2 as follows:

1. **VoIP user:** A VoIP user is referred to the actual person who utilizes VoIP services.
2. **SIP Service Provider (SP):** A SIP SP provides SIP services for VoIP users in a specific SIP domain.
3. **SIP URI:** A SIP URI is a VoIP user's identifier on the signaling level.
4. **Networking location:** As voice and signaling packets are transmitted over packet-switched networks, a networking location, especially, an IP address is used for locating a user's equipment. It is a user's identifier on the networking level.
5. **VoIP session:** A VoIP session refers a conversation of two users on media layer.

According to [1], "Linkability of two or more IOIs from an attacker's perspective means that within the system, the attacker can suffiently distinguish whether these IOIs are related or not." Our analysis is based on the simplified VoIP context as described in Section 2. There are three entities involved in the VoIP context, with a caller, a callee, and a SIP SP. We assume a user (either the caller or the callee) would like to withhold "who called whom" for privacy reasons. However, a potential attacker targets at observing "who called whom" from the information in the conversation. We assume that *the SIP SP and the user on the other side of the communication are potential attackers.* From an attacker's view, a VoIP user can be traced according to the links depicted in Figure 1. The links are shaped in this way: Given a VoIP session, one IOI might be fully or partly deduced from another. The representations of the numbered links are as follows:

Link 1 (VoIP session → SIP URI): In order to establish a VoIP session, users on both sides should first exchange SIP messages with each other for

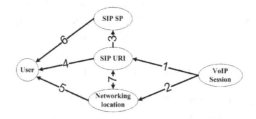

Fig. 1. Linkable IOIs in a VoIP context

signaling establishment. Thus, the users' SIP URIs contained in SIP messages are revealed and related to a certain VoIP session. And it is known by all participates (the caller, the callee, and the SIP SP).

Link 2 (VoIP session → Networking location): A SIP SP knows their users' networking locations in order to relay and to forward SIP messages for them. Furthermore, both the caller and the callee should know each other's networking location to build a VoIP session. In this way, users' networking locations are related to a certain VoIP session, which is known by all participates (the caller, the callee, and the SIP SP).

Link 3 (SIP URI → SIP SP): As introduced in Section 2, a SIP URI contains a domain name of the SIP SP which the user registers to. Thus, it is fairly clear that a user's SIP SP is indicated by the domain name. For instance, given a SIP URI "sip:ge.zhang@kau.se", we say that the user registers to the SIP SP with domain name "kau.se".

Link 4 (SIP URI → User): A SIP URI can be used to trace its owner in the following ways:

- By username: Besides a domain name, a SIP URI also contains a username of a user. Some users take real names as their usernames in favor of others to remember. For example, a SIP URI, "sip:ge.zhang@kau.se", exposes the real name of its owner.
- Linked with calling records: A user can select a pseudonym URI in which the user's real name does not appear. For example, "sip:batman@iptel.org". However, a pseudonym URI does not mean that its owner is untraceable. If a user participated in a set of calls with a single pseudonym URI, these calling records might be useful information to trace the actual user.

Link 5 (Networking Location → User): A Networking location (IP address) can be used to track its owner in the following ways:

- WHOIS lookup: WHOIS [14] provides publicly available information that allows one to query a remote WHOIS database for registration information of a domain name. Generally, a WHOIS record contains a full name, address, telephone number and email address of the Internet Service Provider (ISP). A WHOIS search accepts IP address as an input for querying. In this way, it forms a relationship between the owner of an IP address and its ISP.
- Geographical location: There are a lot of online services [15] which provides mappings between an IP address and a geographical location of its Internet Service Provider (ISP) (including country and city). It can be effective to locate a VoIP user from his/her IP address.
- Linked with other Internet applications: As a user can access a variety of services (e.g., web, email, etc) in the Internet besides VoIP, a user generally may reuse one IP address for different applications. In this case, different applications can be linked by a single IP address, which makes the user easier to be tracked.

Link 6 (SIP SP → User): A SIP SP can be used to trace a user in the following ways:

- Relationship: Since the information of most SP is available in the Internet, it may reveal the relationship between a SP and its users. For example, for a given SP "kau.se", an attacker can find out that kau.se is a domain name of Karlstad University in Sweden. Thus, the attacker can further guess that the users of this SP are either students or faculty members at this university.
- Limited number of users: Some SP may contain only a small number of users, which decreases the user's anonymity set. In this way, users of this SIP SP are easier to trace.

Link 7 (SIP URI ↔ Networking location): Users have to register in their SP domain for services by providing their SIP URI and networking locations. Thus, a SP can deduce a user's networking location from SIP URI and vice versa.

4.2   An Analysis for Anonymity and Unlinkability

In this section, we endeavor to find a mechanism which enables users to achieve caller/callee anonymity, which means to a potential SIP user (whatever caller or callee), each VoIP session is unlinkable. As shown in Figure 1, a user is traceable from the links. Thus, we discuss the feasibility of breaking these links.

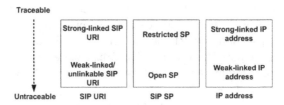

Fig. 2. A brief taxonomy of SIP URI, SP and IP address according to the linkability to their owner

Breaking link 1: To break link 1, a SIP URI should not appear in SIP signaling for a VoIP setup. This obviously contradicts the specification of SIP protocol in RFC 3261 [2]. Therefore, breaking link 1 is unrealistic.

Breaking link 2: To break link 2, networking location (IP address) should not be revealed to build a VoIP session, which defies both SIP protocol[2] and RTP protocol[4]. Thus, breaking link 2 is also not viable.

Breaking link 3: To break link 3 means that the actual domain name of a SIP SP should not appear in a SIP URI. However, a URI is malformed without a domain name, which might cause unexpected behavior of SIP infrastructures. As a result, breaking link 3 is unrealistic as well.

Breaking link 4: We first roughly separate SIP URIs into two category according to the linkability between a SIP URI and its owners.

- **Strong-linked SIP URI:** A SIP URI is defined as a strong-linked SIP URI if personal information exposed from this SIP URI is sufficient to trace its owner. For example, it can be a SIP URI containing the real name of its owner.

- **Weak-linked/unlinkable SIP URI**: A SIP URI is defined as a weak-linked/unlinkable SIP URI if personal information exposed from this SIP URI is insufficient to trace its owner. For instance, It can be a one-time URI only used once per call (unlinkable), or a shared URI which can be potentially used by a number of people (weak-linked).

To break link 4, users should employ weak-linked SIP URI.

Breaking link 5: We first roughly separate IP addresses into two category according to the linkability between an IP address and its owners.

- **Strong-linked IP address**: An IP address is defined as a strong-linked IP address if personal information exposed from this IP address is sufficient to track its owner. For example, an IP address which is used at a specific company, or an IP address which is used at a user's home.
- **Weak-linked IP address**: An IP address is defined as a weak-linked IP address if personal information exposed from this IP address is insufficient to trace its owner. For example, a user made a VoIP call at an Internet cafe in a foreign country. In this case, the IP address used in the internet cafe offers the user a higher anonymity than the one used at home or office. However, different to SIP URI, one-time IP addresses are difficult to provide due to the constraint of current IPv4 address space.

To break link 5, users should employ weak-linked IP address.

Breaking link 6: A classification of SIP SPs is discussed below:

- **Restricted SP**: A restricted SIP SP aims to provide services only to the users in a specific group or an organization. For example, a SIP domain "kau.se" only provides SIP services to the faculty members or the students at Karlstad University. The relationship between a SIP SP and its user is then revealed, which is useful to find out a specific VoIP user.
- **Open SP**: There are a lot of open SIP SPs, of which the services are not limited to a specific group, but available to all Internet users. The relationship between an open SP and its users is simply as VoIP service-client. An open SP provides better anonymity than a restricted SP.

To break link 6, using an open SP is recommended instead of a restricted SP.

Breaking link 7: Users should register their SIP URI and networking locations to their SP according to SIP specification. Thus, breaking link 7 is unrealistic as well.

So far, we have discussed methods to break the links in Figure 1. It is difficult to break link 1, 2, 3 and 7 unless we modify VoIP protocols, but it is possible to break link 4, 5, 6 by using various SIP URIs and IP addresses. A summary of the taxonomy of SIP URI, SP and IP address is illustrated in Figure 2. Weak-linked URIs, weak-linked IP addresses and open SPs are recommended for anonymity. Therefore, for example, a user can make a call anonymously in this way: He/She can setup a call with an one-time URI and an open SP by using a computer at an Internet cafe. However, it is not a scalable solution and it is inconvenience for users to do this in reality. Therefore, we are motivated to design and implement a VoIP anonymisation Service (VAS) to help users to achieve anonymity in an easier way.

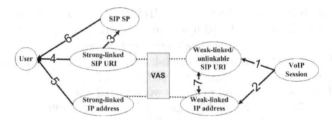

Fig. 3. A perspective VoIP anonymisation service (VAS) provides a higher anonymity to users by mapping SIP URI and IP address

Shown in Figure 3, a VAS should constantly map both the strong-linked SIP URI and IP address to weak-linked or unlinkable ones. Some further requirements of this VAS is discussed in the next section.

5   Requirements for a VAS

Several requirements for the VAS must be taken into account to be suitable for a VoIP environment. These are describes below in the contexts of basic requirements, performance, usability and resistance to traffic analysis.

5.1   Basic Requirements

We consider the following basic requirements of functionalities of a VAS.

- anonymisation service: The VAS provides anonymisation services by mapping a user's strong-linked SIP URI and IP address to the weak-linked or unlinkable ones.
- Compliant to VoIP protocols: A VAS should be compliant to existing VoIP protocols standardized in RFC documents. Although SIP protocol supports extension to some degree, the extension should be minimised for scalability. Furthermore, a VAS should be designed to understand the grammar defined in VoIP protocols since it needs to map SIP URIs and relay VoIP sessions.
- UDP support: The VAS must support UDP communication. TCP, being designed to provide a reliable end-to-end communication with a "flow control" method, has been employed for many Internet services (e.g., web services and file delivery). However, in return, the "flow control" method consumes additional bandwidth. On the other hand, UDP, without a "flow control" method, is more efficient than TCP. Similar to other stream media applications, VoIP session does not need a reliable communication since a small amount of packet loss actually does not prevent users from understanding the whole conversation. Therefore, RTP protocol was designed on the top of UDP to achieve a better performance instead of reliability. Furthermore, SIP protocol can work over both TCP as well as UDP. Thus, to be compatible with existing VoIP protocols, our VAS will be designed to be accessed over UDP.

– No single Trusted Third Party (TTP): Most privacy problems can be easily tackled by introducing a single TTP. However, in reality, a single TTP may not be relied on. Our solution should avoid single point of failure.

5.2   Requirements on Performance

For voice communication over packet-switched networks, three issues generally affect the quality of service including network delay, delay jitter and packet loss. These three issues are frequently taken as criteria to evaluate performance of communication services.

– Network delay: It refers to the time interval elapsed from the moment one user sends a voice packet until the user at another side receives the packet. It is mainly caused by transmission, propagation and queuing of packets. The network delay affects the voice conversation when the delay reaches a certain threshold. According to [16], the delay of a voice communication will not affect users as long as it is less then 150 ms; When the delay is between 150 to 400 ms, the quality of conversation is still acceptable but users will notice a slight hesitation in their partner's response. While the delay is above 400 ms, the performance is unacceptable for voice communication since the users cannot follow the conversation.
– Delay jitter: It is caused by the network congestion and improper routing during the transmission of voice packets. As a result, the packets arrive the receiver side at an uneven rate, which can lead to short-term audio gaps if the delay jitter is too large. According to [16], the performance is unacceptable if the value is above 75 ms for most codecs used.
– Packet loss: Some voice packets may be dropped or discarded during the transmission. As said above, VoIP conversation is able to endure packet loss, however, too much packet loss can lead to an incomplete conversation. Packet loss may occur due to many reasons (e.g., traffic congestion at a router in the middle). The impact introduced by packet loss varies generally depending on the codec design.

Employing a VoIP VAS may introduce negative impact on the performance of packets transferring since signaling and voice packets have to traverse over additional networking nodes as "stepping stones". It probably leads to more network delay, delay jitter and packet loss rate. Thus, to make a VAS useable, the values of network delay, delay jitter and packet loss rate introduced must be kept in an acceptable level as described above.

5.3   Requirements on Usability

A VoIP user may be confused when operating a VAS if its user interface is too complicated. Also, a VoIP user may be too inexperienced to use a VAS. Thus, we are motivated to implement a user-friendly interface which supports following functions. The user interface should be designed easy-to-use. Some predefined privacy settings should be built-in with the interface.

5.4   Requirements on Resistance to Traffic Analysis

Different with Section 4, here we extend the threat model considering more practical requirements: The attackers not only can be the SP and the communication partners, but also can be intermediaries in the network. In this way, we need to take traffic analysis attacks into account. Traffic analysis attack aims to correlate the flows entering and leaving a VAS by observing their characteristics (e.g., size and inter-arrival time of packets) of the flows. A flow entering the networking and a flow leaving the network can be paired if they have similar characteristics. For example, an attacker cannot correlate the flows in Figure 4(a) as all flows look the same. It is hard to say whom user1 communicates with (could be user4, user5, or user6). However, each flow has its own characteristics in Figure 4(b). In this case, attackers can easily correlate the flows by their characteristics (user1 ↔ user5, user2 ↔ user4, user3 ↔ user6). Instead of passively observing, Attackers can also modify a flow to insert more characteristics before it enters the network (active attack), as illustrated in Figure 4(c). Our VAS is designed to prevent both the passive and the active traffic analysis attacks.

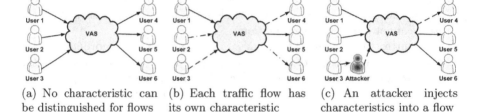

(a) No characteristic can be distinguished for flows

(b) Each traffic flow has its own characteristic

(c) An attacker injects characteristics into a flow

Fig. 4. Traffic analysis attacks on a VAS

6   Work in Progress

We plan to construct a VAS by using anonymous overlay network, which is a virtual network built on the top of other network layers to hide a user's real identifier. The anonymity service is then provided by the nodes in the anonymous network, instead of a single TTP. Some anonymous overlay networks are already available in the Internet to provides anonymity services for different applications, which can be mainly divided into two categories: One for high-latency applications (e.g., mail) and another for low-latency applications (e.g., web surfing). In the later case, both the Tor [17] and the AN.ON [18] have been operated in the Internet for several years. The Tor network forwards users' traffic through several routers with multi-layer encryption, with each router decrypting one layer of the encryption. The end-to-end path is constructed by several circuits between end-points and Tor routers in a telescoping fashion. In this way, each Tor router only knows the previous and the next router in the network, but it has no idea of the whole end-to-end path. Generally, Tor routers are dynamically selected from the network prior to the communications or during the communications.

On the other hand, AN.ON employs *cascades*, which consist of predefined mixing routers. Thus, AN.ON users select cascades instead of routers.

R. Wendolsky, et al [19] provide an empirical study of the performance comparison of Tor and AN.ON. Their results show that Tor is subject to unpredictable performance (with average end-to-end delay from 2000 ms to 7500 ms), while AN.ON can provide more consistent performance in general (with average end-to-end delay from 1000 to 1500 ms). This is mainly caused by their topology. Recently, [20], [21] and [22] addresses the alternatives to enhance the performance of Tor network by router selecting algorithms based on some parameters (e.g., on bandwidth, latency, etc). While optimising performance, the paths are not randomly selected anymore, which reduces anonymity. The authors also proposed their metrics for tradeoff performance and anonymity. However, without a proper measurement mechanism on performance [23], these router selecting algorithms cannot be employed by Tor so far.

Usually, anonymous overlay networks employ different techniques (e.g., packets-padding, dummy traffic and packets-delaying, etc) to eliminate (or hide) the characteristics of flows to mitigate traffic analysis attacks. In return, these techniques usually lead to a worse networking performance, which means they cannot be easily employed for VoIP services. As an alternative, we take the features of VoIP into account and discuss how the features can be exploited to prevent traffic analysis attacks.

- As said, VoIP endpoints will not send packets during silence period if silence suppression is enabled. Thus, it introduces additional timing characteristics to VoIP flows. The work [24] shows that it is easy to pair VoIP flows by these characteristics. Without silence suppression, VoIP endpoints can send voice packet with a fixed rate, which means that less characteristics of inter-arrival time between packets can be used for traffic analysis. *Thus, silence suppression must be disabled for VAS.*
- VoIP endpoints will generate voice packets with different sizes for a given conversation if a VBR is specified instead of a FBR. This also introduces a VoIP flow with more characteristics which makes a VAS more vulnerable to traffic analysis attacks. Besides traffic analysis, [25] and [26] demonstrates that packets size varying can reveal the conversation content between two VoIP users even the traffic is encrypted. *Therefore, FBR is highly recommended for VAS instead of VBR.*
- Similarly to the design in [27], we consider a defensive dropping mechanism to defend active traffic analysis attacks. As mentioned, the voice packets for silence period are meaningless for the actual conversation, but they must be sent to reduce flow characteristics. As an alternative, these silent "packets" can also be randomly dropped at the Mixer routers to obscure the characteristics. In this way, the traffic analysis is difficult even if the attackers actively introduce timing characteristics in the flow (e.g., [28]). The "silence packets" can be marked by the original endpoints, with indicating that which router can drop which packets.

Fig. 5. Two anonymous overlay networks should be used, one for signaling and another for media

- The end-to-end delay for voice conversation should be less than 450 ms. We can also consider a dropping mechanism based on time stamp. We say that a voice packet transmitted for 500 ms is less important than one transmitted for 100 ms. Therefore, we consider a QoS-aware scheme to minimize the impact of traffic congestion. For example, we set a timeout, saying 450 ms. The packets which have already spent more than 450 ms in the transmission should be dropped in case of traffic congestion.
- There are many different features between signaling traffic and media traffic. First, they have different requirements on performance: signaling traffic can suffer more delay (several seconds) but less packet loss, while with media traffic it is just the opposite. Moreover, media traffic can be composed by packets with the same size and inter-arrival time. However, signaling traffic cannot achieve this. Taking these difference in mind, we plan to employ two overlay network for each respectively (shown in Figure 5).
- As introduced in Section 2, endpoints periodically send RTCP control packets to the other side in default. With different packet sizes, RTCP streams are vulnerable to traffic analysis attacks. However, RTCP stream is designed to be optional and independent from RTP voice data stream. In this way, end-points should disable RTCP when they access a VAS. Moreover, the key exchange mechanism should be taken place in signaling traffic instead of media traffic to minimize the characteristic of media traffic.

7   Conclusion and Future Work

This study provided an investigation of VoIP anonymity in terms of unlinkability. We demonstrated that for a VoIP user, the privacy requirements on the signaling level and the session level should not be considered separately. We also proposed requirements towards a VAS including functionality, performance and usability. However, this work did not show any concrete solution of the VoIP VAS, as this is work in progress. In our future work, we are going to design the VAS in more detail. We consider to construct a VAS and do some experiments on the performance. For example, we are curious to find out how much performance can be enhanced by the packet dropping method addressed in Section 6 and in which condition our VAS solution can provide services with end-to-end delay less than 450 ms in a large-scale networking environment (e.g., the Internet).

Acknowledgments. The author would like to thank Stefan Köpsell, Stefan Berthold, Sebastian Clauss and Professor Fischer-Hübner for their comments and suggestions.

References

1. Pfitzmann, A., Hansen, M.: Anonymity, unlinkability, undetectability, unobservability, pseudonymity, and identity management - a consolidated proposal for terminology. Technical report (February 2008)
2. Rosenberg, J., Schulzrinne, H., Camarillo, G., Johnston, A., Peterson, J., Sparks, R., Handley, M., Schooler, E.: SIP: Session Initiation Protocol. RFC 3261 (2002)
3. Handley, M., Jacobson, V.: SDP: Session Description Protocol. RFC 2327 (1998)
4. Schulzrinne, H., Casner, S., Frederick, R., Jacobson, V.: RTP: A Transport Protocol for Real-Time Applications. RFC 3550 (2003)
5. Johansson, I., Westerlund, M.: Support for Reduced-Size Real-Time Transport Control Protocol (RTCP): Opportunities and Consequences. RFC 5506 (2009)
6. G.711, http://www.itu.int/rec/T-REC-G.711/e (visited at October 21, 2009)
7. Spexx, http://www.speex.org/ (visited at October 21, 2009)
8. Zopf, R.: Real-time Transport Protocol (RTP) Payload for Comfort Noise (CN). RFC 3389 (2002)
9. Baugher, M., McGrew, D., Naslund, M., Carrara, E., Norrman, K.: The Secure Real-time Transport Protocol (SRTP). RFC 3711 (2004)
10. Arkko, J., Carrara, E., Lindholm, F., Naslund, M., Norrman, K.: MIKEY: Multimedia Internet KEYing. RFC 3830 (2004)
11. Zimmermann, P., Johnston, A., Callas, J.: ZRTP: Media Path Key Agreement for Secure RTP draft-zimmermann-avt-zrtp-15 (2009) (Internet-Draft)
12. Peterson, J.: A Privacy Mechanism for the Session Initiation Protocol (SIP). RFC 3323 (2002)
13. Shen, C., Schulzrinne, H.: A voip privacy mechanism and its application in voip peering for voice service provider topology and identity hiding (2008)
14. Harrenstien, K., Stahl, M., Feinler, E.: NICNAME/WHOIS. RFC 954 (1985)
15. Geobytes, http://www.geobytes.com/IpLocator.htm?getlocation (visited at May 10, 2009)
16. Karapantazis, S., Pavlidou, F.: Voip: A comprehensive survey on a promising technology. Comput. Netw. 53(12), 2050–2090 (2009)
17. Dingledine, R., Mathewson, N., Syverson, P.: Tor: the second-generation onion router. In: SSYM 2004: Proceedings of the 13th conference on USENIX Security Symposium, Berkeley, CA, USA, pp. 21–21. USENIX Association (2004)
18. Berthold, O., Federrath, H., Köpsell, S.: Web mixes: a system for anonymous and unobservable internet access. In: International workshop on Designing privacy enhancing technologies, pp. 115–129. Springer, New York (2001)
19. Herrmann, D., Wendolsky, R., Federrath, H.: Performance comparison of low-latency anonymisation services from a user perspective. In: Borisov, N., Golle, P. (eds.) PET 2007. LNCS, vol. 4776, pp. 233–253. Springer, Heidelberg (2007)
20. Snader, R., Borisov, N.: A tune-up for tor: Improving security and performance in the tor network. In: NDSS 2008: Proceedings of the Network and Distributed System Security Symposium, NDSS 2008. The Internet Society, San Diego (2008)
21. Sherr, M., Loo, B.T., Blaze, M.: Towards application-aware anonymous routing. In: HOTSEC 2007: Proceedings of the 2nd USENIX workshop on Hot topics in security, Berkeley, CA, USA, pp. 1–5. USENIX Association (2007)

22. Murdoch, S.J., Watson, R.N.: Metrics for security and performance in low-latency anonymity systems. In: Borisov, N., Goldberg, I. (eds.) PETS 2008. LNCS, vol. 5134, pp. 115–132. Springer, Heidelberg (2008)
23. Dingledine, R., Murdoch, S.J.: Performance improvements on tor or, why tor is slow and what we're going to do about it (2009)
24. Vlachos, M., Anagnostopoulos, A., Verscheure, O., Yu, P.S.: Online pairing of voip conversations. The VLDB Journal 18(1), 77–98 (2009)
25. Wright, C.V., Ballard, L., Monrose, F., Masson, G.M.: Language identification of encrypted voip traffic: Alejandra y roberto or alice and bob? In: SS 2007: Proceedings of 16th USENIX Security Symposium on USENIX Security Symposium, Berkeley, CA, USA, pp. 1–12. USENIX Association (2007)
26. Wright, C.V., Ballard, L., Coull, S.E., Monrose, F., Masson, G.M.: Spot me if you can: Uncovering spoken phrases in encrypted voip conversations. In: SP 2008: Proceedings of the 2008 IEEE Symposium on Security and Privacy, Washington, DC, USA, pp. 35–49. IEEE Computer Society, Los Alamitos (2008)
27. Wang, C., Levine, B.N., Reiter, M.K., Wright, M.: Timing attacks in low-latency mix systems (extended abstract). In: Juels, A. (ed.) FC 2004. LNCS, vol. 3110, pp. 251–265. Springer, Heidelberg (2004)
28. Wang, X., Chen, S., Jajodia, S.: Tracking anonymous peer-to-peer voip calls on the internet. In: CCS 2005: Proceedings of the 12th ACM conference on Computer and communications security, pp. 81–91. ACM, New York (2005)

PRIvacy LEakage Methodology (PRILE) for IDS Rules

Nils Ulltveit-Moe and Vladimir Oleshchuk

University of Agder
Servicebox 509
NO-4898 Grimstad, Norway
{Nils.Ulltveit-Moe,Vladimir.Oleshchuk}@uia.no

Abstract. This paper introduces a methodology for evaluating PRIvacy LEakage in signature-based Network Intrusion Detection System (IDS) rules. IDS rules that expose more data than a given percentage of all data sessions are defined as privacy leaking. Furthermore, it analyses the IDS rule attack specific pattern size required in order to keep the privacy leakage below a given threshold, presuming that occurrence frequencies of the attack pattern in normal text are known. We have applied the methodology on the network intrusion detection system Snort's rule set. The evaluation confirms that Snort in its default configuration aims at not being excessively privacy invasive. However we have identified some types of rules rules with poor or missing ability to distinguish attack traffic from normal traffic.

Keywords: IDS, rules, privacy impact, methodology, privacy violation.

1 Introduction

One of the largest threats towards on-line security and privacy today is attacks caused by cyber-criminals. Such attacks can be devastating from a privacy perspective, since they can be used for theft of identity, sensitive information or sensitive transactions. It is important to use counter measures against this threat by using computer security technologies like firewalls, anti-virus and Intrusion Detection Systems (IDS).

However, the operation of IDS systems imply that alarms with potentially sensitive information may be revealed to the security analysts monitoring the alarms. This may be particularly problematic if the IDS monitoring is outsourced to a third party. Contractual means like confidentiality agreements alone cannot hinder potential misuse of this information, for example by a corrupt security analyst performing the monitoring. Such misuse may be subtle and hard to detect. The analyst could for example use sensitive insider information leaked out via IDS alarms for his own gain when buying or selling shares in a monitored company, or he could sell such information to competitors.

It is therefore important to have a methodology that can be used to analyse the privacy impact of Intrusion Detection System (IDS) rules, in order to identify how

M. Bezzi et al. (Eds.): Privacy and Identity, IFIP AICT 320, pp. 213–225, 2010.

privacy invasive the operation of signature-based IDS's are in a given scenario and context.

Our methodology is an engineering approach aimed at keeping the average privacy leakage caused by IDS rules below a certain threshold. The approach does not give any privacy guarantees, although the amount of privacy leakage can be chosen arbitrarily low[1]. It is not a replacement for provably secure methods for improving the privacy of IDS operations like for example cryptographic methods for privacy-preserving IDS. We believe the methodology can be useful in order to tune IDS rule sets to be less privacy invasive than what they typically are today. The usefulness comes both as reduced privacy leakage in the form of less exposure to sensitive information and as improved rule efficiency with less false alarms.

We apply the methodology on a case study of how privacy violating the rule set of the Snort IDS is. The rule set is categorised manually based on expert knowledge into five different categories.

This paper is organised as follows: Section 2 goes through some categorisation examples as an introduction to the problems the methodology is attempting to solve. Section 3 performs a theoretical analysis of privacy leakage from IDS rules. Section 4 describes the PRILE evaluation methodology and section 5 discusses the case study where the PRILE methodology was applied to the Snort rule set. Section 6 presents results from the case study, section 7 presents related work and section 8 contains concluding remarks.

2   Categorisation Examples

This section goes through some categorisation examples based on Snort IDS rules, as motivation for the methodology introduced in section 3 and 4. In subsection 2.1, we go through three clear categorisation examples - two attack rules that are not considered privacy violating and one user surveillance rule that is considered privacy violating. In the next subsection, we go through some less clear examples. The last subsection concludes the privacy against security discussion by recommending that a privacy leakage analysis of the IDS operation from a methodological perspective should be performed independently of security considerations as far as practically possible.

2.1   Clear Categorisation Examples

In some cases, it is relatively easy to determine that IDS rules are violating the user's privacy. IDS rules can often be presumed to contain bad or exceptional traffic if they describe malicious activities, like backdoors, viruses, worms, denial of service attacks, spoofing, shellcode or other attacks. It is further expected that attack rules without a significant privacy impact are reasonably precise, meaning that they most probably will detect the malicious activities without generating

---

[1] There are probably both technological and economical limits for how low the privacy leakage threshold can be set presuming today's IDS technology.

too many false alarms which may reveal privacy sensitive information about ordinary users.

The privacy impact of Snort rules vary greatly. Some rules are very specific and target a given attack. Especially when the rule targets a binary attack vector, for example an incoming worm or virus, then the utility from a security perspective can be expected to be high and the privacy impact from monitoring this event low because the revealed payload consists of binary code, which is more or less unintelligible and the rule is precise at matching an attack. One example of such a rule, is the rule with Snort ID (*sid:*) 2003 "MS-SQL Worm Propagation attempt". The modeled vulnerability (CVE-2002-0449) has a Common Vulnerability Scoring System (CVSS) score in the Common Vulnerabilities and Exposures (CVE) Database[2] of 7.5 out of 10, so this is considered a quite serious attack from a security perspective. This rule looks like the following:

```
alert udp $EXTERNAL_NET any -> $HOME_NET 1434 (\
msg:"MS-SQL Worm propagation attempt";\
content:"|04|"; depth:1;\
content:"|81 F1 03 01 04 9B 81 F1 01|";\
content:"sock";\
content:"send";\
reference:bugtraq,5310;\
reference:bugtraq,5311;\
reference:cve,2002-0649;\
reference:nessus,11214;\
reference:url,vil.nai.com/vil/content/v_99992.htm;\
classtype:misc-attack;\
sid:2003;\
rev:8;)
```

The rule matches MS-SQL worm propagation attempts. These are UDP requests from any port on the external network towards the well known port number of Microsoft's SQL server on the home network. Snort usually presumes that alerts can only be caused by traffic to or from your own network, which is why it defines the variable $HOME_NET. The *msg:* field shows the IDS alert message that will show up in the IDS console when this rule is triggered. In this case, "MS-SQL Worm propagation attempt". The *content:* field matches specific strings or patterns in the payload. Four different content patterns are required to be present in an UDP packet to trigger this rule. Some of the matched content is binary data whereas other is ASCII text. The first *content:* field matches at depth (offset) 1 into the payload. The rule contains 5 authoritative references to other sources that describe the vulnerability, including Bugtraq and the Common Vulnerabilities and Exposures (CVE) databases of publicly known security vulnerabilities. *Classtype:* is Snort's rule classification. This rule is classified as a *misc-attack* rule, which indicates that the rule matches a known attack. *Sid:* is the unique Snort rule identity and *rev:* is the rule revision.

---

[2] Common Vulnerabilities and Exposures http://cve.mitre.org

This is a specific rule, backed up by authoritative references. It is a quite serious exposure for vulnerable systems, as indicated by the CVSS score of 7.5. It is targeted against a system service that is not normally exposed to end-users on the Internet and should be reasonably precise at only matching attacks. The utility from a security perspective can in other words be expected to be high and the privacy impact low for this rule. We therefore categorised this as an attack rule, that is not regarded as sensitive from a privacy perspective.

A rule that can be expected to violate users' privacy, is *sid:1437* "MULTI-MEDIA Windows Media download". This is a broad policy rule that matches download of any windows media files via the web. It does however not indicate which file that was downloaded[3].

```
alert tcp $EXTERNAL_NET 80 -> $HOME_NET any (\
msg:"MULTIMEDIA Windows Media download";\
flow:from_server,established;\
content:"Content-Type|3A|"; nocase;\
pcre:"/^Content-Type\x3a\s*(?=[av])(video\/x\-ms\-(w[vm]x|asf)|
     a(udio\/x\-ms\-w(m[av]|ax)|pplication\/x\-ms\-wm[zd]))/smi";\
classtype:policy-violation;\
sid:1437;\
rev:6;)
```

This rule matches TCP traffic originating from the external network and with destination to any port on the home network. It is in other word an HTTP reply message. The alert message given in the IDS console is "MULTIMEDIA Windows Media download" and it matches established TCP sessions originating from the server. The rule first performs a case insensitive string match on the HTTP header element "Content-Type:" in the payload. If the *content:* rule matches, then the regular expression as indicated in the *pcre:* field will be executed to match the Windows Media multimedia MIME types for *wvx, wmx, wma, wmv, wax, wmz* and *wmd* files. This rule is *not* backed up by any external references like CVE or Bugtraq, so the rule does not present any evidence of having any significant security impact. It is purely a rule for detecting violation of an IT usage policy, where downloading media files is not allowed. This is also indicated in Snort's *classtype:* field which classifies it as a "policy-violation", which broadly means a violation of corporate IT policy[4]. A user being monitored will probably regard such monitoring as a privacy violation, since the monitoring effectively limits what a user can see and do, and it affects both legal and illegal activities. This rule is therefore categorised as a privacy violating rule. Further information about interpreting Snort rules can be found in the Snort user's manual included in the source code distribution[5].

---

[3] It is technically possible to record all network traffic over a limited time span using network forensic interfaces [1]. The monitoring organisation can therefore still detect downloaded media files, if they desire to do so.

[4] It should however be noted that the policy-violation rules not are enabled by default in Snort.

[5] Snort is available from http://www.snort.org

2.2 What about Conflicting Rules?

Some IDS rules are designed to monitor entire applications. For example SID 2372 is a rule that monitors all access to the file *showphoto.php*. The IDS rule detects two critical SQL injection vulnerabilities (CVSS score 10) that are remotely exploitable. SQL injection vulnerabilities can often be attributed to poor software engineering practices, so if one such vulnerability is detected, then it is reasonable that other similar vulnerabilities may exist as well in the vulnerable application. Another reason for adding general application monitoring, is that SQL injection attacks often have a large set of potential SQL-based attack vectors that can target the vulnerability, which means that it may seem easier and simpler for the author of the IDS rule to safeguard and write one rule that catches all application activities, than to cover all potential SQL injection attack vectors. Another complication, is the variety of encoding schemes used on the web, which can be used to evade attack detection. Examples of such encoding schema are URL encoding, HEX or Unicode[6].

This means that there is a significant chance that real attacks, hidden by a particular encoding scheme, may go undetected by a security analyst viewing the alert. It would be better in this case to use a more complex rule, that is able to trigger on the core of the problem, instead of general application activity monitoring.

However, there also exist some vulnerabilities where it can be harder to avoid general application monitoring. For example vulnerabilities that give direct or partial access to an unrestricted execution environment like the underlying operating system. These vulnerabilities are often due to lack of input data validation before external programs are called.

An example of such an input validation error is SID 1717, WEB-CGI simplestguest.cgi access. This is covered by the vulnerability CVE-2001-0022, which has a CVSS score of 10. The vulnerability allows remote attackers to execute arbitrary commands via shell meta characters in the guestbook parameter of the CGI script due to lack of parameter checking. It is not possible to know in advance which set of commands that may be attempted executed, so the safest thing to do, is to monitor all access to the vulnerable parameter of the CGI-script. However, it would be even better if the rule could simulate the input validation and let the most common normal use cases of the vulnerable parameter pass through without any alerts, to reduce the amount of false alarms and privacy leakage from using the rule.

2.3 Privacy against Security

IDS rules used in Managed Security Services (MSS) can in other words leak private and sensitive information. Customers will have particular concern about this for outsourced MSS. On the other hand, outsourcing MSS is usually cost effective and more efficient than running the service in-house from a security

---

[6] See Ofer Maor and Amichai Schulman SQL Injection Signatures Evasion
  http://www.imperva.com/docs/SQLInjectionSignaturesEvasion.pdf

standpoint. Few companies can for example afford running their own 24x7 monitoring service. There is in other words a trade off between potential privacy leakage caused by a monitoring organisation running an MSS, and the privacy leakage caused by adversaries.

It should in this respect be noted that the effects of privacy leakage to criminals can be devastating and is without any regulatory control, whereas the privacy leakage from MSS are presumed to be measurable and under regulatory control. The MSS providers will however be liable if they breach the confidentiality agreement with the customer. It should therefore be a goal for the monitoring organisation to minimise the harm on privacy and confidentiality for the subjects being monitored, both as work ethics and because this reduces potential liabilities for the MSS provider.

The privacy invasiveness of IDS rules vary a lot. As the discussion above has shown, there are both specific and unspecific IDS rules with both high and low CVSS score. Analysing the *privacy impact* of IDS rules should in general be done *independently* of the security relevance of the IDS rule[7]. In conflicting situations where there is a privacy against security dilemma for an IDS rule, then the privacy leakage as a result of false alarms (false positives) can almost always be reduced significantly by investing some more effort into the design of the IDS rule. For example by making a more specific IDS rule that performs a more accurate test for the attack pattern and that also only matches vulnerable versions of applications instead of monitoring all versions of a given application or service. This can in many cases be done without significantly affecting the amount of missed real attacks (false negatives), as we have indicated in the examples in section 2.2. As an additional benefit, the MSS provider will probably reduce the costs of processing false IDS alarms.

3   Quantifying Privacy Leakage

We will in this section attempt to quantify the privacy leakage from IDS rules. An IDS rule signature R can be considered to consist of two parts as shown in Figure 1:

- *A protocol specific part P consisting of one or more patterns used to address a specific part of a session. The protocol specific part(s) trigger for every session for the chosen scope (platform, service, program or file level).*
- *An attack distinguishing part A consisting of one or more patterns, which aims at matching an attack vector, for example given by a software vulnerability.*

---

[7] It can for example not be claimed that a high CVSS score in general warrants more privacy invasive monitoring, since this disregards privacy rights. More privacy invasive monitoring can only be warranted if this is the only practical solution for detecting the attack. If it is viable to detect the attack in a more privacy-friendly way, then this should be attempted.

IDS rule R

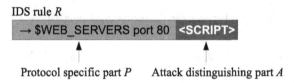

     Protocol specific part P Attack distinguishing part A

Fig. 1. Illustration of the protocol specific part and attack distinguishing part for an IDS rule (SID 1497, WEB-MISC cross site scripting attempt)

The privacy leakage of an IDS rule describes how much potentially sensitive information that leaks out from applying the rule, that is not attack relevant. The privacy leakage is defined as:

Definition 1. *Let S be a sufficiently large set of communication sessions[8], $S = \{s_i | i = 1, ..., n\}$, identified by the protocol specific part P of an IDS rule R. Let $E \subseteq S$ be a set of sessions that have been exposed by the IDS via alert messages that are false alarms. The privacy leakage p can then be calculated as the fraction $p = \frac{|E|}{|S|}$ of exposed communication sessions that are not attack related to all communication sessions.*

From this, it is apparent that the privacy leakage is proportional to the false positive rate for attack rules, however it is not the same measure. The false positive rate is the fraction of false alarms to the total number of alarms, whereas the privacy leakage instead is related to the total number of data sessions for a given scope.

It should be noted that this definition of privacy leakage implicitly presumes that real alarms (true positives) do not leak private or sensitive information. This may not necessarily be the case for rules identifying attack vectors where the user is lured into performing the attack by the adversary. Examples of such attacks are trojans and web bugs. It may be important from a security standpoint to investigate such attacks, regardless of whether it was the attacker or the user who initiated the attack. This means that real alarms (true positives) must be investigated, however additional privacy enhancing techniques like pseudonymisation or anonymisation of the alert data should be considered in these cases to protect the user's privacy.

We can now proceed with analysing the privacy leakage p for a group of commonly used IDS rules: match of an attack pattern in b different byte positions within each session s_i. It is in particular interesting to analyse the borderline case with a one byte wide attack distinguishing pattern A, since that occurs relatively frequently, and it is not obvious that a one byte wide pattern is sufficient to keep the privacy leakage below a chosen maximum privacy leakage threshold.

It is presumed that the occurrence frequency f of the attack distinguishing pattern A for a byte stream of normal traffic is known or can be measured.

---

[8] Data on session level is preferred to data on packet level since the data forensics involved in determining whether an alert is a false positive or a real attack often requires that the entire data session is loaded from a data forensics tool like a Time Machine http://www.net.t-labs.tu-berlin.de/research/tm/

On average $1/f$ bytes between each attack distinguishing pattern A

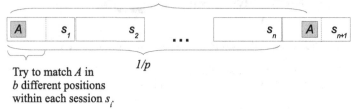

Fig. 2. Match of attack pattern in b different positions within each session s_i

The privacy leakage caused by matching the attack pattern A in b different byte positions can then be calculated using the relation $f \leq \frac{p}{b}$, as indicated in Figure 2, which gives:

$$bf \leq p. \tag{1}$$

This means that the number of byte positions matched times the occurrence frequency must be less than or equal to the privacy leakage.

Example 1. The IDS rule (SID 2666) for a format string vulnerability in the Courier-IMAP server uses the following regular expression:
$/\hat{}PASS\backslash s+[\hat{}\backslash n]*?\%/smi$. In this regular expression, it is only one character, the '%' sign, that differentiates this IDS rule from a normal IMAP password authentication session. Furthermore, the regular expression matches the percent sign in any position of the password. It is in other words only the *percent sign* that is the *attack distinguishing part* of the IDS rule. The maximum privacy leakage threshold is chosen to be $p = 1\%$.

Presuming that the probability of hitting a percent sign in a random password has been measured[9] to $f = 0.0017$, and that the average password size is $b = 8$ bytes, this means that $bf = 1.35\%$ by using Equation 1. Since this is larger than 1%, this means that the IDS rule is considered privacy violating.

This example shows that IDS rules with a one byte wide attack distinguishing pattern can be privacy violating. In general, the occurrence frequency of the attack pattern f is not available. It is therefore only possible to get good estimates of the privacy leakage for some special cases like this. It is however in many cases still possible to estimate the privacy leakage for extreme cases where one can argue that the attack distinguishing pattern either occurs sufficiently frequently to cause a a privacy leakage or sufficiently infrequently to not cause a privacy leakage based on qualitative arguments. For example can rules that detect attacks based on protocol violations in many cases be expected to have little or no privacy leakage, presuming that they seldom or never happen in ordinary traffic. Also, many overflow detecting rules match so wide patterns for typed user input that they probably not will be privacy leaking for normal traffic.

---

[9] Matt Weir Reusable Security - Character Frequency Analysis Info
http://reusablesec.blogspot.com/2009/05/character-frequency-analysis-info.html

4 Evaluation Methodology

The aim of our evaluation methodology is to provide a gold standard for evaluating the privacy impact of Network-based IDS rules. We have defined a 5 level scale for privacy invasiveness that focuses on how wide scope the privacy violation has. This scope is also important for the privacy leakage calculation, since it defines the split between the protocol specific part P and the attack distinguishing part A for a given IDS rule. The privacy leakage scale is defined below:

0-None No privacy leakage expected from the IDS rule. This can for example happen for rules detecting protocol violations or denial of service attacks that can not happen from normal user behaviour.

1-Vulnerability The IDS rule models attacks based on a known *vulnerability* in a specific way. This means that the IDS rule can be expected to expose less than a given percentage p of all sessions being investigated by it. Another way of interpreting this level is as a *tolerable* average privacy leakage.

2-Program file More than p percent of all sessions targeted at a given *program file or module* as part of an application are being monitored.

3-Application More than p percent of all sessions targeted at a given *application* or *service* are being monitored. An *application* is presumed to consist of several program files.

4-Platform More than p percent of all sessions targeted at a given *platform* are being monitored. For example monitoring of specific files or file types across all services for a given operating system, which potentially can cause monitoring of any application on that given platform. The scope of all sessions S must here be limited to the number of relevant sessions. If specific files or file types are being monitored on platform level, then S must only consist of sessions that contain the monitored files or file types.

5-Policy The IDS rule is applied on *network-wide level* and is not necessarily relevant from a security perspective. It is defined to monitor or control usage of services being monitored. The legality of Level 5 rules in a given legislative area must be investigated before such rules are enabled. For example, monitoring use of end-user services like chat, instant messaging, VoIP, email or web.

The enumerated scale from 0 to 5 can then be used for quantitative measurements of privacy invasiveness. The scale is bounded and naturally lends itself to further aggregation over a group of rules. Furthermore, we define a *privacy violating rule* as a *rule that leaks more information than level 1*. That means that level 2, 3, 4 and 5 IDS rules are privacy violating by definition.

5 Discussion

Manual categorisation of 3669 Snort rules from the community rule set was done according to our PRILE methodology. We presume a network environment where all typical end-user services (HTTP,FTP,POP,IMAP,...) are provided on the Internet in their normal configuration. We furthermore presume English localisation (language) of the environment where the IDS rules are applied. For file storage services, like FTP, we presume that some end-users can have access to both upload and download of data.

The main problem we identified during categorisation, is IDS rules that perform full monitoring of all access to an application or program file as part of an application. This is quite common for web application monitoring rules. The problem with this practice is the privacy leakage that full access monitoring causes.

Our opinion is that IDS systems and rules should be improved to reduce the scope of monitoring in order to only detect attack traffic and preferably only trigger on vulnerable applications. General application monitoring can be so noisy that the utility of it also from a security standpoint can be disputed. However, rules should not be made so specific that they reduce the risks of identifying likely variants of a given attack. So there will in practice often be a trade off between privacy leakage reduction and IDS rule generalisation. However, section 2.2 shows that the current practice often goes too far in the direction of monitoring all access to a given service or application.

Another type of vulnerabilities that often have weak attack distinguishing patterns are format string vulnerabilities. Most of these have only got an attack distinguishing pattern of one byte. For example, SID 2666 targets a format string vulnerability for the password handling of Courier-IMAP. This is the rule that was analysed in Section 3.

6   Results

487 of the 3669 manually categorised Snort rules (13%) appear to have a significant impact on privacy as shown in Table 1. However, in a default Snort installation 15 rule files with 270 rules are disabled. All the level 5 policy specific rules (117 rules) were contained within the set of disabled rule files, which is encouraging. This shows that Snort in its default configuration aims at not

Table 1. PRIvacy LEakage (PRILE) classification of Snort rule sets

PRILE	Privacy invasiveness	Default rule set	Disabled rules	All rules
0	None	13	4	17
1	Vulnerability	3026	139	3165
Total non-privacy violating:		3039	143	3182
2	Program file	333	5	338
3	Application	24	3	27
4	Platform	3	2	5
5	Policy		117	117
Total privacy violating:		360	127	487
Percentage privacy violating:		11%	47%	13%

being excessively privacy invasive. The policy specific rules detect content like chat, pornography, peer-to-peer or multimedia. The complete rule set has 370 privacy violating rules on level 2 to 4. These are general file, application or platform monitoring rules, which are founded on a known vulnerability. Even if these rules account for only 10% of all IDS rules, they can be expected to cause significant privacy leakage, false alarms and draw processing power from the IDS sensor. This means that there is a large improvement potential from a privacy and efficiency perspective if these rules are tightened up to fall within PRILE 1. In fact, 76% of all rules categorised as privacy violating fall into this category.

7   Related Work

There exists, as far as we know, no similar scoring system that can be used to analyse the privacy leakage of IDS rules. There are however similar scoring systems for system vulnerabilities. The Common Vulnerability Scoring System (CVSS) is an industry standard metric for the characteristics and impacts of IT vulnerabilities [2]. This score is useful to indicate the security relevance of a given IDS rule. It has also got a confidentiality indicator which measures the level of potential confidentiality loss from a vulnerability. However, it does not cover the potential confidentiality loss that can occur from IDS monitoring activities.

There is also some relevant work within the area of privacy metrics. Privacy violations of internet sites are described in [3], however this paper is quite general and does not mention any indicators that capture the amount of privacy violations. Other metrics for privacy are entropy-based [4] or based on the combination of k-anonymity [5, 6, 7] and l-diversity [8]. These measures focus more on how anonymous data are than to measure to what extent a network monitoring organisation's operation is privacy-intrusive.

Another related area is privacy enhanced intrusion detection systems. The BRO IDS for example supports a way to anonymise the payload of a packet instead of removing the entire payload [9]. There also exists some earlier work on privacy-enhanced host-based IDS systems that pseudonymise audit data and performs analysis on the pseudonymised audit records [10, 11, 12, 13, 14, 15].

8   Conclusion

This paper introduces a new methodology - PRILE for identifying privacy leakage in IDS rules. The methodology itself is intended to be generic and should also be useful for privacy leakage evaluation of other network intrusion detection systems than Snort. A limitation with the methodology is that it does not specify how to define the scope for preprocessors and similar IDS rules that present aggregated data[10]. In these cases, the false alarm rate can be used as an

---

[10] False alarms from preprocessors or composed IDS systems may also contain aggregated data with sensitive information. For example false alarms from the Snort portscan preprocessor which may reveal information about user behaviour like web browsing habits.

alternative indicator of privacy leaking rules, since it is proportional to our privacy leakage metric for a given IDS rule.

We have performed a proof-of-concept evaluation of the Snort rule set using the PRILE methodology. This evaluation confirms that Snort in its default configuration aims at not being excessively privacy invasive. Level 5 policy rules are for example switched off by default. Problematic areas we have identified are rules with poor or missing ability to distinguish attack traffic from normal traffic. For example general file, application or platform monitoring rules, which are founded on known vulnerabilities. Even if these rules account for only 10% of all IDS rules, they can be expected to cause privacy leakage, false alarms and draw a significant amount of processing power from the IDS sensor. This means that there is a large improvement potential from a privacy, cost and efficiency perspective if these rules are tightened up to fall within PRILE level 1.

In addition, optimisations of the IDS rule set can and should be considered both in the temporal domain based on "smart" IDS rules that disable themselves when a system is patched up and also based on the environment - whether rules are relevant for the platforms and appliances in the network being monitored.

Future research includes adding support for measuring the privacy leakage and occurrence frequency of attack distinguished patterns on an existing IDS system, in order to get better privacy leakage estimates and improve the model. Another possibility is to do a broader study where a representative set of experts perform the same classification to achieve a more objective interpretation of the PRILE methodology. Experiences by applying the methodology can then be used to further improve it. Last, but not least - this methodology may open up a possibility for privacy impact testing tools for IDS systems.

Acknowledgments. This work is funded by Telenor Research & Innovation under the contract DR-2009-1.

References

[1] Maier, G., Sommer, R., Dreger, H., Feldmann, A., Paxson, V., Shneider, F.: Enriching network security analysis with time travel. SIGCOMM Comput. Commun. Rev. 38(4), 183–194 (2008)

[2] Mell, P., Scarfone, K., Romanosky, S.: CVSS a complete guide to the common vulnerability scoring system version 2.0 (2007),
http://www.first.org/cvss/cvss-guide.pdf

[3] Klewitz-Hommelsen, S.: Indicators for privacy violation of internet sites. Electronic Government, 219–223 (2002)

[4] Sebastian Clauß, S.S.: Structuring anonymity metrics. In: Proceedings of the second ACM workshop on Digital identity management, pp. 55–62 (2006)

[5] Ti, P.S.: Protecting respondents' identities in microdata release. IEEE Transactions on Knowledge and Data Engineering 13, 1010–1027 (2001)

[6] Sweeney, L.: k-anonymity: a model for protecting privacy. International Journal on Uncertainty. Fuzziness and Knowledge-based Systems 10, 557–570 (2002)

[7] Ciriani, V., di Vimercati, S.C., Foresti, S., Samarati, P.: k-Anonymity. In: Secure Data Management in Decentralized Systems, pp. 323–353. Springer, Heidelberg (2007)

[8] Machanavajjhala, A., Kifer, D., Gehrke, J., Venkitasubramaniam, M.: l-diversity: Privacy beyond k-anonymity, March 2007, p. 52. Cornell University (2007)

[9] Pang, R., Paxson, V.: A high-level programming environment for packet trace anonymization and transformation. In: Proceedings of the 2003 conference on Applications, technologies, architectures, and protocols for computer communications, Karlsruhe, Germany, pp. 339–351. ACM, New York (2003)

[10] Sobirey, M., Fischer-Hübner, S., Rannenberg, K.: Pseudonymous audit for privacy enhanced intrusion detection. In: Proceedings of the IFIP TC11 13th International Conference on Information Security (SEC 1997), May 1997, pp. 151–163 (1997)

[11] Fischer-Hübner, S.: IDA - An Intrusion Detection and Avoidance System, Aachen, Shaker (2007) (in German)

[12] Sobirey, M., Richter, B., König, H.: The intrusion detection system aid - architecture and experiences in automated autid trail analysis. In: Proceedings of the IFIP TC6/TC11 International Conference on Communications and Multimedia Security, pp. 278–290 (1996)

[13] Büschkes, R., Kesdogan, D.: Privacy enhanced intrusion detection. In: Müller, G., Rannenberg, K. (eds.) Multilateral Security in Communications, Information Security, pp. 187–204. Addison Wesley, Reading (1999)

[14] Flegel, U.: Privacy-Respecting Intrusion Detection, 1st edn. Springer, Heidelberg (October 2007)

[15] Holz, T.: An efficient distributed intrusion detection scheme. In: COMPSAC Workshops, pp. 39–40 (2004)

Digital Personae and Profiles as Representations of Individuals

Arnold Roosendaal

Tilburg Institute for Law, Technology, and Society (TILT)
Tilburg University
PO Box 90153, 5000 LE Tilburg, The Netherlands
A.P.C.Roosendaal@uvt.nl

Abstract. This paper explores the concepts of digital personae and profiles and the way they represent individuals. Even though their manifestation as data sets seems similar, they originate in different ways. The differences between the two forms of digital representations have major implications for their connection and application to known individuals. Digital personae are connected to known individuals in the real world, whereas profiles are not. However, different types of identification can establish the connection between a profile and an offline individual. A profile can then transform into a digital persona. The differences between digital personae and profiles have implications for the applicability of data protection regulations and influence the amount of control individuals have over their representations and decisions based on these. This paper shows the relation between digital personae and profiles and indicates where privacy and autonomy of individuals can be at stake.

Keywords: Digital Persona, Profile, Representation, Individual, Data sets.

1 Introduction

The enormous amount of electronic data inherent to the information society facilitates the establishment of digital personae [1], representations of individuals in the form of data sets. These digital personae are used by governments or businesses to take decisions that affect the represented individual. Digital personae are consciously created with a specific, indicated purpose, and the concerned individual is usually aware of the representation being created. Another form of digital representations are profiles. These are the result of automated processes where large data sets are processed in order to arrive at (a set of) characteristics which can be used as a basis for decision making. Usually, in particular in the case of group profiles, the represented individual is not known in the real world beforehand, but a profile can be connected to a known individual later on.

This paper presents the concept of a digital persona (section 2) and of a profile (section 3) and explores similarities and differences between the two (section 4). It appears that the manifestation of both forms is basically similar, namely as a data set comprising attributes instantiated with values associated to the individual, but the differences in the way they are constructed and the intended purpose and connection

M. Bezzi et al. (Eds.): Privacy and Identity, IFIP AICT 320, pp. 226–236, 2010.

to individuals in the real world are essential to gain further insight in how the represented individuals are affected. Section 5 analyses this connection between individuals and data sets from a legal perspective. The real world individuals are the underlying entities which are represented by data sets (identities) [1]. These data sets can contain personal data. Personal data means: "any information relating to an identified or identifiable natural person ('data subject'); an identifiable person is one who can be identified, directly or indirectly, in particular by reference to an identification number or to one or more factors specific to his physical, physiological, mental, economic, cultural or social identity" (Art. 2(a) Data Protection Directive (DPD)[1]). Thus, for the applicability of the DPD it is important to know whether the connection between a digital persona or a profile and the underlying entity can be made based on the data in the representation. It appears that the DPD might be applicable in the case of a digital persona as well as in the case of a profile as a basis for taking decisions. The main focus is to clarify to what extent digital personae and profiles can be connected to entities and to come to a common understanding of the two concepts. In section 6 the conclusions are drawn.

2   Digital Personae

A digital persona is a representation of an individual, identifiable[2] by the one who creates and/or uses the data set. The concept of a digital persona was introduced by Roger Clarke, who used the following definition: "a model of an individual's public personality based on data and maintained by transactions, and intended for use as a proxy for the individual" [2]. The representational capacity is a key element. It follows from the definition that functioning as a proxy for a specific individual is intended, so the representations that qualify as a digital persona are limited to those data sets which contain an identifying link to an entity. To compare, Solove, for instance, takes a much broader perspective when he talks about a digital person. He states that "it is ever more possible to create an electronic collage that covers much of a person's life – a life captured in records, a digital person composed in the collective computer networks of the world" [3]. Solove's digital person includes digital personae as well as profiles, which will be discussed later on in this paper, and other data sets. In the case of a digital persona, the purpose of its creation is known beforehand, and therefore the data that are needed to form the representation are also known or at least to a certain extent. This implies that creating a digital persona can be compared to filling out a template since it is known which attributes one needs.

Clarke distinguishes between projected personae and imposed personae. A projected digital persona is "an image of one's self that an individual conveys to others by means of data", for instance by creating a personal page on a social network site, whereas the imposed digital persona is "an identity projected onto a person by means of data, by outside agencies such as corporations and government agencies" [2], for instance a record created by a credit rating agency. A combined form is also possible,

---

[1] Directive 95/46/EC of the European Parliament and of the Council of 24 October 1995 on the protection of individuals with regard to the processing of personal data and on the free movement of such data, No L 281/31.

[2] Identifiability can take different forms. See below, section 3.1.

for instance when an electronic patient record (usually called a 'profile') is created. The concerned individual is closely involved in the creation and provides a major part of the data. The health provider stores the data and adds personal interpretations and other data (e.g. diagnoses and personal observations). The creation and maintenance of the digital persona is based on transactions, which can be any kind of interaction between the concerned individual and persons or technical devices.

The data that form a digital persona can function as or are a representation of a partial identity of the individual. A partial identity is a subset of attributes of a complete identity, where a complete identity is the union of all attributes of all identities of this person [4]. Usually, a digital persona is created for use in a specific context, so the data that are relevant for the purpose are limited to this context. For instance, data concerning the income and taxations of an individual are not relevant for a medical dossier, so they should not be included there. Even though the represented individual is aware of the existence of digital personae, she does not always know what the contents exactly are. In particular in the case of imposed personae, the individual may be aware of part of the data, mainly those data that are obvious to be included, such as name and address and specific context related data, but the individual may not know which additional data are part of the representation (e.g. a medical diagnosis).

3 Profiles

Another form of digital representations of individuals are profiles. These are the result of an automated process where large data sets are processed in order to come to (a set of) characteristics which can be used as a basis for decision making. A profile is a set of correlated data which is created with the use of profiling technologies, a set of technologies with as a common characteristic the use of algorithms or other techniques to create, discover or construct knowledge from huge sets of data. Profiling can be defined as "[t]he process of 'discovering' correlations between data in databases that can be used to identify and represent a human or nonhuman subject (individual or group) and/or the application of profiles (sets of correlated data) to individuate and represent a subject or to identify a subject as a member of a group or category" [5] or the creation of a representation based on automated monitoring of individual behaviour. The data can be aggregated from different sources. In first instance, there is no direct connection to an entity, so individuals that can be affected later on are not (necessarily) aware of the data collection.

Profiles concern groups or individuals. Group profiles describe a set of attributes concerning a group of people and are created with a data mining process. Group profiles can be distributive or non-distributive. In the case of a distributive group profile, the attributes of the group are also the attributes of all the members of the group. For instance, the attribute of 'not being married' for a group of bachelors also counts for each individual member of the group. For non-distributive group profiles, matters are more complicated. Consider again the group of bachelors, and suppose an indication is added that this group has a higher risk of getting a liver disease. This higher risk applies to the group, but not to each individual, because other factors, like drinking behaviour, are also relevant. The association is statistical rather than determinate.

Here, the information contained in the profile envisages individuals as members of groups; it does not envisage the individuals as such [6].

In the case of an individual profile automatic monitoring processes are executed to collect and analyse data from a specific individual. This individual does not have to be identified (yet) when data is added to the profile, but only recognized, for instance based on a cookie. The profile is created based on monitoring behaviour of the concerned individual.

The table below gives an overview of the main characteristics of digital personae and profiles. As can be seen, the main differences between the two lie in the creation and whether the represented individual is aware of the data set. A profile can be connected to an individual later on, while the connection between a digital persona and an individual is ingrained beforehand.

Table 1. Characteristics of digital personae and profiles

Characteristics	Digital Persona		Profile	
Creation	Desired attributes in 'template'	Projected persona	Result of profiling technologies: automated process	Distributive profile
		Imposed persona		Non-distributive profile
				Individual profile
Awareness	Individual is aware		Individual is not (necessarily) aware	
Connection to individual	Ingrained beforehand		Can be connected/applied to a specific individual later on	

3.1 From Profile to Digital Persona

Even though there is no direct connection to a specific entity, a profile can be connected to or applied to an individual later on. The connection to an individual can be made based on the identification of an individual as having one or more attributes contained in the profile. Leenes [7] distinguishes between different forms of identifiability. Depending on the data in the data set, in his terms, the identifiability can be L-identifiability for Look-up identifiability or R-identifiability for Recognition identifiability. L-identifiability means that there is a register or table that provides the connection between an identifier and an individual, such as a phone directory which links phone numbers to names. In case of a digital persona, the data set always contains an L-identifier, like a name or a passport number. This implies that there is a direct connection to an individual and that data protection regulation applies.

Profiles do not contain L-identifiers, but they connect to individuals in an indirect manner. As seen above, an individual profile may contain an R-identifier, such as a cookie, which facilitates the recognition of the individual when she returns to the site of the profiling one (e.g. Amazon). A group profile refers to a number of people. People that show certain behavior or an attribute that is in the profile can be identified as belonging to a certain class. After recognition as a member of a group, an identifier can be issued to enable R-identification in the future. So, according to Leenes [7], the typical procedure will be: after the group profile is instantiated to the individual an

R-identifier (e.g. cookie) is issued to the individual to maintain the link. The group profile is now an individual profile. It is important to note that at this point (R-ID in profile) there is no link to an entity.[3]

An individual profile can become a digital persona when an L-identifier is added. For instance, an individual at a certain point in time gives identifying information, or the information is obtained from another source. The L-identifier makes the connection between the individual profile and an offline individual. Since the data in the profile is provided by a third party it takes the form of an imposed digital persona. With regard to data protection, group profiles are excluded. Individual profiles, however, are in a grey area, because there can be discussion on whether an R-Identifier can indirectly identify an individual. An example of such a discussion can be found in IP-addresses [9]. The figure below gives a schematic overview of the relation between profiles and digital personae.

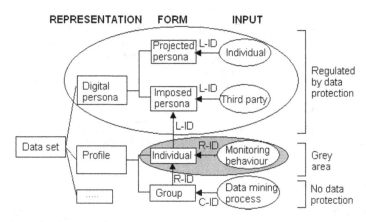

Fig. 1. The relation between digital personae and profiles. The C-ID is a non-individual identifier as belonging to a class and applies to all individuals in the group.

4   Digital Personae and Profiles: Similarities and Differences

This section describes the similarities and differences between digital personae and profiles. As shown above, their main differences lie in the way they originate and in the link to an individual. A digital persona is created with the aim of representing a specific known individual and often the concerned individual herself is involved in providing (parts of) the data in the digital persona. A profile is usually created with profiling technologies out of a set of aggregated data and is meant to reveal patterns. A profile refers to a group of people or to an individual without identification. After

---

[3] The used theory as developed by Leenes is helpful to distinguish between different identifiers. To calculate the probability of an R-identifier, additional tools, such as the Shannon/Weaver theory [8], are needed. This paper is, however, not on information theory, so that complementing aspect is not included here.

the identification of an individual that fits the profile the individual profile becomes an imposed digital persona.

Profiles as well as digital personae are meant as representations. Whether they are capable of representing a known individual or not distinguishes the one from the other, but they both have representational capacity. Presenting something in text or images is always a form of representation, since it refers to an original (absent) object. How this representation works can be explained with the help of semiotics, in particular the theory of the 'triad of meaning' as developed by C.S. Peirce. His triad is a model of how things get meaning [10]. There are conflicting views on this triadic theory, including proposed adaptations to the model. For instance, there have been proposals for a category of Fourthness which question the sufficiency of Peirce's semiotic, and proposals for a reduction to dyadicity which would render the semiotic triad unnecessary.[4] However, the aim of this paper is not to set out semiotic theory and the different possible viewpoints. Since Peirce's triadic model is widely accepted, I take this model as a starting point for illustrating my view on representation and the differences between digital personae and profiles. According to Peirce, the process of ascribing meaning to a certain object is always an interactive process between three things: the object, the sign, and the interpretant. The object is the thing to which a certain meaning, the knowledge of the object at a specific moment (the interpretant[5]), is ascribed. This object can be anything, physical as well as virtual. The only precondition is that the receiver of information that leads to the interpretant is able to have an idea about the object, for instance based on past experiences. The sign is something that stands for the object, since it is impossible to have knowledge on an object in a direct manner. "The sign is an instruction for interpretation, a mechanism which starts from an initial stimulus and leads to all its illative consequences" [11]. This implies that for each person the interpretant can be different, since the sign is interpreted and this interpretation can lead to different outcomes. Peirce's theory can be visualised as follows:

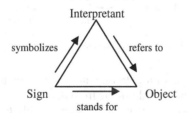

Fig. 2. Peirce's Triad of Meaning

When applied to the situation of a digital persona related to an individual the triad can be filled in as follows:

---

[4] See, for instance: http://www.paulburgess.org/triadic.html
[5] The interpretant is an interpretation in the sense of the result of the process of interpretation. It is formed in the mind of the receiver of the information.

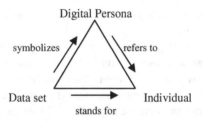

Fig. 3. The Triad of Meaning applied to a Digital Persona

Here, the individual is the object, the element to which a certain meaning is ascribed. The data set is the sign that there is an individual and shows information which can be interpreted and leads to the interpretant, a digital persona. The interpretant has to reveal the knowledge concerning the individual at a certain moment. The digital persona can become the starting point for a new semiotic process in the function of a new sign. This sign is interpreted and leads to a new interpretant and further knowledge about the original object, the individual.

Now, consider the same process with the digital persona replaced by a (distributive) profile. In this case, the data set can be interpreted, leading to a profile. The data, however, are now related to an unknown or potential individual instead of to a known individual, known to the one who interprets the data set, as is the case with a digital persona. Once the individual is known, the profile can become an imposed digital persona in the sense that the individual is considered to be in conformity with the profile. It is an image projected onto a person by others.

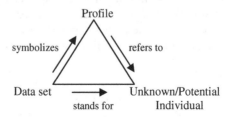

Fig. 4. The Triad of Meaning applied to a Profile

A digital persona stems from data that are directly related to and coming from a specific individual. A group profile stems from data that are collected from numerous individuals and forms an image that might be applicable to one or more of the individuals in the group. It appears that digital personae can be seen as explicit representations of individuals, whereas profiles are implicit, or more indirect, representations. Nevertheless, the manifestation of both is similar; a data set. The major difference lies in how meaning is ascribed to the individual. In the case of a digital persona, the meaning is ingrained beforehand, while in the case of a profile certain attributes or patterns can reveal information. Due to the differences, profiles and digital personae should be treated differently by those who use the representations as a basis for taking decisions concerning individuals, although their manifestation as a data set is similar.

This statement will be discussed now from a legal perspective. So, the next section will explore whether the applicability of the DPD really is dependent on whether a data set is a digital persona or a profile.

5 Legal Embedding

Essentially, regardless whether one is dealing with a digital persona or a profile, individuals can be affected by decisions that are taken based on the data sets. When personal data are involved in the processing, data protection legislation applies. At a European level, this means that the data processing has to comply with the provisions of Directive 95/46/EC (DPD). With regard to decisions taken based on the processing of (personal) data, Article 15 of the DPD is very relevant. It grants the right to every person not to be subjected to decisions that are taken based solely on the automated processing of data. So, the involvement of a human being is always required when it concerns decisions that affect an individual. In particular this means that a decision can be taken based on a profile, even when this profile is created by automated means only, but the involvement of a natural person in actually taking the decision is required [12].

In industry and commerce, automated decision-making is common practice [13]. This is not strange in our modern society where data and information are important assets and where automation is a standard business process. In the light of Article 15 of the DPD, it is relevant whether the processing is meant to reveal a certain aspect of the personality of an individual on which a decision can be based. This implies that, usually, personal data are at stake in the processing. Then, the decision is based on a digital persona. However, even in the case of profiles the DPD might be applicable. Regardless of whether the data contain personal data, the decision will be connected to an individual, thereby constituting the identifiability which is necessary to speak of personal data. Thus, also the combination with personal data afterwards makes the DPD applicable to the processing.

The core problem is that identifiability is difficult to define. In the grey area (see section 3.1 above), where personalised profiles are at stake, but the only identifier is an R-identifier which establishes recognition as the same person, the decision will be applied to an individual. The characteristics in the profile may be too general to speak of personal data when not connected to a known individual. However, the R-identifier establishes the connection and makes that a decision, based on these (personal) characteristics can be applied to an individual. For instance, an online store recognizes a visitor and knows some general preferences. Based on earlier visits, where the person was recognized because of an issued cookie, a profile is created that shows that this person is interested in heavy metal music and books about fishing. Based on this profile, it is decided (in an automated manner) that this person receives an online offer of price reduced tickets for a heavy metal concert. In this example, the individual is affected in a positive way by the decision, but, obviously, there can often be negative effects, for instance when someone is excluded from a price reduction, because she buys her heavy metal music at another store. Nevertheless, being affected in a positive or negative way is not the key issue. The key issue is that individuals are affected, even when their names are not known. Because the decisions are applied to individuals, perhaps even without processing personal data in a strict sense[6], the DPD should apply.

The previous paragraph had the implied assumption that there is one single user bound to a computer. This is, obviously, not completely true, since often computers are shared with a family or colleagues. However, technological development makes that electronic devices become more and more personal. Smartphones and laptops allow Internet access, regardless of one's location, and are usually used by only one individual. Besides, even when a computer is used by more than one individual, it is still possible to distinguish between the different users. Clicking behaviour and web analysis reveal patterns that relate to individuals, simply by comparing click trails and visited web sites. After a certain amount of information is revealed a fingerprint threshold is met which enables the identification (recognition) of an individual user [14].

The opposite of personalization is possible as well. Individuals can choose for so-called deliberate disinformation, which basically means that individual identifiers, such as a bar code or customer number, are posted on the Internet, allowing others to use it. When a number of individuals is using the same identifier it is no longer personal and opportunities to make appropriate individual profiles are blocked. Nevertheless, this practice can occur in the case of identifiers issued by companies, but in ordinary circumstances IP addresses and account data or login details reveal whether one is dealing with the same individual, or at least a restricted number of individuals, such as a family.

Article 15 of the DPD is meant to protect individuals from decisions being taken about them without any human involvement. This, because the lack of a human factor was deemed to be conflicting with human dignity. Another function of the DPD is to ensure transparency towards data subjects as supported by the information duties laid down in Articles 10 and 11 of the DPD. Since it was concluded that even the use of anonymous profiles as a basis for decision taking lead to affected individuals afterwards, this automated decision-making is not allowed at all, because it conflicts with the DPD. Whether the regime is meant to be so strict has to be researched further, but at least there is an important issue concerning the way data are processed in today's society. In any case, this section showed that the distinction between digital personae and profiles in the light of automated decision-making is not so relevant, even though public (and academic) debate focuses on the scope of the term 'personal data' as determining whether the DPD is applicable in a certain case or not.

Deciding that the DPD is applicable to all processing of data in the form of digital personae as well as profiles would have major consequences for the information society, which might not be the most desirable. Besides, it is always important to read and interpret legal texts while keeping an eye on the context to which the provisions are applied. This context is nowadays a different one than the context in 1995, when the DPD was written. However, research is needed to find out when the DPD should apply and when not. As long as there is no clarity, the protection goals of the DPD may not be achieved. The individual has to be the central factor around which data processing and data protection takes place. That means that the changing technologies should not be leading in deciding whether the DPD is applicable or not.

---

[6] Unless the cookie is considered to be personal data, but that is a discussion on itself.

6 Conclusion

This paper described the concepts of a digital persona and a profile. Both are forms of representations that are used by governments and businesses to take decisions. However, there are some important differences between the two concepts, which also have implications for the way they possibly affect represented individuals. A main difference lies in the connection to a known individual and whether this connection is made before or after the representation is created. A digital persona is a direct, explicit representation, whereas a profile usually represents a group and reveals attributes that may be applicable to individuals in the group, or the profile represents an individual whose behaviour is monitored. However, the concerned individuals are not identified.

Digital personae and profiles both consist of data. Thus, their basic manifestation is similar. However, the individualisation of a data set and the way the data are collected may imply differences in the impact of the application of the representations. An important aspect is the awareness of the concerned individual of the data set being created. Without awareness, as is the case with profiles, the individual cannot influence the way the data set is used for decision taking. Another important aspect is whether individuals can exercise rights from data protection regulations. A digital persona always contains an L-identifier which establishes the connection to an offline individual, so the data in the digital persona do qualify as personal data. In group profiles this is not the case. Individual profiles are somewhat unclear in this respect, because they may very well facilitate identification, even though there is no L-identifier included.

In the end, individuals are affected by decisions taken based on the data sets. Important questions are whether it is problematic that some parts of the data processing are not regulated by data protection regulations, and whether there is a significant difference for the individual between a profile and a digital persona as a starting point of a digital representation. It is important to know how privacy and autonomy of the represented individuals are affected by these decisions and the way the representations are made. Privacy is in this context related to the applicability of data protection regulations. Autonomy relates to the amount of control an individual has in the establishment and processing of her data set and informational self-determination. This paper clarified the concepts of digital personae and profiles and their relations in order to enable further research on these implications for individuals. It also became clear that in a strict sense the DPD might be applicable to all data processing aiming at automated decision-making, regardless of whether digital personae or anonymous profiles are used as input. Applying the DPD to all processing might have major, probably undesirable, consequences for the way industry and commerce are organized. Further research is needed in order to find out whether the DPD currently should be interpreted as including these types of data processing. A general factor in this research should be that the DPD gives certain rights to individuals to protect them. Developments in technology should not lead to the case that the DPD is not applied, while individuals and their rights are influenced anyway.

Acknowledgments. The author wants to thank prof. dr. Ronald Leenes for his stimulating supervision, as well as the reviewers for their comments on the draft version of this paper. Part of the research leading to these results has received funding from the

European Community's Seventh Framework programme (FP7/2007-2013) under grant agreement No. 216483.

References

1. Clarke, R.: Authentication Re-visited: How Public Key Infrastructure Could Yet Prosper. In: 16th Bled eCommerce Conference eTransformation, Bled, Slovenia, pp. 632–648 (2003)
2. Clarke, R.: The Digital Persona and it's Application to Data Surveillance. The Information Society 10 (1994)
3. Solove, D.J.: The Digital Person; technology and privacy in the information age. New York University Press, New York (2004)
4. Pfitzmann, A., Hansen, M.: Anonymity, Unlinkability, Undetectability, Unobservability, Pseudonymity and Identity Management - A Consolidated Proposal for Terminology. TUD/ULD, Dresden/Kiel (2008)
5. Hildebrandt, M.: Defining Profiling: A New Type of Knowledge? In: Hildebrandt, M., Gutwirth, S. (eds.) Profiling the European Citizen; Cross-Disciplinary Perspectives, pp. 17–45. Springer, Heidelberg (2008)
6. Vedder, A.H.: KDD, Privacy, Individuality and Fairness. In: Spinello, R.A., Tavani, H.T. (eds.) Readings in CyberEthics, pp. 462–470. Jones and Bartlett Publishers, Sudbury Massachusetts (2004)
7. Leenes, R.: Do They Know Me? Deconstructing identifiability. University of Ottawa Law & Technology Journal 4 (2008)
8. Shannon, C.E., Weaver, W.: A Mathematical Theory of Communication. Bell System Technical Journal 27, 379–423, 623–656 (1948)
9. Article 29 Working Party: Opinion 4/2007 on the Concept of Personal Data. Vol. WP136 (2007)
10. Driel, H.v.: Het semiotisch pragmatisme van Charles S. Peirce. Benjamins, Amsterdam (1991)
11. Eco, U.: Semiotics and the Philosophy of Language. Indiana University Press, Bloomington (1984)
12. Cuijpers, C.M.C.K.: Privacyrecht of privaatrecht? Een privaatrechtelijk alternatief voor de implementatie van de Europese privacyrichtlijn. Wolf Legal Publishers, Tilburg (2004)
13. Leenes, R.E.: Reply: Addressing the Obscurity of Data Clouds. In: Hildebrandt, M., Gutwirth, S. (eds.) Profiling the European Citizen; Cross-Disciplinary Perspectives, pp. 293–300. Springer, Heidelberg (2008)
14. Conti, G.: Googling Security; How much does Google know about you? Addison-Wesley, Boston (2009)

Anonymous Credentials in Web Applications
A Child's Play with the PRIME Core

Benjamin Kellermann and Immanuel Scholz

Technische Universität Dresden
Faculty of Computer Science
D-01062 Dresden, Germany
{Benjamin.Kellermann,Immanuel.Scholz}@tu-dresden.de

Abstract. Web applications dealing with personal data in a privacy-friendly way have the need for anonymous credential systems. While there are already protocols describing anonymous credential systems and libraries, implementing the protocols, application using the libraries are rare. Without applications supporting anonymous credentials, companies will not start building a credential infrastructure and vice versa. This paper presents an easy way to issue and use anonymous credentials for web applications. By reducing the initial cost for both parties, the barrier of "starting first" can be lowered.

1 Introduction

Imagine a web application dealing with some personal data. It lets the user register and enter his age and nationality as well as a username and password for access control. The service operator does not want to worry about checking the accuracy of the personal data, so he uses a third party to certify these attributes. This kind of application has some disadvantages, e. g., in a naive implementation, the third party learns about the users intention to use the service. Additionally, the access control credentials (username and password) could be given to other people and finally the user is traceable through different sessions. All these problems can be avoided with anonymous credentials, introduced by Chaum [1].

Anonymous credentials, presented by Camenisch and Lysyanskaya [2], provide several features not present in "classic" credential systems. They are unlinkable, i. e., two subsequent presentations of the same credentials can not be linked with each other. Partial information on the attributes can be released, which means if a credential contains multiple entries (e. g., "age is 20", "gender is male" and "first name is John"), only some can be revealed, hiding the remaining entries. Relational proofs can be used for numerical entries (e. g., if a credential states "age is 20", the relation "age is greater than 18" can be shown without revealing the actual value.) Finally, they offer the so called "all-or-nothing sharing", which means sharing one credential leads to sharing all of the owners credentials, making it unattractive for users to disclose their credential information to others.

M. Bezzi et al. (Eds.): Privacy and Identity, IFIP AICT 320, pp. 237–245, 2010.
© IFIP International Federation for Information Processing 2010

Many developers believe that implementing access control via anonymous credentials and building an infrastructure for credential issuers is very complicated. From a first point of view, it looks like a "hen-and-egg" problem. Companies, will not start to issue anonymous credentials without applications using them. Application developers will not start implementing access control via anonymous credentials, when there is no infrastructure issuing them.

This paper presents an easy way to enroll and verify anonymous credentials with the PRIME core [3], which uses the Idemix library [4]. This library already implements many features of the Camenisch-Lysyanskaya credentials system. A larger tutorial has been created during the development which shows additional features not covered in this paper [5].

The document is structured as follows. Section 2 explains the communication flow, which is done by the basic scenario and discusses, what has to be done to set up everything on the users side. The few web application modifications, which have to be done to use anonymous credentials with the PRIME core are shown in Section 3 and the steps to issue credentials are given in Section 4.

2   Setup

2.1   Architectural Overview

The setup and communication flow is shown in Figure 1 on the facing page. One can see that in addition to the users web browser and the web application, two other instances are needed. These are needed to exchange data through cryptographic protocols. We call these instances "PRIME core". They can be compared to PGP[1], in a scenario, where an E-mail application wants to send an encrypted E-mail. Two small programs, which intercepts the normal communication flow to do the cryptography, are needed there as well. Note that the communication is always initiated by the client, to ensure connectivity from behind a firewall or NAT.

Users are solely concerned with the client PRIME core installation. Administrators of issuer services and developers also have to cope with running and configuring a server. We will explain in the following, how a PRIME core is launched at client side. The administrators and developers perspective is considered at the beginning of the Sections 3 and 4.

2.2   Running PRIME on Client Side

Using the PRIME core at the users side is pretty much the same as running any other program. After unpacking the archive `prime.zip`, the `prime.jar` can be run without any parameter. This provides a tray icon with several menu functions to execute the different user functions.

There are two possibilities to deflect his web traffic through the PRIME core. The PRIME core may act as web proxy, which can be configured within the

---

[1] Pretty Good Privacy. An application for encrypting data, especially E-mails.

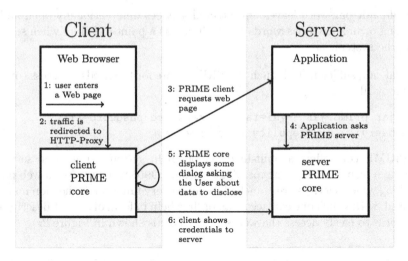

Fig. 1. Overview of the communication flow with PRIME. The arrows indicate the initiation of communication links.

config interface. The other possibility is to install a Firefox extension, which watches the traffic and calls the PRIME core if needed.[2]

3   How to Use PRIME in an Application

3.1   Launching PRIME as a Developer

Each PRIME core offers its functionality through a set of web services. Common web services are launched by default, which are sufficient, if the PRIME core should act as client. At server side, additional web services have to be launched as well as the graphical user interface has to be disabled. Because of disabling the user interface, passwords for some components (e. g., the Java secure key store) cannot be entered interactively. Therefore, the required passwords have to be given on the command line or in a configuration file.

Some of the PRIME core's web services are only launched when a password has been specified for them to access. These passwords are there to authenticate external programs accessing the PRIME core. They should not be confused with credentials or data that may have to be provided to access personal information within the PRIME data storage. If an application wants to access personal information, it may have to provide additional authorization information.

The web services are grouped in categories (like "common", "system", or "simplepolicy"). The mechanism of launching a category which is not launched by default is specifying a password for it. This ensures that

---

[2] This requires using Firefox of course, but it has other advantages, which might be desirable.

1. no default password leaves unprotected services unintentionally open and
2. wrong or unknown passwords are excluded as a point of failure when setting up the system.

A typical call, sufficient to launch the PRIME core for the needs of access control would look like:

```
java -jar prime.jar --gui=false --keystore.password=XYZ \
  --webservice.simplepolicy.password=YZX
```

The PRIME core offers a built-in developer help system for its web services. Directing a web browser to `https://localhost:9906`,[3] one can see a web page, describing which services are launched. Behind every function, a question mark is displayed, with which one can access an on-line help in form of a short description and a form to easily access the web service. This is shown in Figure 2.

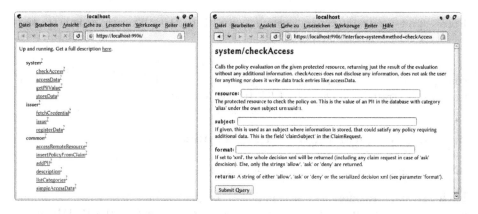

Fig. 2. Two help pages offered by the PRIME core. The overview page (left) and the description of `checkAccess` (right).

For debugging and developing, a set of very powerful **debug** web services is available, including a direct SQL access to the database and example implementations for typical server administrative services, like configuring policies or approving credentials.

3.2   PRIME Enabled "Hello World!"

Assume a very simple "Hello World" web application consisting of one line of code (Figure 3 on the facing page). This application does nothing more than printing out the string "Hello World!", which should be the placeholder for a point, where access control is checked in a more complex application.

---

[3] For the rest of the document it is assumed, that the server runs on `localhost` and uses the default port `9906`.

```
1  <?php echo "Hello␣World!"; ?>
```

Fig. 3. Hello world web application in PHP

Now, we want to implement access control to our "Hello World!" application by means of an anonymous credential. For this, we have to

1. create a policy in the server's database, and
2. modify the source code so that it asks the PRIME core to evaluate the policy and grant or deny access.

Inserting a Policy. A policy requires a so-called "protected resource" which defines what data item the policy is about. The protected resource can be any URI[4] chosen by the developer – for example the URL of the web site to protect. This is also called "object", or just "resource" in some policy languages. In our example we use the self-chosen URI "urn:hello" as identifier for the protected resource.

PRIME supports very sophisticated policies. Different actions like read and write are supported. Policy rules can simply depend on the disclosure of any data or the data can be required to have a specific value. For numerical data like the age, relations can be specified (e. g., greater than 18 years old). Developer-specific relations are possible as well. It can be required that disclosed data is certified by anonymous or non-anonymous credentials. Data handling policies can be attached to data categories to specify meta information like the intended purpose or time period which the disclosed data is used for. These policies are specified in an XML policy language using the `policy/insert` web service. For the most common case "require existence of one data category", the much simpler web service `simplepolicy/insert` can be used.[5] After choosing the data category, which a user has to show to get access, the policy is ready for use.

Modifying the Source Code. We already illustrated the communication flow of the application in Figure 1 on page 239. Figure 4 on the next page tries to show this in more detail. When a user tries to access the web page (arrow 1 and 2 of Figure 1, or the first two "GET URL" arrows of Figure 4), the web application will ask the server-side PRIME core, if the user is allowed or not. The web service `system/checkAccess` can be used for this policy evaluation.[6]

---

[4] Uniform Resource Identifier. A character string to identify a resource.

[5] The on-line help (question mark next to the function) provides a simple web interface for sending the request (cp., Section 3.1 on page 239). However, if you like to use a more convenient reference implementation, browsing to `https://localhost:9906/debug/managePolicies` tries to show how a simple policy manager may look like.

[6] The on-line help can be used again to quickly check the policy while developing (cp., Section 3.1).

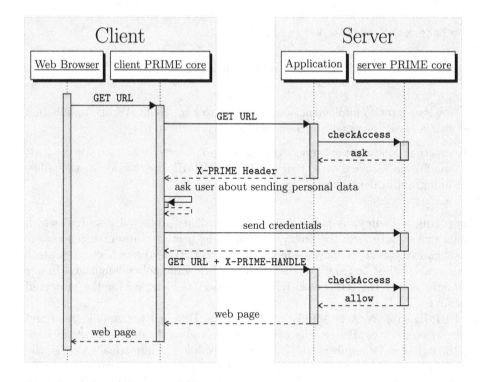

Fig. 4. Sequence diagram of the communication flow with PRIME

It returns one of three possible values: "allow", "deny", and "ask". The state "ask" denotes that not enough information has been provided and the authorization should be started. Most developers using access control frameworks are only familiar with the two states: "allow" and "deny". Usually, the time when authentication checks are done has to be known to the developed application and some kind of logged-in state is maintained. It is possible but not encouraged with the PRIME framework to track and maintain a logged-in state (which usually comes with linkability between individual user transactions). However the best practice approach here is, to let the policy evaluation decide directly for each individual transaction. If this is technically feasible, it enables that a user's activities become unlinkable, say the browsing for books (remain anonymous) and the actual ordering (disclosing contact information).

For interpreting the three return values in PHP, a `switch` environment can be used. In case of "allow" or "deny", the server's output is `"Hello World!"` or any error message, respectively. In case of "ask", the policy evaluation determined that it cannot decide, yet, whether the user is allowed to access the protected resource (this is also the case in Figure 4). It needs more information, e. g., a proof of possession of an anonymous credential. This proof can be triggered by the server by inserting two HTTP-headers in the response to the client: "X-PRIME" and "X-PRIME-Protected-Resource". The first header defines the address, the client should contact to show his credential, and the second one states the protected resource under which the policy is stored. The client-side PRIME core will interpret these headers, trigger the credential proving process with the client-side PRIME core ("ask user" and "send credential" arrows of Figure 4 or arrows 5 and 6 of Figure 1), and repeat the HTTP request to the web server including another HTTP header "X-PRIME-HANDLE", which contains a session id. The web application has to pass the session id to the server-side PRIME core, which evaluates the policy again and now hopefully returns "allow".

Figure 5 shows the complete PRIME-enabled "Hello World!" application. Lines 2–4 queries the web service system/checkAccess of the server-side PRIME core. Lines 5 and 6 reply the easy cases, where access is allowed or denied. Lines 7–10 return HTTP-headers which causes the client to show the required credentials.

```
1   <?php
2   switch (fread(fopen("https://localhost:9906/"
3           ."system/checkAccess?resource=urn:hello"
4           ."&subject=$_SERVER[HTTP_X_PRIME_HANDLE]","r"),10)){
5   case "allow": echo "Hello␣World!";   break;
6   case "deny":  echo "Access␣Denied"; break;
7   case "ask":
8           header("X-PRIME:␣https://example.org:9906");
9           header("X-PRIME-Protected-Resource:␣urn:hello");
10          break;
11  }?>
```

Fig. 5. Example source code of the PRIME enabled "Hello World!" application

With these additional 10 lines of code, the developer has integrated whole access control and credential verification features of the PRIME core.

4   Credential Issuing

4.1   Running PRIME as Issuer

If one wants to issue credentials, the restricted web services have to be launched in addition to the ones one has to launch for access control. An appropriate command line to launch the server could look like:

```
java -jar prime.jar --gui=false --keystore.password=XYZ \
    --webservice.simplepolicy.password=YZX \
    --webservice.restricted.password=ZYX
```

Also, some configuration has to be done to specify for which cryptographic key and which data categories the service will issue credentials. A reference implementation has been made within the debug web services. Browsing to https://localhost:9906/debug/configIssuer will provide an easy click-through interface, which does the necessary configuration for issuing credentials.

4.2 Issuing Credentials

Issuing of credentials is one of the functionalities, built into the PRIME core. There is no need for developers to do additional programming to offer credential issuing for end-users. Steps to a successful issue a credential are

1. submitting data to be certified to the issuing service,
2. convincing the service provider about the correctness of the data[7], and
3. fetching a credential for this data.

Submitting Data. To fetch any credential, the option "Fetch Credential" in the send personal data dialog can be used.[8] Alternatively, the fetching can be initiated by the menu option "Register Data" in the tray icon.[9]

After entering and sending the data, a 4-digit number is displayed. This number is needed in the next step.

Convincing the Issuer. During the registration process, a shared secret[10] is stored at the client and the server. A 4-digit hash of this secret is displayed to the user as described previously. By revealing this hash value, the user proves to the credential issuer that the data at the server was indeed provided by his client computer. The 4-digit hash is used here for usability reasons, a longer value or even the whole secret can be used in other scenarios.

When the credential issuer is convinced, that

- the person is authorized to get a credential for this data (e. g., by verifying the id-card) and
- that the credential in the server database is the credential from the persons' computer (by checking if the data stored under the shared secret is correct),[11]

he approves the credential by calling to the web service `restricted/setProven` and informs the user, that his client can fetch it.

A minimalistic sample implementation has been realized within the `debug` web services. Browsing to `https://localhost:9906/debug/managUnprovenPii` delivers an easy interface which displays all unapproved hashes and personal data together with a link to approve them.

Fetching the Credential. After approving the request, the user can obtain the credential via the "Fetch Credential" menu option in the clients tray icon.

---

[7] In practice it may often be the case that the issuing party already has the data it wants to issue. However, the user still has to convince the service provider, that the data was submitted from his personal device.

[8] The send personal data dialog is the dialog that pops up when browsing on a protected web site with a PRIME-enabled web browser.

[9] In this case, the issuing service URL has to be specified manually.

[10] Here, the shared secret is a 122 bit long random number.

[11] Imagine an attacker, submitting the same information to trick the clerk verifying the id-card into approving his credential request instead.

5   Conclusion

We showed, that anonymous credentials are easy to handle with the PRIME core. Most of the features of modern anonymous credential systems were provided without any additional effort. Obviously, the authentication with the PRIME core could be implemented in addition or as an alternative to an existing one, which improves acceptance and ability to integrate PRIME into existing projects.

Our simple example showed a way to present an unlinkable, partially-provable credential which also supports relational proofs. If access control is bundled at one point of the application, about 10 lines of code are necessary to replace the normal authentication.

Acknowledgments. The authors want to thank Mike Bergmann, Sebastian Clauss, Martin Meinhold, and many others for the development on the PRIME core. Helpful comments from Rainer Böhme, Sebastian Clauss and Stefan Köpsell have been incorporated. In addition, we want to thank Jan Camenisch and the other anonymous reviewers.

The research leading to these results has received funding from the European Community's Seventh Framework Programme (FP7/2007–2013) under grant agreement №216483. The information in this document is provided "as is", and no guarantee or warranty is given that the information is fit for any particular purpose. The above referenced consortium members shall have no liability for damages of any kind including without limitation direct, special, indirect, or consequential damages that may result from the use of these materials subject to any liability which is mandatory due to applicable law. Copyright 2009 by TU Dresden.

References

1. Chaum, D.: Security without identification: Transaction systems to make big brother obsolete. Commun. ACM 28(10), 1030–1044 (1985)
2. Camenisch, J., Lysyanskaya, A.: An efficient system for non-transferable anonymous credentials with optional anonymity revocation. In: Pfitzmann, B. (ed.) EUROCRYPT 2001. LNCS, vol. 2045, pp. 93–118. Springer, Heidelberg (2001)
3. Casassa-Mont, M., Crosta, S., Kriegelstein, T., Sommer, D.: Architecture v2. PRIME, Deliverable D14.2.c (March 2007),
   https://www.prime-project.eu/prime_products/reports/arch/
   pub_del_D14.2.c_ec_WP14.2_v1_Final.pdf.
4. IBM Research, "Identity mixer" (November 2009),
   http://prime.inf.tu-dresden.de/idemix/
5. Kellermann, B., Scholz, I., Wahrig, H.: The PRIME developers tutorial (August 2009), http://turrican.inf.tu-dresden.de/doc/

Reaching for Informed Revocation: Shutting Off the Tap on Personal Data

Ioannis Agrafiotis, Sadie Creese, Michael Goldsmith,
and Nick Papanikolaou

International Digital Laboratory, University of Warwick, Coventry UK
{I.Agrafiotis,S.Creese,M.Goldsmith,N.Papanikolaou}@warwick.ac.uk

Abstract. We introduce a revocation model for handling personal data in cyberspace. The model is motivated by a series of focus groups undertaken by the EnCoRe project aimed at understanding the control requirements of a variety of data subjects. We observe that there is a lack of understanding of the various technical options available for implementing revocation preferences, and introduce the concept of *informed revocation* by analogy to Faden and Beauchamp's *informed consent*. We argue that we can overcome the limitations associated with informed consent via the implementation of EnCoRe technology solutions. Finally, we apply our model and demonstrate its validity to a number of data-handling scenarios which have arisen in the context of the EnCoRe research project. We have found that data subjects tend to alter their default privacy preferences when they are informed of all the different types of revocation available to them.

Keywords: Data Privacy, Consent, Revocation, Requirements.

1 Introduction

In an environment dominated by information systems, e-services and e-commerce whose applications are continually evolving, enterprises have an ever-growing reason and capability to collect, store and process huge quantities of personal data. Increasingly we depend on cyberspace and necessarily disclose personal data in order to gain access to services. But we do so without having any practical control over how our data is handled; once we have handed over our data it physically resides on technology beyond our physical and logical reach, unless a service provider specifically provides functionality offering control. Consider the information uploaded by data subjects of social-networking sites. It is often analysed and sold to enterprises, and data subjects are categorised in profiles according to their commercial preferences. This offers significant value as marketing and products can become personalised and targeted. Mechanisms to enable data subjects to control these actions and, for example, to remove or modify personal data held by others, are missing. This lack of control directly hinders data subjects' ability to protect their own privacy in cyberspace.

The right to privacy has been historically protected. It has been the basis for the stability of all democratic societies, and its importance is highlighted throughout the

M. Bezzi et al. (Eds.): Privacy and Identity, IFIP AICT 320, pp. 246–258, 2010.

published literature [1, 4,13] e.g.. It is difficult to conceptualise privacy because it is multidimensional, subjective and context dependent; people feel differently about what privacy means to them. So unsurprisingly its definitions vary widely and a definition of privacy that is acceptable in one context fails in another. The volatile notion of privacy and the pervasion of technological innovations throughout our daily lives highlight the importance of personal data privacy and the complexity of controlling it.

In the field of privacy there is a constant debate over the relative importance of the individual right to privacy versus the common good for society [1, 4, 5, 13]. Legislation and regulatory procedures endeavour to establish functions that may find a balance between individuals' right to privacy and the common good. But every time a balance is found, the use of new technologies alters old norms either in favour of the individual or in the interest of the common good, and new norms and functions need to be re-established to restore the balance, thus forming a vicious circle.

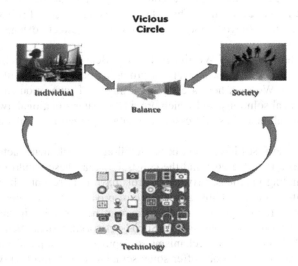

Fig. 1. The constant development of data collection, aggregation and processing technologies results in a vicious circle as society attempts to seek a balance of protection between the individual's privacy and security of society

As technology advances, new ways of gathering private information emerge. This affects the ways in which privacy may be either protected or violated, depending on the purpose for which these advances are applied. Technological developments always proceed faster than the establishment of legislation and regulatory policies, thus fuelling the vicious circle. Thus, society is continuously attempting to achieve a balance between privacy and security without ever fulfilling this goal. Consider the war against illegal drugs in the US: It was thought that using heat sensors to find marijuana growing operations would be acceptable, but in 2001 [Kyllo v United States (533 U.S. 27)] it was ruled that using thermal imaging devices that can reveal previously unknown information without a warrant does indeed constitute a violation of privacy. Our research, and the EnCoRe project more generally [2], seeks to develop methods by which balance can be achieved via consent and revocation controls over the use of personal data.

The need for control mechanisms to deliver privacy of personal data is not a new observation. Many theories [1,4,13] reframe privacy either as individual liberalism or as a fundamental human right and an essential component in the functioning of democratic societies. Westin foresaw the need of the individuals to determine when, how, and to what extent information about them is communicated to others. Similarly, Faden and Beauchamp [5] perceived privacy as the possibility to choose or consent whether to disclose personal information. Solove [11] discusses the various ways in which data collection and aggregation can result in privacy problems and violations, and uses Wittgenstein's concept of family resemblances to identify and classify privacy violations. Seeking an understanding of what can be practically protected and regulated against, he argues that privacy can be conceptualised as having various similar characteristics, but the combination of these similarities makes its nature slightly different every time. Thus, the focus is on classes of privacy violations and not on prevention (beyond the contribution of an effective legal deterrent of course).

In line with the theories of Westin, Faden and Beauchamp, we believe that data privacy can be provided most effectively by providing data subjects with *control* over their personal data. We seek here a conceptual model of revocation suitable for implementing technical solutions, and which provides greater situational awareness as to the state of personal data, thus addressing the data aggregation problems highlighted in Solove's work [11].

Historically, enterprises have often been unwilling to implement such mechanisms in their databases due to the cost and the constraints that these would impose on enterprise data-handling practices. Privacy controls have only recently been introduced in large-scale information systems, and the use of privacy-impact statements is still a maturing discipline (and arguably is part of current best practice in managing risks associated with handling personal data). Social-networking sites such as Facebook and Twitter include embedded mechanisms to capture data subjects' preferences regarding their consent, which does offer some semblance of control. However, whilst data subjects may consent explicitly to sharing, storing and processing data on such sites, they cannot so easily revoke (permissions to hold or process) data that they may already have disclosed. This means that in most cases it is not possible for data subjects to change their privacy preferences in a transparent way; without an explicit revocation capability data subjects cannot have clear and unambiguous control mechanisms to protect data privacy. Unfortunately, there is a general lack of revocation controls in social-networking, e-commerce or indeed almost any cyberspace applications. Indeed, this lack is manifest not only in computer systems but in the relevant legal and regulatory policies also.

2 Revocation Requirements

In order to capture data subjects' requirements for revocation, we conducted a literature review. Due to the limited number of references to revocation mechanisms in the published literature, we extended our investigation to online articles covering realistic case studies. Furthermore, we analysed the transcripts of four focus groups, held by the EnCoRe project, to gain deeper understanding of data subjects' requirements. Within the setting of the EnCoRe[1] project, Edgar Whitley's group at the London School of Economics (LSE) conducted a series of interviews with multiple groups of data subjects to discover what their expectations might be of a system that provided revocation controls.

The focus groups were held at the University of Warwick and at the LSE. In the first group participants were students from Warwick University and unsophisticated data subjects. In the second participants were PhD students from LSE with a background in Information Systems. The third focus group, held also at the LSE, interviewed civil society representatives, and the participants of the fourth focus group were data protection professionals and representatives from the EnCoRe project. Data subjects were presented with various realistic scenarios in which they would need to grant and might wish to revoke consent for access to their personal data.

The focus groups were recorded and transcribed and the participants were informed that "the data from their session will be available to all researchers working on the project but the transcripts will be kept anonymous. The data may also be used in reports and publications and direct anonymised quotations from the transcript may be used in published output" [2]. For the needs of this paper, we used the ATLAS.ti software to analyse the transcripts. In our analysis here, we include relevant excerpts from transcripts in *italics*.

Our initial finding was a gap between the legal and the technical perspectives on revocation. In the legal view there is an ongoing philosophical debate to understand the concept of privacy independently of technology, while computer scientists perceive privacy mechanisms only as security requirements. Even though the examined sample was relatively small, references to revocation requirements were scant and almost without exception revocation was understood as deletion of personal data.

2.1 Context Dependency of Privacy Concerns

The literature [1,4,8,10] suggests that privacy has a context dependent nature. The analysis of the focus groups transcripts verified our literature findings as it emerged that the environment in which data subjects revoke personal data, drastically influences their preferences. In this section, we present and analyse the possible environments that are created, when adopting a data subject's perspective. When stakeholders with different interests in the privacy problem interact, they establish relationships. In these relationships, there are conflicting needs to be balanced, different kinds of requirements arise and, as a result diverse environments are formed. We concern ourselves with three different categories of stakeholder:

- **Data Subjects**, who have a role in protecting their own personal information and specifying how it should be handled by others
- **Society**, which sets the standards, monitors their implementation and ensures compliance
- **Data Controllers**, who play a role in implementing and operating solutions

---

[1] See www.encore-project.info for more information on EnCoRe.

Here, we adopt a data subject's perspective, and we will examine the environments that are created when a data subject interacts with each one of the above three different stakeholders. Understanding the interactions that dominate in each relationship is the first step to capture the contextual nature of privacy. We focus on interactions in order to obtain a representative view of a relationship in motion, as opposed to just a snapshot of a specific situation. Each type of interaction leads to different revocation requirements and we have distinguished four cases of interest depicted in Figure 2 below. The arrow denotes an interaction between the data subject and a stakeholder.

Diverse Environments

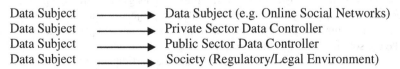

Data Subject ⟶ Data Subject (e.g. Online Social Networks)
Data Subject ⟶ Private Sector Data Controller
Data Subject ⟶ Public Sector Data Controller
Data Subject ⟶ Society (Regulatory/Legal Environment)

Fig. 2. The environments that are formed, when a data subject interacts with the possible stakeholders of the privacy problem

The interactions of the data subject with public and private sector data controllers must be treated separately, as the participants of the focus groups emphasised; privacy preferences of data subjects differ substantially in these two cases, as the asymmetries that emerge especially in the public related environment, create more complex situations for the data subjects to handle. Participants in the focus groups were not asked specifically to distinguish the diverse environments in which they perform the act of revocation. What follows below is an analysis of the identified environments.

2.2   Identifying Data Subjects' Requirements

In this section we present our analysis of the way in which privacy requirements vary across these environments.

2.2.1   Social Networking Interactions

The social networking environment involves interactions between data subjects mediated by a third party. The literature suggests [3, 7] that social networking enables data subjects to control not only their own data, but often that of their friends by providing the means to disseminate information from various data subjects to some extent. Thus, data subjects are now empowered with capabilities that enable the collection process and dissemination of personal information.

In the focus groups, there were a number of references to data subjects' interactions with other citizens, in the context of social networks. People indicated that they use sites such as Facebook and Twitter only for socialising. They do not bother to read privacy terms and conditions as they believe that the information they disclose is trivial. Even though it may be a fallacy, data subjects believe that they are always able to delete data uploaded onto these sites. They feel secure and more confident to disclose data with deletion mechanisms in place, even though they have no guarantee that the act of deletion on the part of the data subject actually puts their data out of use. To quote one participant:

"Twitter's advanced search page allows data subjects to find deleted Tweets, an issue highlighted earlier this week after UK chat show host Jonathan Ross accidentally posted his personal email address in a message. Even though he quickly deleted the message the information was still easily obtainable, because Twitter fails to purge deleted tweets from its system."

On social networking networks there are some privacy controls already available. Facebook provides fine-grained privacy settings[2] [8] that allow data subjects to control with whom to share what, for example. Revocation in this setting is almost exclusively understood as deletion of data, and this is not always possible (as the above quote illustrates). Data subjects generally would like to have more revocation options, including anonymisation and actual deletion (expunging the data from the system altogether).

2.2.2 Interactions with Private Sector

When data subjects interact with private data controllers, they seek to build and enhance a relationship based on trust. Data subjects experience a *lock-in effect*, as they are reluctant to have to disclose data to another controller. They often highlight the importance of *"previous experience"*. In contrast to the social networks, where the interactions between data subjects have similar value for both parties (although there are exceptions [7]), all participants have the same expectations and the environment regarding privacy is not complex, in such an environment the situation becomes far more complex and new asymmetries emerge. These asymmetries take the form of asymmetric expectations, in which "one party expects the other party to behave in ways in which the other party does not expect or intend to behave" [7].

As mentioned above because of "expectations asymmetries," their trust is sometimes violated and data subjects wish to perform revocation mechanisms to balance the situation. Individuals are only vigilant if they happen to have experienced a breach of their privacy, and are unwilling to revoke data when the revocation mechanisms available are not clear in terms of objective and function:

"I don't really think I would actually go and pursue every company I've been shopping with and do that, because it would just be a waste, a lot of a waste of my time".

When data subjects act in this environment they mainly conceptualise revocation as deletion and opt for a regulatory organisation to certify that not only is their data properly deleted in accordance with their preferences, but also that it is not used in an arbitrary way. The importance of revocation mechanisms, understood just as deletion of data, is underlined from both data subjects and enterprises:

"I want the option [to delete my data], *no matter what* [damage] *it does to the public* [good]. "

We observed in the focus groups that participants in this environment would opt for revocation mechanisms, such as revocation of permission to process data and revocation of permission to disseminate data. These mechanisms were not explicitly identified by them at the beginning of the focus groups. Only through discussions and

---

[2] See http://www.facebook.com/privacy/explanation.php?ref=pf for more information on Facebook's new privacy policy.

a presentation of detailed revocation options at the focus groups did participants real-ise in how many ways they could exercise control.

2.2.3 Interactions with Public Sector

According to the literature when data subjects interact with public data controllers new forms of asymmetries occur and thus data subject's preferences differ from the previous environments [7]. We derived from our analysis the following diverse forms of asymmetries:

- *Asymmetry in value*, in which public controllers derive high value from interactions, but data subjects derive low value
- *Asymmetry in expectations,* in the same sense where data subjects experience this form when interacting with a private data controller, as described above.
- *Asymmetry in power,* in which data subject has disproportionate ability to cause "damage" to the public controllers as some times data subjects are forced to consent and have no information on how their data is collected, processed and disseminated among the diverse public data controllers.

From the focus groups, participants indicated that they alter their perception of revocation when they interact with a public data controller. We identified the asymmetries that they experience in this environment. The data collected and processed by the public sector is sensitive private information and citizens' interest in preventing an invasion in their private lives may be by-passed for the sake of national security, to enable medical research, or in the interest of the common good or government policy. In a focus group, a data subject expressed concern about the

"...merging of state and private sector, which is complicating a lot of the services under which data is actually processed, the value of data is valuable to the state for, you know, for anti-terrorist organised crime and so on and that again is making it more complicated..."

Recent incidents of lost or stolen government data [17] have reduced confidence in public authorities. Data subjects are increasingly concerned about preventing arbitrary use of personal data by government services. Although data subjects acknowledge that, in particular cases, the revocation of data will not be permitted (e.g. DNA database), they desire revocation mechanisms so as to deal with the aforementioned problems and to restore a relationship of trust.

Individuals are willing to share personal data for medical research if certain conditions are met. Those participated in the focus groups have indicated that anonymity and traceability are required features of a health database if they are to disclose their medical records. However, these two concepts are in tension, often resulting in solutions based on separation but with the potential for tracing back:

"Patients - who already had the right to opt out of the scheme - now have the right to have their medical records anonymised or masked once they are put onto the system."

Due to the asymmetries, participants believed that they could not perform any revocation. However, when they realised the options that they could have, data subjects opted for revocation of permission to process data, to disseminate data and of delegated revocation. In medical cases, delegated revocation was a popular option.

2.2.4 Interactions with Society

Society could motivate enterprises to enhance their privacy mechanisms by providing revocation controls. Privacy guidelines for large enterprises exist, and law requires that these are used. Smaller enterprises need to abide by the same rules and report to the Information Commissioner Office. On the contrary, in the public sector it appears to be occasions where revocation controls are prohibited for the sake of common good [16]. In the name of society data subjects' right to privacy is invaded and in cases such as criminal records and police's dna data bases data may have a lifetime persistence [18].

To synopsis our findings in this environment, the only revocation mechanism that a data subject could apply, in terms of legislation, is the right to object to:

"unfair/unlawful processing by withdrawing the existing consent – i.e. revoke – and optionally replace it with a new consent; terminating any relevant contract with the data controller/ processor; objecting on the basis that the processing is prejudicial to the data subject's 'rights and freedoms' or 'legitimate interests".

Finding a balance between individuals' privacy and national security is an ongoing debate. [10] As the requirements that emerge from this environment are more of legal nature and were found also in the other three environments, we consider this debate beyond the scope of this paper.

3 Revocation Model

The principal results of our analysis is a novel taxonomy of revocation. We identify four *fundamental* types of revocation (1.-4. below), and four *derived* types of revocation (5.-8. below).

1. **No Revocation At All:** Personal data remains static, and once it has been disclosed, it is either physically impossible to revoke (how could ever revoke reputation) or prohibited for various reasons (e.g. law-enforcement, data from police's DNA database).

2. **Deletion:** Data are completely erased and cannot be retrieved or reconstituted in any way. Certain privacy rights are enshrined in national and European legislation; it is worth mentioning here how our model incorporates some of the stipulations of the EU Data Protection Directive 95/46/EC. In article 12, for example, the directive mentions "the **rectification,** erasure or blocking of data the processing of which does not comply with the provisions of this Directive, in particular because of the incomplete or inaccurate nature of the data." Rectification is a variant of revocation in the sense that a data subject may request the deletion of incorrect data held about him or herself and have it replaced with other data.

3. **Revocation of Permissions to Process Data:** Data subjects withdraw consent that would enable an enterprise to process or analyse their personal data for a specified purpose. EU Data Protection mentions "blocking," which corresponds exactly to revocation of permissions to process data in our model.

4. **Revocation of Permissions for Third Party Dissemination:** Data subjects withdraw consent that would enable an enterprise to disclose information to a third party.

5. **Cascading Revocation** is a variation on any of the above kinds of revocation, whereby the revocation is (recursively) passed on to any party to whom the data has been disclosed. Through this mechanism, data subjects are able to revoke data by only contacting the enterprise that they disclosed their data to originally.

We may remark that offering such a service is only practicable if data is only disclosed to organisations which themselves offer such a control.

6. **Consentless Revocation:** Personal data for whose storage and dissemination no consent has been explicitly given by the data subject, but which may need to be revoked. Again, any of the fundamental types of revocation may be invoked. We introduce this form of revocation to capture the privacy problems identified by Solove [11] . The need to revoke consentless data emerges mainly when a breach in privacy has occurred and the data subject experiences one of Solove's problems.

> Example: A picture of Jane drunk at a party was uploaded onto Facebook without her consent. As a consequence her reputation is ruined. She takes legal action in order to have the photograph removed from the site.

7. **Delegated Revocation:** This is a kind of revocation which is exercised by a person other than the individual concerned, such as an inheritor or parent/guardian.

8. **Revocation of Identity (Anonymisation):** Data subjects may be happy for personal data to be held for certain purposes so long as it is not linkable back to them personally. Anonymisation may be regarded as a variant of revocation, in that data subjects request a change to data held so that it is no longer personally identifiable (but see *Limitations* below).

3.1 Limitations

The model proposed in this paper may be limited in the following ways:

- The issue of *granularity* needs to be considered specifically for the deletion type of revocation.
- Data subjects may want to *partially revoke* their data, or to *scramble* their data instead of having it erased completely.
- The question of *deletion certificates,* namely, non-repudiable proofs that deletion has really been performed, but this is beyond the scope of this paper.
- The possibility of anonymisation poses interesting problems as it makes the origin of data untraceable; there are cases where this is not in the interest of security or the common good in general. A system implementing anonymisation should have safeguards in place to ensure that data subjects will act legitimately. On the other hand, if data is (even partly) identifiable, an enterprise can aggregate it and eventually infer to whom it refers. Such issues need to be taken into consideration when implementing revocation mechanisms.

4 Reaching for Informed Revocation

We found there to be a lack of in-depth understanding of the different ways in which revocation can be performed and/or implemented in practice. Participants at our focus groups perceived revocation simply as deletion of data, and they highlighted the need to be informed about the nature of deletion and the privacy protection it can actually offer. Furthermore, when they were denied the option of deletion, they were reluctant to search for alternatives. We distinguished a significant change in people's preferences when they were informed of all the available types of revocation that they could perform in the context of a particular scenario. People become more selective and seek the revocation mechanism closest to their needs.

Table 1. Initial/Default Choices

	Social Networking	Medical Environment	Public Data Controller	Private Data Controller	Legal Environment
Deletion	✓	✓		✓	✓
No Revocation		✓	✓	✓	✓

Table 2. More Informed Choices

	Social Networking	Medical Environment	Public Data Controller	Private Data Controller	Legal Environment
Deletion	✓	✓		✓	
Anonymisation		✓			
Cascading Revocation				✓	
Revocation of Permissions to Process		✓	✓	✓	
No Revocation	✓	✓	✓	✓	✓
Revocation of Permissions to Disseminate		✓		✓	
Consentless Revocation		✓	✓	✓	✓
Delegated Revocation				✓	✓

Tables 1 and 2 illustrate data subjects' choices of revocation mechanisms for a set of example scenarios. In Table 1 we have captured which revocation mechanisms data subjects expect by default. Table 2 shows the revocation mechanisms that data subjects chose after they were informed of their existence. It is quite evident that, once data subjects are informed of the different variants of revocation, they make more careful choices. Before being informed, they choose either to have data deleted or left intact. When given a choice between the different types of revocation (as identified in Section 3), they take advantage of the different controls available.

In order to explain this phenomenon, we introduce the concept of *informed revocation,* by analogy to Faden's and Beauchamp's *informed consent* [5]. In their research, they argue that consent of data subjects needs to be voluntary – not the result of force or coercion – and they need to be informed about how their data is to be used, and how they can exercise rights over it if needed. When these conditions are met, consent granted for a particular use is considered *informed.*

We define informed revocation as a process that allows data subjects to remove and/or change permissions associated with:

- Personal data held by an enterprise.
- The purpose for which personal data may be processed by an enterprise.
- The sharing or dissemination of data by an enterprise with third parties.
- The identity of a data subject (cf. anonymisation), even for the case where consent has not been given initially.

The key characteristic of the concept of informed revocation is that the data subject should be informed of all the available types of revocation that he or she can perform, without being forced or coerced to give up any of these rights.

The idea of consent is at the heart of codes of research ethics and the writings on that subject [5,14]. Consent may be regarded as the opportunity to decline to take part or to withdraw from the process taking place without such decisions triggering adverse consequences for them. According to the Theory of Informed Consent, people can only consent to something if they have received sufficient information, have understood it and have explicitly expressed agreement [5]. Its early adoption is associated with medical practice and the right of patients to be informed about the risks of medical procedures that might affect their wellbeing. Today its scope has broadened to include, amongst other elements, the right of online service data subjects to be informed of the way their personal information is used.

A criticism of the concept of informed consent has been raised on the grounds that, since consent is elicited only once – before personal data is processed – it cannot be considered 'informed' throughout the lifetime of the data; in other words, consent is granted on the basis of information available at a fixed moment in time, and whether that decision may be deemed 'informed' depends only on how much information was available at that moment. At a subsequent time data might be used for alternative purposes than the data subject initially consented to, so that he or she may not be fully informed.

Another concern surrounding achieving informed consent [6] is how free the individual is to participate. Particularly in medical environments, people often decide to consent before they read the consent form. Patients see the process of giving consent as a mere ritual and they sign the form more as a symbolic act rather than a meaningful process that has illuminated them about the situation to be experienced.

Fisher [6] also argues that researchers experience the same phenomenon. They perceive that participants share the same understanding and have the same perception about the process of consent with them and incorrectly conclude that the form they sign is informative enough for the consent of the patient to be informed.

Our revocation model in itself cannot address the criticisms levied at Information Consent as a concept. However, we believe the EnCoRe methodology can, and so we hope to achieve informed revocation through the nature of the EnCoRe system since data subjects will necessarily engage in a process of setting consent and revocation preferences; the nature of the process tackles the problem of the non experience of the situation. Imagine playing a game of chess where consent is like making the first move where the combination of moves are infinite and revocation is like deciding which move to make when the game is ending where the combination of moves could be calculated and the result could be anticipated. Individuals are aware of the situation and do not experience the procedural misconception effect because they have already evaluate the situation and they want to exercise their right to revoke because of their experience. Furthermore, we have formed informed revocation in such a way that the process of revocation is unambiguous. The definitions are not open to interpretation as some consent forms are. Individuals only need to be informed of the different revocation mechanisms that they may perform and what each mechanism could achieve. However the implications that their act of revocation may have to the data controllers cannot always be predicted. This paper has adopted an individual's perspective and further research needs to be conducted to clarify this aspect.

5 Conclusions and Future Work

Information systems abound in our everyday life, and we are constantly disclosing personal data to enterprises and government in an effort to gain access to products, services, and society's many benefits. There is consequently a need to provide data subjects with mechanisms enabling them to control the storage, use and dissemination of such data.

In this paper we have detailed the different kinds of control that data subjects desire to exercise over personal data concerning them that is held by an enterprise. We have elicited data subject requirements from the literature and from focus groups with actual data subjects carried out within the EnCoRe project, and proposed a model that covers all the different guises of revocation. We are not aware of any other work that specifically addresses revocation and its variants. From our sample, we also noted a tendency by data subjects to alter their choice of revocation mechanism when informed of the many different kinds that exist, and coined the term "informed revocation" to describe this change of behaviour.

There are several avenues for future work. Subsequent research could tackle the issue of granularity and provide a more concrete solution to the conflicting requirements of anonymisation and traceability. Moreover, the model presented could be refined by applying it to more case studies. While this paper has considered only the perspective of the data subject, another direction of investigation is to consider revocation requirements from different perspectives such as the data controller's or the society's perspective. It is highly likely that the requirements elicited from these future researches may not be well aligned or may be even in direct conflict with the findings of this paper.

References

[1] Can, A.S.: What Was Privacy? Harvard Business Review (2008)

[2] Casassa Mont, M., Pearson, S., Kounga, G., Shen, Y., Bramhall, P.: On the Management of Consent and Revocation in Enterprises: Setting the Context. Technical Report HPL-2009-49, HP Labs, Bristol (2009)

[3] Dwyer, C., Hiltz, S., Passerini, K.: Trust and Privacy concern within social networking sites: A comparison of Facebook and MySpace. In: Proceedings of the Thirteenth Americas Conference on Information Systems, Keystone (2007)

[4] Etzioni, A.: Are new technologies the enemy of privacy? Knowledge, Technology & Policy, 20, 115–119 (2007)

[5] Faden, R.R., Beauchamp, T.L.: A History and Theory of Informed Consent. Oxford University Press, New York (1986)

[6] Fisher, J.A.: Procedural misconceptions and informed consent: insights from empirical research on the clinical trials industry. Kennedy Institute of Ethics Journal 16, 251–268 (2006)

[7] Glazer, I., Blakley, B.: Privacy. In: Identity and Privacy Strategies In-Depth Research Overview, Burton Group Reports Version 1.0 (2009)

[8] Grimmelmann, J.T.: Facebook and the social dynamics of privacy. Iowa Law Review 95(4) (2009)

[9] Lipford, R.H., Besmer, A., Watson, J.: Understanding privacy settings in Facebook with an audience view. In: Proceedings of the 1st Conference on Usability, Psychology and Security, San Francisco, pp. 1–8 (2008)

[10] Riley, B.T.: Security vs. Privacy: A Comparative Analysis of Canada, the United Kingdom and the United States. Journal of Business and Public Policy 1(2) (2007)

[11] Solove, D.: Understanding Privacy. Harvard University Press, Cambridge (2008)

[12] Warren, S., Brandeis, L.: The Right to Privacy. Harvard Law Rev. 4(5), 193–200 (1890)

[13] Westin, A.F.: Privacy and freedom. Atheneum, New York (1967)

[14] Wilkinson, T.: Research, informed consent and the limits of disclosure. Bioethics 15(4), 342–361 (2001)

[15] Various authors: On the anonymity "versus" accountability debate (2009), http://hosteddocs.ittoolbox.com/ks070709.pdf

[16] http://www.telegraph.co.uk/news/newstopics/politics/lawandorder/5898488/Sex-offender-register-for-life-breaches-rights-of-rapists-and-paedophiles.html (last accessed on 06/02/2010)

[17] http://www.theregister.co.uk/2008/08/20/uk_gov_lost_records/ (last accessed on 06/02/2010)

[18] http://www.theregister.co.uk/2009/12/21/dna_pnc (last accessed on 06/02/2010)

Multilateral Privacy in Clouds:
Requirements for Use in Industry

Ina Schiering and Markus Hansen

i.schiering@ostfalia.de, markus.hansen@privacyresearch.eu

Abstract. After the virtualisation of single components of computing systems such as storage, networks or computing devices the next step is the abstraction of the infrastructure as a whole: cloud computing. There are already cloud services on the market, but most of them rely on proprietary technology. Hence standards for cloud computing are needed that realise the requirements we have for present systems. In this context it is important to think of requirements for privacy when personal data are distributed in cloud services and on the other hand on restrictions an owner of computing resources wants to impose. It is important to note that the concepts that enable multilateral privacy are also needed by industry for the flexible realisation of service level agreements and governance to incorporate cloud services in business processes and to be compliant with legal regulations as e.g. SOX, EuroSOX. Therefore the methods that are needed to realise business critical IT services as cloud services are the same as for privacy.

Keywords: multilateral privacy, privacy, data security, data protection, cloud computing, clouds, requirements, identity management, compliance.

1 Introduction

Cloud computing refers to methods to dynamically utilise scalable IT services, so called *cloud services,*for a certain purpose over networks, especially the Internet. To achieve this, the abstraction paradigms of virtualisation and scalability are used in combination. While virtualisation allows single physical resources to appear and be used as multiple resources of the same type as the initial single one, scalability allows the cloud users to use IT services as flexible as needed: IT services can be ordered dynamically even for special events as training or testing purposes.

We denote the party (company or private user) that uses a cloud service as a *cloud user*. We concentrate here mainly on companies as cloud users. Cloud computing is offered in the form of a *cloud service*. Cloud services are offered by *cloud providers*. Cloud providers and cloud users are denoted as *interacting partners* in the cloud if we do not need the distinguish between them.

Clouds can be operated by several actors, and the services offered from a cloud can be used in several constellations. In e.g. enterprise environments, spare resources can be offered internally as cloud services to allow for a higher level of utilisation. In this case, where provider and user of the resulting cloud are basically the same instance, the cloud is called an *internal cloud*. On the other hand, cloud services might be

M. Bezzi et al. (Eds.): Privacy and Identity, IFIP AICT 320, pp. 259–265, 2010.

offered from an external supplier, e.g. a company that has specialised in operating clouds and sells services or wants to monetise spare resources and operational competencies. In the case of such *external clouds*, all physical resources that are the basis of cloud services are out of physical reach of the cloud users. It is also possible to extend internal clouds by joining them with external clouds, resulting in *hybrid clouds*.

A cloud service might be a single service as it is the case with storage or compute services as e.g. Amazon S3. That sort of cloud service is named *IaaS* (Infrastructure as a Service). Since for data security and privacy questions we need to describe where the data is located, we denote each cloud provider who owns resources a *resource owner*. Some cloud providers for IaaS cloud services act only as intermediaries, where resource owners rent spare resources to the cloud provider who joins resources from several resource owners to form an IaaS cloud service. But a cloud service can also be the aggregation of multiple physically independent services to appear and be used as a single services. The intention here is to use a combined platform (*PaaS* - Platform as a Service) or even a special software (*SaaS* - Software as a Service) and can lead to the realisation of whole business processes in the form of cloud services.

In more general scenario with cloud providers realising a cloud service based on resource owners and existing cloud services from other cloud providers, a cloud service consists of a dynamically changing network of resource owners, cloud providers and cloud users, the *cloud network* for the cloud service.

Such a cloud network is represented by a finite, directed graph where the vertices denote the cloud users, cloud providers and resource owners. There is an edge from a cloud provider to the cloud user that utilises a cloud service of that provider and there is an edge from a cloud provider resp. resource owner to a second cloud provider, if that second cloud provider incorporates the services or resources of the first one in his own cloud services. The following restrictions concerning graphs representing cloud networks apply: A vertex associated to a cloud user has no successor and a vertex associated to a resource owner has no predecessor.

The subnet of the cloud network servicing one cloud user is named the *cloud subnet* of that cloud user. This subnet is represented by the sub-graph of the cloud network induced by the vertices of the cloud user and all cloud providers, resource owners that are utilised to provide the cloud service for that user.

Cloud users can dynamically decide to begin or end using a cloud service. They can in an automated way request more entities of the cloud service e.g. more resources as storage and system instances. In the case of SaaS the cloud users implicitly scale the cloud service by changing the number of users, transactions or by a different choice of software modules. The cloud provider has to provide the cloud service and needs potentially to involve a dynamically changing number of resource owners and other cloud services as needed. A resource owner or cloud provider might want to sell services or resources only for a certain amount of time, e.g. spare resources that are needed later. Hence we speak of a cloud network or a cloud subnet of a cloud user at a certain point of time.

Cloud services are a interesting alternative especially for small up to medium size companies. Companies of that size have a limited amount of IT personnel, know-how and a limited IT Budget. Instead of investments in IT it could be an interesting to use cloud services for complex processes e.g. email, customer relationship management (CRM), enterprise content management (ECM), enterprise resource planning (ERP), data archiving, project management or the desktop. Also it could be interesting to use IaaS services for e.g. storage if the cloud provider offers interesting service levels that are difficult to realise as mirroring over different physical sites, off-site backup or high availability of the computing platform.

Beside the advantages of using the know-how and the resources of the cloud services using cloud services incorporates also several risks: The cloud user needs legal warranties concerning data security and privacy from the cloud provider and the whole cloud subnet that realises the cloud service for him at any point in time, since personal and business critical data are operated in the cloud subnet.

In this context we need to consider an adequate generalisation of the concepts of security and privacy: Multilateral security and multilateral privacy. The concept of multilateral security [7] aims at allowing all parties of an interaction to express their security objectives, at recognising conflicting objectives and (automatically) negotiating compromises, and at enforcing objectives within the scope of the compromises negotiated. To enforce the objectives, mechanisms have to be established to allow effective control. Analogously the concept of multilateral privacy refers to clouds that address the privacy (or secrecy in case of legal entities) objectives of all participating parties, with no party taking precedence over another [8].

2 Cloud Requirements

In the case of IaaS the basic functional requirements are concerning type and clock rate of the CPU, the amount of memory or disk space. For SaaS there are functional requirements for the software used, e.g. collaborative work on documents. Beside the functional requirements there are typically operational requirements: The cloud user needs to start, stop and configure the service. For full flexibility of the service automatic provisioning must be possible. Beside these requirements there are non-functional requirements that are normally formulated in the form of an SLA[1] (service level agreement): for example requirements concerning availability, reliability, scalability, data integrity, data security, privacy, access control, legal regulations.

Directive 1995/46/EC of the European Parliament and of the Council (Data Protection Directive) and Directive 2002/58 on Privacy and Electronic Communications (E-Privacy Directive) are EU directives on data protection and privacy. They provide a regulatory framework to the EU member states that must provide legislation accordingly. With regard to the specifics of cloud computing, the most important regulation concerns transfer of personal data[2] to third countries, i.e. countries outside the EU. Personal data may only be transferred outside the EU if those third countries provide an adequate level of privacy protection. For transfer of data to the USA, the Safe Harbour Agreement applies. Companies in the USA can opt-in to Safe Harbour,

---

[1] For terminology concerning IT services and service level agreements see [1].

[2] The term 'personal data' is defined in the European Data Protection Directive 1995/46/EC, Article 2(a): "'personal data' shall mean any information relating to an identified or identifiable natural person ('data subject'); an identifiable person is one who can be identified, directly or indirectly, in particular by reference to an identification number or to one or more factors specific to his physical, physiological, mental, economic, cultural or social identity."

thereby stating that they follow adequate data protection principles. Then EU companies are - as a general rule - allowed to transfer personal data to them.

In addition to the principle that personal data may only be transferred to countries with adequate protection, further principles that must be complied with according to the Data Protection Directive are that any personal data has to be fairly and lawfully processed, may only be processed for limited purposes, has to be adequate, relevant and not excessive, has to be accurate, must not be kept longer than necessary, may only be processed in accordance with the data subject's rights, and has to be secure.

Examples for other legal regulations cloud users have to comply with are in the USA SOX (Sarbanes-Oxley Act), enacted as a reaction to accounting scandals around companies like Enron, WorldCom, etc. SOX demands e.g. an internal control system for corporations in the USA and all subsidiaries. Similar requirements have evolved in the EU as Directive 2006/43/EC of the European Parliament and the Council of 17 May 2006 on statutory audit of annual accounts and consolidated accounts, and Directive 2008/30/EC of the European Parliament and of the Council of 11 March 2008 amending Directive 2006/43/EC on statutory audits of annual accounts and consolidated accounts (also named EuroSOX).

To comply with e.g. SOX, EuroSOX organisations need as a prerequisite transparent and documented business processes. Since most processes are supported by IT systems this implies a transparent and documented IT environment. Based on this concrete controls can be defined: For a business process concrete control objectives are formulated, the legal regulation that is the cause for the control objective and the proceeding to monitor the control objective. An example for such a control objective is that an invoice is only paid for if there is a valid quote and the responsible person confirms that the goods resp. services are delivered in correspondence with the quote. Monitoring of control objectives can often be realised in IT systems.

Cloud providers and resource owners on the other hand have requirements concerning monitoring, measuring, reporting and billing for services. They are interested in an easy way to integrate services to create new cloud services on the basis of existing services. Cloud providers have to comply with legal regulations for their services, e.g. export control regulations. So there are restrictions concerning the countries where a cloud provider is allowed to sell services.

3   Methods

To realise the requirements of legal regulations in a cloud environment, e.g. internal control systems, similar mechanisms are needed as for ensuring data security and privacy: Federated identity management can realise access control and monitoring and reporting on access. Since it does not correspond to the flexibility and dynamic of cloud services if the cloud user has to negotiate an SLA with each cloud provider in the form of a contract, there must be an automatic process for the communication of these requirements in the cloud interface, oftena cloud API (application programming interface). Finally the cloud user needs control and certification mechanisms to check that the requirements are fulfilled. In the following we describe cloud interfaces and control and certifications mechanisms in more detail. For an overview about federated identity management see [2].

3.1 Cloud Interface

Concerning cloud interfaces resp. cloud APIs there are currently two different approaches: For SaaS, a web browser is mainly used as interface. In the case of IaaS several APIs exist that are specific for the respective cloud provider, e.g. Sun Cloud API, Amazon EC2 API, etc. They are mainly based on XML or JSON (JavaScript Object Notation). They are generally used to represent functional requirements. Therefore it represents a risk to use these cloud services for business critical environments where at least requirements concerning compliance, availability, privacy and data security have to be assured. In addition, as each provider uses his own API, changing the cloud provider will lead to a change of the software of the cloud user as a different API has to be used. Hence the goal is the development of standardised cloud APIs that allow the formulation of non-functional requirements.

There are initiatives that try to develop cloud APIs for at least IaaS environments where it is possible to formulate non-functional requirements as e.g. the Open Cloud Computing Interface Working Group (OCCI-WG). The OCCI-WG works on an API for IaaS cloud services based on cloud APIs in industry. Some draft documents do already exist that line out use cases [4]. They rely on the RESERVOIR architecture where the architecture consists of resource owners, cloud providers that work as intermediaries, and cloud users [3]. For further examples of initiatives that work on cloud APIs in the IaaS field see [5] (SNIA), [6] (DMTF).

Each interacting partner in the cloud network has requirements that need to be fulfilled. Because of the dynamic change of the cloud network the requirements have to be interchanged and checked automatically. Hence they can be formulated as in the example of the OCCI-WG in XML.

As a first step to the formulation of requirements in an API they must be categorized: categories as e.g. high, medium or low availability are created where each category is documented by the service provider. A cloud user begins using a cloud service. Hence he requests the cloud service from the cloud provider where requirements are expressed in XML. The cloud provider checks if all requirements are fulfilled. If that is the case, he acknowledges the request. Otherwise he starts requests to all direct successors in the cloud network that are needed to provide the service with the defined quality. These requests should be derived automatically. The requests are tagged with the initial cloud provider and a number for the request. Each cloud provider and resource owner answers only once to each request and stores all requests and answers. This assurance process is executed recursively. It terminates since the graph representing the cloud network is finite. At least all resource owners, whose corresponding nodes in the graph do not have predecessors, can acknowledge or non-acknowledge the requirements. When the cloud provider has received all acknowledge or non-acknowledge messages from his direct successors in the graph, he derives from the messages if he can deliver the service with the requested quality or not. Hence he can acknowledge resp. non-acknowledge the request. The request is acknowledged if the cloud user receives an acknowledge message. Then the cloud subnet delivering the cloud service for that cloud user is represented by the sub-graph induced by the following nodes: The cloud providers and resource owners that acknowledged the requirements and where there is a path in the graph from the node corresponding to that interacting partner to the cloud user such that all nodes on the path have also acknowledged the requirements.

A cloud user can e.g. express the requirement that any data may only reside and be processed on systems located within the European Union, that only systems and services from companies outside (or, respectively, inside) a certain jurisdiction may be used, that systems and services from a business competitor may not be part of the specific cloud subnet, or that all parties have to have signed the Safe Harbour Agreement. The cloud user would submit these requirements as an XML document through the cloud API, the cloud provider would then select the resources that match the requirements in appropriate quantity and join them into the specific cloud subnet. Analogously, the resource owners can themselves also define their specific requirements to be matched against through the API, e.g. that any resources must not be used for military purposes, or that no medical data may be stored. Also, the cloud providers may have certain requirements that can be expressed and matched alike. Thus, in IaaS scenarios, security and privacy requirements can be expressed and interpreted in an automated process when initiating a cloud subnet. For SaaS scenarios, a similar approach can be followed by adding meta-data to the data to be processed to express e.g. purpose limitations that the SaaS environment has to enforce.

While multilateral security includes mechanisms for automated negotiation and, therefore, compromises (e.g. about what cryptographic algorithms and what key lengths are to be applied), privacy objectives usually are not open to compromise. The process of deciding whether a certain resource can be a node within the cloud of a certain cloud user therefore is a simple binary function, a the resource can only meet the requirements from the privacy objective of the cloud user or not.

3.2 Certification and Control

A means to allow control can be to make use of certification. Systems and services forming the cloud can be certified to meet certain security and privacy standards. Certification according to e.g. IT-Grundschutz [9] or ISO 27001 could replace actual hands-on control for security while the ICPP Privacy Seal [10] can certify privacy compliance. These certificates could be handed through from each resource to the cloud providers and the cloud users using the API. Therefore, cloud users would not have to check the resources from the resource owners for compliance themselves but would rather rely on trusted third parties, i.e. the certification authorities. Protocols using e.g. Trusted Computing components could then be used to allow remote attestation of the state of any system joining the cloud and to allow detection in case the state of a system is not according to certification or contracts.

Still, even when certified, a closed source resource can not actually be controlled and therefore has always to be regarded as a security risk, although probably a low one as for the certification. But as closed source resources also ease vendor lock-in situations, it might be wiser for cloud users to avoid them.

4   Conclusion

In case cloud providers and resource owners take care that only resources certified to meet security standards are integrated into cloud subnets, they can offer transparent and well documented IT to the cloud users that e.g. also allows to establish the location of data. Cloud users can then rely on the certification to use applications on that IT that process personal data. If such applications have received certification as for that they comply with privacy legislation, they can furthermore be offered in an SaaS scenario. But if today's certification frameworks are already capable of representing the specific requirements of dynamically interacting system is currently an open question.

Comprehensive use of combined security and privacy certification could allow SaaS to be a valid business model for processing personal data. Using the API and the certificates, cloud providers can automatically generate clouds for which certain requirements have been proven to be met. Another option would be to only offer certified clouds. Providers of certified software in SaaS making use of hardware offered by other parties have to make sure, that they will use certified systems to still be able to prove that requirements are met. Still, cloud users will have to make sure within their scope that privacy requirements for the processing of personal data are fulfilled.

References

[1] ITIL IT Service Management - Glossary of Terms and Definitions, OGC (2007),
    http://www.itsmfi.org/files/
    ITILV3_Glossary_English_v1_2007_0.pdf
[2] Maler, E., Reed, D.: The Venn of Identity: Options and Issues in Federated Identity Management. IEEE Security and Privacy 6(2), 16–23 (2008)
[3] Rochwerger, B., Breitgand, D., Levy, E., Galis, A., Nagin, K., Llorente, I., Montero, R., Wolfsthal, Y., Elmroth, E., Caceres, J., Ben-Yehuda, M., Emmerich, W., Galán, F.: The RESERVOIR Model and Architecture for Open Federated Cloud Computing. IBM Journal of Research & Development 53(4) (2009)
[4] Open Cloud Computing Interface WG (OCCI-WG),
    http://forge.ggf.org/sf/projects/occi-wg
[5] SNIA Cloud Data Management Interface, http://www.snia.org/cloud
[6] DMTF Cloud Incubator, http://www.dmtf.org/about/cloud-incubator
[7] Federrath, H., Pfitzmann, A.: Bausteine zur Realisierung mehrseitiger Sicherheit. In: Müller, G., Pfitzmann, A. (Hrsg.) Mehrseitige Sicherheit in der Kommunikationstechnik, pp. 83–104. Addison-Wesley-Longman, http://www.semper.org/sirene/
    publ/FePf_97MehrsSicher.inBuch.ps.gz
[8] Cissée, R.: An agent-based approach for privacy-preserving information filtering, dissertation (2009),
    http://deposit.ddb.de/cgi-bin/dokserv?
    idn=994920466&dok_var=d1&dok_ext=pdf&filename=994920466.pdf
[9] IT-Grundschutz,
    https://www.bsi.bund.de/cln_155/EN/topics/ITGrundschutz/
    ITGrundschutzHome/itgrundschutzhome_node.html
[10] ICPP Privacy Seal,
    https://www.datenschutzzentrum.de/guetesiegel/index.htm

PET-USES: Privacy-Enhancing Technology – Users' Self-Estimation Scale

Erik Wästlund[1], Peter Wolkerstorfer[2], and Christina Köffel[2]

[1] Dep. of Psychology – Karlstad University, Sweden
erik.wastlund@kau.se
[2] CURE – Center for Usability Research and Engineering, Vienna, Austria
wolkerstorfer@cure.at, koeffel@cure.at

Abstract. This paper describes the "Privacy-Enhancing Technology Users' Self-Estimation Scale (PET-USES)", a questionnaire that enables users to evaluate PET user interfaces for their overall usability and to measure six different PET aspects. The PET-USES is intended to be used during usability testing and evaluation of PET user interfaces. The focus of the PET-USES is the subjective experience of the user rather than the intrinsic PET functionality of the application being tested. Although the test has been developed within the PrimeLife[1] project to test the usability of PETs developed therein, the test is constructed in such a fashion that it should be applicable to a wide variety of PETs. The objective of this paper is to outline the creation and the background of the PET-USES questionnaire and invite the usability community not only to use the test, but also to contribute to the further development of the PET-USES.

Keywords: PET-USES, HCI, Usability, PET.

1 Introduction

PET-USES (Privacy-Enhancing Technology Users' Self-Estimation Scale) is a questionnaire that enables users to evaluate PET User Interfaces (UIs). The reason for developing and using PET-USES was to be able to measure the perceived usability of UIs, both during single user trails and during large group walkthroughs of screen recordings.

Today there are a number of questionnaires measuring user experience, usability and various HCI (Human-Computer Interaction) aspects such as the hedonic quality [1] of software, websites, and services [2, 3], to our knowledge none includes PET-related issues.

---

[1] The research leading to these results has received funding from the European Community's Seventh Framework Programme (FP7/2007-2013) under grant agreement n° 216483. The information in this document is provided "as is", and no guarantee or warranty is given that the information is fit for any particular purpose. The above referenced consortium members shall have no liability for damages of any kind including without limitation direct, special, indirect, or consequential damages that may result from the use of these materials subject to any liability which is mandatory due to applicable law.

M. Bezzi et al. (Eds.): Privacy and Identity, IFIP AICT 320, pp. 266–274, 2010.

Although there is no single widely accepted definition of PETs, they can be described as:

Privacy-Enhancing Technologies is a system of ICT measures protecting informational privacy by eliminating or minimising personal data thereby preventing unnecessary or unwanted processing of personal data, without the loss of the functionality of the information system. [4]

This above definition is focused on the principle of data minimization whereas others focus more on privacy principles and legislation or how PETs give the user power over his/her own data [5]. There are also attempts to classify PETs into classes such as General PET Controls, Separation of Data, Privacy Management Systems, and Anonymisation Tools [6].

One PET solution currently being investigate within the PrimeLife[2] project is an identity management system that solves a number of the above mentions issues and the usability evaluation of this system is the stepping stone for the development of the PET-USES. In short the system is comprised of a number of subsystems which relate to the handling and release of an individual's personal data. The PrimeLife system also informs the user of the trustworthiness of data recipient and to what extent the data recipient's privacy policy matches the desired privacy policy of the data subject.

The PET-USES consists of two major parts of questions: one part measuring overall usability and one part measuring PET aspects. Thus, the PET usability scales have a dual purpose. They evaluate the software's general usability and the extent to which the software assists the user in learning and understanding privacy related issues. An important feature of the measurement of PET aspects is the modularity of the questionnaire, enabling the inclusion or exclusion of scales measuring specific aspects based on the tasks and features being evaluated.

This text is organized as follows: Section 2 "Related Work" depicts current views on usability testing. The following Section 3 "The PET-USES Approach" describes development criteria for the PET-USES questionnaire and sketches the main modules. This is followed by a discussion in Section 4 on when and how the PET-USES can be employed. Section 5 gives a conclusion and shows next steps in testing the perceived usability of some PETs with the PET-USES questionnaire which version 1.0 is published in the Appendix.

2 Related Work

The PET-USES questionnaire is based on the ISO 9241 general standard of usability [7] as well as the more PET specific HCI guidelines presented by Patrick et al. 2003 [8] and utilized in the work with the PRIME[3] integrated identity management prototype [9]. The former defines usability as the "extent to which a product can be used by specified users to achieve specified goals with effectiveness, efficiency, and

---

[2] "PrimeLife – bringing sustainable privacy and identity management to future networks and services" is an EC FP7 project: http://www.primelife.eu/
[3] "PRIME – Privacy and Identity Management for Europe" was an EC FP6 project: http://www.prime-project.eu/

satisfaction" whereas the latter promotes the four categories comprehension (to understand or know), consciousness (be aware or informed), control (to manipulate or be empowered) and consent (to agree). Although the two views might seem divergent at first they can readily be combined within the structure of usability testing proposed by Hornbæk [10]. Based on a review of 180 studies, published in core HCI journals and proceedings, he argues for a change in terminology from the ISO 9241, to better encompass what is actually being measured. The relationship between the concepts of Hornbæk, ISO 9241, HCI Guidelines and generally often used measures of usability can be seen below (Table 1).

Table 1. The table shows possible constructs of interest for the PET-USES, their relationship to other usability constructs and how they relate to the framework proposed by Hornbæk

Hornbæk	ISO 9241	HCI Guidelines[4]	Other measures/concepts of usability
Outcomes	Effectiveness	Consent (agree)	User Value
		Comprehension (to understand or know)	Usefulness
		Consciousness (be aware of, be informed)	Functionality
Interaction-Process	Efficiency	Control (to manipulate or be empowered)	Efficiency
			Ease of Learning
			Ease of Use
Attitudes & Experiences	Satisfaction		Satisfaction
			Affect / Likeability
			Trust
			Helpfulness
			Awareness of PET-Related Issues

Thus, by using the terminology of Hornbæk, one can for instance investigate the outcomes of using a particular interface in terms of Effectiveness of Goal Completion but also in terms of User Value and what the user learns from the interaction. This framework makes it easy to integrate the above-mentioned constructs into one model as well as adding further constructs if that should be deemed necessary.

3 The PET-USES Approach

The PET-USES scale General Usability is measured as a composite of the sub-scales Ease of Learning, Ease of Use and User Value. The rationale for differentiating between the sub-scales Ease of Learning and Ease of Use is that intuitive interfaces are perceived to have a better learnability whereas a less intuitive interface can be used easily only once the user gets accustomed to it. It is also noteworthy that the General Usability value will be less influenced by perceived User Value than Ease of Learning

---

[4] As defined by Patrick et al. 2003 [8].

and Ease of Use. This reflects the fact that, although user value is an important driver for software adoption the focus of the PET-USES lies more on the usability than on the perceived benefits of a system.

The PET aspects modules currently developed are derived from the user-controlled identity management approach of the projects PRIME and PrimeLife: Data Management, Credential Management, PrivPrefs[5], Recipient Evaluation, Data Release, and History. They can all be used to evaluate specific PET-related functionality of software or websites. The entire PET-USES questionnaire (including all modules) and its items can be found in the appendix.

The focus of the scales are the following privacy-critic areas:

- Data Management: The extent to which the system makes it easier to store and organize personal information. This scale can be used to evaluate all types of identity management software and services.
- Credential Management: The extent to which the system makes it easier to store and organize credentials and other certificates. This scale can be used to evaluate identity management systems that include issued claim credentials (e.g. the Higgins project[6]).
- PrivPrefs: This scale is designed to measure the extent to which the system makes it easier to set general and excessive levels for data release policies and to what extent the user is informed of unwanted data dissemination. Thus, an aspect of this scale is the decision support qualities of the system.
- Recipient Evaluation: the extent to which the system helps users to evaluate the data recipients' credibility and trustworthiness. This scale can also be regarded in terms of decision support.
- Data Release: The extent to which the system clarifies what personal information is being released and who is the recipient of the data.
- History: The extent to which the system can show the user when, what and, to whom personal information has been released and thus provide an overview of what data any given service provider might have accumulated.

Effectiveness and efficiency are often measured in a more objective fashion than the user self-estimations of the PET-USES. The effectiveness of a given interface can for instance be measured in terms of task completion time and efficiency in terms of quality of task solution [11] and, of course, optimally usability evaluations should be comprised of a combination of self-estimation and more objective measurements. It should, however, be pointed out that these types of measurement requires fully functional interfaces and both logging of behavior and knowledge of desired outcomes whilst the PET-USES can be used in a much earlier stage to measure users perception as estimates of effectiveness and efficiency.

Practical considerations such as time and effort to answer the questions can prevent the PET-USES to measure all of the categories mentioned in Table 1 in separate

---

[5] PrivPrefs (Privacy Preferences) is a method that is currently being investigated in the PrimeLife project for defining personal privacy preferences (see for example [12]) which will be used for automated evaluations of the appropriateness of data-requests. The PrivPrefs are evaluations of polices as defined in P3P (http://www.w3.org/TR/2006/NOTE-P3P11-20061113/#P3PPolicies).

[6] http://wiki.eclipse.org/Password_Cards#Required_Claim_Types

scales and hence several of the categories will have to be combined into more general domains.

4   Discussion

A fundamental principle of self-estimation scales is that all questions are thought to measure an aspect of construct of interest. Thus, all questions are thought to be exchangeable with other questions that also measure a related aspect of the same construct. An important aspect of this fact is that the focus of measurement is rather the aggregated data of all the questions of a module than on the specific questions themselves. This idea, of course, is analogous to any type of sampling and point estimation. As with any sampling procedure more observations lead to better estimations. However, when it comes to self-ratings, time constraints are the biggest obstacles to extensive sampling.

In essence, all self rating scales are constructed in a similar fashion containing a stimuli and some way for the participant to rate this stimuli. The PET-USES is constructed as a number of Likert scales [13]. Thus, in accordance with the principle of Likert scales, the stimuli used are a number of statements and users are asked to rate to what extent they agree or disagree with these statements. The response format used in the PET-USES is a five point scale. Thus it is possible for the user to respond in a neutral fashion unlike in a forced choice scale. It should be noted that it is possible to utilize other response formats such as any number of values or a Visual Analogue Scale [14]. There is quite some debate (see for example [13, 15]) over the level of measurement of the added values of the Likert scales and if they should be treated as ordinal or interval data. The basic argument for viewing the scales as being ordinal is that it is impossible to create a subjective scale with equal distances between response options. On the other hand, it is possible to argue that there are in fact equal distances between the response options as respondents are using the numbers one to five, not the verbal descriptions. The main reason for purporting the notion of the scales being interval is of course the possibility to use parametrical tests.

4.1   Evaluating Scales

All measurement needs to be evaluated in terms of reliability and validity. As the individual questions of a scale are thought to measure the same construct, the most fundamental evaluation of a scale is one of internal consistency. The basic principle is that respondents should answer the questions in a coherent manner, that is, if a respondent scores high on one statement of a given scale s/he should score rather high on other statements measuring the same underlying construct. If this is not the case, the items are thought to measure different constructs. Additionally, as different underlying constructs are supposed to be independent from each other, items measuring different underlying constructs should not correlate highly. The statistical technique used to estimate internal consistency is Chronbach's alpha and factor analysis to assess the underlying constructs as such [16].

Tests such as Chronbach's Alpha, however, say nothing about what the test actually measures even though it might measure it satisfactory. In order to understand what a scale actually measures we need to assess its external validity. As some aspects of the PET-USES measure constructs which are also possible to measure in other ways, the questionnaire should be evaluated against these criteria. For instance, as the sub-scales Ease of Learning and Ease of Use both are aspects of Efficiency they could be correlated with measurements of quality of solutions or such.

4.2 When to Use the PET-USES

The main reason for conducting usability tests is to discriminate between usable and not usable interfaces either during the design process or in comparisons between different systems. Typical use-cases for the PET-USES include both of these scenarios. Thus, PET-USES can be used both in order to compare the perceived usability strengths and weaknesses between different interfaces, and, in order to aid interface designers during the design process through administrating the test at various steps in the process. However, as during all statistical testing, the possibility to find significant results is dependent on the power of the investigation. As usual there are only two ways to achieve statistical power: a bigger sample or a bigger effects size. When it comes to comparing existing interfaces a bigger effects size can be achieved both by choosing interfaces that are evaluated as being extremely good and bad and by inviting more of the current user base into the evaluation. During interface design, especially during fast iterations, the differences between versions are usually quite small and the tested user group rather small and hence the power of a test such as the PET-USES will become quite small. This should be taken into consideration when planning when to use the PET-USES as it will be more useful evaluating clear steps in the design process. In order to gain power by adding more respondents without having to do a great number of complete user tests it is possible to do large group walkthroughs of screen recordings. An additional feature of this method is that it is possible to do user tests on interfaces without any functionality.

So far the usage of PET-USES is rather limited, but it has been incorporated in usability studies performed by Center for Usability Research and Engineering (CURE). Although not enough data has yet been collected for formal statistical evaluation of the PET-USES, feedback from both practitioners and users show that the test is easy to use.

4.3 The CURE Web Service

In order to facilitate both the use and the evaluation of the PET-USES, a web service is set up at CURE[7]. The site enables research companies to use the PET-USES questionnaire for their evaluations and will be open to all who wish to use the PET-USES on the premises that the collected PET-USES data will be used to gather feedback and further develop the questionnaire and its scales. In addition to using the scales of the PET-USES researchers in this area will have the possibility to suggest new modules for inclusion in the sub-scale battery to reflect the ever changing field of PETs. Data provided on the website will be anonymized and treated confidentially. Only those conducting the research and the creators of the PET-USES (i.e. Karlstad University and CURE) will have access to the data provided. Users of the site who wish to retain

---

[7] http://pet-uses.cure.at/

data from other sources than the PET-USES are of course allowed to do so, but in order to evaluate the PET-USES users are encouraged to provide data, such as the maturity of the tested system or correlations with other measurements as a part of the validation of the test.

5 Conclusion

The PET-USES presented in this paper is a questionnaire which focuses on measures of both aspects of General Usability and specifically tailored scales that measure the usability of PET solutions. The test is grounded in current views on usability and the experience so far of using the test show that both practitioners and users report that the PET-USES is easy to use. The CURE web service for using the PET-USES is open to PET researchers who wish to evaluate PET UIs.

References

1. Hassenzahl, M., Burmester, M., Koller, F.: AttrakDiff: Ein Fragebogen zur Messung wahrgenommener hedonischer und pragmatischer Qualität. In: Ziegler, J., Szwillus, G. (eds.) Mensch & Computer 2003, Interaktion in Bewegung, pp. 187–196 (2003)
2. Brooke, J.: SUS: a "quick and dirty" usability scale. In: Jordan, P.W., Thomas, B., Weerdmeester, B.A., McClelland, I.L. (eds.) Usability Evaluation in Industry, pp. 189–194. Taylor & Francis, London (1996)
3. Tullis, T.S., Stetson, J.N.: A Comparison of Questionnaires for Assessing Website Usability. In: Usability Professional Association Conference (2004)
4. ISO. Ergonomic requirements for office work with visual display terminals (VDTs)-Part 11: guidance on usability-Part 11: guidance on usability (ISO 9241-11:1998) (1998)
5. Patrick, A.S., Kenny, S., Holmes, C., van Breukelen, M.: Human Computer Interaction. In: Handbook for Privacy and Privacy-Enhancing Technologies: College bescherming persoonsgegevens, pp. 249–290 (2003)
6. Pettersson, J.S. (ed.): HCI Guidelines, PRIME Deliverable, D6.1.c (2005), https://www.prime-project.eu/prime_products/reports/arch/pub_del_D06.1.c_ec_wp06.1_V4_final.pdf
7. Hornbæk, K.: Current practice in measuring usability: Challenges to usability studies and research. Int. J. Human-Computer Studies 64, 79–102 (2006)
8. Frøkjær, E., Hertzum, M., Hornbæk, K.: Measuring Usability: Are Effectiveness, Efficiency, and Satisfaction Really Correlated? In: Proceedings of the ACM CHI 2000 Conference on Human Factors in Computing Systems, April 1-6, pp. 345–352. ACM Press, New York (2000)
9. Edmondson, D.: Likert Scales: A History. In: CHARM – the Conference on Historical Analysis and Research in Marketing, pp. 127–132 (2005)
10. Butler, P.V.: Linear Analogue Self-Assessment and Procrustean Measurement: A Critical Review of Visual Analogue Scaling in Pain Assessment. J. Clin. Psychol. Med. Settings 19, 111–129 (1997)
11. Göb, R., McCollin, C., Ramalhoto, M.: Ordinal Methodology in the Analysis of Likert Scales. Quality and Quantity 41, 601–626 (2007)
12. Anastasi, A., Urbina, S.: Psychological Testing, 7th edn. Prentice Hall, Upper Saddle River (1997)

13. van Blarkom, G.W., Borking, J.J., Olk, J.G.E.: PET. In: van Blarkom, G.W., Borking, J.J., Olk, J.G.E. (eds.) Handbook of privacy and privacy-enhancing technologies (the case of intelligent software agents) (2003), http://www.andrewpatrick.ca/pisa/handbook/handbook.html

14. Harbird, R.: Privacy enhancing technologies. In: Information Commissioner's Office, UK, Privacy by design. Wycliffe House, Cheshire (2008)

15. Koorn, R., van Gils, H., ter Hart, J., Overbeek, P., Tellegen, R.: Privacy-enhancing technologies: White paper for decision makers. Ministry of Interior and Kingdom Relations, The Netherlands (2004)

16. Bergmann, M.: Generic Predefined Privacy Preferences for Online Applications. In: Fischer-Hübner, S., Duquenoy, P., Zuccato, A., Martucci, L. (eds.) The Future of Identity in the Information Society Boston, pp. 259–273. Springer, Heidelberg (2008)

Appendix: PET-USES [1.0]

Modules

The PET-USES questionnaire comprises the following modules (the detailed content can be seen in the Appendix):

Part I – Usability:
- Ease of Learning
- Ease of Use
- User Value

Part II – PET-related aspects:
- Data Management
- Credential Management
- PrivPrefs
- Recipient Evaluation
- Data Release
- History

Instructions

This test is designed to measure your experience with the system you've tested today. Your answers will be used to evaluate the system so please answer the questions as truthfully as you can. As the questions are designed to measure various aspects of the systems usability there are no right or wrong answers. Please use the scale below to indicate to what extent you disagree or agree to the statements that follow.

1 Strongly disagree
2 Disagree
3 Neither agree nor disagree
4 Agree
5 Strongly agree

General Usability
1. I found it easy to learn how to use the *system*	1 2 3 4 5
2. I had to learn a lot in order to use the *system*	1 2 3 4 5
3. I keep forgetting how to do things with this *system*	1 2 3 4 5

4. I need a lot of assistance to use this *system*	1 2 3 4 5
5. I find the *system* interface easy to use	1 2 3 4 5
6. I find the organisation of the *system* interface understandable	1 2 3 4 5
7. I get confused by the *system* interface	1 2 3 4 5
8. I find it very difficult to work with the *system*	1 2 3 4 5
9. I find that the benefits of using the *system* are bigger then the effort of using it	1 2 3 4 5
10. I would like to use this *system* regularly	1 2 3 4 5

Data Management

11. I get a clear view of my personal *data* from the system	1 2 3 4 5
12. I find organising my personal *data* easy with this system	1 2 3 4 5
13. I find keeping track of various user names and passwords is easy with this *system*	1 2 3 4 5

Credential Management

14. I find it easy to add personally issued credentials into the *system*	1 2 3 4 5
15. I find it easy to add / import certificates into the *system*	1 2 3 4 5
16. I find it easy to manage my credentials with this *system*	1 2 3 4 5

PrivPrefs

17. I find it easy to use settings for how much or how little *data* to be released with this *system*	1 2 3 4 5
18. I find that the *system* helps me understand the effects of different privacy settings	1 2 3 4 5
19. I feel safer knowing that I will be notified by the *system* if I'm about to release more personal *data* than my chosen preference	1 2 3 4 5

Recipient Evaluation

20. The *system* makes it easy for me to decide if it is safe to release my data	1 2 3 4 5
21. I don't understand how the *system* determines if a data recipient is trustworthy	1 2 3 4 5
22. I feel safer releasing my personal data when the *system* states it's OK	1 2 3 4 5

Data Release

23. I know what personal information I'm releasing when I'm using this *system*	1 2 3 4 5
24. The system makes it easy to decide how much or how little *data* to release in a given transaction	1 2 3 4 5
25. I get help from the system to understand who will receive my *data*	1 2 3 4 5

History

26. I can easily find out who has received my personal *data* with this *system*	1 2 3 4 5
27. I get a good view of who knows what about me from this *system*	1 2 3 4 5
28. I can easily see how much I've used a particular user name with this *system*	1 2 3 4 5

Headings and numerals are mainly for presentational purposes and thus optional during the use of PET-USES. Items 2, 3, 7, 8, and 21 should be reversed before summated.

Addressing the Privacy Paradox by Expanded Privacy Awareness – The Example of Context-Aware Services

André Deuker

Goethe University Frankfurt
Chair of Mobile Business & Multilateral Security
D-60629 Frankfurt a.M., Germany
Andre.Deuker@m-chair.net

Abstract. When interacting with applications, users are less restrictive in disclosing their personal data than if asked in an application-independent context. On a more general level this behavior is termed as privacy paradox. The creation of privacy awareness can assist users in dealing with context-aware services without harming their privacy unintentionally, thereby addressing the privacy paradox. The paper in hand provides a research approach towards the integration of privacy awareness on an application-specific level, especially taking into account conflicting interests between users and providers of context-aware services. It shows that expanding privacy awareness towards knowledge about methods and tools to react turns out to be useful.

Keywords: Privacy Paradox, Privacy Awareness, Economics of Privacy, Context-Aware Services.

1 Introduction

When thinking about the usage of context-aware services, many people may wonder what consequences it has to provide personal information to a (unknown) service provider[1]. Does the service provider process the information properly; in a way the user intends and expects him to? Does the information a user reveals in fact comply with what he wants to reveal, or is it possible to use disclosed information to convey additional information the user may want to keep private? On the other hand, the provision of personal information is often a necessity for the creation and provision of services and providing less, wrong, or inaccurate information could mean that the service is not performing in a way the user expects it to. One example is location based recommendations [12].

In reality fewer people care about such questions than one would expect, especially with regard to the associated risks of disclosing information imprudently [14]. Having a look at the privacy paradox, one has to admit that this might be not due to very relaxed attitudes towards privacy, but rather because of a lack of awareness with regard to which data is disclosed, and possible consequences a disclosure might bear. The

---

[1] A definition of the terms "context" and "context-awareness" can be found in [6].

M. Bezzi et al. (Eds.): Privacy and Identity, IFIP AICT 320, pp. 275–283, 2010.

goal of the research approach presented in this paper is to assist average individual users in dealing with context-aware applications without harming their privacy unintentionally. To build the theoretical basis, Chapters 2, 3, and 4 focus on the underlying theories of the privacy paradox, and on the creation of privacy awareness itself. Chapter 5 then builds on the insights of the previous chapters, and applies this knowledge on the creation of privacy awareness in context-aware services. Chapter 6 gives a summary of the article, states the scientific contribution, and opens the discussion for further research in this area.

2 The Privacy Paradox

Privacy economists are investigating users' trade-off between benefits and costs of disclosing personal information by means of utility functions for a number of years. The utility function of AWAD and KRISHNAN for instance derives benefits by the degree of the received service personalisation, whereas costs are influenced among other factors by consumers' privacy concerns [3]. To give an example: By providing personal information to a recommendation system as employed by Amazon.com, one could expect to benefit from better recommendations. On the other hand, this might be related to concerns with regard to the protection of the disclosed data, thus creating costs. The inherent assumption of this approach and economic approaches in general is that users seek to maximise their utility constantly by balancing costs and benefits.

Research on rationality in individual decision processes has shown that in principle people are quite clear and well able to articulate their desired level of privacy, at least on an abstract level. Nonetheless, having a look at their behaviour in privacy relevant decision scenarios, it has been observed that peoples' actual decisions do not correspond to their claims regarding their own privacy [2][14].

In literature this phenomenon is discussed as "Privacy Paradox" – human behaviour that does not correspond to the behaviour one could expect given the articulated attitudes towards privacy [9].

Although the existence of the privacy paradox seems to be evident, and might be underlined by personal experiences of many readers, the following section attempts to show that the underlying mechanisms responsible for the paradox are manifold, hard to catch, and even harder to combine within one meta-theory.

3 Three Dimensions of the Privacy Paradox

Research has been performed in order to understand reasons and draw connections to existing theories of human behaviour. Within this article, emphasis is put on three different approaches that can be found in literature. The approaches are motivated by [2]. They correspond well with each other, give explanations on different aspects of the paradox, and can thus be termed as dimensions of the privacy paradox. Further dimensions may exist.

The first two dimensions, the state of *incomplete information* and *bounded rationality*, are commonly used in economic theory. Homo Oeconomicus – the economic prototype of an individual – constantly seeks to maximise his benefits by making rational decisions, whereas the decisions are based on the information he has and he can process. Objectively irrational decisions and actions (as in case of the privacy paradox) can be explained by individuals' limited capabilities in accessing and processing decision relevant information. Although objectively irrational, the behaviour of individuals is considered to be subjectively rational within the given boundaries of perception.

With regard to the limitations in accessing information essential for an objective decision on privacy matters, two facets of incomplete information are worth to be considered:

- **Incomplete information about disclosed data:** Users may not be aware of data they disclose. This refers to a situation in which users' behaviour is observed, stored, and processed without their knowledge. Thus, risks arising from this cannot be considered.

- **Incomplete information about consequences of disclosed data:** Disclosing some information explicitly does not mean that only this information is available to others. Additional information might be derived e.g. by linking the disclosed data with other sources of data. Information the individual wants to keep private might be derived. In a profiling challenge, students were able to capture the Wikipedia user-pseudonym the target person used in his business life. As the target person was very active in Wikipedia the students were able to derive an approximation on working hours and the potential periods of holidays within the last two years by analysing dates and times of entries in forums and contributions to articles[2].

Incomplete information can be considered to explain at least one part of the privacy paradox; but also considering a world in which every piece of decision relevant information is accessible to the user, the vast amount of information available itself would constitute a problem.

- **Bounded rationality results in wrong or biased conclusions:** As described by SIMON in the concept of bounded rationality [13], users' capabilities in processing information and drawing the right conclusions are restricted by nature. This can e.g. result in an over- or underestimation of risks associated with the disclosure of data. The approach of bounded rationality is a concept often considered in theories of human behaviour in the context of new media and services [15].

Beside these two more economic driven theories, *psychological variables* also contribute to give explanations for the privacy paradox. Having a look in psychological literature, one can find detailed research results describing individuals' attitudes towards benefits, costs, and risks in different horizons of time.

- **Users draw less attention to privacy risks than to other types of risk:** BREHM differentiated between different types of risk and their meaning for individuals. Threats that rise within a horizon of time (e.g. threats to privacy) are considered to be less important than immediately arising threats. Threats that

---

[2] The profiling challenge took place as part of the information and communication security course at University Frankfurt in winter term 2007/2008. The exercise was inspired and based on a similar exercise within the 2005 FIDIS PhD Consortium (www.fidis.net).

can be mitigated by personal behaviour (e.g. threats to privacy) are considered to be less important than threats users are exposed to passively [5].

- **Immediate gratification can influence users' (privacy) risk perception:** The presence of immediate gratification can affect users' perception of potential future threats [1]. Thus, privacy risks are likely to be underestimated in the presence of immediate beneficial incentives.

When striving for the best possible explanation, the above-mentioned factors need to be considered as well. Beyond previously mentioned dimensions further factors may influence individuals' behaviour in privacy relevant decision scenarios. Examples are group pressure in social networks or the impact of media and society in general.

4 Privacy Awareness

When aiming to resolve the privacy paradox it makes sense to reflect on how dimensions as incomplete information, bounded rationality, and various psychological factors can be addressed. This may be easier and more successful within concrete privacy sensitive applications. With regard to the aspects of incomplete information and bounded rationality, it seems to be very clear that individuals need to be supported with regard to the collection and processing of their personal data. As an initial step, awareness has to be created or raised in order to motivate individuals to take care of this problem. In this chapter we understand privacy awareness as individual users' ability to identify and assess risks associated to the disclosure of personal information. This approach will be extended in chapter 5.

4.1 A Precondition for the Employment of PETs

Several methods and technologies have been developed in order to mitigate risks that are connected to the disclosure of personal data. Within the domain of computer science and related fields, concepts and implementations for systems supporting anonymity, pseudonymity, unlinkability, or untracability, were developed. Other disciplines may contribute to support users in protecting their privacy as well. Nonetheless, applying privacy enhancing techniques in a reasonable way requires users initially to be aware of the problem's dimensions or of the existence of the problem at all. To give an example: Privacy Enhancing Technologies (PETs) are well able to cope with certain threats, but:

- If users are not able to identify risks, they will not get the idea to employ PETs.
- If users are aware of risks only on a very general level, they might want to take countermeasures, but they will not be able to assess whether costs for embodying PETs are justified.

Being aware of risks associated with the disclosure of personal data is the precondition to deal with them in an appropriate and rational manner.

Raising privacy awareness is thus a first and essential step for motivating individuals to reflect on privacy issues in concrete usage scenarios. Privacy awareness can be raised in different contexts and in different fashions. A valuable segmentation of dimensions of privacy awareness has been provided by PÖTZSCH distinguishing between user-independent vs. user-specific, and application-independent vs. application-specific privacy awareness [10]. In the following, emphasis is put on the application-specific dimension of privacy awareness; in particular on the integration of privacy awareness raising mechanisms in context-aware services. Moreover, the concept of privacy awareness is expanded from awareness of problems towards awareness of possible solutions, as a means to overcome the privacy paradox.

4.2 Privacy Awareness on an Application Level

Privacy awareness in context-aware services can be raised by different means. On a general level privacy disclaimers can contribute to mitigate the effects of users' incomplete information on what is going to be done with their data. The effectiveness of privacy disclaimers with regard to raising privacy awareness is nonetheless questionable, and suffers from the extensive amount of information that comes with them. Because of bounded rationality, users are not able or willing to appreciate this information. As privacy risks are systematically underestimated, described in chapter 3, users will probably not even get the idea to employ advisory tools as e.g. privacy bird [11] to overcome bounded rationality. On a situation specific level, privacy awareness can be raised directly before the actual disclosure of personal data. This has the advantage that the properties of the specific type of information that is going to be disclosed, can be taken into account. Research on how to implement privacy awareness on a situation specific level is still in its infancy. First approaches can be found in related research areas: Within a study on transparent mobile recommendation systems, design criteria have been developed on how users can be supported in understanding what personal information has influenced the actual recommendation [12].

5 Towards a Research Approach

The previous chapters laid out the theoretical ground for an initial research approach that is presented within this section. Following, the problem domain of the research approach is outlined and hypotheses are derived. The chapter closes with an outlook on the application of the design science paradigm that is going to be used to address and probe the hypotheses.

5.1 Problem Domain: Establishment of Application-Specific Privacy Awareness

The motivation of this research approach is to contribute to the establishment of privacy awareness on an application-specific level of context-aware services. "Average" users that are not aware of pitfalls related to the disclosure of personal information in context-aware services should be enabled to assess risks more objectively. Thereby the discrepancy between actual and desired behaviour should be reduced.

Different challenges arise when it comes to the establishment of mechanisms contributing to raise users' privacy on an application-specific level. Beside the questions on how these mechanisms have to be designed and integrated in the processes on a technical basis, it needs to be considered which parties are involved in this process.

In contrast to the establishment of privacy awareness on an application-independent level, e.g. by tutorials and exercises as in the above-mentioned profiling challenge, different parties and their interests have to be considered and harmonised when striving for privacy awareness on an application-specific level. Most important parties in this process are service provider and user of context-aware services.

Knowledge about users' identity attributes is crucial and an essential asset for every provider of context-aware services. It determines the degree of personalisation that can be achieved and thus the quality and price that can be charged for the service. This holds true for different types of context-aware services, among of them mobile services based on location information, e.g. mobile recommendation systems, mobile social communities or services based on individualised mobile advertising.

In principle there are two ways how privacy awareness can be established on an application-specific level. On the one hand, the legislator might oblige providers of context-aware services to establish privacy awareness enhancing mechanisms. This can easily run into a very complex process, as it is not clear whether a one-fits-all regulation is appropriate to address the issue. On the other hand, economic incentives can motivate providers to spend money on raising privacy awareness.

At first glance there seem to be no economic incentives for providers to invest in privacy awareness. On the contrary, disadvantages seem to be predominant: Research on the impact of consumers' privacy concerns gives indications that users will be more likely to provide less, or incomplete information when their concerns with regard to the protection of their privacy rise [8]. This is also underlined and even amplified by the psychological effect of reactance, an emotional overreaction with regard to a presented threat, risk, or confinement of alternatives [5]. As a consequence, users are even likely to disclose less information than with a neutral perspective. Raising privacy awareness in a sense of raising consumers' concerns thwarts providers' attempts to collect as much data as possible for the process of personalisation. How to overcome this?

5.2 Expanded Privacy Awareness: A Means to Address the Privacy Paradox on an Application-Specific Level

The Theory of Psychological Reactance by BREHM states that users will attempt to regain the threatened freedom, in this case their privacy, by whatever method available [5]. If users are not enabled to disclose personal data while preserving their privacy, it can be assumed according to [8], that they will indeed provide less information or even completely abstain from providing information; as this is the only method to regain the threatened freedom. Therefore we propose:

P1: To overcome the privacy paradox, raising privacy awareness on an application-specific level should be closely connected with raising knowledge about methods and tools essential to satisfy needs with regard to the protection of privacy in a meaningful way.

By this proposition we expand the meaning of privacy awareness from awareness of problems towards awareness of possible solutions as a means to overcome the privacy paradox.

In addition to P1 we propose that raising privacy awareness on the one hand, and providing means that allow users to react on their needs with regard to the protection of privacy on the other hand, positively affects the relation between user and provider of a service.

P2: Raising privacy awareness in connection with providing privacy enhancing technologies on an application level can strengthen the relationship between user and provider of a context-aware service.

This constitutes an economic incentive for providers to accept or even support the creation of privacy awareness within their applications. Focussing on potential incentives that could motivate providers to enforce the creation of privacy awareness, the goal of the research approach is to assess whether a combined approach of enhancing privacy awareness on the one hand, and providing privacy enhancing means on the other hand, can motivate customers to provide more or more accurate personal data than before. This is reflected in Proposition 3.

P3: The combined approach of raising privacy awareness and providing means to react will result in more or more accurate disclosed personal data.

The Propositions P1, P2 and P3 are based on a literature review on the underlying theories of the privacy paradox, as well as on privacy awareness and related topics.

5.3 Outlook: Applying the Design Science Paradigm

Research on information systems (IS) is still young compared to related disciplines of computer science and economics. Methods to address problems in IS research are not confined to a traditional and established set of alternatives. This, among other factors, led to a discussion on the discipline's identity [4]. Nonetheless, on an abstract level the paradigms of behavioural-science and design science exposed to be predominant for research in IS [16]. The focus of behavioural-science is on the discovery of truth to explain or predict human or organisational behaviour. Design science seeks to discover artefacts that proactively address relevant problems in the area of IS. Design science is inherently a problem solving process, whereas a problem is defined as discrepancy between a goal state and the current state of a system [7].

Several theories from the area of behavioural-science were used within Chapters 2 to 4 to derive and underline the problem description laid out in Chapter 5.1. In future research, the propositions derived in Chapter 5.2 will be addressed, substantiated and evaluated mainly by following the design science paradigm.

The article in hand derives a problem description and gives substantiated evidence for the problem's relevance. A first rudimentary version of an artefact was proposed by describing a method on how to integrate privacy awareness on an application-specific level[3]. In a next step the insights of this paper will be embedded into the design science framework provided by HEVNER [7] to allow for a proper enhancement of propositions, e.g. to consider the heterogeneity of user in the process of awareness creation, and to derive provable hypotheses. The author plans to create a context sensitive mobile application to implement privacy awareness in a way as described in

---

[3] In the context of the design science framework by HEVNER [7] this can be classified as a contribution to Guideline 1 (Design as an Artifact) and Guideline 2 (Problem Relevance).

Proposition 1. Following up on this the hypotheses should be validated by an experimental comparison against already existing, less privacy focussed, context-aware mobile applications.

6 Summary and Concluding Remarks

Within this paper a research approach in the area of privacy in context-aware services was presented. Based on a literature review the phenomenon of the privacy paradox has been described and explanations were given by referring to economic and psychological theories.

Based on the theoretical ground laid out in chapters 2, 3, and 4, chapter 5 particularly addressed the establishment of privacy awareness on an application-specific level. In contrast to the application-independent creation of privacy awareness, interests and perspectives of more involved partners need to be considered when creating privacy awareness on an application-specific level, as e.g. in context-aware services.

It has been shown, that raising privacy awareness alone can result in a conflict of interest between users and providers of services, as users might disclose less of their personal information than before. In contrast to that, it was proposed that combining the creation of privacy awareness with tools that allow users to react in a meaningful way can end up in a win-win situation. By these propositions we expand the meaning of privacy awareness, from awareness of problems, towards awareness of possible solutions as a means to overcome the privacy paradox.

Acknowledgements

I would like to thank Prof. Kai Rannenberg and my colleagues at the Chair of Mobile Business & Multilateral Security for many helpful discussions and inspirations. In addition to that I received many valuable comments in the course of the PrimeLife Summer School and during the final review.

The research leading to this results was supported by the European Union Projects Future of Identity in the Information Society (FIDIS, project number 507512, www.fidis.net), PrivacyOS (project number 225044, www.privacyos.eu) and the German Federal Research Ministry project PREMIUM-Services (project number 01IA08003C, www.premium-services-projekt.de/).

References

1. Acquisti, A.: Privacy in electronic commerce and the economics of immediate gratification. In: Proceedings of the 2004 ACM Electronic Commerce Conference (2004)
2. Acquisti, A., Grossklags, J.: Privacy and rationality in individual decision making. IEEE Security and Privacy 3(1), 26–33 (2005)
3. Awad, N.F., Krishnan, M.S.: The personalization privacy paradox: An empirical evaluation of information transparency and willingness to be profiled online for personalalization. MIS Quaterly 30(1), 13–28 (2006)

4. Benbasat, I., Zmud, R.W.: The Identity Crisis within the IS Discipline: Defining and Communicating the Discipline's Core Properties. MIS Quarterly 27(2), 183–194 (2003)
5. Brehm, J.: A Theory of Psychological Reactance. In: Festinger, L., Schachter, S. (eds.) Social Psychology. A series of monographs, treatises, and texts, Academic Press, London (1966)
6. Dey, A.K., Abowd, G.D.: Towards a Better Understanding of Context and Context-Awareness. In: CHI 2000 Workshop on the What, Who, Where, When, and How of Context-Awareness (2000)
7. Hevner, A.R., March, S.T., Park, J., et al.: Design Science in Information Systems Research. MIS Quarterly 28(1), 75–105 (2004)
8. Hoy, M.: Flaming, Complaining, Abstaining: How Online Users Respond to Privacy Concern. Journal of Advertising 28(3), 41–45 (1999)
9. Norberg, P.A., Horne, D.R., Horne, D.A.: The Privacy Paradox: Personal Information Disclosure Intentions versus Behaviors. Journal of Consumer Affairs 41(1), 100–126 (2007)
10. Pötzsch, S.: Privacy Awareness – A Means to Solve the Privacy Paradox? In: Matyáš, V., et al. (eds.) The Future of Identity. IFIP AICT, vol. 298, pp. 226–236 (2009)
11. Privacy Bird Website,
    http://www.privacybird.org (accessed on 2009-07-22)
12. Radmacher, M.: Design Criteria for Transparent Mobile Event Recommendations. In: Proceedings of the 11th Americas Conference on Information Systems, Toronto (2008)
13. Simon, H.A.: Models of bounded rationality. MIT Press, Cambridge (1982)
14. Spiekermann, S., Grossklags, J., Berendt, B.: E-privacy in 2nd generation E-commerce: privacy preferences versus actual behavior. In: Proceedings of the 3rd ACM Conference on Electronic Commerce, New York, pp. 28–47 (2001)
15. Zerdick, A., Picot, A., Schrape, A.: Die Internet-Ökonomie: Strategien für die digitale Wirtschaft. In: European Communication Council Report. Springer, Berlin (2006)
16. Zmud, R.W.: Editor's Comments. MIS Quaterly 21(2), xxi-xxii (1997)

Secure Logging of Retained Data for an Anonymity Service

Stefan Köpsell[1] and Petr Švenda[2]

[1] TU Dresden, Germany
sk13@inf.tu-dresden.de
[2] Masaryk University, Czech Republic
svenda@fi.muni.cz

Abstract. The recently introduced legislation on data retention to aid prosecuting cyber-related crime in Europe also affects the achievable security of systems for anonymous communication on the Internet. We have analyzed the newly arising risks associated with the process of accessing and storage of the retained data and propose a secure logging system, which utilizes cryptographic smart cards, trusted timestamping servers and distributed storage. These key components will allow for controlled access to the stored log data, enforce a limited data retention period, ensure integrity of the logged data, and enable reasonably convenient response to any legitimated request of the retained data. A practical implementation of the proposed scheme was performed for the AN.ON anonymity service, but the scheme can be used for other services affected by data retention legislation.

1 Introduction

The recently introduced legislation on data retention affects—at least in some countries (e.g., Germany)— systems for anonymous communication on the Internet such as AN.ON [BeFK00] or TOR [DiMS04]. These systems alter the source IP-addresses of users and these alterations should be logged and accessible on request from legal authorities (cf., [BeBK08] for a description of the legal obligations and the usefulness of the retained data).

Standard secure logging mechanisms such as [MaTs09] protect the logged records sufficiently against unauthorised access (confidentiality), unauthorised modification (integrity) and in some cases attempt to ensure availability of records. But when applied to the needs of data retention logging on the logging entity side, newly arising risks remain unsolved as the attacker model has changed. Potentially sensitive data are present on logging entity side as a result of compliance with data retention legislation. The logging entity can be forced to reveal, delete or modify this data—threats that did not exist before as there was no need to store such data in the first place. Specifically, threats related to the data retention period must be addressed and mitigated.

Note that the risk for a user to be deanonymised, if the operators of the chosen anonymity servers behave *dishonestly*, exists before the introduction of

M. Bezzi et al. (Eds.): Privacy and Identity, IFIP AICT 320, pp. 284–298, 2010.

data retention. But if the operators are *honest*, the attacker gains an additional advantage of mounting a successful attack on the anonymity of a given user with the help of retained data. Moreover, it is now possible for the attacker to start his attack *after the fact* (i.e. after the activity, the attacker wants to deanonymise took place). This was not possible before, as the attacker had to log the anonymised and encrypted traffic at the time of this activity in order to analyze it later on.

Completely new risks arise from the fact that the logged data is used for law enforcement. One such attack results in the risk of the attacker modifying the logged data so that an innocuous user of the anonymity service becomes suspicious. For an operator of an anonymisation server, the new risk is that an attacker forces him to modify the logged data in such a way (or at least in a way which hides the criminal activities of the attacker). So, our solution should not only protect the users of the anonymity service but also its operators.

A demand for the practical implementation originates from the needs of the AN.ON anonymity service. This anonymity service has been open to public since 2000 and has to fulfil the legal obligations given by the data retention legislation. But the proposed logging scheme can be used for other services affected by the data retention legislation as well. More generally, the scheme can be used for any logging service where the logged records are accessible only for a limited time period or where knowledge of cryptographic secrets might lead to personal threats of the holder.

Our paper is organised as follows: the first section describes the requirements for data retention logging and summarizes related work. The second section describes the logging scheme and analyzes security of the scheme. This section also provides an overview of the steps involved in logging and answering requests. Selected properties of practical implementation and results of the performance analysis are given in section three, followed by conclusions in section four.

1.1 Legal and Operational Requirements on Logging of Retained Data

In this section, we summarize the requirements for the retained data and the logging procedures. These are general requirements applicable to any service which needs to be compliant with the EC data retention directive. They can be derived from the legal obligations (R1–R4) and the operational needs (R5). Moreover, they can be classified as functional requirements (R1; what the system should *do*) and non-functional requirements (R2–R5; how the system should *be*).

R1: Logged data has to include all statutory categories of data. Article 5 of the data retention directive describes what types of services have to retain which data categories. National implementations of the directive could extend this. This functional requirement basically states that some meaningful data has to be logged and that logging of (e.g.) random data would not be sufficient.

R2: Logged data have to be deleted after a specific period of time. This means that logged records cannot be accessed outside a given data retention period. In the following text we use the term "outdated" to describe a property of a given item (cryptographic key, log entry etc.) to which the access should be prevented because the related retention period already expired.

R3: Logged data need to be accessible, so that requests from law enforcement agencies can be answered without undue delay.

R4: Logged data have to be secure, so that no access to the logged data by unauthorised person is possible. This requirement covers confidentiality as well as integrity of the logged records. Note that in our case the integrity means that the operator can detect if the logged data have been altered—it is not necessary that the operator proves something to the third party.

R5: The cost of logging has to be reasonable. It includes the monetary costs (e.g. initial necessary investments, operational costs) but also the degradation of the overall performance of the system as well as the organisational overhead.

1.2   Related Work

Mechanisms for secure logging were previously described in the literature, e.g. [BeYe97, ScKe99, Acco05, Holt06, WSBL08, MaTs09]. One of the presented ideas was the use forward-secure MACs to protect the integrity of log entries. The use of hash chains ensures *forward integrity*, which means that any alterations of the log entries stored *before* the system was compromised could be detected.

The common idea of all of the mentioned schemes is to divide the timeline into several epochs. All log entries which belong to the same epoch are protected by the corresponding epoch key. Once the epoch is over, the key of that epoch is destroyed and a new one is generated for the next epoch. Usually the so-called key evolution scheme is used to derive the next key from the current one. Normally, one way function is used for key evolution. Thus, it is hard for an attacker who knows the key of the current epoch to calculate a valid key of any previous epoch.

But as analysed in [MaTs09] the systems described in [BeYe97,ScKe99,Holt06] suffer from a so-called *truncation attack*—"a special kind of deletion attack, whereby the attacker deletes a contiguous subset of tail-end log entries." The idea of using hash chains for log file protection (used in [ScKe99,Acco05,Holt06, WSBL08]) is patented (US patent 5978475).

The solution presented in [MaTs09] is based on the Forward-Secure Sequential Aggregate (FssAgg) authentication techniques. The key component of the FssAgg scheme is the sign-and-aggregate algorithm. This algorithm—which can be seen as a substitution of the forward-secure MACs used in other secure logging schemes—takes as an input the private key, certain data to be signed and the aggregate signature generated so far. It computes a new aggregated signature which covers the given input data and a new private key which is used for generation of the subsequent aggregate signature. The performance comparison of the various FssAgg schemes given in [MaTs09] demonstrates that even the fastest scheme still needs 5.55 ms for signing a single log entry. This means that the overall performance of our anonymity system would be significantly diminished.

2   The Proposed Scheme for Secure Logging

The following roles are represented in the scheme:

1. Mix **operator** – is responsible for general maintenance of Mix server(s) and logging required traffic data into protected log files. Mix operator does not need to be able to access content of the log files afterwards.
2. Law enforcement agency **officer** – will issue the data retention request backed up by court order. The usual procedure is to issue the order and receive the response in the plaintext. One cannot assume that the law enforcement agencies can easily change such procedures e.g. integrate new cryptographic mechanisms.
3. Data retention request **responder** – the entity responsible to collection and accession of protected log files, search for entries relevant to particular data retention request and responding to law enforcement officer. Serves as communication party for an officer.
4. External **storage(s)** – responsible for the keeping of the log files with redundancy required to provide the reliable backup and integrity protection.
5. Trusted **time source(s)** – responsible for providing the current date and time for the decision process about data retention period validity.

As the responsibility of Mix operator is only to keep logging software running and is usually the same person as the data retention requests responder, we will refer to both simply as an *operator* in the following text.

2.1   General Assumptions and Settings

We have developed a secure logging scheme primarily for our anonymity service called AN.ON. which is based on Mixes. A Mix [Chau81] is a server which forwards messages thereby ensuring that an outsider (e.g. an eavesdropper) cannot link incoming and outgoing messages. This is accomplished by a combination of several (cryptographic) mechanisms. In order to enhance the trustworthiness of the anonymity system, several Mixes are chained together. The sender of a given message can only be deanonymised if all Mixes along the path of his message reveal the linkage between the appropriate incoming and outgoing messages. Therefore, the use of multiple Mixes offers some protection against the dishonest Mix operators.

One can imagine our anonymisation service described below as a simple proxy which a user uses to hide its own IP-address, e.g. towards a Web-Server. Therefore, the proxy exchanges the IP-address of the user (IP_U) with its own IP-address (IP_P). This alteration of the source IP-address (together with a timestamp t) has to be retained (cf. requirement R1). For simplicity, we assume that the IP-address of the proxy will change rarely so that it is not necessary to store it with every log entry. Finally each log entry can be seen as a pair of IP-address and timestamp (in our example: (IP_U, t)). Multiple log entries are stored within one log file.

In addition to the Mixes, which are the logging servers generating and storing the logged data, two other parties are relevant to our setting: the Mix operators and law enforcement agencies. Mix operator is a legal or natural person responsible for the operation of a given Mix, and for the implementation of data retention, which include includes answering the requests for retained data by the law enforcement agencies.

As IP_P of the proxy will be visible in suspicious requests, the law enforcement agencies ask questions in the form of: "Who was using IP-address IP_P at time t_R". In order to answer such questions we need to search through our log files for all records with timestamps t_i for which: $t_R - \epsilon \leq t_i \leq t_R + \epsilon$. The need for the parameter ϵ reflects the fact that we cannot assume that all clocks of all servers are synchronised. The specific value of ϵ is usually given by law through technical regulations.

In order to facilitate the search process, log entries are stored and organized according to increasing timestamps t_i. This is also the natural order they were generated by the proxy.

We decided that not all log entries should be stored within a one single log file but rather multiple log files should be generated. In our case we store one log file per day. The reasons for this are twofold. On one hand, storing log entries in multiple files would simplify the process of deleting of outdated log entries. On the other hand, we propose that a dedicated machine, which has no connection to any communication network should be used for the processing of the law enforcement requests. Therefore the stored log file related to the timestamp in question needs to be transferred to that machine. This in turn would result in an overwhelming overhead if all log entries are stored within a single file.

The logged data has to be stored encrypted and integrity protected (cf. requirement R4). The encryption ensures that the content of the logged data can not be revealed without the knowledge of the secret key. Of course this is only true, if the server which logged the data was not compromised at the time of the data logging. The advantage of encrypting the logged data is that the data can be protected using available (probably insecure) backup mechanisms. Note that because of this backup, it is in generally not possible to (provably) delete the retained data. So the "deletion" has to be accomplished by cryptographic means (e.g., by destruction of a decryption key[1]).

2.2   Confidentiality

Confidentiality can be achieved by either symmetric or asymmetric encryption[2]. Asymmetric encryption has the advantage that no secret key needs to be stored on the logging server but suffers from poor performance compared to the symmetric encryption. The use of symmetric cryptography leads to the problem

---

[1] Deletion of a single decryption key, which is not part of any backup, is much easier compared to ensuring that every backup copy of a given log file is deleted. This is especially true if the backup in place is not under full control of the operator of the anonymisation server itself. This in turn is the usually setting in dedicated hosting service scenarios.

[2] Basically we could also use tamper resistant trusted devices. But as such devices which are able to store large amount of logged data are not available for reasonable price to the operators of our anonymity servers we do not consider them here.

where the secret key used for the encryption becomes vulnerable to attack. If the same key is used for the encryption of multiple log entries the attacker might be able to decrypt log entries generated *before* gaining control over the logging server.

As a compromise, we utilize a hybrid encryption scheme where the symmetric encryption is used for the log entries itself. The corresponding symmetric key k is stored within the log file using asymmetric encryption.

For efficiency reasons, we use an authenticated encryption scheme for symmetric encryption, AES-128 in Galois/Counter Mode (GCM). GCM [GrVi05] is a combination of counter mode for confidentiality and universal hashing (based on polynomial operation in the finite field $GF(2^n)$) for integrity protection. GCM is one of the NIST approved modes of operation [SP 800-38D] and is part of many (Internet) network protocols. GCM offers very good performance and is believed to be patent free.

We use the position of a log entry within a log file as initialisation vector (counter) for GCM. This allows random access to log entries based on their position within the log file. Thus, it is not necessary to decrypt the whole log file while answering a request of a law enforcement agency.

The same symmetric key is used for all log entries of a given log file and for every log file a new symmetric key is generated. Thus our "epoch" (cf. Section 1.2) is related to a single log file. As mentioned before, the key itself is encrypted using an asymmetric algorithm. Only the operator of the proxy is in possession of the private key. Of course, the keys for the asymmetric scheme change from time to time—but they cannot be changed to often (e.g. on a daily basis) due to the organisational overhead implied by the necessary key management.

Note that because we use the same symmetric key for a whole log file and generate log files on a daily basis, an attacker which compromises the logging server just before midnight might get the knowledge of the symmetric key for that day and thus compromise the confidentiality and integrity of the related log file. One way to mitigate such risk is to generate new log files more frequently. But if the attacker is smart enough to compromise the system and read out the symmetric key from the somewhat protected main memory, he is very likely to be smart enough to hide his traces. Thus the fact that the machine was compromised might be detected only after weeks or even months—making the protective advantage of more frequently generated log files negligible.

We decided to store the private key on a trusted device. Here, trusted device is a device able to control access to the private key. Note that we use this trusted device not only to prevent unauthorised access of third parties to the private key. Additionally, the access to outdated log files (cf. requirement R2) is prevented and the risk that the operator is forced by the attacker to decrypt outdated log files is mitigated by the use of trusted device usage. Therefore, an important property of the access control to the private key implemented by the trusted device is, that it not only depends on proper authorisation (e.g. password of the operator) but *on the current time*. The idea is, that the trusted device denies decryption of a symmetric key if the related log file is outdated. Basically any device which has a TPM and fulfils the requirements on Sealed Storage of the Trusted Computing Group could be used. But as they are not yet widely deployed, we decided to use smart cards as a possible alternative.

In order to prevent access to outdated log files the date of the log file has to be bound to the symmetric key used for that log file. This binding can be accomplished by three different mechanisms. The first one uses a key derivation function to calculate the symmetric key k from the date d of the related log file and a random value k_r. We use KDF3 as proposed in [Shou01] with SHA-512 as hash function. Thus, the symmetric key k is calculate as: $k = \text{SHA-512}\left(0^{64}|k_r|d\right)$. k_r is stored in asymmetrically encrypted form within the log file. If later a decryption of the log file is required, the encrypted value of k_r is send together with d to the smart card which, after proper authorisation and verification that d is not outdated, outputs k.

Note that the key derivation function is a one-way function, i.e. calculating k while knowing d and k_r is straightforward. But calculating either d or k_r from the other two values ($\{k, k_r\}$ resp. $\{k, d\}$) is difficult. Thus, the key derivation construction ensures that someone who knows $k = \text{KDF3}(k_r, d)$ and d cannot learn $k' = \text{KDF3}(k_r, d')$ for any value $d' \neq d$. Otherwise an attacker who wants to learn k' of an outdated log file with date d' and who has access to the smart card can send a valid date d together with the encrypted version of k_r to the smart card.

The second line of defence is to include the date d within the asymmetric encryption of k_r. We use RSA-OAEP for that asymmetric encryption: $Enc = \text{RSA-OAEP}(k_r, d)$. Derived from the non-malleability security property of RSA-OAEP, one can conclude that it is hard for an attacker who knows only Enc and the public RSA key used, to construct a valid $Enc' = \text{RSA-OAEP}(k_r', d')$; where d' is a valid date, such that he can learn anything about k_r from k_r'.

The third and final line of defence is to include MAC over d using k_r as a key within the asymmetric encryption. Thus $Enc = \text{RSA-OAEP}(k_r, d, \text{MAC}_{k_r}(d))$. For calculating the MAC we use AES-128-GCM. This construction should make it even harder to construct valid Enc' using valid date d'.

Note that the smart card needs to know the current date in order to check if d is valid or not. How this can be achieved is described in section 2.5.

2.3   Integrity Protection

So far we have described the mechanisms used to protect the confidentiality of the log entries. Now, we want to explain how the integrity of a log file is protected. Note that the integrity of a single log entry can be verified through MAC generated during the authenticated encryption (GCM) of that log entry. As already stated in section 2.2, we use the position of a log entry as initialisation vector for GCM. Therefore, copying a log entry to another position could be detected. Finally, we append a footer to the log file which consists of the encrypted and integrity protected number of log entries stored within the log file. Thus deletion of log entries could be detected and as a result provides protection against the truncation attack.

The alternative attack on integrity is to delete a whole log file and create a completely new one. This is possible, because knowledge of the public key alone, used to encrypt k_r (see above), is needed.

In order to prevent this attack it is sufficient to protect the integrity of the pair (k_r, d). We propose multiple mechanisms to achieve this kind of protection, namely: digital signatures, distribution and trusted timestamping. As for every single mechanism the security depends on different assumptions, we propose to use all of them for enhanced protection.

The "digital signature" mechanism means that the logging server signs the encryption of the pair (k_r, d). Note that the private signature key used by the logging server has to be changed frequently (in our case on a daily basis). Otherwise an attacker might generate a valid signature even for a log file generated before the logging server was compromised. In order to facilitate the key installation and management process, the digital signature key pairs can be generated in advance (e.g. one for each day of the year). The date (d) for which a given key pair is valid is encoded as the validity period of the public certificate of the signature test key.

The "distribution" mechanism means that every artefact involved in the integrity verification process should be distributed in a way so that it is hard for the attacker to manipulate all of the copies simultaneously. One way to achieve this is to utilise censorship resistant P2P-networks such as FreeNet [CSWH00] or Free Haven [DiFM00]. Another possibility is to send an artefact to a number of people. In order to prevent denial of service attacks by compromising only one copy, some form of threshold voting can be introduced. The set of artefacts to be distributed should include at least a hash value of the encryption of the pair (k_r, d). If digital signatures are used, the public key certificates should be distributed immediately after their generation.

The "trusted timestamping" mechanism means that every artefact mentioned above should be timestamped. As mentioned in section 2.2 and further explained in section 2.5, trusted timestamping servers are already used to prevent access to outdated log entries. Thus, we can use the same set of servers with little reorganization.

2.4   Searching for Log Entries

In order to answer requests of the law enforcement agencies (i.e. search for log entries) it is not necessary to decrypt a whole log file nor to check the integrity of a whole log file. It is sufficient to:

V1 verify the integrity of the encryption of the pair (k_r, d) (depending on the protection mechanisms chosen).

V2 verify the integrity of the number of log entries stored within the footer of the log file. This includes checking if the stored number of log entries equals the actual number of log entries found in the log file. This can be easily done, because each log entry as well as the header and the footer of a log file is of constant size.

V3 verify the integrity of every log entry "touched" during the search process. We use a binary search to find the first entry i for which $t_i \geq t_R - \epsilon$ and $t_{i-1} < t_R - \epsilon$. Starting from this entry, we sequentially decrypt the individual entries until we find the last entry i' for which $t_{i'} \leq t_R + \epsilon$.

The need for of V1–V3 follows directly from the considerations in section 2.3. V1 ensures that the whole log file is not generated by the attacker, whereas V2 ensures that any deletion of records from the end of the log file can be detected.

The fact that V1–V3 are sufficient derives basically from the observation that data, which is not input to the search algorithm cannot influence the result of that search algorithm. Therefore, it does not matter if log entries not "touched" during the execution of the search algorithm are manipulated by the attacker. Also, the integrity verification of a given log entry ensures that this log entry is in the correct position within the log file, as this position is used as initialization vector.

2.5   Trusted Timestamping Servers as Reliable Time Source

For the enforcement of data retention period, the smart card needs to know the current date. Smart cards usually do not have an internal clock. Therefore, the current date has to be set from the outside. An operator can set the current date, but this introduces the risk of operator being forced to set an expired date, enabling the attacker to get access to outdated log entries.

In order to mitigate this risk, we decided that the only the source of time for the smart card should be (external) trusted timestamping servers (TTS). Therefore, an additional logical step is introduced in the process of answering data retention requests, which is activated during every key recovery process. When a key recovery from the smart card is requested, the smart card creates its own unique nonce, sends it to the PC application which then creates a time stamp request according to the "Internet X.509 Public Key Infrastructure Time-Stamp Protocol (TSP)" [RFC 3161] for every TTS with this nonce included. The TSP requests are then sent to the trusted time servers[3]. The smart card verifies the signed TTS responses, including its own challenge nonces and eventually updates the internal time according to the time stamps provided (i.e. by means of some majority decision algorithm). The irrelevant parts of TTS response (e.g., chain of TTS certificates) outside digitally signed part with time and nonce can be stripped off on the PC console to speed up the processing on the smart card. Note, that the public certificates of the trusted time servers can be installed immutably on the smart card during initialisation.

2.6   Overall Overview

The overall process of initialisation, generation of log entries and answering law enforcement requests is depicted in figure 1 and figure 2.

---

[3] As the smart card itself has no ability to directly communicate with time servers we use the PC console as a transparent proxy, with no possibility to undetectably modify TTS response.

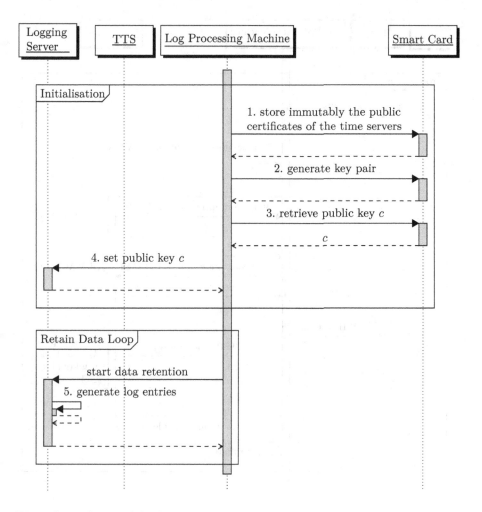

Fig. 1. Logical steps of the data retention compliant logging—initialisation and logging

The following steps are executed only once during smart card initialisation:

1. The public certificates of the signature keys of the trusted timestamping servers are immutably stored on the smart card,
2. A unique RSA-2048 key pair is generated on-card (the private key never leaves the card),

3., 4. The public key c is exported to the logging server.

After this initialisation, the logging server can generate encrypted and integrity-protected log files (step 5) as described in section 2.

Finally, a request for the retained data is answered by executing the following steps:

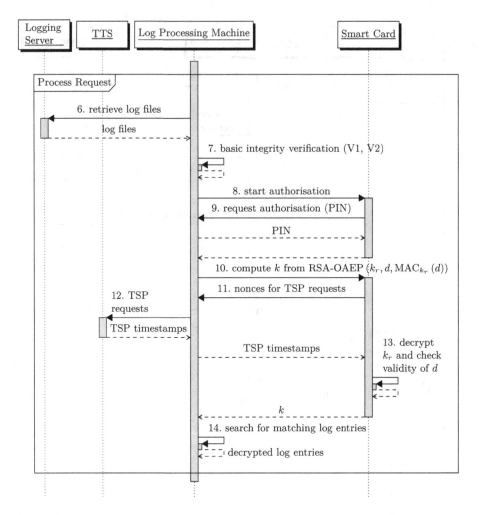

Fig. 2. Logical steps of the data retention compliant logging (continued)—processing requests

6. The log files in question (according to the date) are transferred to a dedicated machine used for a processing of data retention requests.

7. After initialization of the log file processing tool, the basic log file integrity is verified according to V1 and V2 of section 2.3.

8., 9. The smart card is inserted into the reader connected to the dedicated machine. The user authenticates himself with his user PIN. Note, that in the case that the smart card reader has its own display and keypad, the PIN is entered directly on the smart card reader and not on the dedicated machine as shown in figure 2 step 9.

10. The encryption of k_r stored in the log file is sent to the smart card.

11.,12. The smart card generates the nonces used for the requests to the remote
trusted timestamping servers. These requests are generated by the log
processing tool and sent to the trusted timestamping servers (step 12).
The responses from the trusted timestamping servers are received and
relayed by the log processing tool to the smart card. The smart card
verifies the validity of the received timestamps.

13. The smart card decrypts the encrypted value of k_r. If the enclosed value
d is still valid, the smart card calculates k and returns k to the log processing tool.

14. The log processing tool searches for the requested records and generates
a report which can be sent to the law enforcement agency.

3 Remarks on the Practical Implementation

3.1 Smart Card

We used the smart card with JavaCard platform for our implementation.

We use RSA-2048 as a basic asymmetric encryption primitive, which is implemented in hardware on the smart cards we used (JCOP-4.1 with JavaCard
v2.2.1, SmartMX cryptographic processor). The key generation and the basic
decryption functions are fast. The OAEP mode and SHA-512 hash function are
not available on our platform[4] so it was necessary to implemented it on the software level with significant performance impact on decryption of k_r. The time
required for retrieval of one key was approximately 90 seconds with the current
setup. Nevertheless this time period is still practically useful, provided that the
law enforcement agencies do not request hundreds of files per day. Significant
performance improvement can be obtained with 32-bit smart cards, which might
increase the speed more than twice due to the faster execution of arithmetic operations with larger operand. Smart cards with hardware support for SHA-512
algorithm will provide key recovery process with less than ten seconds. Although
such smart card chips already exist, they were not available to us for our implementation. But driven by the new JavaCard 3.0 specification, it is anticipated
that more powerful smart cards will be available for end users in the near future.

Note that the GCM mode is not supported by the current JavaCard specification as well as TSP timestamping requests. Both need to be implemented in the
software. Fortunately, TSP uses only standard cryptographic primitives (RSA,
SHA-1) which are part of the hardware in current smart cards.

3.2 Logging Performance

So far we assumed that for every log entry a separate authenticated encryption
using AES-128-GCM is performed. Given that the size of a log entry is relatively small compared to the AES-128-GCM block size this would lead to poor

---

[4] In fact, these functions are not available on most of the currently available smart
cards.

encryption performance and significant storage overhead. Therefore, we decided to group multiple log entries into a single block. As a consequence, the authenticated encryption carried out in blocks. According to [GrVi05], the block sizes between 256 and 1024 bytes lead to good performance results. Moreover, the block size should be a multiple of the AES-128 block size. On the other side not too many log entries should be grouped together within a single block as this could negatively impact the possibility of random access to an arbitrary log entry. Given these constraints and the actual size of a log entry, the number of log entries per block are calculated automatically by the logging server.

It is important to mention that we use this vector size as it requires no pre-processing of the initialization vector.

For our implementation of the cryptographic operations on the logging server we used the "Zork GCM 0.9.5" code (http://www.cryptobarn.com/gcm/). Without any extensive optimisations, we measured a speed of more than 85 MByte/s for block sizes ranging from 256 to 4096 bytes. The measurements were performed using an Intel Core 2 DUO T7700 2.4 GHz CPU. In case of our AN.ON system a single log entry requires less than 20 bytes with the cryptographic overhead for a single log entry being less than 0.25 μs. This is notably faster than the 5.55 ms previously reported by [MaTs09] for an Intel dual-core 1.73 GHz.

Given that every log entry is related to an asymmetric decryption operation of the anonymisation algorithm, which takes roughly 1 ms, the computational overhead introduced by the data retention is negligible (cf. requirement R5).

3.3   Search Performance

Our dedicated search tool is written in Java utilizing the "Bouncy Castle" cryptographic library (http://www.bouncycastle.org/). The mostly used servers of our AN.ON system generated log files with speed of roughly 85000 blocks per day. Because each block contained 128 log entries, the whole log file contains more than 10 million log entries.

Processing of the whole log file (i.e. decrypting and checking the integrity of every single block) required about 630 seconds (measured using SUN Java 1.6 and an Intel Core 2 DUO T7700 2.4 GHz CPU). Thus, we needed approx. 7.5 ms per block. Altogether the processing time needed by our tool (e.g. less than 30 seconds for the search leading to roughly 2800 log entries ($\epsilon = 10$ s)) is negligible compared to the overall time need for answering a request by the law enforcement agency (i.e. checking the validity of the request itself, transferring the right log files to the dedicated machine, obtaining the decryption key from the smart card etc.). In summary, we conclude that our logging scheme fulfils the requirement R3.

4   Conclusions

The compliance with the new data retention directive introduces not only benefits for the law enforcement agencies, but also additional risks for the users and operators of the communication service need to be mitigated. We have proposed, implemented and start into the practical usage a secure logging service based on a combination of log file encryption, key recovery with smart cards and data retention period enforcement via trusted timestamping servers. Several categories of attackers with different capabilities and levels of access to the system were analyzed.

The main contribution lies in the design and implementation of a practical system that allows logging required data with only modest impact on performance of our anonymity service, which complies with the legal requirements and does provide additional protection for the holder of cryptographic secrets necessary to access the logged records. The records can be accessed only if a cryptographic smart card and its owner are present and the retained data is not outdated. An operator cannot be forced to reveal logged records outside the data retention period, because the period is enforced directly on the smart card with the help of trusted timestamping servers.

The log data of selected German AN.ON servers are protected with the proposed mechanism since 1st January 2009. So far, we did not receive any valid request for retained data from the law enforcement agencies. Therefore, at present, we can not evaluate how efficiently will the large number of log entries be handled, and we hope to provide further practical details in the near future.

Future work will focus on the problem of receipt creation. These receipts will contain provable information on all of the retained data that were released to the law enforcement agencies and serve as a official record (e.g., based on digital signatures and fair exchange protocols). While a seemingly straightforward task, the solution to this problem will have to avoid introduction of new risks for an operator (caused by possession of additional sensitive data on his side). Additional requirement that complicates the problem further is a need for a protection of the AN.ON users' privacy. The official record itself must not reveal any sensitive information (e.g. content of the retained data) to an outsider.

The authors would like to thank all anonymous reviewers, Jan Camenisch and Jakub Švenda for their valuable comments and Microsoft Research for the generous support which allowed the presentation of this work.

References

[Acco05]   Accorsi, R.: Towards a secure logging mechanism for dynamic systems. In: Proc. of the 7th IT Security Symposium, São José dos Campos, Brasilien (November 2005)

[BeBK08]   Berthold, S., Böhme, R., Köpsell, S.: Data Retention and Anonymity Services. In: Proc. The Future of Identity in the Information Society - Challenges for Privacy and Security, FIDIS/IFIP Internet Security & Privacy Fourth International Summer School. IFIP Advances in Information and Communication Technology, vol. 298, pp. 92–106. Springer, Boston (2009)

[BeFK00]   Berthold, O., Federrath, H., Köpsell, S.: Web MIXes: A System for Anonymous and Unobservable Internet Access. In: Federrath, H. (ed.) Anonymity 2000. LNCS, vol. 2009, pp. 115–129. Springer, Heidelberg (2001)

[BeYe97]   Bellare, M., Yee, B.S.: Forward integrity for secure audit logs; Techni-
              cal Report, University of California at San Diego, Dept. of Computer
              Science & Engineering (1997)
[Chau81]   Chaum, D.: Untraceable Electronic Mail, Return Addresses, and Digital
              Pseudonyms. Communications of the ACM 24(2), 84–88 (1981)
[CSWH00]   Clarke, I., Sandberg, O., Wiley, B., Hong, T.W.: Freenet: A Distributed
              Anonymous Information Storage and Retrieval System. In: Federrath,
              H. (ed.) Anonymity 2000. LNCS, vol. 2009, pp. 46–66. Springer, Hei-
              delberg (2001)
[DiFM00]   Dingledine, R., Freedman, M.J., Molnar, D.: The Free Haven Project:
              Distributed Anonymous Storage Service. In: Federrath, H. (ed.) Design-
              ing Privacy Enhancing Technologies. LNCS, vol. 2009, p. 67. Springer,
              Heidelberg (2001)
[DiMS04]   Dingledine, R., Mathewson, N., Syverson, P.F.: Tor: The Second-
              Generation Onion Router. In: Proc. of the 13th USENIX Security Sym-
              posium, August 2004, pp. 303–320 (2004)
[GrVi05]   McGrew, D.A., Viega, J.: The Security and Performance of the
              Galois/Counter Mode (GCM) of Operation. In: Canteaut, A.,
              Viswanathan, K. (eds.) INDOCRYPT 2004. LNCS, vol. 3348, pp. 343–
              355. Springer, Heidelberg (2004)
[Guer09]   Gueron, S.: Intel's New AES Instructions for Enhanced Performance
              and Security. In: Dunkelman, O. (ed.) FSE 2009. LNCS, vol. 5665, pp.
              51–66. Springer, Heidelberg (2009)
[Holt06]   Holt, J.E.: Logcrypt: forward security and public verification for se-
              cure audit logs. In: Proc. of the 2006 Australasian Workshops on Grid
              Computing and E-Research, January 2006, pp. 203–211 (2006)
[MaTs09]   Ma, D., Tsudik, G.: A new approach to secure logging. ACM Transac-
              tions on Storage (TOS) 5(1) (2009)
[RFC 3161]   Adams, C., Cain, P., Pinkas, D., Zuccherato, R.: Internet X.509 Public
              Key Infrastructure Time-Stamp Protocol (TSP), Proposed Standard
              (August 2001), http://www.rfc-editor.org/rfc/rfc3161.txt
[ScKe99]   Schneier, B., Kelsey, J.: Secure Audit Logs to Support Computer Foren-
              sics. ACM Transactions on Information and System Security (TIS-
              SEC) 2(2), 159–176 (1999)
[Shou01]   Shoup, V.: A proposal for an ISO standard for public key encryption;
              Version 2.1 (December 20, 2001),
              http://www.shoup.net/papers/iso-2_1.pdf (last accessed Juli 28,
              2009)
[SP 800-38D] Dworkin, M.: Recommendation for Block Cipher Modes of Operation:
              Galois/Counter Mode (GCM) and GMAC; U.S. Department of
              Commerce, National Institute of Standards and Technology (NIST),
              Information Technology Laboratory (ITL) (November 2007),
              http://csrc.nist.gov/publications/nistpubs/800-38D/
              SP-800-38D.pdf (last access on December 1, 2008)
[WSBL08]   Wouters, K., Simoens, K., Lathouwers, D., Preneel, B.: Secure and
              Privacy-Friendly Logging for eGovernment Services. In: Proc. of the
              2008 Third International Conference on Availability, Reliability and Se-
              curity, pp. 1091–1096. IEEE Computer Society, Los Alamitos (2008)

Adding Secure Transparency Logging to the PRIME Core*

Hans Hedbom, Tobias Pulls, Peter Hjärtquist, and Andreas Lavén

Department of Computer Science, Karlstad University, Karlstad, Sweden
Hans.Hedbom@kau.se, tobias@pulls.name, peter@hjartquist.se,
a.laven@gmail.com

Abstract. This paper presents a secure privacy preserving log. These types of logs are useful (if not necessary) when constructing transparency services for privacy enhancement. The solution builds on and extends previous work within the area and tries to address the shortcomings of previous solutions regarding privacy issues.

1 Introduction

PrimeLife [6] is aiming at understanding the privacy implications for a user[1] in a networked world and at constructing concepts and tools that can help a user to regain control over her personal sphere. One goal is to increase the possibilities that a person has to know what really happens with her personal data, i.e., what data about her are collected and how they are further processed, by whom, and for what purposes. This is important in order to judge if the data are processed in a legal manner and whether they are correct. The concept usually used to describe these properties is the notion of transparency. Consequently, one of our goals within PrimeLife is to develop tools and concepts for increased transparency.

In order to audit or verify that custodians of personal information (usually called data controllers) are behaving according to agreed policies, some form of event log is needed to track the processing and access of data at the data controller's side. This log must be built in such a way that it cannot be tampered with and since the log itself also contains personal information it must be encrypted in order to protect these data. Ideally, the only entity able to read

---

* Part of the research leading to these results has received funding from the European Community's Seventh Framework Program (FP7/2007-2013) under grant agreement n° 216483. The information in this document is provided "as is", and no guarantee or warranty is given that the information is fit for any particular purpose. The above referenced consortium members shall have no liability for damages of any kind including without limitation direct, special, indirect, or consequential damages that may result from the use of these materials subject to any liability which is mandatory due to applicable law.
[1] We imply that "user" and "end user" throughout this paper are also data subjects in the system.

M. Bezzi et al. (Eds.): Privacy and Identity, IFIP AICT 320, pp. 299–314, 2010.

the log entry should be the one that the log entry concerns (i.e., the data subject). Currently there exists some examples of secure logs (e.g., the secure log pattern in [9] and the Schneier-Kelsey log [8]) The Schneier-Kelsey log has been further developed by Holt [2] addressing problems of public verification and by Ma and Tsudik [3] discussing solutions to attacks on integrity using forward secure sequential aggregation. There is also an example of a secure log built in a privacy setting based on a Schneier-Kelsey log [7]. The paper by Sackmann et al. is primarily on detecting policy breaches using a secure log and protecting user's log entries from each other by using the userid as part of the symmetric encryption key. However, these solutions all have their shortcomings from a privacy perspective and none of them addresses the question of unlinkability of, and secure anonymous access to log entries. Some work of unlinkability in connection with logs have been addressed by [10]. However, this work primarily addresses the unlinkability of logs between logging systems in a eGovernment setting rather than unlinkability of log entries within a log. Further, they do not address the problem of an inside attacker nor provide anonymous access to log entries. Because of this we decided to design and build a privacy-preserving secure log module in Java that can log events to an SQL database in such a way that the different events are only accessible[2] by the data subject that the entry refers to while minimizing the linkability of the log entries referring to a specific data subject. The result of our design work will be described in this paper. In the following, Section 2 will give a short overview of the PRIME core while Section 3 discusses requirements for the log and the assumed attacker model. In Section 4 an overview of the different components in the log system is given and Section 5 explains the different internal states and secrets needed in the solution. Section 6 gives an explanation of the structure of the log and discusses how the different fields are used to fulfill the different requirements and Section 7 presents an analysis of the solution. Finally, Section 8 concludes the paper.

2   The PRIME Core

Within the scope of the PRIME [5] project a working prototype of a privacy-enhancing Identity Management System has been developed. This prototype is referred to as the PRIME middle-ware and is situated between an application and the different underlying data sources. The purpose of the middle-ware is to monitor and control access to any stored or released personal data and to track what data has been released and to whom. The middle-ware consist of a server-side component and a client-side component. However, both these components have the same functionality and capabilities and thus only play the role of client or server in a specific setting by configuration and not by design. The middle-ware component by itself consists of a number of components divided into

---

[2] By accessible in this case we do not mean the log entry itself but rather the plain-text content of the log entry.

the PRIME core and external components. In Figure 1 the external components are the PII LCM that handles obligation management, i.e, the upholdment of negotiated rules for use, storage, deletion and release of personal data, the crypto module and the assurance manager that among other things handle the verification of code integrity in the PRIME middle-ware. The PRIME core consists of the system application interface and the primary access control (PAC) module. It is the PAC module and its different sub modules that control the access and release of stored and released data and keeps track of released information. For a more in-depth and thorough discussion of the PRIME middle-ware we refer to [1].

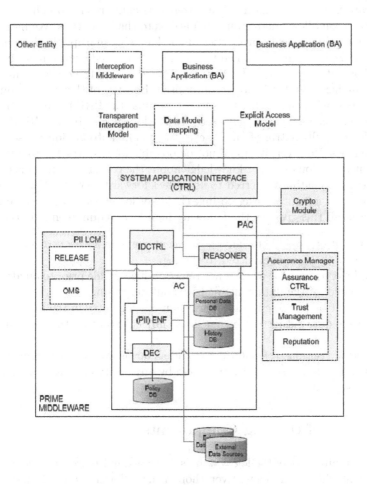

Fig. 1. The PRIME middle-ware [1]

3 Requirements and Attacker Model

As was mentioned briefly in the introduction we build this work on the secure log presented by Schneier-Kelsey [8] and further developed by Sackmann et al. [7]. However, we have modified and extended their ideas in order to further address the privacy problem and to try to overcome what we believe to be shortcomings in the previous solutions. The big differences are that we try to address the linkability problem in the log and that we use asymmetric encryption in some parts where the original solution uses symmetric encryption. The asymmetric encryption is used partly to solve the authentication problem and partly to guarantee irreversibility of committed log entries to any entity except the owner of the private key, i.e., the data subject that this entry refers to. The effect of this is that we can allow anonymous read access to the log entries. We have also tried to expand the integrity properties of the log using multiple hash chains.

The PRIME core itself is assumed to execute in a trusted environment having full control over its own data and execution. Thus the PRIME core is assumed to not behave maliciously if it is not compromised. Because of this we are concentrating on an attacker that either tries to compromise the PRIME core or that in one way or another manages to get access to the log entries. If the PRIME core is ever under the full control of an attacker there is little to be done in securing future log entries. However, it should not be possible for the attacker to alter the past without detection or to get knowledge about the content of previous events and log entries (sometimes referred to as perfect forward secrecy). Furthermore it should be hard for an attacker to link chains of log events to a specific data subject. All in all this gives us the following high level requirements on the log:

- It should not be possible for anybody except the data subject to decrypt log entries once they are committed to the log.
- It should not be possible to alter nor remove entries made prior to an attacker taking control of the data controller without detection.
- It should not be possible to link more than one log entry in the log referring to a specific data subject with that data subject except by the data subject herself[3].
- For efficiency reasons the solution should as far as possible not require that the whole log database is fully traversed by any entity or sent as a whole to the data subject.

4 Overview of the Log Components

The general architecture of the log system is described in Figure 2 and consists of the components described below. Even though the full architecture is described, only the gray components have been developed in the first attempt.

---

[3] Ideally we would like to make it impossible to link any entry, however, our current solution makes one entry per data subject identifier linkable to that data subject identifier.

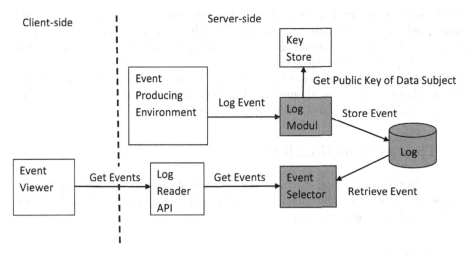

Fig. 2. Components in the log system

Each component in the figure is briefly described below:

The event producing environment: This is the component that is under audit and produces log event objects. These event objects consist of at least the subject (i.e., the identifier of the entity performing an action), the action (i.e., what was done), the purpose (i.e., why it was done), the object (i.e., the personal data that the action was performed on), and the data subject (i.e., the identifier of the "owner" of the personal data)[4].

The key store: This is a server side protected storage that contains public keys of data subjects and can hand them out to the log module if handed a data subject identifier. Where the key store is situated and what type of public key that is used is dependent on the application. However, in the PRIME case the key will be a self signed public key stored together with the PRIME data subject identifier (see foot note 3) in the personal data DB (see Figure 1) on the server side.

The log module: This is a module that receives log events and transforms them into secure privacy preserving log entries with the help of the public key of the data subject and stores them in the log.

The event selector: This is a module that given an entry identifier retrieves the requested log entry in the log to the requester.

The log reader API: This is a wrapper API that provides controlled or anonymous access to the Event selector depending on the requirements of the service.

---

[4] Please note that as soon as personal data is stored in any way in the PRIME system an identifier is generated. This is true even for anonymous access. However, the identifier might not be linked to a known user i.e., it might be a transaction pseudonym.

The event viewer: This is a module that presents and decrypts the events associated with a data subject in a user friendly fashion. It also contains functionality for searching, sorting, and comparing events as well as functionality for deciding if policy violations have occurred.

In the general case the event producing environment can be any trusted module capable of calling the log module. However, in our solution it is assumed to be the PRIME middle-ware configured as a server.

5   The Log Functionality

This section describes and discusses the different states needed in the client and the server in order for the solution to work. It also describes the procedures for storing and accessing log entries.

5.1   Secrets

The following secrets are needed in the scheme.

Secrets known and stored by the server:

1. SAS_0- A random number constituting the initial server secret used to authenticate all entries in the log for the server. This is also used as part of generating all the ServerIDs in the log.
2. $ServerID_0$- A random number constituting the initial ServerID seed.

Ideally these values are never directly stored on the server but securely stored somewhere else and only used when the integrity of the whole log needs to be verified (see Section 5.6). Instead the server initially stores SAS_1 and $ServerID_1$ calculated using formula 1 and 3 (see Section 5.2).

Secrets known and stored by each client for each data subject identifier used by a data subject using the client:

1. DSS_0- A random number constituting the initial data subject's secret used to authenticate all entries relating to the data subject identifier for the client. This is also used as part of generating all the data subject identifier's EntryIDs in the log.
2. $EntryID_0$- A random number constituting the data subject's initial EntryID seed for the data subject identifier.

The server gets DSS_1 and $EntryID_1$ in its first contact with the data subject and never needs to know DSS_0 and $EntryID_0$. The client calculates DSS_1 and $EntryID_1$ using DSS_0, $EntryID_0$ and formula 2 and 4 (see Section 5.2).

5.2   Log Field and State Value Calculations

This section describes the calculations needed when adding an entry to the log. The states stored outside of the log is described in Section 5.3. Please note that values stored outside of the log are overwritten when new values are calculated, e.g., DSS_i is overwritten by DSS_{i+1}.

The following notation is used:

$hash(x)$ =any cryptographically secure one-way hash function.

$ENC_{PU_{DS}}(x)$= encryption of x under the public key of the data subject.

$SIGN_{PR_s}(x)$ =a digital signature on x using the private key of the server.

$HMAC_Y(x)$= The HMAC of x using the key Y.

i and j are indices where i is defined from $0..m$ and j from $0..n$; where m is the maximum number of log entries related to the data subject and n is the maximum number of log entries in the entire log.

The following calculations need to be performed for each log entry where DS always refer to the data subject identifier related to the log entry.

1. $SAS_{j+1} = hash(SAS_j)$ The SAS is used as an authentication key for the server fields used for integrity validation in the log. When new values are calculated the old SAS is permanently overwritten by the new one i.e., SAS_i is overwritten by SAS_{i+1}. This makes it computationally hard for anyone not knowing SAS_0 to recreate already used keys and thus computationally hard to alter stored entries.

2. $DSS_{i+1} = hash(DSS_i)$.The DSS is used as an authentication key for the data subject fields used for integrity validation in the log. When new values are calculated the old DSS is permanently overwritten by the new one, i.e., DSS_i is overwritten by DSS_{i+1}. This is used for the same reasons as SAS but for the data subject fields.

3. $ServerID_{j+1} = hash(ServerID_j, SAS_{j+1})$. This value is used by the server to identify the different log entries in the integrity verification process. It is hashed to make it computationally hard for anyone not knowing $ServerID_0$ to order the entries (see Section 6). The SAS parameter is used to make it computationally hard for anybody not knowing SAS_0 to forge $ServerIDs$.

4. $EntryID_{i+1} = hash(EntryID_i, DSS_{i+1})$. This value is used by the data subject to identify the different log entries in the integrity verification process. It is hashed to make it computationally hard for anyone not knowing $EntryID_0$ to order the entries or to link them to a specific data subject identifier(see Section6). The DSS parameter is used to make it computationally hard for anybody not knowing DSS_0 to forge $EntryIDs$.

5. $Data_{i+1} = ENC_{PU_{DS}}(SIGN_{PR_s}(logData), logData, nonce)$. The data field is encrypted with the data subject's public key and contains the $logData$ to be stored in the log, a signature of the $logData$ and a $nonce$. The signature, created using the server's private key, allows the data subject to prove that the data was committed to the log by the server. The $nonce$ is used to make it harder for an attacker, once having gained access to the log database, to

link entries to data subjects by generating common log entries and matching them to entries stored in the log.

6. $DataSubjectChain_{i+1} = HMAC_{DSS_{i+1}}(DataSubjectChain_i, EntryID_{i+1},$ $Data_{i+1})$. The $DataSubjectChain$ authenticates the log entry and all previous log entries for the data subject. The $DataSubjectChain$ is keyed with the current DSS value for the data subject.

7. $ServerChain_{j+1} = HMAC_{SAS_{j+1}}(ServerChain_j, DataSubjectChain_{i+1},$ $Data_{i+1}, EntryID_{i+1}, ServerID_{j+1})$. The $ServerChain$ authenticates the log entry and all previous log entries in the entire log for the server. The $ServerChain$ is keyed with the current SAS value.

5.3   Server State

The server is assumed to have some form of persistent data structures storing information needed for the algorithm. We will refer to these persistent data structures as state tables. After each new log entry created the "next authentication key" and "latest entry" part of the state is updated for the server state table completely overwriting the old values in the process. The same procedure is repeated for the "next authentication key" and "latest entry" part of the state table for the specific data subject associated with the log entry.

Data subject states stored at the server
One entry in the state table for each data subject identifier that includes:

1. Data Subject Identifier - the PRIME Core system identifier.
2. Next authentication key - if i is the index of the latest entry made for the data subject then DSS_{i+1} is stored here.
3. Latest entry - the pair (EntryID, DataSubjectChain) of the latest entry in the log for the data subject. The DataSubjectChain is used by the server when generating the next log entry (as part of the new entry's DataSubjectChain) and the EntryID is used to generate the next EntryID.

Server states stored
Only one entry in the state table that includes:

1. Next authentication key - SAS_{j+1}.
2. Latest entry - the pair (ServerID, ServerChain) of the latest entry in the log made by the server. The ServerChain is used by the server when generating the next log entry and the ServerID is used to generate the next ServerID.

5.4   Adding a Log Entry

The following section describes the steps needed in order to add a log entry. The data for the event is assumed to be present in the *logData* variable.

1. Create an empty log record X.
2. Retrieve the stored SAS_j and $ServerID_{j-1}$ and calculate $ServerID_j$ according to formula 3 Section 5.2. Store $ServerID_j$ in X and overwrite the server state $ServerID_{j-1}$ with $ServerID_j$ (see Figure 3).
3. Retrieve the stored DSS_i and $EntryID_{i-1}$ and calculate $EntryID_i$ according to formula 4 Section 5.2. Store $EntryID_i$ in X and overwrite the data subject state $EntryID_{i-1}$ with $EntryID_i$ (see Figure 3).
4. Retrieve the stored data subject's public key DS_{PU}, the server's signing key PR_S and $logData$. Generate a random nonce and calculate $Data_i$ according to formula 5 Section 5.2 and store it in X.
5. Retrieve the stored $DataSubjectChain_{i-1}$ and calculate $DataSubjectChain_i$ according to formula 6 Section 5.2. Store $DataSubjectChain_i$ in X and overwrite the data subject state $DataSubjectChain_{i-1}$ with $DataSubjectChain_i$ (see Figure 4).
6. Retrieve the stored $ServerChain_{j-1}$ and calculate $ServerChain_j$ according to formula 7 Section 5.2. Store $ServerChain_j$ in X and overwrite the server state $ServerChain_{j-1}$ with $ServerChain_j$ (see Figure 4).
7. Calculate SAS_{j+1} and DSS_{i+1} overwriting the old values in the process and store X in the log.

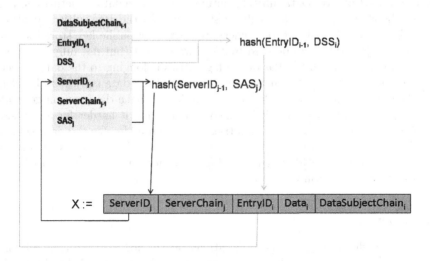

Fig. 3. Steps 2 and 3 in the algorithm

5.5   The Log API

1. GetLogEntry(EntryID) - returns the object(s) with the supplied EntryID. Since only a data subject knowing the right private key can decrypt the data field this method does not need the data subject to be identified and authenticated.

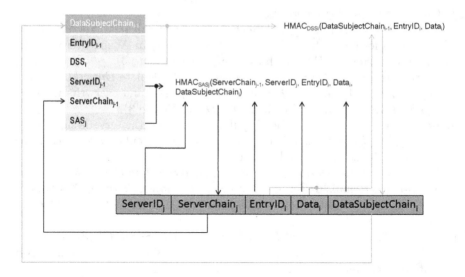

Fig. 4. Steps 5 and 6 in the algorithm

2. GetLatestEntryID(DataSubjectIdentifier) - returns a data structure containing the EntryID in the data subject state table for the data subject identifier and a nonce. The structure is encrypted with the public key stored for the data subject. This can be used by the data subject (but not fully relied on) when generating all the IDs of the log entries belonging to the data subject identifier. As above this method does not need the data subject to be identified and authenticated. The nonce is added to make the function generate different values each time it is called thus making it harder for an outside attacker to learn that new log entries have been added for the data subject identifier. Further this function should return seemingly valid responses for invalid DataSubjectIdentifiers making it harder for an outside attacker to deduce valid DataSubjectIdentifiers.

5.6 Operations

This section describes some key operations on the log i.e the client fetching entries in the log and the validation procedure on the server and the client side. All communication between the server and the client is assumed to be on an encrypted channel (the PRIME core uses SSL) and if anonymity is required the underlying network needs to be an anonymizing network, e.g., Tor as used in the PRIME Architecture [1]. We realize that the client behavior as described below can affect the linkability of entries to data subjects if not done properly. This issue is further discussed in Section 6.5.

Fetch all entries for a data subject identifier from the server. The client is assumed to have knowledge of the initial data subject identifier's secrets DSS_0 and $EntryID_0$ for the data subject identifier.

1. Request GetLatestEntryID() from the server log API.
2. Generate and make a list of all IDs from $EntryID_1$ to the latest ID returned from the server using the formulas $EntryID_i = hash(EntryID_{i-1}, DSS_i)$, $DSS_i = hash(DSS_{i-1})$.
3. Request all the log entries based on EntryID in random order from the server (please see Section 6.5 where we discuss the need for the client to behave properly in order to keep unlinkability from an inside attacker).

Log Integrity Validation by the Client side

1. Fetch all the log entries from the server from $EntryID_1$ to GetLatestEntryID("your identifier") (see 5.6 above).
2. Generate the DataSubjectChain and compare it to the stored values in the entries. If it at any point doesn't match the validation fails.
3. Generate at least one more EntryID and request it from the server. If any entry is returned the validation fails.
4. Compare the recently downloaded entries in step 1 with the old entries (if any) stored in the client. If any entry differs or was not found on the server the validation fails.

Log Integrity Validation by the Server side (or trusted third-party)
The server (or a trusted third-party) can validate the integrity of the entire log by knowing the initial server secrets (SAS_0 and $ServerID_0$).

1. Starting from $ServerID_0$:
   (a) Generate a ServerID and match it to an entry. Each time you match an entry note it down on a list.
   (b) Generate the ServerChain and compare it to the stored value in the entry; if it doesn't match the validation fails.
   (c) Repeat until a generated ServerID is not found in the log.
2. Compare the list from step 1 with the log. If there is any entry in the log that is not on the list the validation fails.
3. Examine the entry for the server in the server state table and verify that the correct server authentication key and previous entry are set.

6   Analysis of the Solution

Like in the Schneier-Kelsey log[8] we are concerned about the security of the log entries committed to the log prior to an attacker compromising the server; once compromised little can be done to secure future commits to the log. When analyzing our solution we assume that all cryptographic primitives are ideal and that the anonymity set is of sufficient size, i.e., the event producing environment has produced events to log for a number of different data subjects for some time prior to the attacker taking control of the server.

6.1   The Confidentiality of the Log

The confidentiality of the data field in a log entry is dependent on how well the private key that decrypts the data field is kept secret by the corresponding data subject.

Claim. It is computationally hard for anybody except the data subject to decrypt log entries once they are committed to the log.

Justification. The properties of public key encryption and the use of the data subjects public key gives the property that it is computationally hard for anybody except the data subject to decrypt log entries once they are committed to the log.

6.2   The Integrity of the Log

The signature of the log data, as part of the data field once decrypted, allows the data subject to both validate the integrity of the log data and to prove that the log data was committed to the log by the server.

The DataSubjectChain and ServerChain, similar to the hash chain and MAC used by Schneier-Kelsey[8], serve to authenticate the log entry and all previous log entries for the data subject and server respectively. In fact, our chains are similar to what Holt discusses as a modification to his solution to enable cumulative verification ([2] Section 7). If we use a hash function instead of a MAC for the DataSubjectChain an attacker can simply use it to link all entries belonging to a data subject together. In the same way for the ServerChain, if we use a hash instead of a MAC, an attacker could order all entries in chronological order.

Claim. It is computationally hard to alter or remove entries made prior to an attacker taking control of the data controller without detection.

Justification. For an attacker to be able to modify an entry in the log in an undetectable manner she has to have knowledge of the right authentication keys for the DataSubjectChain and ServerChain fields for that entry. As stated in Section 5.3, all authentication keys are irretrievably overwritten as soon as a new key is generated. When an attacker takes over the server, all previously used authentication keys will therefore be inaccessible for the attacker. This prevents the attacker from falsifying either chain for any of the entries committed to the log prior to the attacker taking over the server. The process which detects any modifications made, for both a data subject and the server, is described in Section 5.6. The DataSubjectChain is used by the data subject to verify the integrity of the chain of log events relating to this data subject and the ServerChain makes it possible to verify the integrity of the whole log. Thus, the DataSubjectChain empowers the data subject to verify its log parts without having access to the whole log and the ServerChain can for example be used by auditors to verify that the log as a whole has not been tampered with.

6.3 Linking Log Entries to Data Subjects

Compared to the secure logs described by [8] and [2] the order of entries in our log is considered sensitive due to our requirement for a high degree of unlinkability between log entries and data subjects. The notion of order among our log entries is given by the EntryID and ServerID generation as described in Section 5. If an attacker was able to order all entries in the log in chronological order something as simple as an access log (like the Apache default access log) for a service using the PRIME Core together with some statistical analysis would probably aid an attacker greatly in linking entries to data subjects.

Claim. It is not be possible to link more than one log entry in the log referring to a specific data subject with that data subject except by the data subject itself.

Justification. An attacker, once having compromised the server and gained access to the log database, can by examining the server's state (see Section 5.3) link the latest entry in the log to a data subject for each data subject. The attacker can further deduce which entry was the latest entry made in the log and to which data subject it belongs to. Beyond what's already mentioned, barring any shortcomings as discussed in Section 6.5, an attacker needs to gain further knowledge about the secrets in the system to be able to link more entries to data subjects. To link all entries in the log belonging to a data subject an attacker needs to learn the initial data subject's secrets (DSS_0 and $EntryID_0$). This holds true as long as at least one other data subject's secrets are unknown to the attacker. If an attacker manages to learn the initial server secrets (SAS_0 and $ServerID_0$), all the entries in the log can be ordered in chronological order (based on the ServerID generation or by following the ServerChain as outlined in Section 5.2) which may severely affect linkability. Since we allow access to log entries based on EntryID anonymously, as stated in Section 4, an attacker will not be able to break unlinkability by simply waiting for data subjects to authenticate themselves towards the server as they download entries. However, an attacker looking at which entries are being accessed in the database and at what time might very well be able to link entries together; it all depends on how the client software behaves.

6.4 Two Important Scenarios Explored

Imagine a very powerful attacker that at time t manages to compromise the server, accesses the log, learns the server's initial secrets and private key used for signing, learns the initial secrets and private keys for every data subject in the system with the only exception of the data subject identifier Bob's initial secrets and private key. The consequences are that the attacker can:

– Link all entries in the log to a data subject by generating all entry IDs belonging to each data subject except for Bobs. Bob's entries are the entries that remain unlinked to a data subject once all known data subject secrets have been used to generate IDs. Thus Bob's entries are also linkable.

- Read the contents of every entry in the log except for those belonging to Bob.
- Generate a valid ServerChain for every entry in the log and generate a valid DataSubjectChain for every entry in the log that doesn't belong to Bob.
- Sign any data with the server's private key.
- Update everything stored in the server's state (see Section 5.3), except for the entry concerning Bob, to a valid state.

This means that the attacker can replace any entry in the log, except for those belonging to Bob, with contents of her choosing with valid chains. She can also delete any entry except for those belonging to Bob and update the chains (and in some cases the server state) to a valid state. However, several factors prevent the attacker from in any way modifying any entry in the log without running a high risk of detection:

- Any of the compromised data subjects may already have downloaded an entry which the attacker has modified or deleted. This will be detected by the validation process as outlined in Section 5.6.
- Any modification to any entry belonging to Bob will result in an invalid DataSubjectChain due to a lack of authentication keys. In addition, the attacker will be unable to successfully update the server's state table for Bob with a valid DataSubjectChain or valid authentication key in the case of deletion. Last but not least, if any modifications are made to entries belonging to Bob all future entries committed to the log for the data subject Bob will have an invalid DataSubjectChain. All all of the above is detectable by Bob's validation process.
- Any modification to any entry in the log will result in the need to recreate the ServerChain for all the entries committed to the log after the modified entry. This change in the ServerChain will be detectable by every data subject's client upon validation if any entry committed to the log after the modified entry has been downloaded by any data subject prior to the modification.

Even with extensive knowledge of the secrets in the scheme and with access to the server an attacker is still severely limited when it comes to making undetected modifications to any entries in the log committed prior to compromising the server.

Another scenario that is of particular interest is if an attacker at time t has managed to compromise the server, gained access to the log and learned the initial secrets and private keys of all data subjects in the system leaving only the initial server secrets and the server's private key unknown to the attacker. For every entry in the log the attacker can link it to a data subject and read its contents. However, the ServerChain for any entry made prior to time t remains impossible for the attacker to modify without detection due to the lack of server authentication keys. In addition to having any change to any entry being detectable by the server validation process, there is also the chance that a data subject's client has downloaded an entry prior to the attacker modifying it.

6.5   Drawbacks and Shortcomings

One drawback of our solution is that the authentication keys used for the Data-SubjectChain and ServerChain fields are also used as part of the EntryID and ServerID generation respectively. This leads to a weakest link scenario where a flaw in either the MAC or hash algorithm used in an implementation will affect both the degree of unlinkability and the integrity of the log.

A problem is also that the behavior and functionality of the client software will play a role in the degree of unlinkability between data subjects and log entries in the scheme. For example, the validation process described in Section 5.6 can be used by an attacker who has compromised the server to link entries to data subjects simply by looking at when entries are requested (validation will cause a burst of requests that can be assumed to be from the same source). In addition the client also needs to have anonymous access to log entries based on entry ID; otherwise something as simple as tracking the IP-address of each request for an entry in the log would potentially allow an attacker to link log entries to data subjects (or at least to determine that some entries belong to the same data subject). It might be possible to address this issue using private information retrieval (see [4] and references there in). However, this is still subject for future work.

In [3] two security-related drawbacks are discussed for the Schneier-Kelsey log[8] and Holt [2] secure logs; a truncation attack and what the authors refer to as delayed detection. We claim that the truncation attack is only possible to a degree on our secure log when an attacker has extensive knowledge of the secrets in the scheme as discussed in the two examples in Section 7.3. Our secure log doesn't suffer from delayed detection from the server's point of view, since the server can validate the entire log independently.

7   Conclusions and Future Work

In this paper we have described the design of a privacy-friendly secure log for the purpose of making it possible for data subjects to get information on events relating to them on a server. The log builds on previous work and addresses primarily the questions of secure anonymous access to and unlinkability of log entries which previous work as far as we know have not addressed. We have implemented our design in Java as a standalone log thus showing that it is implementable. However, the lessons learned during the implementation have made us change the API slightly. These changes have not been implemented and thus the implemented version differs somewhat from the API presented in the paper. Further, we have not been able to do any extensive testing on the implementation regarding performance and penetration testing. When going from an idea to an actual implementation of the log system several questions are raised which could affect security and privacy;

1. Is it really possible to irreversibly overwrite the old authentication keys once stored in the server's state, i.e., memory?

2. Will the actual database used to store the log entries to some extent leak the order in which the entries were added to the database due to some internal structures or functionality?

Further research to find how these questions affect our solution is needed. We will also integrate the solution in to the PRIME core and implement a log view reader on the client side. By doing this we hope to find answers to the open issues on the optimal client behavior and the optimal logging strategy in order to balance performance and transparency.

Acknowledgment

The authors like to thank Professor Simone Fischer-Hübner for valuable input and suggestions during the work and Stefan Köpsell for fruitful discussions in connection with secure logs. We would also like to thank the participants and session chairs of the PrimeLife/IFIP Summer School for valuable inputs and suggestions.

References

1. Casassa-Mont, M., Crosta, S., Kriegelstein, T., Sommer, D.: Architecture v2. PRIME Deliverable D14.2.c (March 2007)
2. Holt, J.E.: Logcrypt: forward security and public verification for secure audit logs. In: Proceedings of the 2006 Australasian workshops on Grid computing and e-research. ACM International Conference Proceeding Series, vol. 54, 167, pp. 203–211. Australian Computer Society (2006)
3. Ma, D., Tsudik, G.: A new approach to secure logging. ACM Transactions on Storage (TOS) 5(1) (March 2009)
4. Pfitzmann, A., Juschka, A., Stange, A.-K., Steinbrecher, S., Köpsell, S.: Digital Privacy: Theory, Technologies and Practices, ch. 2, pp. 19–47. Auerbach Publications (2008)
5. PRIME Project, https://www.prime-project.eu/
6. PrimeLife Project, http://www.primelife.eu/
7. Sackmann, S., Strüker, J., Accorsi, R.: Personalization in privacy-aware highly dynamic systems. Communications of the ACM 49(9) (September 2006)
8. Schneier, B., Kelsey, J.: Cryptographic support for secure logs on untrusted machines. In: The Seventh USENIX Security Symposium Proceedings, January 1998, pp. 53–62. USENIX Press (1998)
9. Steel, C., Nagappan, R., Lai, R.: Core Security Patterns: Best Practices and Strategies for J2EE. In: Web Services and Identity Management. Pearson Education Inc., London (2006)
10. Wouters, K., Simoens, K., Lathouwers, D., Preneel, B.: Secure and privacy-friendly logging for egovernment services. In: 3rd International Conference on Availability, Reliability and Security (ARES 2008), Barcelona, Catalonia, ES, pp. 1091–1096. IEEE, Los Alamitos (2008)

Author Index